CULTURE, PLACE, AND NATURE

Studies in Anthropology and Environment

K. SIVARAMAKRISHNAN, SERIES EDITOR

CULTURE, PLACE, AND NATURE

Centered in anthropology, the Culture, Place, and Nature series encompasses new interdisciplinary social science research on environmental issues, focusing on the intersection of culture, ecology, and politics in global, national, and local contexts. Contributors to the series view environmental knowledge and issues from the multiple and often conflicting perspectives of various cultural systems.

Forests of Belonging

IDENTITIES, ETHNICITIES, *and* STEREOTYPES
in the CONGO RIVER BASIN

STEPHANIE RUPP

UNIVERSITY OF WASHINGTON PRESS | SEATTLE AND LONDON

FOR MY PARENTS, NANCY AND GEORGE . . . FOR EVERYTHING.

THIS PUBLICATION IS SUPPORTED IN PART BY THE DONALD R. ELLEGOOD
INTERNATIONAL PUBLICATIONS ENDOWMENT

THIS PUBLICATION IS ALSO SUPPORTED BY GRANTS FROM
LEHMAN COLLEGE, THE CITY UNIVERSITY OF NEW YORK,
AND THE PROFESSIONAL STAFF CONGRESS / CUNY

UNIVERSITY OF WASHINGTON PRESS, P.O. Box 50096, Seattle, WA 98145-5096, USA
www.washington.edu/uwpress

All photographs are by the author.

LIBRARY OF CONGRESS CATALOGING-IN-PUBLICATION DATA
Rupp, Stephanie.
Forests of belonging : identities, ethnicities, and stereotypes in the Congo River basin /
by Stephanie Rupp.
        p. cm. — (Culture, place, and nature)
Includes bibliographical references and index.
ISBN 978-0-295-99105-4 (cloth : alk. paper) — ISBN 978-0-295-99106-1 (pbk. : alk. paper)
1. Group identity—Cameroon. 2. Group identity—Congo River Valley. 3. Stereotypes
(Social psychology)—Cameroon. 4. Stereotypes (Social psychology)—Congo River Valley
5. Ethnicity—Cameroon. 6. Ethnicity—Congo River Valley 7. Cameroon—Ethnic relations.
8. Congo River Valley—Ethnic relations. I. Title.
GN655.C3R87 2011   302.4—dc22   2011003506

COVER ILLUSTRATION: Kwok Shin Hua, *Congo Basin Forest*, 2010

Contents

Acknowledgments

As I near the end, I circle back to the beginning. Dozens of teachers and advisors, colleagues and friends, and three families in dramatically different parts of the world have contributed to this project in unique and essential ways. My sense of gratitude is overwhelming and humbling.

This book is based on my doctoral research in the Lobéké region of southeastern Cameroon, which I undertook as part of my graduate studies in anthropology at Yale beginning in 1996. But the roots of this project lie many years earlier, in my seventh-grade history classroom. Mrs. Virginia Satterfield introduced me to the history, geography, and people of Africa — including the Mbuti "pygmies" of Colin Turnbull's ethnography. After I graduated from college, I followed this childhood interest in African forests to the Ituri Forest in northeastern Democratic Republic of Congo (DRC). I thank John and Terese Hart for including me in their circle of researchers and in their family in Epulu, giving me the opportunity to engage with many of the ideas at the core of this book. I thank Marti Burkert, Carolyn Bocian, Howie Frederick, and Karl and Rosie Ruf for their friendship in Epulu. I thank Richard Tshombe for including me as a novice member of the Équipe Socioéconomique, and extend my gratitude to Bryan Curran, without whose support in DRC and in Cameroon this research would not have taken the shape it has.

Following the devastating Rwandan genocide in 1994 and the waves of instability that subsequently surged through regions on the eastern edge of the Congo River basin, it was Bryan who suggested that I continue my research in Cameroon on the western rim of the basin, focusing my studies on the Bangando community as a comparative study to the work I had undertaken in the Ituri Forest. I am also grateful for the guidance offered by David Wilkie in conceptualizing early stages of my research in southeastern Cameroon. Arriving in Cameroon in 1995, I found kind support in Cheryl and Rob Fimbel, who directed the Lobéké project in southeastern Cameroon under the auspices of the Wildlife Conservation Society. Encouraging my research and opening their project to my interests, Cheryl and Rob quickly became close friends and mentors. My thanks go to Leonard Usongo and Lucie Zouya-Mimbang, whose companionship in southeastern Cameroon brought deep insight into the ecological and cultural contexts of the region, as well as gales of laughter over shared pots of beans and rice.

After one year of field research in southeastern Cameroon, I arrived at Yale in 1996 to begin my doctoral studies. I was fortunate to enroll in courses with each of my future dissertation advisors; throughout my graduate studies Eric Worby, Jim Scott, and Bob Harms challenged me to read, write, and think in new ways. I am inspired by their scholarship, their teaching, and their welcoming ways, and am honored to be their student—always. I am thankful for the abiding friendship of Yuka Suzuki and Yoonhee Kang; we have been through much together, and our friendship and shared intellectual adventures have been tremendous. I thank Rebecca Hardin and Heather Eves for their collaboration as we organized the Sangha River Conference at Yale, and thank Rebecca for her companionship during memorable field trips to France, Cameroon, and the Central African Republic.

I gratefully acknowledge the generous support for my field research and writing that I received from many sources: Fulbright-Institute of International Education; the Mellon Foundation; the Agrarian Studies Program and African Studies Council at Yale University; the Samuel K. Bushnell Fellowship; the Social Science Research Council; the Philanthropic Educational Organization; the National University of Singapore; Robert I. Rotberg and the Program on Intrastate Conflict and Conflict Resolution, together with Steven Miller and the International Security Program at the Harvard Kennedy School; Lehman College, the City University of New York, and the professional Staff Congress/CUNY.

I am grateful for the institutional support I received while undertaking my research in Cameroon. I express my thanks to Dr. Robert Nemba and the Ministère de la Recherche Scientifique et Technique for granting research clearance to conduct my studies in southeastern Cameroon. I am grateful to numerous individuals at the Ministère des Forêts et de la Faune for granting me permission to conduct research in the Lobéké forest region: Yadji Bellow, Mengang Mewondo Joseph, Fonki Tobias Mbenkum, and Ndoh Mkoumou Jean-Claude. I am grateful to the administration in Moloundou, including the mayor, Ipando Jean-Jaques and the sous-préfet, Edjimbi Simon. In Cameroon I also received kind assistance from representatives of both the World Wide Fund for Nature and the Gesellschaft für technische Zusammenarbeit. I thank Steve Gartlan, Leonard Usongo, Henk Hoefsloot, Tim Davenport, Mathias Heinze, and Karin Augustat for their collegiality. At the Université de Yaoundé I and the École Normale Supérieure, I thank Dr. Ango Mengue and Dr. Ella.

While in Yaoundé and France, I was fortunate to become integrated into a network of researchers who offered invaluable guidance at various stages of this project. Serge Bahuchet and Alain Froment have offered steadfast intellectual support for my work over the years. The wider community of APFT (Avenir des Peuples des Forêts Tropicales) offered a tremendous resource for engaging divergent perspectives and a wonderful community of friends. I benefited enormously from the intellectual guidance and warm friendship of Edmond Dounias, Daou Joiris, Christian Leclerc, Philippe Auzel, Stéphanie Carrière, Corinne Dallière, Jean-Marc Sinnassamy, Hillary Solly, and Serge Cogels.

While conducting research in Germany, I received kind hospitality from Lisa Brunkhorst as I explored commercial links to southeastern Cameroon in Hamburg. Professors Andreas Mehler, Albert Wirtz, Peter Seebald, Heike Schmidt, and Georg Deutch offered support in Hamburg and Berlin as I pieced together the German colonial history of southeastern Cameroon at the Institut für Afrika-Kunde in Hamburg and the Humboldt Universität and Bundesarkiv in Berlin.

In southeastern Cameroon I had the pleasure and good fortune to meet many individuals who enriched my experiences in the Lobéké forest. I am particularly grateful to Sisters Geneviève, Simone, and Jacqueline for supporting my research interests, my morale, and my health when I conducted research in the region of Salapoumbé. I also thank volunteer nurses Véronique, Barbara, Marielle, and Cécile for their companionship during my stays. I thank Pierre Roulet and Anthony Sajous for their friendship in Mbanjani, and for celebrating several of my birthdays with extraordinary chocolate cakes. I am grateful for the hospitality of René and Maïthé Duchatelet at the SOCALIB timber company in Congo, and for helping me arrange transport from the forest back to Douala, Cameroon. I am grateful to Dr. Sato Hiroaki, Koji Hayashi, and Charlie Jones for assisting me in my research in Ndongo in 1999.

My deepest thanks go to the Bangando, Baka, Bakwélé, and Mbomam of southeastern Cameroon, who patiently endured my awkward presence and persistent questions over numerous years of fieldwork. Thanks to the early and generous help of Maga Jacques and Jeanne in Lopondji, I was able to find my footing linguistically, culturally, and socially within the Bangando community. Their family offered a warm and gracious welcome during my many trips to southeastern Cameroon. The generosity and support offered by Ambata Philippe and his family—Kebikibele, Salo, Maddé, Ngola, Asila, Pascaline—allowed me to visit Dioula regularly during 1995-96, and then to focus my research on Dioula from 1997 to 2000. Kebikibele and Ngola were my closest companions in southeastern Cameroon, explaining details and stories as many times as I needed until I understood. Salo and Maddé, Ambata and Pascaline, Ndjumbe and Nakola, Wanguwangu and Iindeko, Mungoi and Gnangue formed the core of my closest friends, supporters, and informants. To all the villagers of Dioula and Lopondji, and to the many, many others who welcomed me into their homes throughout the Lobéké forest region: ákìbà ɛ́nɛ́ súlòwè!

Marriage brought me from Cameroon to Singapore as I wrote up my dissertation, and my continuing work was generously supported by the Centre for Advanced Studies at the National University of Singapore, where I was a visiting scholar from 2000 to 2001. I am grateful to professors Alan Chan, Lily Kong, Brenda Yeoh, and Thang Leng Leng for so warmly offering me an academic home away from home. I am immensely thankful for the resourcefulness of librarians Kannagi Rajamanickam and Vimala Nambiar, who procured innumerable and obscure sources through interlibrary loan and document delivery service. I am grateful for the constant friendship and the reading of many drafts of my work by Dr. Medha Kudaisya. Even from halfway around the world, Tamara Giles-Vernick remained a regular correspondent and a wonderful colleague, patiently reading early drafts.

Turning a two-volume dissertation into a publishable book has been a task that has also involved many steadfast mentors and supporters. I am grateful to K. Sivaramakrishnan for his early interest in the manuscript, and for his faithful endurance through several years of reducing and revising the manuscript. Lorri Hagman, Pat Soden, Marilyn Trueblood, Kerrie Maynes, Pamela Canell, Tom Eykemans, and Mary Ribesky at the University of Washington Press have provided invaluable guidance as the project moved through the stages of review, revision, and publishing. I am grateful to an anonymous reader and to Peter Geschiere for reviewing the manuscript. Peter Geschiere went above and beyond the call of duty in shaping the final book, offering incisive suggestions for improvement, and steadfast support for the book. My thanks go also to Dr. Suzanne Smith at Harvard for her fantastic ability to see where to prune the manuscript. Mark Denil produced the lovely maps, often from handdrawn sketches full of obscure symbols and languages. I thank Dorothy Woodson, curator of the African collection at Sterling Memorial Library, Yale University, for agreeing to archive digital copies of my field notes for future use by other researchers. I extend my gratitude to Kay Mansfield for combing through the page proofs, and to Scott Smiley for preparing the index. It is only with the help of this tremendous team of talented, patient contributors that this book has been possible.

Finally, I thank my families. My Bangando family in Dioula supported me emotionally, intellectually, and practically as I tried my best to learn Bangando ways. I have been honored to be one of their family, and I cherish the affection that we share. My parents-in-law in Singapore—Ben and Shin Kwek—have supported me in the best ways possible, by offering alternatives to work when I needed to escape, understanding and space when I needed to work, and enthusiastic help in looking after small children. Deep thanks to my mother-in-law, Shin, for painting the beautiful illustration for the book's cover. I warmly thank my sister, Kathy, whose partnership as sisters and anthropologists has been joyous and enriching. I thank my parents, George and Nancy, for the decades of guidance and support that they have provided, including the tremendous freedom that they granted me from a very young age to explore Africa independently, even when they fervently wished I would just come home. Thanks to Mom for her editorial prowess, to Dad for his honest criticisms and patient guidance of the manuscript, and to them both for their unending and loving support of our family. Words fall short in capturing my gratitude to Ju-Hon, my husband, for his provocative challenges to my ideas and his abiding love and partnership. Finally, I am grateful that Kai-Lin, Kai-Shan, and Kai-Jin, our children, pull me away from my computer as often as possible, reminding me that life is about much more than books. *Tòkídí tòkídí bò dɔ́ɔ dà wè.*

Foreword

S tudies of the relationships between ethnicity and environment, having grown and matured over several decades, have moved beyond the familiar dichotomy between positivist determinism and relativism. New scholarship observes that identities animating human group and individual behavior should be understood as dynamic and historically fashioned. Equally, the ecological conditions in which these identifications operate are now recognized as patterned by the shifting nature of nonhuman life, associated landscapes, and human entanglements in them. How, then, does an anthropologist pursue questions relating to environments and ethnic identifications? In this painstakingly researched, compassionately written, and erudite study, Stephanie Rupp suggests some very compelling ways to answer this question.

Based on long and detailed fieldwork in the central African nation-state of Cameroon, Rupp presents valuable new information and refreshing new analysis of the lives of forests and their inhabitants in one of the most contested forest regions in Africa, and possibly the tropical world. For at least two hundred years, powerful nations have entered this area to mine resources, and peoples there have dealt with these intrusions to negotiate their own life paths and relations with each other in conditions of great hazard and unpredictable opportunity. Rupp takes as her central focus the dynamics of belonging and the production of social and ethnic identities in this turbulent history, demonstrating how such identities remain fluid, take particular temporarily stable forms at specific historical conjunctures, and then are remade in violent contexts of change, from colonial rule to independent nation-state formation. She discusses complex ideas with deceptive simplicity and keeps her study immersed in the lives of the people whose livelihoods, stories, memories, and suffering provide the substance for her argument.

At the heart of the book, a series of compelling chapters develops important themes—marriage and kinship; lineage structures, shared work, and ritual; and the impact of commercialized farming—as the basis for building an argument about how identities become fluid and then congeal around specific concerns and conflicts. Rupp attends closely to the lives of Bangando and Baka alike, the two main groups in the central African forest zone in which she worked. Comprehending the changing social and ecological landscape in Bandango and Baka terms, Rupp has produced a sharp, elegant, and rich ethnographic account that situates the making of identity and lives in the shadow and light of historical memory and contemporary compulsions arising from commercial hunting, forest conservation, and projects of sustainable development. This is a systematic analysis of the patterns of identity change and stabilization in the context of unequal relations among southeastern Cameroonians, as well as among central Africans and colonial traders, officials, and missionaries. Apart from adding a gem to African studies, Rupp charts a new direction for the study of ecology and ethnicity anywhere in the world, and does so in lucid prose and a caring voice.

K. Sivaramakrishnan
Yale University
August 2011

Forests of Belonging

Introduction

The forest supplies all of the necessities of life—food, shelter, clothing, and fuel for the family hearth. Bark, vines, saplings, leaves, and various resins are all the hunters need to build and furnish their homes. Above all, the sense of belonging to the forest unites the pygmy hunters against nearby village farmers, who cut it down to plant crops. The hunters trade with them, mainly to stop their searching the forest for needed meat and supplies.

—*"Mbuti Pygmies" diorama at the American Museum of Natural History, New York City*

During the early days there was a separation between Bangando and Baka. Bangando lived in their villages, and Baka lived in the forest. You could say that Baka did more hunting and Bangando did more farming. But today Baka and Bangando are mixed together. Bangando and Baka live together in villages along the road. . . . Today there is no difference between Baka and Bangando because of what they do. To call one group "hunters" and one group "farmers" doesn't make sense today, because today we all hunt, we all farm, we all gather—so that we can eat and also sell something.

—*Maga, Bangando elder in Lopondji, southeastern Cameroon*

This book is about identities that defy simple categorization. It addresses the conundrum of formal, prescriptive categories that identify people according to where and how they live, but that do not fit with the lived experiences and sentiments of belonging among the people themselves. While images of forest people in the Congo River basin reflect intellectual and institutional models that are unitary, oppositional, and paradigmatic, the social realities of belonging in the forest reflect identities that are multiple, cross-cutting, and integrative.

This ethnography focuses on the Bangando, a forest community living in southeastern Cameroon that is identified in academic and policy literature as consisting of "villagers" or "farmers." The research complements existing studies of the Baka "pygmies" or "hunter-gatherers" conducted in the same region,[1] and the innumerable studies of "pygmy" communities that scholars have undertaken throughout the Congo River basin of equatorial Africa throughout the twentieth century. This study examines dynamics of belonging and processes of identification, as forest communities encounter profound political-economic, ecological, and social change, and as they reconfigure senses of self and other, negotiate multiple ways and means of intercommunal belonging, and engage with the nation-state as well as international actors and agencies.

The Bangando community is numerically small, including approximately 5,000 people who reside primarily in southeastern Cameroon, near the articulation of the borders of Cameroon, the Republic of Congo, and the Central African Republic. The region is distinguished as a region by "Lake" Lobéké, a swampy and verdant inland delta of the Lobéké River, a tributary of the Sangha River. This forest is a pocket of semideciduous, tropical forest within a much larger cultural and ecological sphere of interaction on the western rim of the Congo River basin. The Lobéké region is home to four locally based ethnic groups—Bangando, Baka, Bakwélé, and Mbomam—as well as people from other regions of Cameroon and central Africa who identify themselves with many other communities.

Despite this evident diversity, scholars who work in this tropical forest seldom consider the possibility that the identities and sentiments of belonging of forest peoples may be based on experiences, relationships, and understandings that derive from neither the forest environment nor an economic mode of subsisting in the forest environment. Where scholars, practitioners, and observers recognize evident categories of self-identification, such as affiliation with speakers of a shared language, they tend to overlay and equate members of this community with predetermined categories of environment and economic subsistence. Thus for example, in the context of southeastern Cameroon, people who are identified ethnically as Baka by virtue of their language are also considered by categorical equation to be "people of the forest" and "hunter-gatherers"; at the same time, their immediate neighbors, the Bangando, are identified by categorical opposition as "people of the village" and "farmers." As a toddler's set of stacking cups aligns similar, graduated, and functionally substitutable containers, so categories of identity are assumed to be interrelated and even interchangeable. "Baka," "pygmies," "people of the forest," "hunter-gatherers," and "indigenous people" all operate as categorical and rhetorical synonyms considered sufficient to identify, delimit, and contain this particular community, usually placing the community in structural opposition to its neighbors in southeastern Cameroon. These neighboring communities are categorized (usually by rote dichotomization) into another predetermined set of graduated and functionally substitutable containers: "Bangando," "villagers," "people of the village," "farmers," and "immigrants." In other words, the categorical stacking cups that scholars and practitioners use to identify forest peoples treat ethnicity, place-based identity, mode of subsistence, and aboriginality as equivalent, interchangeable markers of identity.

What happens to these neatly stacking categories, however, when an individual expresses an environmental or economic orientation that is not consistent with the correlated ethnic label? For example, do Baka who rely primarily on agriculture for their subsistence continue to "count" as "hunter-gatherers"? Ethnicity as measured by some scholars is directly related to what people do. Thus when an informant states, "I am a hunter [I hunt; I go hunting]. That is what I am. That is what I do," the researcher takes this statement (together with empirical studies of this individual's economic activities) as evidence that this individual is in essence a "hunter-gatherer," and, moreover, that the category of "hunter-gatherer" has fundamental meaning as an expression of basic identity for individuals of that community (Kent 1996: 20). In this case, as in many others, the researcher equates ethnicity and social identity with the categorical stereotype of "hunter-gatherer," as if this categorical reduction is sufficient to represent the individual, and community, in totality. This conflation of stereotype, ethnicity, and social identity is problematic because it blinkers outside observers from recognizing and taking seriously other salient—and perhaps even more salient—relationships, experiences, and lifeways that contribute to processes of identification and senses of belonging. The facile blurring of these distinct modes of identification constrains our ability to perceive, appreciate, and analyze how communities—especially communities that are intimately integrated with neighboring communities—generate social cohesion and negotiate social conflict (Barth 1969).

The categorical conflation of stereotype, ethnicity, and social identity is problematic, furthermore, because it does not allow for the possibility that stereotypes, ethnic identities, and social identities are *not* equivalent and substitutable. In contemporary southeastern Cameroon, certainly some people identify themselves as "hunters." But these "hunters" belong to all four communities that inhabit the Lobéké forest region, not just the Baka community. Furthermore, the experience of hunting is by no means the only social experience that shapes these hunters' senses of self; their processes of identification as individuals and their sentiments of belonging within groups are not limited to the economic activity of hunting or their experiences of working and living in the forest. What began as skepticism about stereotypes, such as "hunter-gatherers" and "pygmies" that are ubiquitous in academic, policy, and popular literature, has resulted in a sustained, ethnographic analysis of the diverse processes of identification and dynamics of belonging in southeastern Cameroon.

I conducted research in southeastern Cameroon as a result of linked coincidences of previous studies, travels, and political contingencies. I read Colin Turnbull's *The Forest People* (1961) in social studies class as a schoolgirl; like many young readers of Turnbull's account of idyllic "pygmy" life in the forest, I was enchanted by the stories of the Mbuti community in the leafy thick of the Ituri Forest and came to view the "pygmies" as a unique and special community. Years later, my childhood interest became an opportunity to learn about forest peoples firsthand. After my undergraduate studies in anthropology, I volunteered as an intern for the Wildlife Conservation Society (WCS) in the Ituri Forest, where conservationists were undertaking long-term research to create conservation policies for managing the Okapi Wildlife Reserve. I worked as part of a small team of social scientists based in Epulu, Democratic Republic of Congo (then Zaïre) on ways to encourage community participation in the conservation efforts. Finding myself in one of the hubs of "hunter-gatherer" research in the Ituri Forest, and in the village that featured prominently in Turnbull's work, I read as many resources as I could find concerning the "pygmies," assuming that these academic and policy models reflected actual social dynamics in the Ituri Forest in particular, and throughout the Congo River basin in general.[2]

Because of the turmoil that began with the Rwandan genocide of 1994 and quickly engulfed neighboring areas on the eastern edge of the Congo River basin, I was unable to return to the Ituri Forest in 1995 to continue field research as I had intended. Instead, at the suggestion of my mentor, I explored a similar ecological context on the western rim of the Congo River basin, hoping to learn about forest communities in the Ituri Forest and the Lobéké forest region in southeastern Cameroon in comparative perspective. Thus I arrived in southeastern Cameroon as a Fulbright Scholar for a year of field research on the ethnoecology of Bangando women, again in collaboration with the Wildlife Conservation Society. WCS was in the process of designing and implementing plans for a new protected area in southeastern Cameroon, with its core protected area centered on the Lobéké forest region. My research was designed to examine patterns of resource use, agricultural technologies, and land tenure systems practiced by the Bangando "farmers," who live in the Lobéké forest ecosystem but pursue agriculture as their primary mode of subsistence, thus presenting an apparent contradiction between their economic way of life and the sustainable use of their ecological surroundings.

The research I had proposed to conduct in southeastern Cameroon was riddled with assumptions. First, I assumed that subsistence farming in tropical forests, negatively portrayed by many conservationists as swidden agriculture, is necessarily detrimental to forest ecosystems.[3] I set out to understand Bangando agricultural patterns, land tenure, and resource-management strategies so that conservationists could more effectively understand and monitor itinerant agriculture, with the ultimate goal of minimizing the ecological impacts of these farmers' swidden practices on the Lobéké forest. Second, I assumed that the Bangando community ought to be the subject of my research: the Bangando community had been identified as "villagers" and "farmers" in colonial, historical, socioeconomic, and conservation literature, based on the perception that they are the village-dwelling, agriculture-practicing neighbors of Baka "pygmies" or "hunter-gatherers." Third, I assumed that whereas Bangando "farmers" exemplify the relatively recent arrival of agricultural entrepreneurs in the forest environment, Baka "pygmies" or "hunter-gatherers" represent the autochthonous "people of the forest," the "indigenous people" celebrated in literature and promoted by policies of conservation, development, and missionization. Fundamentally, I assumed that "farmer" and "villager" were accurate summations of who the Bangando *are*, quite suitable to identify the community in academic analyses as well as in conservation and development policy documents.

I arrived in southeastern Cameroon in August 1995 and began Bangando language lessons with the second wife of the lineage head of a small hamlet called Lopondji, on the outskirts of the larger Mambélé village, which is located near the intersection of two logging roads. As my research progressed, I visited the dozen villages in the region of the Lobéké forest where Bangando make up a significant proportion of the population. During my first weeks in southeastern Cameroon, I was puzzled that I often had difficulty distinguishing between "pygmies" and "villagers," who in the literature had been portrayed as distinctly different and easily identifiable communities. But in Mambélé, the great majority of people lived in square, wattle-and-daub houses by the edges of the logging roads. Although a handful of leaf-shingled, dome-shaped houses suggested that Baka families lived in the Mambélé community, there were not nearly enough "pygmy" houses to accommodate the entire population of Baka living in the area. Men, women, and children—of all groups—passed through and loitered at the junction of the logging roads, where a few lean-to shops sold blocks of grease soap, salt, sardines, school notebooks, and pens. Young men of various heights and speaking various languages arrived at the WCS camp in search of employment as guides and trackers for the biologists conducting research in the forest. Shrouding any social distinctions that I could perceive by casual observation, people's clothes seemed equally worn and tattered throughout the multiethnic community. I developed the habit of initiating conversations with people by smiling broadly, hoping that they would smile back at me so that I could see if their teeth were filed or straight. If the teeth are filed to sharp points, I thought, this person must be a Baka "hunter-gatherer"; if the teeth are unfiled, perhaps this person is a Bangando "farmer," a potential subject for my research. This approach to judging who was who was certainly simple-minded, but reflects the difficulty in recognizing who is who among these intermingled forest communities.[4]

It was when I made an extended visit to the village of Dioula, approximately in the middle of the region of the Lobéké forest where the Bangando are prominent, that I began to question fundamentally who was who, and whom I should be studying if I wanted to understand the intersection between local agricultural systems and the surrounding forest ecosystem. In Dioula, the family that produced the most plantains to sell on the regional, commercial market was a Baka family. Another Baka family produced a sizeable crop of cocoa beans for sale on the international market. Up until then, and in accordance with other research and literature, I had understood Baka to be hunting-gathering "pygmies" rather than farming "villagers." Yet these Baka families not only produced a large quantity of surplus plantains and crops of cocoa to sell, they also lived in square mud-and-thatch houses in the village, sent their children to the local school (when it was open), and could afford a variety of clothes, a portable radio, and other household items. These socio-economic characteristics ought to apply to the market- and consumption-oriented "villagers," not to the economically marginalized, nonmaterialist, and seminomadic "pygmies," according to institutional stereotypes and academic models. In anthropological literature, the social category of "villager" was consistently linked with farming and contrasted with "pygmy," yet these Baka "pygmy" families seemed to be village-based and agriculture-oriented.

FIG. I.1 Kilombo, Baka elder who initiates the elephant-hunting ceremony (*Yéli*) harvesting her family's substantial cocoa plantation, Dioula Village, 1995

Meeting these families forced me to widen the scope of my initial research on farming systems in the Lobéké forest. As I met and engaged with Bangando and Baka families alike, I learned of Bangando families who do not live in the village alongside the logging road, but instead live fifteen kilometers into the forest, pursue some agriculture for subsistence and commerce, and *also* engage in a preponderance of hunting and gathering of forest products. These Bangando individuals described themselves, in their own language and using their own metaphor, as "people of the forest." I learned of Baka families that produce significant quantities of cocoa for the semiannual cocoa market and rarely make extended trips into the forest for hunting or fishing. I learned of the complex relationship between Bangando and Baka men as they hunt elephants together, collaboratively capitalizing on the demands of the (illegal) ivory and bushmeat markets. I learned about the tension between cooperation and competition, as Bangando and Baka share historical experiences and future opportunities, intermarry, and participate together in each community's—as well as intercommunal—rituals and ceremonies.

As I gradually realized that the whole basis for my research project on Bangando "farmers" was crumbling under the weight of my assumptions, I also realized that the fundamental assumptions that Euroamerican scholars, missionaries, and aid practitioners have made and continue to make about forest peoples need to be challenged if we are to understand social relationships and processes of identification in equatorial Africa beyond slotting people into convenient stereotypes. And, if we strive to understand the complexities of social interactions among various forest communities, we must pay attention to who the people we study understand *themselves* to be. Researchers, policy makers, and observers must move beyond elementary models of "pygmies" and "villagers" or "hunter-gatherers" and "farmers" if our goal is to make sense of the complexities of contemporary life in the forest, and for practitioners, to devise viable policies for the conservation of forest resources and the socioeconomic development of forest communities. It was to analyze processes of identity formation, belonging, and social change that I returned to the Lobéké region to continue my research in 1997, 1998-99, and 2000.[5] Once I had set aside preconceived models of forest peoples, it became apparent that the diverse communities of southeastern Cameroon pursue numerous and flexible economic strategies that may or may not be related to their sense of who they are, engage in manifold and changing social and ecological relationships that affect their sentiments of belonging, and identify self and other in multiple and shifting ways.

At the same time, outside observers who were active in the Lobéké region—including fellow researchers, conservation and development agents, Cameroonian officials, missionaries, and safari hunters—strenuously resisted the notion that perhaps the categorical stereotypes on which they rely for identifying forest peoples might represent incomplete or even inaccurate models of social identities and relations of belonging. In each of these areas of practical engagement with forest communities, the ability to identify and categorize people according to standards that appear to have stood the test of time and seem to be based on (at least partial) empirical reality, offers a practical solution for simplifying the complex interwoven communities of southeastern Cameroon. These categorical models offer convenient conceptual handles for identifying who is who in the multiethnic setting of the Lobéké forest. Thus, identifying certain people as "pygmies" and "hunter-gatherers" and relegating all other groups to the unmarked category of "villager" facilitates external interventions by indicating which people will be the objects of study; the recipients of special concessions and benefits of conservation and development; the targets for missionization, conversion, or subsidized medical care; and the main focus for attracting the tourists' gaze. The issue of who counts as a "pygmy," "hunter-gatherer," or autochthonous and rightful dweller in the forests of tropical Africa is a matter of political importance: research agendas, policy priorities, and economic resources tend to be directed at those communities deemed by external experts to be "indigenous," a category that is conflated with "pygmies" and "hunter-gatherers" but does not include "villagers" or "farmers."

Thus, beyond attempting to point out the inadequacy of models of "pygmies" and "hunter-gatherers," there is political urgency and moral obligation to take seriously people's own perceptions of belonging and experiences of identity. It is through the political projects of colonialism and exploitation, conservation and development, health care and missionization, that stereotypes of "pygmies" as "indigenous people" of the forest and "villagers" as recent and opportunistic arrivals have assumed their potency. The persistence of these polar categories has resulted in incomplete studies of partial societies throughout equatorial Africa (Vansina 1990, 1986), inaccurate conclusions about contemporary relationships between power and social status, as well as unrealistic conclusions about the relationship between cultural identity and natural resources. The danger of such partiality—in the double sense of incompletion and bias—is that policies for the conservation of forest resources and the development of forest communities based on such research will be compromised from the outset. Policies that enshrine particular groups such as "pygmies" and "hunter-gatherers" as "indigenous people" risk overlooking the shared realities of poverty and marginalization that these communities share with their "nonindigenous" neighbors, partners, and even spouses (Gupta 1998; Li 2000; Burnham 2000). While the goals of development and conservation in central Africa are extremely important to the well-being of all forest communities, the common misunderstandings of how local people express and experience who they are has led to unanticipated tension and conflict among local communities as misguided policies, based on misrepresentations of identity, are implemented.

Having had my assumptions shattered during my initial fieldwork in southeastern Cameroon, I consciously attempted to set aside the categories "hunter-gatherer" and "farmer" to try to understand how the various communities—self-articulated as Bangando, Baka, Bakwélé, and Mbomam—experience and express who they are as individuals and as members of communities; what their position in their world is, has been, and might be; and what they think about these things. Silberbauer echoes my unease with the simplifying models that typically define "hunter-gatherers":

> [A] people's social construction of reality is a necessary element in understanding its social and cultural behavior. To leave out of the account their way of construing their experience of reality is to present the people as bereft of rationality, or, for lack of anything better, to impose on them the anthropologist's own set of constructions. . . . My quibble with my own and others' use of reductionist explanations is that it leaves us blind to the possibility of alternative patterns and to additional relevant factors. (Silberbauer 1994: 122)

I suggest that taking a closer look at these alternative patterns, other ways of thinking about self and other, might help us to understand the dynamics of contemporary forest communities from their own points of view, using terms and images that are salient to their experiences over the past two centuries of tumultuous change. This book attempts to understand what people think about their lives, social relationships, and experiences with the broader political-economic system, as they remember the past, as they contend with today's contexts, and as they imagine the future.

Simplified structures that delineate and identify subjects distill complex social realities into compact, conceptual containers. The power of such models lies in their abstraction and universality (Scott 1998). Rather than taking such abstract, codified models of identity as the starting point, the research at the heart of this study has examined social relations in southeastern Cameroon as one might study the dynamics of a multi-layered forest. This study sets aside the flat, cadastral map of identities—"pygmy," "villager," "hunter-gatherer," "farmer"—categories that typically define the outlines of sociality for researchers and administrators, and categories through which policies for "indigenous people" are prescribed and implemented. Instead I have examined the qualities and processes of identification and belonging among the forest communities of southeastern Cameroon, finding that careful study of these integrated communities presents new and compelling insights about spatial, ritual, social, and political relations—in both historical and contemporary contexts—in the equatorial African forest. This study looks at belonging *as* a forest, as a living, dynamic, interrelated system. Some identities and relationships in the Lobéké forest region are rooted in particular places, languages, and memories. Some structures have a vertical, almost trunk-like quality to them, such as lines of descent. But the dynamism of the forest comes from lateral connections that are formed at many layers. Historical relations of cooperation—in the precolonial, colonial, and contemporary periods—connect individuals, families, and communities as systems of roots spread laterally, becoming entangled and intertwined. Solidarities based on shared participation in a soccer team, common experiences in a timber camp, and interethnic hunting teams connect individuals of these forest communities as vines, lianas, and creepers tie together trees of all kinds in the forest. Disruptive experiences in the forest—forced labor during the colonial period and unrest during the tumultuous years of post-independence rebellion—have brought forest communities in southeastern Cameroon together in dynamic, mutually engaged and supportive relations, much as forest disturbance caused by cutting a pathway or the falling of a tree creates spaces in the forest for particularly dynamic, robust, and tangled growth. Rather than being schematically organized according to the simple models that make the forest legible to outside researchers, administrators, or travelers, the contours of belonging of the Lobéké forest resemble the forest itself: layers of interpenetrating individuals and processes of dynamic interrelationships constitute this complex, multiethnic community.

The ethnographic research at the heart of this study takes a multiangular approach, explicitly making room for the diverse and sometimes divergent articulations, relationships, and experiences that drive the formation and transformation of identities and shape sentiments of belonging. The research methodology insists on the consideration of articulations between a given community and its neighbors, rather than privileging evidence from the focal community in isolation. This research is multiangular in spatial-cultural dimensions as well, examining the social interfaces among Bangando, Baka, and Mbomam communities at the northern region of the study, and among Bangando, Baka, and Bakwélé communities in the southern part of the research area. Noting historian Jan Vansina's challenge that research on forest communities tends to overlook the "farmers" who are inextricably intertwined in social, political, economic, and ecological relations with "hunter-gatherers," my research and discussion consider all four of the communities in southeastern Cameroon: Bangando, Baka, Bakwélé, and Mbomam (Vansina 1990: 29). However, out of methodological necessity, this book is not balanced in its presentation of the four communities; the presentation and analysis emphasize Bangando perspectives, analyzing Bangando relationships with Baka, Bakwélé, and Mbomam, respectively.

Even as this multiangular ethnographic methodology has proved invaluable in orienting the fieldwork, it also poses an analytical challenge. For if investigations of identity must necessarily be multiangular, as people's experiences of identity and belonging are undeniably multifaceted, then referring to any particular individual or community by a particular term — whether that term references a social identity, an ethnic affiliation, or a stereotype — lends the discussion a misleading sense of fixity. At the same time, however, accepting this lack of fixity enables the researcher (and reader) to acknowledge that expressions and experiences of a particular category of identity are multiple in both experience and expression. Thus even categories such as "pygmy" and "villager," categories that I argue are firmly rooted in external stereotypes, are deployed in varied and meaningful ways in local contexts. Because of the strategic flexibility of people's uses and experiences of identities, the boundaries of "outside" and "inside" identities become blurred, reflecting the social reality that people strategically embrace identities — even essentialized identities based on stereotypes — for particular purposes in particular contexts (Spivak 1988).

The chapters that follow make the fundamental argument that in order to make sense of contemporary experiences of belonging and identification, it is crucial to differentiate among social identities, ethnic affiliations, and stereotypes. Each of these elements is a distinct component of larger processes of identification, and often these elements are intertwined in social relationships and discourse. To conflate social identities, ethnic affiliations, and stereotypes and treat them as if they were equivalent, substitutable markers of identity is to misunderstand the fundamentally different ways that people experience and express the multifaceted, varied senses of who they are and how they relate to others. By "social identities" I mean the everyday categories that individuals use to describe themselves and others in a wide variety of contexts, categories that people move into and out of with ease and rapidity. To offer a preliminary example, "people of the kitchen" refers to individuals involved in kitchen activities: people who belong in the kitchen at a particular moment, whether they are cooking a meal, bathing children, or sharing news in the kitchen house. Such markers of social identity are expressed using a particular linguistic format to specify that it is a category of identity. By "ethnic affiliations" I refer to the language groups that people in southeastern Cameroon use to distinguish membership in broader linguistic and cultural communities: Bangando, Baka, Bakwélé, and Mbomam. Although membership in a particular language group generally implies shared history and descent, in southeastern Cameroon it is the speaking of a common language as a first language that overtly signals the boundary of ethnic affiliation and a basic sense of ethnic belonging (Barth 1969). By "stereotype" I refer to categories of identity such as "pygmy" and "villager" or "hunter-gatherer" and "farmer," categories that reflect external values and assumptions about forest people, what they do, and where they belong, even if these stereotypes come to be used in complex ways in local contexts.

This ethnography demonstrates that social identities, ethnic affiliations, and stereotypes operate as distinct components in processes of identification and belonging. In particular, they have varying qualities of viscosity, congealing and softening at different rates and for different purposes. For example, social identities are highly malleable. People express and project social identities to emphasize their social roles in everyday contexts, and can assume and shed these identities with ease. Social identities form and disintegrate with frequency, reflecting shifting social, political, economic, and ecological contexts. Ethnic affiliations are more viscous than social identities. Whereas ethnic affiliations held by people in southeastern Cameroon have changed over time in name and meaning, they emerge and solidify as a result of specific historical conditions and remain relatively firm (although not solid) over several generations. Stereotypes are the most rigid markers of identity, having been established through the distillation of social information to a few, salient elements that crystallize into rigid form. Although the prevalent stereotypes that typify forest peoples in equatorial Africa are rooted in perceptions and policies of outside observers, they can and do take on local valences that are often emotionally cutting and socially divisive. Stereotypes seem to be intractable. Local communities in southeastern Cameroon have little control over either the application of stereotypes to describe their social lives or the prescriptive use of stereotypes to form policies that affect their livelihoods.

Social identities, ethnic affiliations, and stereotypes work together as distinct but interrelated components in larger processes of identification. Each component involves internal as well as external definitions of identity, in varying proportions (Jenkins 1994). As a result, each component is differentially malleable in the hands of a given individual or community. An experience of categorizing oneself or being categorized by others into a particular, stereotypic category may contribute to a person's experiences of ethnic affiliation and social identification. Fundamentally, however, social identities, ethnic affiliations, and stereotypes are not interchangeable markers of identity. Fluid identities—ways of relating oneself to others that are relatively easy to adapt and manage—offer many ways for people to emphasize shared attributes and interests; congealed identities—ways of identifying oneself and others that are rigidly prescribed—tend to emphasize social differences and divisions.

The communities of southeastern Cameroon shape their identities and their relations with other people with reference to three interrelated clusters of issues: paradigms; processes of identification; and cultural relations with their neighbors. Each cluster itself involves several interrelated values, processes, and sets of relationships. The first cluster, paradigms, includes stereotypes such as "pygmies" or "villagers," models such as "hunter-gatherer" studies, and discourses such as "indigenous people's" rights; these structures provide the larger framework for the politics of belonging in the Lobéké forest region. Individuals may align themselves strategically with such paradigms in order to gain access to economic or social resources, which often are provided by external institutions. Elements in the second cluster, processes of identification, vary in their manipulability. Although individuals are constrained in their ability to shape stereotypes that are imposed on their communities by external images or policies, communities do alter their senses of ethnic affiliation over time, and individuals shift and manage their expressions of social identities frequently. The third cluster of interrelated factors is the multiethnic community of the Lobéké region: Bangando, Baka, Bakwélé, and Mbomam engage in dynamic, changing relationships that vary throughout the region and over time. Individuals negotiate these interrelated values, identities, and relationships in the broader context of forest exploitation and conservation in southeastern Cameroon.

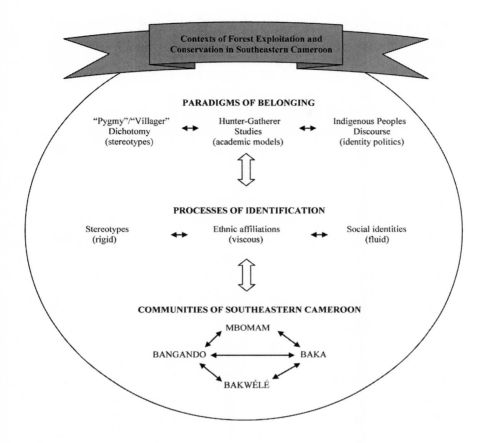

PARADIGMS OF BELONGING

"Pygmy"/"Villager"   Hunter-Gatherer   Indigenous Peoples
Dichotomy   ↔   Studies   ↔   Discourse
(stereotypes)   (academic models)   (identity politics)

⇕

PROCESSES OF IDENTIFICATION

Stereotypes   Ethnic affiliations   Social identities
(rigid)   ↔   (viscous)   ↔   (fluid)

⇕

COMMUNITIES OF SOUTHEASTERN CAMEROON

MBOMAM

BANGANDO ⟷ BAKA

BAKWÉLÉ

FIG. 1.2 Forests of Belonging: Interrelated Identities in the Lobéké Forest Region

The chapters that follow offer ethnographic illustrations and analysis of the elements within each cluster, as well as synthetic analysis of the interactions among the clusters. Chapter one introduces paradigms of forest peoples that are employed by scholars, policy makers, and practitioners alike to determine who is who. The chapter discusses stereotypes of "pygmy," "hunter-gatherer," and "indigenous people" as they are deployed in southeastern Cameroon, analyzing the assumptions that are fundamental to these paradigms. The next five chapters present the core ethnography, examining the contemporary realities and social relationships among the multiethnic community of southeastern Cameroon, highlighting the degree to which Bangando, Baka, Bakwélé, and Mbomam come together in intimate and varied social relations. Together, these chapters demonstrate the historic, spatial, emotional, ritual, and social integration among the communities of southeastern Cameroon. The ethnography highlights the varied ways that people construct identities and experience belonging; the evidence challenges expectations that one community in southeastern Cameroon—the "pygmies"—can be privileged as uniquely "indigenous" by virtue of their aboriginal relations to place and nature, cultural purity and social distinctiveness, political subjugation and marginalization within the nation. Chapter seven highlights institutional plans for the Lobéké region that reify stereotyped, dichotomous models of identity such as "pygmy," "hunter-gatherer," and "indigenous people." As a result of recent conservation, development, and missionary projects, as well as safari hunting activities, new strains of tension have emerged among the communities of southeastern Cameroon as they jockey and adjust to new economic, political, and social constraints—and opportunities.

In anticipation, the conclusion argues that distinguishing among three components of identification—social identities, ethnic affiliations, and stereotypes—accomplishes three primary tasks. First, this distinction facilitates analysis of social relationships and dynamics of belonging in complex, polyvalent contexts such as southeastern Cameroon. Second, this clarity illuminates the different qualities of viscosity—and manipulability—that the various modes of identification offer. Insisting on the clarification of the differences among social identities, ethnic affiliations, and stereotypes thus contributes to the voluminous theorizing of ethnicity by elucidating these distinct components in processes of identity. Finally, this approach to understanding processes of identification levels a serious challenge to research and policy applications that utilize and reify monolithic, binary categories of people as "pygmies" or "villagers," "hunter-gatherers" or "farmers," "indigenous people" or "immigrants."

By now the reader has undoubtedly grown weary of my continual use of quotation marks around categories of forest people. I consciously and consistently use quotation marks around stereotyped terms such as "pygmy" and "villager" because I wish to emphasize the constructed nature of these glosses. I ask the reader's forbearance with the unwieldy presentation of these terms, and hope that the annoyance caused will underscore the inappropriateness of their continued, unquestioned use in academic literature as well as policy documents concerning diverse forest communities.

CHAPTER ONE

Paradigms

THE FOREST AND ITS PEOPLES

T he western rim of the Congo River basin is a vast, forested region, covering southeastern Cameroon, northeastern Gabon, northwestern Congo, and southwestern Central African Republic. In many ways this area of dense, tropical forest is more comprehensible as an interrelated region than as discrete provinces of several distinct nations, whose capitals are geographically, socially, and politically far removed from the forest areas. Southeastern Cameroon is marginalized from the rest of the nation in terms of socioeconomic development and political integration, even as the forests of this region are of central importance to the nation's economic well-being (Ango 1982; Akolea 1994; Karsenty 1999). As a result of the richness of the forest and the contrasting poverty of forest communities, struggles over access to forest resources have emerged since the mid-1990s. Questions of

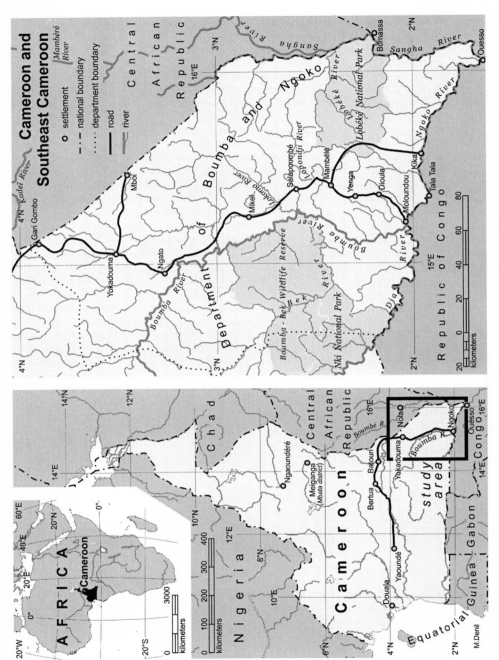

MAP 1.1 Cameroon and the Lobéké Forest region, southeastern Cameroon

belonging have been central to these debates: to whom does the forest right-fully belong, and who rightfully belongs to—or in—the forest?

Contemporary contexts of commercial forest exploitation and conser-vation of forest resources allow individuals and institutions to mobilize stereotyped identities such as "indigenous people," "pygmies," and "hunter-gatherers" to achieve their aims. These paradigms conveniently coalesce and condense social variables of identity that are deemed to be significant by institutions engaged in forest exploitation, forest conservation, and pro-grams for the socioeconomic development of forest peoples; in the process these paradigms generate rigid stereotypes that individuals resist or embrace as evidence of their social and natural belonging within the forest.

The forests of southeastern Cameroon are described, analyzed, and man-aged with reference to boundaries: national parks and protected areas; buf-fer zones and community forests; timber and safari hunting concessions; "people of the forest" and "people of the village"; "indigenous people" and "immigrants." Whose boundaries are these, and what do the boundaries purport to contain? What underlying values are reflected in the outlines and distinctions that the boundaries establish? This ethnography demonstrates that despite the pervasiveness of boundaries that denote natural, spatial, and social differences, there is as much that joins people together in the Lobéké region of southeastern Cameroon as divides them.

The Forest Environment

Heading east from Yaoundé, the capital of Cameroon, toward the East Province, the paved road peters out after 140 kilometers. From the town of Bertoua to Batouri, the road becomes increasingly rutted and bridges pro-gressively more rickety; drivers align the wheels of their vehicles with thick planks or split logs that serve as pontoons for crossing ravines and gullies. The road narrows as it turns southward and passes through Yokadouma, the last town with reliable electricity and markets. Trees tower over the road, and undergrowth crowds toward the open light. Entering Cameroon's Boumba-Ngoko district, small clusters of houses appear from time to time along the road, with long stretches of forest in between.

The marginalization of this far southeastern corner of Cameroon is evi-dent through absences. Vehicles are few and far between; markets are sparse and inconsistent. The limited network of unpaved roads is maintained by international timber companies, to the extent that the roads are passable by large timber trucks. Moloundou is a town of approximately 5,000 inhabitants on the Ngoko River, offering the only public services available—even haltingly—in the region. In the forest villages surrounding Moloundou, schools are limited to the primary grades, are sporadically open, and offer inadequate preparation for any kind of formal employment. National medical services are limited to Moloundou and, even there, procedures are expensive, often ineffective, and occasionally downright dangerous. The public availability of electricity in Moloundou is recent, rare, and irregular. A municipal generator was installed in Moloundou in 2000 and provides spotty power for several hours each day, offering the only public source of electricity for more than two hundred kilometers, until one reaches Yokadouma. The national postal system barely reaches this corner of Cameroon; rather than sending mail through the dysfunctional post office in Moloundou, residents of southeastern Cameroon send messages and letters via travelers on logging trucks and small passenger buses that negotiate the tortuous road that tenuously connects this region to the rest of the nation.

In contrast to the political isolation of the region, the forest of the Boumba-Ngoko district is a verdant tangle of resources that are central to the national economy. The majestic, columnar trunks of tropical hardwood trees such as *ayous* (*Triplochyton scleroxylon*), *sapeli* (*Etandophragma cylindricum*), and *moabi* (*Baillonella toxisperma*) extend high into the forest canopy, unfolding their branches under the equatorial sun and offering cooling shade below. These branches provide habitats for many hundreds of species of plants, animals, and insects, and offer important sources of food and materials for forest peoples. Bromeliads and epiphytes, lichens and mosses, strangler figs and creepers cling to and climb over the structures of the trees in dynamic consociation. Black-and-white colobus monkeys, African gray parrots, tree hyraxes, and dozens of other animal species forage for food and take refuge in the branches. Innumerable insects—especially caterpillars, which make a delicious stew—also populate these trees. The Lobéké forest is also home to an astonishing array of charismatic and endangered fauna: the region is thick with forest elephants and leopards, bongo and sitatunga, as well as dozens of species of primates, including lowland gorillas and chimpanzees (Stroymayer and Ekobo 1991; Wildlife Conservation Society 1995). From canopy to forest floor, stretching in all directions, the forest provides a wealth of natural resources that support the plants, animals, and people that make up this tightly tangled ecosystem.

The forest also offers a pocket of wealth for external intervention and exploitation. The very trees that provide the structure and canopy of the forest—in particular *ayous* and *sapeli*—are commercially valuable and actively exploited by timber companies throughout the region. By the late 1990s, Cameroon was the fourth largest exporter of tropical hardwood in the world, the second in Africa (Burnham 2000; International Tropical Timber Organization 1998). By 2008 Cameroon had fallen in the global ranks of timber exporters, as other African nations have dramatically expanded their timber production in response to China's surge into African natural resource markets. Cameroon's export production has also declined recently as a result of changes in the licensing of logging concessions, including the requirement that 70 percent of Cameroon's timber be processed locally before it is exported. Nevertheless, as Cameroon's oil reserves are depleted and commodity prices for export crops such as cocoa and coffee have fallen in the first years of the twenty-first century, it is likely that Cameroon's reliance on timber exports will continue and increase. In 2007 the forestry sector contributed 11 percent to Cameroon's gross national product, and constituted 20 percent of its exports (Njoh 2007). Much of the timber that continues to buoy Cameroon's economy originates in the East Province. Indeed, the far southeastern corner of the East Province—the Boumba-Ngoko district—contributed an astonishing 10 percent of Cameroon's overall gross domestic product in 1998 (Forni and Karsenty 2000).

Cutting secondary logging roads through the forest to access these valuable trees has also opened the forest up to hunters who come from various regions of Cameroon to exploit the dense populations of animals, which they sell in local, regional, and national bushmeat markets. In addition to hunting small mammals, bushmeat hunters also target forest elephant; the highly valued meat and ivory offer high returns to local hunters, in part because of the illegality of their commercial sale. Miners in search of seams of gold and diamonds in forest streams, and poachers eager to capture African gray parrots, green pigeons, and young gorillas and chimpanzees for exotic pet markets also arrive in southeastern Cameroon and penetrate the forest to conduct their illegal, clandestine activities. Safari hunting operations have also been active in southeastern Cameroon since the 1980s, bringing wealthy tourist-hunters into the forest for a chance to kill graceful and elusive bongo, forest elephants, and other forest mammals.

As a result of the remarkable biodiversity and chaotic exploitation of natural resources in southeastern Cameroon, international conservationists have been working actively since the mid-1980s to set aside substantial tracts of forest for protection. Research and planning began through efforts by the Wildlife Conservation Society, gaining local support and momentum during the mid-1990s (Curran and Tshombe 2001; WCS 1995). Since 1998 these conservation efforts have been spearheaded by the World Wide Fund for Nature (WWF), with coordinated socioeconomic development programs undertaken by the German organization Gesellschaft für technische Zusammenarbeit (GTZ); as a result, Lobéké National Park was legally established in 2001.

The Forest Peoples

Many communities live together in southeastern Cameroon, forming an extended, multiethnic mosaic in the Lobéké forest region. The Bangando community includes approximately 5,000 individuals who speak Bangando, a Ubangian language that falls within the larger family of B-1 Gbaya languages (Greenberg 1955, 1963; Moñino 1988, 1995). Most Bangando live in the relatively small area of southeastern Cameroon extending from Moloundou northward along the main logging road to Salapoumbé, the northernmost village in which Bangando are prevalent. Some Bangando, particularly women, live in Bakwélé-dominated villages along the Ngoko River, and a handful of Bangando live in Ngola and Mikel, villages where Mbomam are preponderant. Baka live throughout the region. Whereas southeastern Cameroon includes villages of all four ethnic groups—Bangando, Baka, Bakwélé, and Mbomam—in various proportions, the region that is socially and politically dominated by the Bangando lies between the Lokomo River in the north and the Ngoko River in the south, and between the Sangha River in the east and the Boumba River in the west.

The Bangando community has not remained exclusively in this extreme southeastern corner of Cameroon, however. Numerous Bangando (as well as Baka, Bakwélé, and Mbomam) have dispersed beyond their dozen or so villages in this corner of southeastern Cameroon to follow educational, occupational, and marriage opportunities. Significant numbers of Bangando also work at logging company sites throughout southeastern Cameroon. Several dozen Bangando live, work, and study in other Cameroonian towns and cities, where they remain in close contact with fellow urban Bangando, Baka, Bakwélé, and Mbomam. Three Bangando have pursued university degrees in Yaoundé and serve as secondary school teachers in various Cameroonian towns. One Bangando woman lives in France, having married a French merchant. Although the Bangando community is far-flung, the majority of people who call themselves Bangando still live in the small area of southeastern

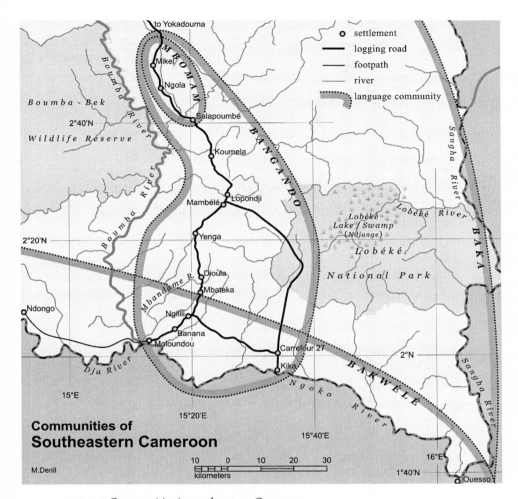

MAP 1.2 Communities in southeastern Cameroon

Cameroon outlined above, which spans only 100 kilometers north to south and approximately 60 kilometers east to west. All Bangando with whom I have spoken throughout Cameroon, whether in a village in the Lobéké forest region, in a logging camp, or in a distant city, expressed strong, sentimental attachments to the forest region of southeastern Cameroon.

Individuals who identify themselves as Baka and speak a Ubangian language of the same name, comprise a second major community that lives in southeastern Cameroon. Researchers and missionaries estimate that the overall Baka community, which covers a vast area of southern Cameroon and extends into northern Congo and Gabon, includes at least 40,000 individuals. In the Lobéké region, Baka families inhabit each of the main villages together with their Bangando, Bakwélé, and Mbomam neighbors and are often numerically the largest ethnic community within a given village. Social relations differ markedly between Baka individuals and each of the other communities, although in each case Baka individuals are generally less politically and economically powerful than their neighbors from the other language groups.

A third major group living in southeastern Cameroon is the Bakwélé community, which shares historical as well as contemporary experiences, social networks, economic markets, and political systems with its Bangando and Baka neighbors, and to a lesser degree with the Mbomam community. The Bakwélé, whose language falls within the Bantu linguistic group (A 85), tend to live in the southern portion of the Lobéké forest region and are concentrated in Ngilili, in Moloundou, and along the Ngoko and Dja rivers. In addition, the Bakwélé community extends southward into the republics of Congo and Gabon, including approximately 12,000 individuals overall.

The Mbomam community constitutes the fourth and smallest group living in the Lobéké region today, including approximately 400 individuals. The Mbomam language falls into the same linguistic group as the Bakwélé language. Mbomam share a particular history with their Bangando neighbors, a past based on tension, conflict, and, according to some people, slavery. Contemporary relations between Bangando and Mbomam are based on intermarriage, cooperation, and a degree of tension because of the diminishing number of Mbomam. The Mbomam community is concentrated in Ngola and Mikel, two villages just north of Salapoumbé on the northern bank of the Lokomo River. These villages were founded by Mbomam elders during the first decade of the twentieth century, during the German colonial period.

Each of the villages in this far, southeastern corner of Cameroon is divided into several neighborhoods. These neighborhoods often have an internal integrity, usually based on a particular family and its constellations of individuals who are linked through kinship and friendship, creating deeply emotional bonds that endure across numerous generations and frequently traverse ethnic boundaries.

Dioula, the village where I concentrated my field research from 1995 to 2000, includes inhabitants of all four ethnic groups in a total population of approximately 500 (the population of adults and children in September 1998 was 489). Bangando and Baka comprise the bulk of the population in roughly equal proportions, while Bakwélé and Mbomam are each represented by a handful of women who have married into Bangando families.

FIG. 1.1 Multiethnic household, including Bangando and Baka

Today, the villages, neighborhoods, and some households are mixed: Bangando, Baka, Bakwélé, and Mbomam reside in the shared space of the village and utilize the common resources of the forest. The interethnic community of southeastern Cameroon has been forged by histories of accommodation and adaptation (Spear and Waller 1993) and is marked by dynamics of both alliance and ambivalence.

The Forest: People, Place, Power

Throughout Cameroon's history, state authorities have sought to constrain the ability of local people to exploit forest resources for commercial gain. As forest regions became intensively integrated into local, regional, and global markets for tropical forest products over the course of the twentieth century, colonial and postcolonial governments sought to ensure that the maximum share of profits would be captured in state coffers. Until the mid-1990s local questions of belonging—who belongs to which lands, and who has access to the resources that the land provides—have been subordinate to the overarching state objectives of control over land and resources. However, Cameroon's Forestry, Wildlife, and Fisheries Law (1994) acknowledges the importance of community involvement in the management of lands and resources, leading to questions about what "community" means, and who belongs to it (Burnham 2000; Geschiere 2004).

Under German, French, and Cameroonian authority, control over land and resources favored—and continues to favor—the state. The German Crown Land Acts of 1896 legalized the appropriation of all lands by the colonial state, except for lands that were actively in use by "natives" as either areas of residence or cultivation. On both crown and "native" lands, however, the right to harvest forest resources was reserved by the German colonial regime (Vabi and Sikod 2000). After France took control of the colony in 1919, legislation to manage land rights followed a similar authoritarian pattern. Forests were classified, catalogued, and placed under the purview and authority of the French colonial government. In 1921, all "unoccupied" land was declared the property of the colonial state (Thigio 2007), and a 1946 decree granted explicit, exclusive control over forests to the French colonial government (Oyono et al., 2006). Power was vested in the French Commissioner to grant forest concessions of up to 10,000 square hectares to individuals or private companies, giving them the right to extract forest resources such as timber, rubber, ivory, and other products that could regenerate naturally. Local people, although not legally entitled to own land, were accorded user-rights access to fallen wood and nontimber forest products (Vabi and Sikod 2000).

Strategies to institutionalize and monopolize access to forest lands were upheld and intensified in independent Cameroon after 1961. While the government centralized power in the hands of the national administration, forest communities were relegated to the margins of decision-making processes that determined access to the forests in which they lived. In 1974 Cameroon abolished traditional land tenure systems in favor of land and resource tenure controlled by the state. Two decades later, this centralization of legal authority over natural resources culminated in the 1994 Forestry, Wildlife, and Fisheries Law, under which all natural resources—including all plants and trees—were nationalized (Vabi and Sikod, 2000). The conditions for an individual or company to apply for private ownership of land are arduous, and require the area under question to be permanently occupied and under exploitation. This regulation effectively precludes all forest lands in southeastern Cameroon from private ownership and control, as these areas consist primarily of forest that is intact or only periodically uncultivated (Karsenty 1999; Oyono et al. 2006; Vabi and Sikod 2000). National discourse depicts these forests as populated by elusive communities of forest peoples, iconically represented by "pygmies."

Illustrating various ethnic communities of Cameroon, several maps are widely circulated among Cameroonian school children that identify the entire population of the East Province as "pygmies." Maintaining the illusion that the population of southeastern Cameroon comprises only "pygmies" serves the political-economic interests of various state and nongovernmental actors. Because the official discourse depicts the forests of the East Province as inhabited by itinerant "pygmies," government officials and policymakers imagine and then legislate that the administration and exploitation of these seemingly uncontrolled, uncontested forest resources ought to be the prerogative solely of the state and its officials. Furthermore, from the points of view of nongovernmental agencies, such as conservation and development NGOs and missionaries, perpetuating the image of "pygmies" as the focus of their work ensures broad popular appeal and financial support from Euroamerican donors. The image of southeastern Cameroon as peopled by "pygmies" remains unchallenged in institutional paradigms.

At the same time that the Cameroonian state has consolidated control over forests throughout the nation, the exceptional biodiversity of and extreme commercial pressures on these resource-rich forests has induced international agencies, notably the World Bank and conservation organizations, to prevail on the government to introduce clauses into the 1994 Forestry Law that grant the possibility of community access to and control over forest resources in their locality as a means to promote community-based conservation. Legal rights to a "community forest" may be established by a group of villagers, providing that they form a "communal initiative group" (Groupe d'Interêt Communitaire, or GIC) whose constitution prescribes criteria for membership (Burnham 2000). This newly constituted "community" must draw up a detailed management plan proposing how they will utilize and conserve "their" community forest, a concession of up to 5,000 hectares on forest lands designated within the "nonpermanent forest" domain. In southeastern Cameroon, these community forests run along the eastern side of the main road, giving local peoples access to the secondary forests that they have utilized for generations, but precluding the rich hunting, fishing, and gathering areas in the denser forest, where Lobéké National Park has been established.

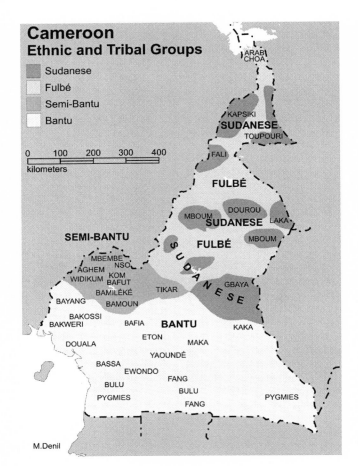

MAP 1.3

"*Pygmées,*" the "ethnic/tribal" group of southeastern Cameroon (after Neba 1987: 47)

The process of constituting a GIC, drawing up the management plan for a community forest, and navigating the channels of bureaucracy necessary to obtain official access to a community forest is exceedingly complicated, requiring a degree of local coordination and institutional fluency that is not common in many villages in southeastern Cameroon. As of 1999, no community forests had been legally established in Cameroon (Burnham 2000). By 2004, the provisional "simple" management plans for sixty-seven community forests have been approved nationwide (World Resources Institute et al. 2005), in large part due to village coordination by international conservation organizations, such as WWF, or to efforts by local elites who return to their villages to spearhead the effort, often resulting in tremendous conflict (Geschiere 2004, 2009). But, significantly, dozens of applications for community forests have been rejected by the Ministère des Forêts et de la Faune (MINFOF),[1] the ministry responsible for forest resources, including several proposals from the Lobéké region. By 2004, more than 300 official proposals for community forests had already been submitted to MINFOF; by 2006, many of these applications appear to have stagnated in the bureaucratic pipeline. Further complicating the slow process of establishing community forests, in 2004, fourteen permits for community forests were revoked because of "bad management" (World Resources Institute et al. 2005).

But even more problematic than the bureaucratic procedures for establishing a community forest is the issue of defining the "community" to which the forest belongs (Geschiere 2004). According to conservation guidelines, the community is marked by shared membership in the "interest group," the people whose interests are served by accessing forest resources. While the legislative guide to forming community forests remains vague on just how such a community is identified or established, NGOs' procedures for collecting data on local communities are premised on categories that identify communities by highlighting differences among them, perpetuating stereotypic, binary paradigms of who people are and how they relate to each other.

Analyses of the social contexts in southeastern Cameroon by conservation and development researchers typically pivot on the presumed division between nature and culture, differentiating people of nature ("pygmies" or "indigenous people") from people of culture ("villagers," "farmers," or "non-indigenous people"). An initial field report set the foundation for conservation work and set the tone for future research and activities by offering preliminary biological data, as well as a brief sketch of the social context, of southeastern Cameroon. The authors describe the communities living alongside the Yokadouma-Moloundou road as "predominantly Bantu agriculturalists who practice small-scale subsistence and cash crop farming, and Baka hunter-gatherers, who are now largely sedentarized and economically dependent on the Bantu" (Stromayer and Ekobo 1991: 22). This description both reflects and reinforces stereotypes embraced by other researchers, conservation and development practitioners, missionaries and government officials, and the general public. This paradigm is based on the assumption that central African forest communities can be identified by means of straightforward, opposing social categories (here "Bantu" and "Baka") derived from their basic subsistence techniques, which are taken to be indicative of the communities' innate relationship with the land. Starting with this assumption, the conclusion emerges that Baka—as the "hunter-gatherers," "pygmies," and "indigenous people" of southeastern Cameroon—are the only appropriate group of people to qualify as the traditional custodians of the land. WWF promotes its efforts to protect the apparently pristine Lobéké forest along with its "primitive" human inhabitants, specifically the Baka "pygmies":

Cameroon's Gift to the Earth: The Lobéké Forest
This *Gift to the Earth* is the traditional home of the Baka pygmies, and it is hoped that by preserving their forest, it will help to preserve their threatened culture and way of life. This is seen by WWF as important as preservation of the forest and its flora and fauna. The Baka are the indigenous peoples of this forest; they depend on it and their way of life is deeply intertwined and enmeshed with the forest ecosystem.[2]

Conservation policies designed, legislated, and implemented by the WWF in southeastern Cameroon wholeheartedly embrace the symbol of the "pygmies" as the "indigenous people" of the forest to promote their activities and raise funds.

As the management plan for Lobéké National Park was being designed, the Cameroonian anthropologist, who had been employed by WWF to oversee social science research and community relations, argued that Baka "hunter-gatherers" must be allowed to enter the core protected area of the Lobéké forest, where the swampy forest provides fertile hunting and fishing grounds, because the Baka are the original inhabitants of the Lobéké forest. The *"villageois"* (his term) would be formally excluded from the national park in the conservation management policy, because they are not "indigenous" to the forest.[3] This perspective assumes that the hunting, gathering, and fishing activities undertaken by *"villageois"* are unsustainable because villagers are, by conventional definition, recent arrivals in the forest who do not intimately tend the forest resources, people whose subsistence depends primarily on agriculture, and whose economic activities are likely to involve production for commercial gain. Despite the fact that all contemporary communities in the Lobéké forest practice myriad economic activities, including cultivation, hunting, gathering, fishing, and some degree of wage labor, WWF accepted as legitimate only the penetration of the deep forest by Baka, because, as "hunter-gatherers," they are the indigenous "people of the forest" whose needs can be met through their allegedly inherently conservationist utilization of forest resources. As this ethnography demonstrates, Baka, Bakwélé, and Bangando have for many generations relied extensively on the rich forest centered on Ndjàngé, the swamp at the heart of Lobéké National Park, for hunting, gathering, and fishing. The differential treatment of two of these communities, based on their presumed conformity with external stereotypes of "villagers" and "farmers," has generated unanticipated friction between local people and international conservation and development organizations, as well as among local community members themselves.

In March 2001 Lobéké National Park was officially legalized as a protected area. True to WWF's social scientists' intentions, the core zone of the reserve was specially legislated as a zone of nonhuman activity, except for the permissible, dry-season entrance of Baka "pygmies" for the purposes of fishing, shrimping, and the gathering of yams, wild honey, and bush mangoes. The director of the Lobéké Project for WWF, Dr. Leonard Usongo, explained in a radio interview for *Radio Deutsche Welle* in July 2002:

> WWF: [The Baka] have a special way of looking at the forest, and they also value the forest more than the Bantus, that is the non-Bakas. Take the lifestyle of a typical Baka man. He lives in the forest. He depends on the forest for his survival, mainly in terms of food and in terms of refuge. So basically the forest is just everything in his life.
>
> *Radio Deutsche Welle*: 20,000 Baka who live in the peripheral areas of the park are only allowed limited access to the core zone. The original idea was to keep Lobéké Park free of all human interference, to only allow settlements on its edges. But when the Park was established, the World Wide fund for Nature and the Government of Cameroon made an exception.
>
> WWF: We realized that certain forest areas of the National Park that contain quite a lot of resources like the fish, shrimp, bush mangoes are very, very important to the Baka. And in the process we had to negotiate with them on access to these areas in particular periods of the year. . . .
>
> *Radio Deutsche Welle*: For this purpose the WWF, with technical assistance from the German development agency GTZ, identified and mapped out the key areas used by the Baka. Meanwhile the pygmies have accepted the notion of limited access to preserve their way of life. (*Radio Deutsche Welle* broadcast, 30 July 2002)

The broadcast also emphasizes that

> Baka knowledge of the rainforest is vastly superior to that of other tribes who settled more recently in the region. . . . [Baka] still use time-honored hunting techniques. The Baka hunt smaller prey with a type of crossbow. A tiny wooden

arrow is fixed to the shaft with wild honey and a strong cord made from a vine is pulled back, and the arrow is released. (Ibid)

This icon of the "primitive pygmy" hunting with a tiny arrow and thus sustainably harvesting forest resources is emphasized time and again in the rhetoric of conservation and development organizations operating in southeastern Cameroon and in other areas of the Congo River basin. Stereotyped notions of Baka as "pygmies" and "hunter-gatherers," and therefore as the "indigenous people" of the Lobéké forest region, and the expectation that all other inhabitants of the forest exist in contentious, oppositional relations with both the forest and the "pygmies" by virtue of their status as "nonindigenous people," "villagers," and "agriculturalists," have become formally inscribed through the process of legislating Lobéké National Park.

Yet people whose lives are intimately entangled with the forest and with their neighbors include Baka as well as Bangando, Bakwélé, and Mbomam. In the contemporary context of southeastern Cameroon, Baka live alongside Bangando, Bakwélé, and Mbomam neighbors; individuals from all of these communities participate in the economic activities of cultivation, hunting, gathering, and fishing as well as wage labor, often in parallel, cooperative relations. Baka, Bangando, Bakwélé, and Mbomam all rely on the forest not only for their subsistence, but also for their spirituality. Furthermore, Baka, Bangando, and Bakwélé rely on fishing, shrimping, and gathering of forest products in Ndjàngé—the swamp that is now the core restricted zone of Lobéké National Park—during the dry season. Contrary to the portrayal by WWF, these resources have historically been shared by all communities in the Lobéké region. Finally, and perhaps most ironically, the hunting technologies that outside analysts point to as representing archetypal "indigenous" hunting—the crossbow, as mentioned above, and hunting nets, as frequently mentioned in other sources—are technologies that Bangando hunters introduced to their Baka neighbors, and that are still used by hunters from both communities. Contrary to conventional images of Baka "pygmies" as the unique and prototypical hunters of southeastern Cameroon using primitive hunting techniques, according to elders' accounts Baka learned how to make and use both crossbows and hunting nets from their Bangando neighbors, who are generally stereotyped as "farmers," "immigrants," and "nonindigenous" forest peoples (Bahuchet 1993a, 1993b; Gnangue 1998; Joiris 1998). This history of technological collaboration alludes to the reality that Bangando are also hunters in their own right, and highlights the historical intimacy of relations between Bangando and Baka as they learned forest skills from each other.[4] The common

FIG. 1.2 Hunter with "indigenous" crossbow

misrepresentation of Baka "pygmies" as the singular primitive "hunter-gatherers" of the forest perpetuates monolithic images of "indigenous people" but does little to clarify the pertinent realities of multiethnic collaboration, integration, and cooperation that take place in the Congo River basin and are critically relevant to the success of conservation and development initiatives.

Simplifications: "Pygmies," "Hunter-Gatherers," and "Indigenous People"

Simplified general images help coalesce relevant information about complex situations into convenient categories. The notions of "pygmy," "hunter-gatherer," and "indigenous people" serve as conceptual containers whose parameters reflect abstract, condensed social realities of the people who "belong" in each category. These categories are useful for simplifying, sifting, and sorting information about communities, providing basic building blocks for creating management policies. Yet each of these categories—

"pygmy," "hunter-gatherer," and "indigenous people"—is based on social qualities that external observers have deemed to be relevant, reflecting Euroamerican values and preoccupations more directly than social realities and relationships in southeastern Cameroon.

The terms "pygmy," "hunter-gatherer," and "indigenous people" are used synonymously and interchangeably in describing equatorial African forest people, providing convenient conceptual handles for expressing idealized—and oppositional—qualities. Throughout five millennia of intellectual history, the idea of "pygmy" has represented an interstitial human form that straddles oppositional qualities: culture and nature; humanity and animality; civilization and savagery (Bahuchet 1993c; Rupp 2001; Klieman 2003). Since the nineteenth century, the category "hunter-gatherer" has been used as an analytical model of the human condition at its most basic and most pure: people embedded in nature, situated in opposition to village-based, agriculturally oriented people. The concept of "indigenous people," as it has emerged over the past three decades in the geopolitical contexts of development and conservation, celebrates people on the margins of modernity who live harmoniously with their natural surroundings and suffer discrimination by neighbors, national states, and multinational corporations. Each of these categories is compelling because each claims to identify a community that is distinctive (from its neighbors and from ourselves), that represents an ideal society (simple, nonaccumulative, inherently conservationist), and that warrants analytical attention and protective policies. "Pygmies," "hunter-gatherers," "indigenous people": each paradigm positions an ideal type of society in contrast to notions of cultured, corrupted civilization.

Pygmies

The earliest accounts of "pygmies" emerge from ancient Egyptian iconography, in which "pygmies" were portrayed as the "horizon dwellers" and the "dancers of the gods," people at the edge of the known world, whose talents charmed even deities. The term "pygmy" is derived from the Greek word for fist—*pugme* (πγμη)—and refers specifically to the distance measured from elbow to knuckle. According to ancient Greek accounts, "pygmies" stand one and one-half to two *pugmes* tall. Their diminutive distortion of human stature fueled Greek explorers' and later scholars' perceptions of "pygmies" as extraordinary and aberrant examples of humanity.

Beginning with Aristotle and continuing through the nineteenth century, philosophers, naturalists, and social scientists speculated about the place of "pygmies" in the natural order. As scholars sought to identify boundaries between different states of being and various categories of people, "pygmies" were consistently positioned as an interstitial form that linked discrete states of being. Thus, for Aristotle, the "pygmy" came to represent the nearly human form of a developed fetus. In describing the gestational process, Aristotle describes the progression "from sperm to a fungus-like shape, to that of an unshaped animal, to the shape of an ape, and finally—one stage before the fully human configuration—to the shape of a Pygmy" (Aristotle, cited in Friedman 1981: 191).

For Albertus Magnus (c. 1200-1280), the puzzle of how to locate "pygmies" in the natural order resulted from his observation that both the physical and the psychological characteristics of "pygmies" seemed to straddle the divide between animality and humanity. According to Magnus, "pygmies" and apes share basic similarities based on their facial structure, such as the inability to wiggle their ears. And yet, Magnus noted that "pygmies" possessed the faculty of language, a basic human trait. He postulated that although "pygmies" utilize language, their rudimentary utterances are not sufficient for the expression and communication of concepts, and relegated "pygmies" to an imprecise, subhuman status. While Albertus Magnus acknowledged a qualitative difference between apes and "pygmies," he also reinforced the division between "pygmies" and other humans. He argued that "pygmies" form no regular communities, lack morality and shame, and have neither art nor science (Jahoda 1999).

Four hundred years after Albertus Magnus's comparisons between apes and humans, in 1699 anatomist Edward Tyson dissected a "pygmy" in order to disprove ancient Egyptian and Greek scholars whose accounts documented the existence of "pygmies." Through his dissection, Tyson attempted to demonstrate that "pygmies" were not able to speak, and thus did not constitute a particular race of humans, being no more than apes (Tyson 1895 [1699]). In an ironic twist, Tyson was correct in his suspicion that his "pygmy" specimen did not exemplify a human form; he later acknowledged that the specimen he had dissected was, in fact, a chimpanzee. Although Tyson's work failed to dispel belief in monstrous races such as "pygmies," it ushered in a new era of research that sought to demonstrate scientifically the boundary between humans and nonhumans.

During the Enlightenment, the model of the "Great Chain of Being" emerged as an extension of Plato's idea of the plentitude of the universe, and of Aristotle's notion that the fullness of the universe is structured through continuity and gradation. The Great Chain of Being was understood to be composed of innumerable—indeed, infinite—links, from the most lowly of all creatures in the universe to the most exalted, from fungi to angels (Lovejoy 1936). The search to understand the interconnectedness of the universe brought into focus once again the compellingly elusive links between known categories of beings; "pygmies" were positioned as the link between humans and animals in the Great Chain.

During the nineteenth and twentieth centuries, "pygmies" were exhibited to Euroamerican audiences as living relics of ancient primitivity, as people who straddle the boundary between nature and culture. King Leopold II exhibited a small group of "pygmies" in his Congo display at the colonial exhibition of 1897. At the 1904 St. Louis World's Fair, a small coterie of "pygmies" brought from the Congo River basin represented a panoply of paradoxical values: primitive savages and endearing children; clever, cheerful individuals who were nevertheless trapped in their depravity. One "pygmy" man did not return to Africa, but was housed at the American Museum of Natural History and later displayed in the monkey house of the Bronx Zoo, evoking his apparently liminal status as something or someone between ape and human. He eventually retreated to rural Virginia and committed suicide (Bradford and Blume 1992). In 1906 another group of "pygmies" was exhibited to parliamentarians in the British House of Commons, dressed in children's sailor outfits, highlighting their ignorant, innocent primitivity (Jahoda 1999). Popular fascination with "pygmies" continued throughout the twentieth century, culminating in an astonishing and controversial display of Baka "pygmies" from Cameroon at the Oasis Nature Park in Yvoir, Belgium, in 2002. In public displays of "pygmies," from ancient Egypt to contemporary Europe, "pygmies" have been presented as embodiments of boundaries between existential states of being.

Hunter-Gatherers

During the second half of the twentieth century, academic models of "hunter-gatherers" developed alongside public fascination with "pygmies." At that time, Colin Turnbull's momentous and influential book *The Forest People* (1961) was both a symptom and a cause of continued fascination with the "pygmies" in particular and "hunter-gatherers" in general. In the opening pages of his classic ethnography of the Mbuti of the Ituri Forest, Turnbull introduces the "pygmies" as the quintessential forest people, embedded in nature and providing a contrast to "villagers," people of culture:

[T]he BaMbuti are the real people of the forest. Whereas the other tribes are relatively recent arrivals, the Pygmies have been in the forest for many thousands of years. It is their world, and in return for their affection and trust it supplies them with all their needs. . . . The BaMbuti roam the forest at will, in small isolated bands or hunting groups. They have no fear, because for them there is no danger. For them it is a good world. . . . [The Pygmies] may well be the original inhabitants of the great tropical rainforest which stretches nearly from coast to coast. They were certainly well established there at the very beginning of historic times. . . . They were a people who had found in the forest something that made their life more than just worth living, something that made it, with all its hardships and problems and tragedies, a wonderful thing full of joy and happiness and free of care. (Turnbull 1961: 13-14, 26)

This idyllic conception of the forest and its original inhabitants profoundly shaped popular and scholarly notions of "pygmy" and "hunter-gatherer" societies for the next forty years. While the impact of Turnbull's work was profound, so too was the way in which his portrayal of the "pygmies" reflected his own values of equality and liberty, his aspirations for social harmony, and his search for intimate relationships at least as much as it revealed the realities of the Mbuti (Grinker 2000). Even so, the model for "pygmy" life that Turnbull offered provided an enduring template for basic perceptions as well as academic analyses of "hunter-gatherer" societies. Turnbull's personal search for a society that demonstrated basic human equality and equilibrium with nature resonated with deeply held values and concerns of Euroamerican audiences during the second half of the twentieth century.

The basic paradigm at the core of "hunter-gatherer" studies posits that modes of production provide the salient lines of social and political differentiation that mark "hunter-gatherers" as something special. For example, the practices of hunting and gathering produce particular techniques for storage and distinct patterns of mobility, which result in specific patterns of social and political organization. The different modes of production of "hunter-gatherers" and "farmers" also reflect distinct ideologies of space, resources, morality, and spirituality. As a result of these differences in ecological, economic, and social and political structures, "hunter-gatherers" have more divergent relations with states and other statelike institutions than do neighboring "farmers." Many studies parenthetically indicate that "hunter-gatherers" also engage in cultivation, either on their own terms or on behalf of their partners, and that "farmers" participate in significant hunting, gathering, and fishing, too. This overlap of subsistence practices is usually glossed over; researchers point to distinctions in cultural orientation, ideology, social and political relations that stem from basic subsistence patterns, regardless of whether communities categorized as "hunter-gatherers" exclusively hunt and gather, or whether "farmers" exclusively farm. Despite such niggling evidence of boundary-blurring, in analyses of their social relations the two groups are typically presented as conceptually distinct entities, identified by paired, oppositional categories.

The vast majority of ethnographic studies on "hunter-gatherer" societies indicate that relations with neighboring communities are a significant feature of their social context, resulting in close if uneven relationships with neighboring communities. During the periods for which ethnographic research can yield data—including oral historical data that reference the previous two centuries of interaction—there is strong evidence across the literature on "hunter-gatherer" societies that they have been intimately involved both with neighboring groups and also with the historical trends, economic pressures, and political institutions that shape the larger context of their social relations.

In his unparalleled contributions to ethnographic analysis of the historical and cultural dynamics of "pygmies," Serge Bahuchet argues that "hunter-gatherers" in equatorial Africa existed apart from "farming" communities in the distant past. Reconstructing exchanges of vocabulary and technologies and integrating genetic evidence and oral histories, Bahuchet paints a detailed picture of an ancient prototype of forest people, which he calls *Baakaa "pygmy" society, and its relationship with "Grands Noirs." His analysis offers important evidence of lines of integration among the communities, but fundamentally underscores the distinctiveness of "pygmies." Because of the potential for "pygmy" communities to be independent of neighboring groups, Bahuchet emphasizes that relationships between these distinct communities have been forged and sustained by the *choice* of both groups, each for its own advantage:

Relations between the Pygmies and the Big Blacks are voluntary, from the start. For the Pygmies, associating with farmers presents a consistent, secular strategy. At the same time, that there is choice in relations between Pygmies and Big Blacks is also proved by the fact that the villagers have no technical need for the Pygmies to obtain for them the things they want from the forest. . . . The Pygmies of yesterday and today are specialists who have chosen to remain hunter-gatherer specialists in a world of farmers in which they are an integral part. (Bahuchet 1993b: 152-53)

Emphasizing the strategic ability of "pygmies" to choose to relate with "villagers" also grants them the agency to disengage from such partnerships. Bahuchet argues that, from a historical perspective, the communities were not only distinct but also separate; other research undertaken by Bahuchet supports his contention that they once did—and still could—physiologically survive, in nutritional terms, exclusively on resources hunted and gathered from the equatorial African forest. Bahuchet makes invaluable contributions to our understanding of how "hunter-gatherer" and "villager" communities came together; however, his analytical orientation rests on identifying and emphasizing differences between "pygmies" and their neighbors.

The bulk of research on relations between "hunter-gatherers" and "farmers" highlights their interdependent ecological and economic relationships, in combination with sociopolitical and ideological relationships of domination and subordination. In studies that locate interrelations in this middle range of interdependence, "hunter-gatherers" live alongside their "farmer" neighbors but are relatively autonomous as individuals and families. These relationships are often described as symbiotic. Within this framework, relations between the communities focus on the exchange of hunted protein and cultivated starches (for example, Peterson 1978). Variations on the theme of economic exchange include exchange of forest products for commodities such as salt, cloth or clothes, and tools. These exchange partnerships are often formalized as partnerships between men, which can be inherited from generation to generation, presenting an enduring social ligament between "hunter-gatherers" and "farmers." As a result of these partnerships, communities may offer each other support in other social, political, or ritual contexts. Hart and Hart (1978) describe these relations as generalized reciprocity, characterized by a "fluid give-and-take" that builds long-term relations of mutual support.

While many studies offer evidence of intimate integration and ties of mutual affinity, they tend to de-emphasize these socially affirming relations in favor of analyses of relations of domination and subordination (Turnbull 1965; Terashima 1986; Waehle 1986; Headland and Reid 1989). Colonial-era ethnographies posit frameworks of colonial domination and paternalism as providing models for understanding relations between "pygmies" and their neighbors (Schweinfurth 1918; Schebesta 1940, 1952). Even as the bulk of colonial as well as contemporary analyses of relations highlights the interdependence of communities, analytical categories such as "master-servant" relations or "patron-client" relations are common, emphasizing the domination of "pygmies" by "villagers," thereby underscoring oppositional relations (Bahuchet and Guillaume 1982; Pederson and Waehle 1988). Similarly, some recent research has highlighted issues of discrimination and prejudice, presenting unidirectional analyses of discrimination by "villagers" against "pygmies" and emphasizing tensions and divisions between interdependent communities (Woodburn 1997; Kenrick and Lewis 2004).

Roy Richard Grinker's study of the relations between Lese "farmers" and Efe "foragers" stands out as a notable exception to the narrow focus on "hunter-gatherers" when evaluating intercommunal relationships. Grinker's accounts of Lese-Efe interactions offer a unique analysis from the perspective of the "non-pygmy" partners in interethnic social and economic relationships, in this case the Lese community. Because of the overwhelming preponderance of research on "pygmies" and other "hunter-gatherers," Grinker's analyses (1990, 1994) offer a much-needed balance in our understanding of the complexities of relationships between "hunter-gatherers" and their neighbors. Importantly, Grinker argues that Lese and Efe must be seen as parts of a larger, ethnically differentiated society. Grinker examines the Lese-Efe relationship as a multiethnic system comprising two communities. By taking ethnicity as his analytical focus, Grinker's analysis prioritizes relations between groups over focusing on one particular group in isolation (Grinker 1994: xi–xii), answering Jan Vansina's call to examine forest communities as complex societies that include *both* "hunter-gatherer" *and* "farmer" groups (1990), or, as Bahuchet describes it, two sides of the same mountain (1993a).

Despite this significant departure from the pattern of studying sociality of forest communities from the perspective of "pygmy" groups, Grinker's argument runs parallel to the corpus of "hunter-gatherer" research in two important ways. First, Grinker does not analytically move beyond the essentialist categories of "forager" and "farmer." Instead, he argues that "forager" and "farmer" are markers of ethnicity rather than ecological adaptation. Second, in building his nuanced, structural argument about the nature of Lese-Efe relations, Grinker emphasizes layers of structural inequality. Using the household as his overarching model for social relations, he compares the subordination of Efe to Lese to the subordination of wives to husbands and children to parents. Although novel for its attention to both "farmers" and "foragers," Grinker's attempt to identify ethnic boundaries contributes to the pattern of highlighting relations of inequality and difference, while de-emphasizing positive affiliations that are also significant in the intimate context of the family and household.

Several analytical patterns characterize academic research on relations between "hunter-gatherers"/"farmers" and "pygmies"/"villagers." First, analyses seem to reflect canalized relations of distinction, difference, and opposition. Second, relations of contention have a prominent place in these analyses, despite consistent evidence that affirming relations also take place between the communities and may be prominent. Third, research methodologically and analytically privileges "hunter-gatherer" groups, with attention to "farmer" groups only secondarily. Finally, studies that examine inter-relations focus on dyads comprising one "hunter-gatherer" group and one "farmer" group, even though in many—perhaps most—cases, each group is *also* in contact with other neighboring communities, widening and complicating the sphere of social relations and identities for both "hunter-gatherers" and "villagers."

A final example of research on relations between "pygmies" and "villagers" falls outside of the conventional patterns of analysis. Daou Joiris (1998) has examined relations between Baka and Bakwélé in southern Cameroon, bringing both communities into ethnographic consideration, following the approach advocated by Vansina and undertaken by Grinker. Going beyond analyses of ecological or economic interdependence and setting aside models that focus on relations of domination and subordination, her analysis demonstrates that Baka and Bakwélé relations are characterized by durable ties that create both vertical and horizontal alliances between individuals and groups of the two communities. Joiris illustrates that Baka and Bakwélé—while being historically, linguistically, and socially distinct communities—have forged and continue to sustain alliances of ritual friendship, ritual solidarity, and pseudo-kinship that hold the communities together.

Despite the breadth and depth of "hunter-gatherer" studies over the past half-century—research that reveals the diversity and dynamism of "hunter-gatherer" societies throughout the world—the subfield remains curiously dedicated to the flawed concept at its core. Although scholars have endeavored to demonstrate that "hunter-gatherers" really exist and deserve special attention, the analytical delineation of "hunter-gatherer" societies separates contemporary communities from the complex contexts in which they live, pursuing flexible economic, social, and political strategies that cannot be distilled to a subsistence type or a binary opposition to others. The categorical entity "hunter-gatherer" has been collectively created by generations of scholars and observers who have used this category as a convenient gloss to identify, describe, and refer to the people whom they observe, even as analytical models pertaining to "hunter-gatherers" have changed in approach and nuance over time. As argued by Robert Kelly, "[H]unter-gatherer is a category we impose on human diversity—it is not itself a causal variable. . . . That is, the history of the field, rather than some other criterion, defines the subject" (Kelly 1995: 3; emphasis in original). Having begun as descriptive models *of* particular communities, categories such as "hunter-gatherer" have become prescriptive models *for* the ecological and social conditions and relationships that prescriptively typify communities thus labeled (Geertz 1973).

The reductive categories of identity such as "pygmy" and "hunter-gatherer" that are often attributed to forest communities are misleading for several reasons. First, they suggest internal social, economic, and ecological homogeneity among members of the category, obscuring salient social differences within the category. Second, they suggest that people categorized in opposition to these groups—as "villagers" or "farmers"—are primarily and fundamentally *different*, masking important relationships, alliances, and mutual interests that unify rather than divide neighbors. Third, the categories are based on criteria deemed to be relevant by outside observers, often ignoring criteria for defining, discussing, and debating identity that forest peoples themselves deem significant. Fourth, the rigidly reductive nature of these categories does not allow for sustained analysis of social variation and change. Finally, these categories have taken on a dominance in paradigms of forest peoples that squelches alternative narratives, experiences, and understandings of self and other as viewed by forest peoples themselves. In light of the volume of detailed, rigorous ethnographic research on forest communities, I recognize that perhaps in certain temporal and cultural contexts the analytical categories such as "pygmy" or "hunter-gatherer" did, perhaps, reflect social realities of certain forest peoples. Yet certainly in the ethnographic context of southeastern Cameroon at the turn of the twenty-first century, and, I suspect, in other cultural settings as well, these categories have outlived their usefulness.

It is important to recognize the difference between a category that is intended to be analytical, such as "hunter-gatherer" as it is often used by anthropologists, and an identity, one of several possible ways that an individual either presents himself or herself or is represented by others. I do not mean to suggest that scholars of "hunter-gatherers" believe that the analytical category at the focus of their studies encompasses the lived identities of the people they study. Nevertheless, the category "hunter-gatherer" has become a convenient gloss and even substitution for local categories of identity regardless of how, and often ignoring the ways in which, people thus categorized express their own senses of self. Similarly, the publication in the last decade of several collected volumes of "hunter-gatherer" studies, including the seemingly comprehensive *Cambridge Encyclopedia of Hunters and Gatherers* (Lee and Daley 1999), continues to reinforce the notion that the category "hunter-gatherer" does, in fact, represent the fundamental and central identifying criterion of the communities under examination. Among some scholars, and especially among practitioners of development, conservation, and missionary work, as well as popular audiences, categories such as "hunter-gatherer" and "pygmy" have become synonymous with the fundamental, culminating identities of "indigenous" forest communities. The consistent use and tacit acceptance of categorical stereotypes such as "pygmy," "hunter-gatherer," and "indigenous people" as equivalents for people's identities and as terms that appropriately identify these people in scholarly, practical, and political discourse reestablishes and reinforces the notion that these categories actually do constitute the most fundamental means of individual self-identification as well as collective mobilization and action (Wilmsen and McAllister 1996).

I wish to emphasize that, although this book challenges the flat categorization of forest peoples as either "hunter-gatherers" *or* "farmers," "pygmies" *or* "villagers," I argue neither that "hunter-gatherers are us" nor that "hunter-gatherer" is a "noncategory," a fictitious construction that exists only in the imaginations of scholars and outside observers (Lee 1992, in critique of the "revisionist" school of the Kalahari Debate). The central conundrum in the context of the Congo River basin is that, although manifold social experiences and identities are meaningful in contexts *other* than subsistence and are realized through relationships *other* than economic or ecological interactions, the categories of "hunter-gatherer" and "farmer" or "pygmy" and "villager" *are also* relevant and used politically in certain contexts. However, the analytical and political focus on "pygmies" and their oppositional relations with "villagers" has rendered these other identities and relationships invisible and irrelevant to institutions with the power to effect social change, resulting in unanticipated frictions among forest peoples themselves.

While I concur with Bernard Arcand's fundamental skepticism about the analytical value of the term "hunter-gatherer," I respectfully recognize that anthropologists and other specialists do understand, analyze, and appreciate the level of complexity, dynamism, and capacity for change that characterize many of the communities referred to as "hunter-gatherers" (Arcand 1988). The great proliferation of studies on the historical and contemporary articulations of "hunter-gatherer" societies in trading networks, tributary systems, and political processes has dispelled any lingering notions of "foragers" as isolated or socially stagnated. Nevertheless, by consistently relying on narrowly construed, heuristic models that identify some people as "pygmies" and "hunter-gatherers" and others as "villagers" and "farmers," this field of otherwise rigorous and profound research has overlooked a vast and fundamental aspect of basic social realities and experiences. How do people who live within tropical forests and other remote areas construe, express, and alter their own sense(s) of identity and relationships? Who do they understand themselves and others to be?

Recognizing the error of insisting that people who no longer rely on hunting and gathering for subsistence are "hunter-gatherers," some scholars have recently adjusted their categorization of these communities as "former-foragers" or "post-foragers" (Lee and Daly 1999; Lee 2005; Woodburn 2005). While these updated categories indicate that perhaps "hunter-gatherer" communities have moved beyond the boundaries dictated by subsistence—or the social, political, or qualitative characteristics associated with this particular way of life—the model remains rooted in the assumption that subsistence is a causal and necessary indicator of identity and status. Rather than rejecting the category "hunter-gatherer" or "forager" as imprecise, these researchers retain continuity with the analytical models of "hunter-gatherer" studies and the field's underlying assumptions.

Indigenous People

The emergence of "indigenous people" as an academic and political category has brought new energy to "hunter-gatherer" studies. The basic assumptions inherent in "hunter-gatherer" studies run parallel to requirements for claiming an "indigenous" identity. As with "hunter-gatherers" and "pygmies," the category "indigenous people" is premised on ancient, intimate relations with nature and place, sustainable subsistence, and oppositional relations with neighboring communities and the nation-state. Just as the field of "hunter-gatherer" studies was reeling from internal debates about whether "hunter-gatherers" were "real or spurious" (for example, Wilmsen 1989; Solway and Lee 1990; Lee 1992), scholars responded enthusiastically to the emerging discourse on "indigenous peoples." By identifying "hunter-gatherers" as "indigenous people," academic researchers have identified an emotive field of applied work that validates models of "hunter-gatherers" as people whose unique relations with landscapes and natural resources, combined with their suppression by domineering and exploitative neighbors, warrant further intellectual attention, public acclaim, political representation, and research funding. This academic enthusiasm for the intersection of "hunter-gatherers" and "indigenous people" has been bolstered by the interest in such communities by officials (and donors) in the world of conservation, development, and social justice advocacy.

Most institutions that "promote the rights, voices, and visions of indigenous peoples" refrain from specifying whom they define as indigenous.[5] Yet the notion of indigeneity has gathered political power since 1989, when the International Labor Organization (ILO) issued the definitive paradigm of "indigenous people." According to the ILO, "indigenous people" are differentiated from other communities in a given nation by virtue of their prior origin in a territory; their cultural distinctiveness from the majority or national population; their subjugation by external political structures; and their self-definition as indigenous or "first peoples" (International Labor Organization, 1989). Until the ratification of the United Nations Declaration on Indigenous People in 2007, the ILO's definition of "indigenous people" was the only legally binding statement about what constitutes "indigeneity" (Saugestad 1999) and was seminal in shaping institutional policies of community engagement. Influential international organizations, such as the United Nations Environmental Program and High Commission for Human Rights, the World Bank, and the International Union for the Conservation of Nature (IUCN, the parent organization of the WWF), have explicitly embraced the ILO's delineation in their own definitions of and policies for "indigenous people."

In the context of southeastern Cameroon, these definitions of "indigeneity" can apply equally and without distortion to many forest communities, regardless of whether these communities conform to Euroamerican paradigms of "pygmies" or to academic models of "hunter-gatherers." Yet the fundamental assumption made by practitioners and supported by "hunter-gatherer" scholars is that the "indigenous people" of equatorial African forests are, and can only be, the "pygmies" or "hunter-gatherers." At a World Bank conference concerning the management of forest resources in western and central Africa, this explicitly narrow application of the concept of indigeneity was clear:

> [T]he Bank's definition of indigenous forest peoples, in practice, evidently excluded all agriculturalists from the "indigenous peoples" category, since papers were commissioned on Pygmy peoples only. By this dubious logic, all the millions of people inhabiting the forested zones of West and Central Africa could be passed over in the planning of the environmental future of the region. However convenient this may be for World Bank planners or conservation NGOs, it is clearly not a conception that accords with on-the-ground political or cultural realities. (Burnham 2000: 47)

Using narrow anthropological models for "pygmies" and "hunter-gatherers" facilitates the application of the vague concept of "indigeneity" in equatorial African forests by excluding forest communities that are classified as primarily agriculture- or village-based. By identifying the "indigenous people" of central African forests as "pygmies" or "hunter-gatherers," policy makers are able to simplify the intricate details of local political, social, economic, and ecological relations between diverse communities, distilling the object of their activities to a clearly identifiable community—"pygmies" or "hunter-gatherers."

As has been noted by numerous scholars (Saugestad 1998, 1999; Burnham 2000; Barnard and Kenrick 2001), in the perceptions of many African governments, and from the points of view of various nongovernmental organizations, the notion of "indigenous people" in Africa is contested; the application of the international notion of "indigenous people" implies that some Africans are more indigenous than others. Yet in their preface to a small volume of conference papers entitled *Africa's Indigenous Peoples: "First Peoples" or "Marginalized Minorities"?* editors Alan Barnard and Justin Kenrick are explicit in stating that "not all peoples indigenous to Africa are 'indigenous peoples.'" They go on to define "indigenous people" in terms that echo conventional policy definitions as

> those who legitimately claim a prior origin in a territory, as well as maintaining cultural distinctiveness from the majority populations. Typically, indigenous, autochthonous, or aboriginal peoples the world over are subjugated by external

political and economic structures (whether nation states or oil companies). And they maintain a self-definition *as* indigenous or "first" peoples. (Barnard and Kenrick 2001: vii-viii, emphasis in original.)

Later in the preface, the leap from "indigenous people" to "hunter-gatherers" and "pygmies" is made clear:

Thus relative to colonial or neo-colonial powers, all Africans are indigenous, but relative to most of their African neighbours Central African forest hunter-gatherers, for example, are seen by their neighbours as indigenous, as the first peoples who truly belong to the forest and know how to ensure its blessings. Where, formerly, their farming neighbours relied on them to facilitate their relationship with the forest (whether through knowledge or through rituals), today the increasing domination of the forest environment is replicated in the domination and marginalization of these Forest Peoples. (Barnard and Kenrick 2001: xi-xii)

Thus the transition from "Forest People" to "First People" to "Indigenous People" is complete; the assumptions that underlie the field of "hunter-gatherer" studies are reinscribed in policy documents and reaffirmed in the practice of integrating the concept of "hunter-gatherers" and "pygmies" as "indigenous people" into conservation and development programs.

In response to the institutionalization, legalization, and celebration of "indigenous people," Adam Kuper issued a scathing critique of the concept, prompting a firestorm of controversy among anthropologists. The core of Kuper's argument is that the concept "indigenous" is a euphemism for the unfashionable term "primitive"; it is an illusory construction reflecting the presumed opposition between "indigenous" values and those exemplified by mainstream, industrialized Euroamerican society (Kuper 1988, 2003). Kuper argues that the evidence presented to justify "indigenous" claims to land and resources relies "on obsolete anthropological notions and on a romantic and false ethnographic vision" (Kuper 2003: 395). In the heated debate that has ensued, the many outspoken defenders of the concept "indigenous people" have been scholars who specialize in "hunter-gatherer" studies in general and "pygmy" communities in particular. This defense has been spirited but insufficient to defend "indigenous people" (or "hunter-gatherer" or "pygmy," for that matter) as an analytically valid concept.

As this ethnography illustrates, the self-evident nature of indigeneity may not be so clear in the specific, multiethnic contexts in which most "indigenous people" are actually situated. In the context of the Congo River basin, for example, "primal culture" (Klieman 2003) is an amalgam of components mixed through millennia of interaction among communities, resulting in the sharing of natural, cultural, and genetic endowments. In equatorial Africa, distinguishing "indigenous" from "nonindigenous" is no straightforward historical or even genetic matter (Klieman 2003; Vansina 1995; Cavalli-Sforza et al. 1993). Furthermore, if the distinction between "indigenous" and "nonindigenous" makes a tangible difference in accessing natural or economic resources, as in politicized contexts of conservation and development, then identities are likely to be intentionally managed, as individuals variably emphasize qualities of "indigeneity" that conform to the institutional models on which policies for access and benefits are based. In reality, the people designated "indigenous" are likely to be those who most closely conform to—or align their performance with—the parameters of "indigeneity" outlined by the institutions and individuals empowered to disperse resources and benefits, often extra-local nongovernmental organizations and researchers in equatorial Africa (Mbembe 2001; Simone 2001).

Acknowledging the polyethnic, politicized contexts of African communities, Sidsel Saugestad has argued that "indigeneity" ought to be viewed as a relational concept rather than an essentialized one (Saugestad 2001), much as Fredrik Barth envisioned the ongoing, negotiated dynamics of ethnic relations in his landmark study (1969). Kenrick and Lewis build on Saugestad's argument, claiming that "'indigenous' describes one side of a relationship, the side which has been dispossessed" (Kenrick and Lewis 2004: 263). At times the relational argument positions "indigenous people" against the nation-state and corporate interests, and at times this argument positions "indigenous people" against neighboring communities. While it makes sense to think of indigeneity in the context of how people relate to others—to neighbors, to the nation, to corporations—this line of argument risks overlooking several important factors in the context of equatorial Africa. Although "indigenous people" may be invisible, inconvenient, and irrelevant vis-à-vis their national governments, their situation may not differ markedly from that of their "nonindigenous" neighbors. The focus on "indigenous people" to the exclusion of neighboring communities may lead to problematic exclusion of other, equally marginalized communities. Furthermore, the argument that all "indigenous people" suffer stigmatization, discrimination, and local subjugation by neighboring communities seems strained, given the lack of evidence presented by "hunter-gatherer" specialists to demonstrate the positions, opinions, and actions supposedly undertaken by the "villagers" or "farmers" from their own point of view. Academic activists who seek to position "hunter-gatherers" as the archetypal "indigenous people" rely on claims of a pandemic of discrimination that all "hunter-gatherers" experience in their relations with neighboring communities, without research that fully considers these relations, including the perspectives of these apparently oppressive neighbors (Kenrick and Lewis 2004; Lewis 2001).

This ethnography demonstrates that it is the relational, processual aspect of identities—be they legally inscribed and institutionally recognized or not—that shapes who people are and how they relate to each other, to particular places, and to particular discourses. In both academic models and legal policy frameworks, paradigms of "indigenous people" *require* definitions of exclusion, uniqueness, and difference of particular communities as *the* "indigenous people," providing contrast with and exclusion of neighboring communities. While scholars may argue that indigeneity is theoretically a relational term, once the category is applied to a particular group in practice, indigeneity becomes a rigid marker for prescribing policies and benefits that accrue to certain groups to the exclusion of others. While "hunter-gatherer" specialists who promote the rights of "indigenous people" argue that protecting the rights of "indigenous people" signals and motivates a move toward equality (Kenrick and Lewis 2004; Kenrick 2005), this ethnography demonstrates that channeling resources to certain communities because of projections of stereotyped identities—including "indigenous people"—moves toward new lines of *inequality* among forest communities that have been integrated socially, spatially, emotionally, and ritually for many generations. The notion of "indigenous people" overlays so neatly with other binary oppositions used to describe forest communities—"pygmies" and "hunter-gatherers"—that it is seductively straightforward to apply this category to forest peoples by layering it on top of these earlier paradigms, without careful consideration of how these paradigms came to be, what their underlying assumptions are, what role they play in academic analyses and policy prescriptions, and whether they track with local conceptions of who people are and how they interrelate.

Autochthony: The Politics of Belonging

In Cameroon, belonging determines access to resources and power. Autochthony and allogeneity—belonging and exclusion—have become driving forces in Cameroonian politics as parties, regions, communities, and individuals struggle for access to scarce resources. Whereas Cameroon's first constitution (1972) upheld the rights of each Cameroonian as a citizen of the nation to settle—to belong—anywhere within the nation, the constitution of 1996 enshrines particular rights for people identified as "indigenous" (Geschiere and Nyamanjoh 2000; Monga 2000). As a result, indigenous regional elites retain control over their local base of supporters by channeling state resources back to the community; the ruling party retains its political dominance by granting these elites a place at the national "trough" in return for their unwavering support (Monga 2001). The conjunction of the "politics of the belly" (Bayart 1993) and the politics of indigeneity ensure that those who belong are well-fed.

The definition of "belonging" is strenuously contested throughout Cameroon (Geschiere 2009; Konings 2001; Geschiere and Nyamanjoh 2000). Furthermore, autochthony—local frameworks of belonging—do not always mesh with international expectations of indigeneity (Pelican 2009). Since the early 1990s, the introduction of multiparty politics has produced fierce battles between "autochthones" (original inhabitants) and "allogènes" (strangers, or recent arrivals) in contexts throughout the nation (Sharpe 1998; Burnham 2000; Geschiere 2004; Socpa 2006). This decentralization of Cameroonian politics, combined with the agendas of international institutions that mandated structural adjustment programs and other efforts to roll back the state apparatus, resulted in increasing the political influence of regional associations and nongovernmental organizations (Burnham 2000; Geschiere 2004). In the context of the forests of southeastern Cameroon, the hollowing out of administrative functioning of the Cameroonian state has ensured both that local government officials treat forest resources as a personal inheritance and that decision making and policy implementation for public management of the forest are outsourced to international conservation and development organizations.

The politics of belonging has brought together two powerful political currents: autochthony as a vehicle to ensure that power and resources remain in the hands of the regional elite and their followers, and the international insistence that resources are channeled to communities that conform to Euroamerican, institutional definitions of "indigenous people." In Cameroon struggles over autochthony create tension between elites and villagers about who really represents "local" interests, generate conflicts about ethnicity and kinship and who really belongs to the land, and often result in the violent exclusion of *allogènes* (strangers). Discourses of autochthony generate heated debate in Cameroon, because the criteria for belonging are both slippery and manipulable; in the sliding scales of autochthony, there is always one person who is more authentic than the next (Geschiere 2009, 2004). In this way, autochthony undermines the premise of citizenship as extended to every member of the national community in the 1972 constitution (Geschiere and Nyamanjoh 2000; Geschiere 2004). Similarly, policies based on international frameworks of "indigeneity" undermine the notions of sociality that have held the multiethnic community of southeastern Cameroon together over many generations.

In the contexts of conservation and development initiatives, belonging is defined by NGOs and follows prescriptive categories and guidelines drawn up by global institutions and their representatives. In contexts of forest communities, belonging to the forest is a status reserved for "pygmies," "hunter-gatherers," and "indigenous people." For each of these categories, the salient qualities for membership concern a timeless rootedness within the forest and the concomitant status as a "first comer" or autochthon, belonging to a nondominant (ethnic) group, cultural distinctiveness from neighboring communities, and self-ascription as "indigenous": "hunter-gatherer," "pygmy," or "person of the forest."

Processes of social identification among people of the Lobéké forest call each of the four qualities of belonging inherent in "indigeneity" into question. Oral histories of the confluences of communities in southeastern Cameroon indicate that no single community clearly predated other communities (see also Bahuchet 1993b); instead, social histories emphasize the integration among communities extending across generations. Rather than being rooted in the Lobéké forest, the communities of southeastern Cameroon have moved within and between regional forests. Similarly, social relations are not determined solely by channels of vertical descent as defined by kinship and ethnicity, but are also forged through dynamic, cross-cutting ties that bring individuals and groups together in relations of collaboration and competition on a routine—daily, hourly, and immediate—basis. Lines of identification are not premised on cultural distinctiveness or ethnic boundaries. Cultural features that researchers might expect to identify as distinctive to "indigenous people"—language, particular technologies, subsistence practices, house-forms, clothing, kinship structure, ritual practices—show a remarkable degree of overlap and exchange among the communities. Finally, this research demonstrates that people identify themselves in many flexible ways, reflecting historical associations, maternal language, kinship, gender, senses of belonging to place, communal participation, professions and talents, and emotional qualities. People throughout the Lobéké forest region identify themselves as "people of the forest" in various contexts for various purposes, regardless of whether or how these individuals fit external paradigms of who the "indigenous people" ought to be.

Simplifications derive their potent functionality from the abstract universals that they represent (Scott 1998). If generalized stereotypes remain the monocle through which powerful institutions and individuals view different peoples and places, this administrative vision may remain sharply focused only on particular details that have been deemed to be relevant to particular categories of people, at the risk of losing fine-grained details about other understandings of and conclusions about the social system in question. Determining which details are *relevant* in defining these categories is a profoundly political act, one in which the overarching political objectives of powerful agencies and bureaucracies are intimately involved (Scott 1998). In both academic analyses of and institutional policies for forest communities in southeastern Cameroon, the equivalence and interchangeability among the categories "pygmies," "hunter-gatherers," and "indigenous people" and the simultaneous condensation of social details that are relevant to determining these categories render this trio of concepts as compelling and powerful as each is monolithic and static.

The concepts "pygmy," "hunter-gatherer," and "indigenous people" are all institutionally useful concepts because they simplify complex social realities; by drawing boundaries that purport to demarcate authenticity, the concepts offer a schematic map of who belongs and who does not, and to whom space, resources, or services ought rightly be allocated. Boundary making is a political process, one that is as common in anthropological research as it is necessary in policy making. But in the Congo River basin, where forest communities are characterized by countervailing dynamics of fission and fusion—collaboration and cohesion, as well as competition and conflict—notions of belonging and community are being constantly reconstituted and relocated within, across, and among the communities (Sharpe 1998). Oppositional, binary models—however expedient for researchers or institutions—do not reflect the ambiguous, contested, and often integrated social realities of southeastern Cameroon. In the context of forest exploitation and conservation in southeastern Cameroon, the totalizing glare of stereotypes such as "pygmy," "hunter-gatherer," and "indigenous people" overshadows the particularities of ethnic affiliations and obscures the shifting social identities that bring communities together in dynamic, intimate relations that involve cooperation as well as competition, integration as well as self-interest.

CHAPTER TWO

Belonging

ETHNIC AFFILIATIONS AND CONFLUENCES

B ending over notebooks spread out over the small, tippy table beneath the edge of the window, I tried to hide from both the afternoon heat of *pèmbé swèè*, the long, dry season, and from the curious eyes of neighbors and children who were heading home from baths in the river or from the shady cool of the forest. The cloth that I had hung as a curtain for the crooked, gaping window frame let wisps of white afternoon heat tug at its edges and prance over my work. Metallic purple wasps with gangly, orange legs skirted the edges of my curtain when the afternoon breeze blew the cloth aside; the wasps vibrated through the air with mouthfuls of mud to build canisters for their eggs on the walls of my room. The open window shutter was invitation enough to the wasps and indication enough to passersby that I was home; before long neighbors began to trickle by with their late afternoon greetings.

Coming back from checking his snares in the forest, Wanguwangu leaned against the side of my house and peered around the fluttering curtain, looking down at my back hunched over my notebooks. "*Dèí kíà?*" (What is it?) he asked. "I'm thinking," I replied without looking up, hoping for solitude this afternoon. "What are you thinking about?" he continued. With an inward groan, thoughts muddled through my mind. I blurted out to him, "You Bangando, who *are* you?" He guffawed and replied, "The Bangando are the Bangando! WE are the Bangando! Bangando is our language, and we are Bangando. It's not very complicated!" Looking up at him, I stated the evident social facts—"Bangando are not Baka"—and he smiled, shaking his head, and grunted, "*Àààà.*"(No.) "Bangando are not Bakwélé," I continued, and Wanguwangu said "*àààà*" again through his widening smile. "So to be Bangando is to be *what*?" I pushed on. His eyes shone as he replied, "So you want to know the difference between the Bangando and Baka and Bakwélé?" I nodded. As he turned to walk back to his house, he laughed and said, "We'll talk about that tomorrow!" He headed home, softly laughing and slowly shaking his head.[1]

As he left, Wanguwangu took the unfathomable simplicity of Bangando identity with him and left me stewing over my field notes. Laughing as he dismissed my query "for tomorrow" and walked home, Wanguwangu enacted the paradox of identity's seemingly overt simplicity and its inexplicable complexity. In southeastern Cameroon, ethnic differences are so evident to and deeply ingrained in those who embody and experience them that offering a rationalized explanation of the distinctions seems laughable; but at the same time, because ethnic affiliation entails complex and profound emotions held by individuals and groups, its essence seems elusive. Despite my best efforts to return to this precise yet untenable question, Wanguwangu never did explain to me the difference between the Bangando and the other surrounding communities, not "tomorrow" or any other day.

Bangando, Baka, Bakwélé, and Mbomam of the Lobéké forest region are interlaced in ethnic constellations, whose individual points and overall clustering help to illuminate dynamics of belonging within and among these communities. How do people express who they are at the most basic, inherent level, as individuals and as groups? How did the communities of the Lobéké region come together and generate senses of belonging together?

Affiliation within an ethnic community provides a lowest common denominator of identity among the people of the Lobéké forest region. In southeastern Cameroon, this fundamental sense of belonging brings together individuals who speak a common, natal language. Names of languages and names of the people who speak these languages overlap: Bangando (people) speak Bangando (language); Baka speak Baka; Bakwélé speak Bakwélé; Mbomam speak Mbomam. (Complications about which language *is* someone's natal language, arising when individuals are born of multiethnic parentage, will be addressed in chapter four.) Members of these communities also trace their sense of ethnic affiliation to their community's origins and history of movement into the Lobéké region. At individual and group levels, Bangando, Baka, Bakwélé, and Mbomam all recognize a clear consciousness of separation. These communities are linguistically and historically distinct, and recognize their differences of ethnic affiliation as providing the basic axis for orienting identities and relationships. Bangando evoke the notion of ethnic purity through an analogy to a straight, tall tree that grows in the heart of the forest, which they call *sékéséké sáá ngɔmbé*. This tree is both flexible and strong; even in the strongest winds, it will bend but not break.

But significantly, at the same time that ethnic affiliations provide a stable, social pillar that grounds basic senses of self, there is diversity and variation in sentiments of belonging within and between ethnic groups. Oral histories recounted by Bangando, Baka, Bakwélé, and Mbomam elders clearly indicate that interethnic relations among these communities vary tremendously in substance and meaning. Furthermore, ethnographic accounts of processes of interethnic meetings, settlement, conflicts, and negotiations demonstrate that, in addition to the clear boundaries of ethnic communities in southeastern Cameroon, there exists a robust core of shared experiences that bring individuals and groups together across ethnic lines. Returning to the metaphor of the forest, if notions of shared language and social origin provide the trunks that ground ethnic affiliations in stable and durable—but not immutable—structures, the interlinking roots, branches, foliage, and lianas offer the dynamic processes of interactions and relationships that enable the communities to live and work together as a multiethnic system. This chapter seeks to establish the trunks of the forest, the structural supports that hold each language group together through ethnic affiliations. At the same time, ethnic relations among Baka, Bangando, Bakwélé, and Mbomam are not everywhere and always the same, challenging models of sociality among forest communities that would have "pygmies" and "villagers" ubiquitously and eternally locked in dichotomous, oppositional relations.

Ethnic Affiliations

The subject of ethnicity among "hunter-gatherers" has been avoided by many scholars, perhaps because the overwhelming dominance of economic and ecological paradigms to identify who is who among these communities has been considered sufficient. While the vast and contentious field of ethnicity has produced vibrant debates that could enhance "hunter-gatherer" research, some of the recent work on ethnicity in the context of "hunter-gatherers" has remained superficial. For example, in her introduction to the collected volume on ethnicity among "hunter-gatherers," Kent explains that by the terms *ethnicity* and *ethnic group* she refers to distinct "homogenous cultures" (Kent 2002: 2). This approach to conceptualizing ethnicity echoes early ethnographers who identified particular, bounded groups by means of certain characteristics (such as "hunting and gathering") and assumed that an ethnic identity could be mapped onto these discrete characteristics, as species names are pinned to insect specimens (Worby 1996). Moreover, Kent suggests that the ethnicity of "hunter-gatherers" *is* "hunter-gatherer," and that this category is an emic, or internally generated and meaningful, category.

Studies of forest communities in equatorial African typically begin with the basic assumption that the categories "people of the forest" and "people of the village" constitute the basic rubric that organizes social life. Ethnic attributions are layered over these binary modalities, with the effect that the models appear to be locally specific and ethnographically valid. Taking this approach in the context of southeastern Cameroon, to the stacking categories "indigenous people," "hunter-gatherers," and "pygmies" is added the locally specific ethnonym "Baka"; to the counterposed stacking categories "nonindigenous," "agriculturalists," and "villagers" are added the locally specific ethnic categories "Bangando," "Bakwélé," and "Mbomam."

Acceptance of these oppositional sets of categories produces several results. First, "indigenous people," "hunter-gatherers," and "pygmies," together with their counterparts "agriculturalists" and "villagers," emerge from categorical abstraction as people who are really real: in scholarly analyses and policy agendas alike, these categories of people *are* Baka on the one hand, and Bangando, Bakwélé, or Mbomam on the other. Second, the stark divisions that are assumed in oppositional categories such as "pygmies" and "villagers" are projected through these categories as well. The fundamental relationship that inheres in the categories—difference—is projected onto the ethnic groups to which such oppositional categories are applied. By assuming that the salient feature of relations between ethnic communities in southeastern Cameroon is difference, models of sociality overlook the core of shared experiences, relationships, and values that bring communities together across ethnic lines. Identifying communities through reference to categorical stereotypes obscures the scope of diversity and variation in how people situate themselves and relate to others, even in the most basic, fundamental ways reflected in sentiments of ethnic affiliation.

Rather than taking binary oppositions between "forest people" and "village people" as the starting point, this ethnography of social relations and processes of identity approaches the communities of the Lobéké forest region from a multiangular perspective. This research considers the constellation of social relations among all four ethnic communities and reveals that relationships among the groups vary in structure, history, and sentiment. Interethnic relations in southeastern Cameroon can be spatially and schematically represented in the following figure.

It would not be feasible to grasp the dynamics of sociality in the region by focusing on relations between two groups to the exclusion of the others. Neither would it be accurate to take an example of relations between two communities in the Lobéké region as emblematic of relations between "hunter-gatherers" and "agriculturalists" or between "pygmies" and "villagers" in a general sense. Instead, the multiangular perspective of this research requires accounts of ethnic affiliations, processes of identity, and relations among the communities from the perspectives of all four communities. From this multiethnic, multiangular perspective, it is evident that relations

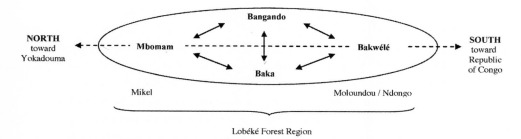

FIG. 2.1 Multiethnic relations among the communities of the Lobéké Forest region

among the communities of the Lobéké region are varied, dynamic, historically contingent, and politically expedient.

Basic outlines of sociality delineate the communities of southeastern Cameroon—Bangando, Baka, Bakwélé, and Mbomam—reflecting how relationships among the communities came to be established and what the broad interethnic dynamics among the communities are like today. Several arguments concerning ethnicity emerge in discussions of belonging in the context of the Lobéké forest. First, ethnic identities and affiliations are not static, but have changed over time. Second, histories of the origins and movements of the communities reveal that no single community is clearly identifiable as the "first-comers," the aboriginal inhabitants of the Lobéké forest. Furthermore, histories of confluence and integration among the communities demonstrate that interethnic ties among the communities are not always and everywhere the same. Contemporary relations among the ethnic groups vary, producing dissimilar lines of amity and tension among the four ethnic groups of the region. As a result, relations of power among the communities of southeastern Cameroon also vary. The elemental senses of belonging held by people of southeastern Cameroon cannot be reduced to a single, dichotomous model that places "pygmies" in relations of distinction from and in opposition to "villagers," with tidy correlation between these categories and ethnic affiliations.

In conversations with Bangando, Baka, Bakwélé, and Mbomam throughout southeastern Cameroon, people articulated experiences of strong, sentimental understandings of self and other that provide the lowest common denominator of who people feel they are. I refer to this sentiment as "ethnic affiliation." The social context of southeastern Cameroon suggests that ethnic affiliations derive their potency from the sense of collective belonging to the inalterable conditions of one's origins: language and social birth. Both of these qualities—language and origins—inhere in individuals as well as groups.

Among the communities of southeastern Cameroon, this sense of belonging to a collectivity united by language and common birth is not inert. The cohesive strength of ethnic sentiments is rooted in the collective embracing of metaphors of belonging by members of the group. Ethnic affiliations are the most stable—but not static—metaphors of existence that individuals call upon to understand themselves and others. During an individual's lifetime, the community's conception of ethnicity varies little and perhaps not at all, barring severe social upheaval. However, ethnicity does change at the group level over numerous generations. Ethnic affiliations change on the social equivalent of the geological time scale: very slowly. The *terra firma* of ethnicity does shift, and when ethnic affiliations do change, these radical transformations often reflect tremendous social (and/or political, economic, ecological) upheavals. These earth-shaking, ethnicity-shaking changes are not frequent occurrences, but take place in extraordinary circumstances such as war, migration, violence, and persecution. Whereas such circumstances of immense social change often build up over time, the transformations that result are often explosive and fundamentally alter the ethnic affiliations of individuals and groups, as they come to experience their senses of self and other in a tectonically altered topography of social relations.

Across individuals of a particular community and in different historical contexts, ethnic affiliations are variable. Different experiences of language and birth result in different emphases in any individual's constitution of ethnic sentiments. In addition, an individual may emphasize different combinations of the metaphors of language and birth in various contexts, evoking and simultaneously resulting in variable experiences of ethnicity. But the fundamental *components* of sociality that reflect ethnic affiliation—language and social origins—remain the metaphors to which an individual turns in expressing ethnic sentiments, even if her experience of those essential metaphors has changed over time. The individual can consciously attempt to shift her presentation of self through manipulating the metaphors, but because ethnic affiliation requires collective recognition and acceptance of an ethnic self, the basic metaphors of ethnic affiliation cannot be dramatically altered.

Ethnographic materials from the Lobéké forest region demonstrate differences between ethnic affiliations and social identities. Ethnicity is distinguished from social identity by the differing degree to which its substance can change. The viscosities of these experiences and expressions of identity vary: ethnic affiliations tend to be thick, sludgy, and slow to move; in contrast, social identities are fluid and shifting. While ethnicity is firmly based on metaphors that are collectively imagined to be stable, understandings of social identity tend to be based on malleable qualities of self and other, attributes which individuals quite freely select and alter according to varying social contexts. Social identities are the attributes of self and other that an individual comes to embody during the course of her life experiences—or over the course of an afternoon—and may include qualities such as gender, religion, nationality, specialty, and occupation. Individuals' experiences of social identity are not necessarily uniform either at a particular moment in time across numerous individuals or for a given individual across time. Metaphors and experiences of social identities tend to traverse the permeable group membranes that are constituted and shaped by ethnic affiliations, and will be discussed in chapters four, five, and six.

Language and Social Birth

Again and again in discussions, language emerged as the most potent idiom of similarity among individuals in southeastern Cameroon: where individuals share the same natal language, their sense of cultural unity and overlapping traditions is secure. The metaphor of belonging that binds Bangando individuals, families, and villages together throughout the Lobéké region is encapsulated in Wanguwangu's brief explanation of who the Bangando are: "Bangando is our language; we are Bangando." The literal translation of Wanguwangu's statement *"Bàngàndò bò nú ɔ̀ɔ̀, kà ɔ̀ɔ̀ bò Bángàndò"* is "Bangando is our language/source/mouth; so we are Bangando." The term *nú* simultaneously refers to "language" (*mí wèlà nù Bángàndò*, "I speak Bangando language"), "source" (*nú kòlò*, "the source of pure drinking water"), and "mouth" (perhaps referring to the mouth as the source of language). The metaphorical connections among these three connotations of *nú* illustrate the sense of ethnic affiliation as a sentiment that bubbles up, flowing and pure, among speakers of a shared, natal language.

The sense of belonging to one ethnic community or another also involves metaphors of birth and origins. As with the particularities of language, which a young child does not choose to speak but which he nonetheless absorbs and incorporates deeply into the core of his self, ethnic affiliation does not inhere in individuals through active choice but is conferred upon people through circumstances beyond their control, circumstances of their birth and upbringing. During an all-afternoon discussion about what it means to belong to their larger linguistic and ethnic communities, Bangando and Baka men gathered under a communal *mbánjó* verandah to while away the heat of the day. The young men unanimously concurred with one particular response to my string of questions. As explained by the village soccer star, being Bangando or Baka is something that an individual is not by choice but by birth. The young men agreed that no one chooses whether he prefers to belong to one community or the other; but they all were equally sure that now, as young adults capable of making decisions, they were unwilling to consider changing ethnic affiliations. The Baka men found it inconceivable and undesirable that they would somehow socially transform into Bangando, just as the Bangando men found it impossible to accept the idea that they would change into Baka, given the possibility. The unwillingness of these men to consider changing ethnic affiliation with their neighbors was underlined by the slow, deliberate shaking of heads, hung low and seriously between their shoulders, and the deep, serious responses of "Àààà" (No). Even though this group of young men hold close, reciprocal social ties as friends, teammates, neighbors, and even bò jáá (brothers—literally, "people of the [same] stomach"), individual ethnic affiliation is deeply ingrained and passionately embraced as the original, authentic essence of oneself and one's community.

But as strong as their senses of ethnic affiliation are, the young men explained that ethnic allegiances change and evolve over time, growing stronger as children grow up and learn the social habits and ways of living espoused by their parents and extended families. Reflecting on the births of two babies on the same day, the men suggested that even as a phenomenon of birth, ethnic belonging is more a function of social relations than of descent. Just the day before our prolonged discussion, two baby boys had been born in neighboring households in Dioula, one to a Bangando family and one to a Baka family. In response to the hypothetical scenario of swapping the babies, so that the Baka infant would be raised by the Bangando family and the Bangando infant would be raised by the Baka family, the men explained that ultimately each baby would "belong" to the ethnic group of the social parents who had raised him, not to the ethnic group of the biological parents who had conceived and given birth to him. Through his hypothetical upbringing by ethnically different parents, the child of Baka biological descent would be Bangando, and the child of Bangando biological descent would be Baka. Once the individual parents and parenting ethnic group had embraced the child, resulting in his social birth, he would remain immutably part of the community that raised him, and this communal sense of self would remain immutably part of his identity. Thus social birth offers a profound metaphor around which an individual's sense of ethnic affiliation is shaped. Although belonging is often expressed through images of blood—both the spilling of blood and the sharing of blood—ethnic affiliation does not necessarily flow from blood, but arises in the process of an individual being shaped into a person within the social context of others who share the same essential characteristics of language and social origin.

Ethnic affiliations provide a stable foundation for collective and individual identification, even as larger social processes shape relationships within and among communities, resulting in changes in the contours and substance of ethnic affiliations over time. From oral historical accounts gathered among the communities in southeastern Cameroon today, consistent narratives emerge indicating that the Baka, Bakwélé, Mbomam, and Bangando have coexisted as neighbors in various relations of mutual support and cooperation as well as tension and competition for at least the past century and a half. These processes of integrating diverse ethnic communities in southeastern Cameroon were neither smooth nor conflict free, yet ultimately the communities arrived at the political and social balance that characterizes the region today.

Confluences among Bangando, Baka, Bakwélé, and Mbomam

Communities of equatorial Africa are notable for their histories of mobility and social dynamics of fission and fusion (Harms 1981; Vansina 1995; Guyer 1995). As a result, many ethnic affiliations have changed over the generations. Communities engage with the political, economic, and social forces that buffet them and either adapt to changed circumstances or move on to new locations and new relationships. The history and social geography of southeastern Cameroon has been shaped by the complex system of rivers, forest paths, and roads that wind through dense tropical forests, connecting disparate communities through networks of kinship, marriage, trading, and conflict. Bangando, Baka, Bakwélé, and Mbomam moved into and within the Lobéké region of southeastern Cameroon as they contended with the political and economic pressures of the eighteenth and nineteenth centuries. In the process, ethnic affiliations changed as individuals negotiated and managed relations among the communities. Examination of what it means to belong to these communities reveals that stories about origins and ancestors, tumultuous flight from violent attacks, movements into and within the forest, and the ensuing social transformations as communities settled in the Lobéké region continue to shape ethnic affiliations, sentiments, and structures of power today.

Bangando: Migration, Ethnic Change, and Settling in the Forest

The case of the Bangando community poses an intriguing question of historical origins and ethnic affiliation. In their current location in southeastern Cameroon, the Bangando are linguistically and culturally isolated from cognate groups, even as they have developed deep and abiding ties with neighboring communities in the Lobéké forest region. Although the Bangando and Baka languages both belong to the Ubangian linguistic family, they are different enough to be mutually unintelligible. Corroborated by linguistic and ethnohistorical research, Bangando oral histories identify Gbaya communities that reside several hundred kilometers north of the Lobéké forest as the closest linguistic and cultural relatives of the Bangando community. If Bangando are indeed closely related to Gbaya speakers in the grasslands to the north, how did they end up living in the dense forest of southeastern Cameroon? And if they are linguistically distinct from the other communities of the Lobéké region, what dynamics led to the inception of relations with Baka, Bakwélé, and Mbomam communities, with whom they share cultural affinities and geographical space today? Have Bangando conceptions of self and other changed as a result of their migrations, movements, and transitions?

In common with many communities in central and western Africa, Bangando elders trace their mythological origins to northeastern Africa, to a Nilotic region beyond the Sudan, variously identified in stories as the Red Sea or the Nile River valley. Bangando elders recount that they were forced to leave this idealized homeland because of hostile invasions, driving the early Bangando community into the desert and then westward beyond the Ubangi River. In these accounts, the aggressors are identified as *Pényé*, light-skinned people whose skin burns rather than browns with exposure to the sun, and who rode horses and abducted slaves, a description that elders then translate into French as "*Arabe*." This earliest positioning of Bangando ancestors echoes histories of Muslim invasions of northern and central Africa, culminating in the spread of the Sokoto Caliphate into eastern Cameroon during the late eighteenth century. Because of continual pressure from the aggressive *Pényé* and the harsh climate of the desert, Bangando forebears fled southward into the grassland-forest mosaic zone of the contemporary Central African Republic. As recounted by Bangando elders,

The Bangando came from *Máánú*, a large territory near the Nile River. The Bangando had to leave this region because they were fleeing the war of the *Pényé*. When the Bangando were at *Máánú*, they were called Ngombé. The Ngombé fought valiantly against the *Pényé*, but finally they fled across the desert. The land was dry and the traveling was hard. The Ngombé couldn't survive in the desert, and so they descended toward the south. Many families stayed there in the grasslands and changed their names. They took the names of Gbaya, Koli, and others.

Other Ngombé continued and arrived at the Boumbé River. The Ngombé were very numerous, and lived among the Yangéré and Bokaré communities, who still understand Bangando [language] today. The Ngombé traveled across the whole area between the Boumbé and the Kadeï rivers. After the Ngombé crossed the Kadeï River, the Yangéré and Bokaré split off from the Ngombé because of an argument. The Yangéré and Bokaré stayed near the Kadeï River, while the Ngombé moved into the forest south of Batouri.[2]

This narrative of conflict, pressure, and flight echoes the discussion of historical events experienced by Gbaya communities offered by Burnham (1996, especially chapter two). During the eighteenth and nineteenth centuries, the Mbéré region of north-central Africa was permeated with trade routes, caravans, and markets bringing resources from the interior of Africa into the global economic sphere via Muslim markets and long-distance trading routes. Central African resources such as palm oil, ivory, and slaves were traded against items such as weapons and cloth (Harms 1981; Burnham, Copet-Rougier, and Noss 1986). The beginning of the nineteenth century saw an intensification of territorial invasions by Muslim North Africans. In the first half of the century, the Fulbé community consolidated power over the grassland town of Ngaoundéré, turning it into a walled city and hub of commerce. The surrounding areas offered the Fulbé an insatiable market for resources — mostly slaves and ivory — that they could access through domination of weaker communities in the grasslands and savanna-forest mosaic of central Africa, including the broad group of Gbaya communities such as the Yangéré, Bokaré, and Koli communities mentioned by Bangando elders (Burnham 1996).

As a result of these political and economic pressures, the confluence of the Mambéré and Kadeï rivers constituted a place of passage and a point of origin for the many migrations that funneled out of the region, often following the Sangha River to the south or along smaller river courses to the southwest (Baumann and Westermann 1948; Copet-Rougier 1998). The accelerating, cascading power of Fulbé political subjugation and religious domination, coupled with the abduction of slaves and extraction of resources, drove smaller groups such as the Ngombé from their villages, following the network of rivers deep into the equatorial forest. Bangando elders' narratives of their migration to the forest fit into the larger patterns and rhythms of events in central Africa during this tumultuous era.

Once the Ngombé had established themselves in the forest along the Boumba River, the community underwent a fundamental schism, resulting in a reorientation of ethnic affiliation. The Bangando elders continue:

> The Ngombé moved into the forest and crossed the Boumba River [Gɓákɔ̀lɔ̀] in the north, where the river is narrower. The Ngombé discovered a bridge of vines called Nyàwúndì, which had been built by Ndjámbé.[3] The Ngombé built two large villages, one on each bank of the Boumba River, one on each side of the bridge.
>
> Then one man fell in love with the wife of his brother. The brothers lived on the western bank of the Boumba. The love between the man and his brother's wife ripened. The couple decided to elope because they could not love each other as long as they lived in the same village as his brother, her husband. So one night the lovers crossed the Nyàwúndì bridge to the eastern bank of the river, and they cut the vines of the bridge so that they couldn't be followed. In the morning the Ngombé despaired because the villages on opposite sides of the river were now separated. But the Ngombé on the western bank were also angry about the love between the man's brother and his wife. So the Ngombé on the eastern side of the river, with the two lovers, left their village on the Boumba River and continued their migration through the forest. Today the Ngombé live in the Congo forest to the east of the Sangha River.[4]
>
> The Ngombé on the western side of the Boumba, including the abandoned husband, were left behind because they had no bridge to cross the river in pursuit of the others. They finally managed to cross the Boumba River using rafts made of small trees and vines, pushing their boats across the river using poles, looking very much like crocodiles swimming across the river. When they arrived on the eastern bank of the Boumba, they abandoned the name Ngombé and took the name Bè Ngándò, which means "little crocodiles," to commemorate their crossing.[5]

The cutting of the Nyàwúndì vine bridge underscores the sense of permanent rupture and social dislocation that Bangando ancestors experienced as they parted ways with Gbaya communities and entered the dense forest of the Lobéké region. Throughout equatorial Africa, social ruptures within communities are commonly expressed through metaphors of cutting vines and vine bridges that span rivers, or by means of stories about an adulterous couple whose transgression divides their community (Harms 1979, 1981; Giles-Vernick 1999, 2002). The story of the Ngombé-Bangando schism in the forest near the Boumba River contains both of these tropes, and can be interpreted as evidence of a profound rift within the community that caused one subset to pull away and strike out on its own, ultimately leading to the emergence of two distinct communities and two distinct ethnic affiliations: Ngombé and Bangando. The breaking of the vine bridge between two communities represents the final rupture in relations between an ancestral social group and a newly constituted social community and ethnic identity. Once the vine bridge was severed and the community managed to cross the Boumba River like crocodiles — *bè ngándò* — the Bangando community remained in the forest of southeastern Cameroon, unified by new sentiments of ethnic affiliation.

Baka: Relations with Bakwélé and Bangando

Despite their relatively late arrival along the Boumba River (c. 1850), Bangando accounts of their arrival make no mention of encounters with other communities, nor do histories of other communities indicate displacement by Bangando (Bahuchet 1993b). Yet oral accounts do clearly indicate that various forest communities were already established in southeastern Cameroon, in the forest to the west of the Sangha River. These forest communities had endured pressures of exploitation of forest resources, slavery, forced migration, and violence similar to those experienced by the Bangando community. In the context of the Congo River basin, however, the pressures stemmed not from equestrian invaders of the grasslands, but from the rush of European and African entrepreneurs to exploit forest resources, control territory, and absorb people. Waves of violent pressures accompanied the spread of guns from the Atlantic coast of Africa toward the interior, following the rivers and tributaries of the Congo River (Siroto 1969; Coquery-Vidrovitch 1972, 1998; Rupp 2001). As a result of these pressures, some communities, such as the Bakota, fled the forests of southeastern Cameroon, while others, such as the Baka and the Bakwélé communities along the Sangha River, formed hardy alliances.

The Lobéké River flows westward from the Sangha River, creating a vast, open clearing in the dense forest, an inland delta known to local communities as Ndjàngé. The seasonal ebbing and flowing of the Lobéké River washes rich organic materials and minerals into the forest clearing, supporting diverse vegetation and attracting a wide array of animal species; the swampy lake of the rainy season is transformed into a lush hunting area during the dry season. Ndjàngé provides ideal hunting and fishing grounds, along with plentiful honey, wild yams, bush mangoes, caterpillars, and even palm oil.[6] This region continues to be the source of vivid imagery of abundance, diversity, and luxurious living cherished by Baka, Bakwélé, and Bangando today.[7]

FIG. 2.2
Buba, Baka elder

Oral histories offered by Baka elders begin by situating the Baka community at Ndjàngé. From the indeterminate past until about seventy years
ago, Baka inhabited the forest to the west of the Sangha River, living in large,
centralized villages near Ndjàngé. Baka elders who remember their youth at
Ndjàngé recall the forest clearing as the source of all good things in the forest. Buba reminisces with sparkling eyes and a toothless smile:

I was born in Ndjàngé. We Baka are migrants from Lobéké. This is why we came
in this direction, toward here, the Bangando region. We were born in the Bakwélé
region.

In this time, when we lived along the Sangha at the clearing called Ndjàngé,
this is what we ate. We ate many kinds of wild yams and much honey. To go with
the wild yams, we ate many kinds of animals: gorillas, wild pigs, chimpanzees,
buffalos. The elephant hunters also killed elephants, and we ate them, too. At this
time, we lived on the edge of the Sangha River. My younger sister and my older
sister, my mother brought us all into this world on the edge of the Sangha. Me, I
was born among the Bakwélé at Ndjàngé.

Really, if you have never been to Ndjàngé, you have never seen a beautiful
thing. There are different parts of Ndjàngé that are filled with different kinds of
animals. The wild pigs, they have space for themselves. The buffalo, the bongo,

the snakes, the elephants all have their space too. It's where I can get everything. . . . Ooooo! Is there honey at Ndjàngé!⁸

The Baka did not live at Ndjàngé in isolation, but lived in close association with the Bakwélé. Buba offered the following rich narrative, describing the complexity of social, economic, and political ties between the Baka and Bakwélé, underscoring the level of deep friendship and support between the two communities:

At Ndjàngé there were four separate villages. At the time when we were with the Bakwélé, Ndjàmbò was the [Baka] chief of our village on the edge of Ndjàngé. Then there was the village of Ngòlú and his father. The third village was Sèmbá, whose chief was Wéétì, a Bakwélé elder. There was also the village of Mègùmlá, who was part of the family of Ngòlú.

In each Baka family group there was one person who was the chief. The entire community at Ndjàngé was governed by Wéétì [the Bakwélé chief], Baka as well as Bakwélé. The meat of all the elephants that were killed came back to Wéétì. All of the ivory tusks that we hunted were collected and stored in a room at Wéétì's house.

Wéétì's most reliable friend was a Baka man named Bàndàmbá, the big brother of Mòténgá. Bàndàmbá was like a manager to Wéétì. They had a very close collaboration. They spoke in each other's ears. After discussions between Bàndàmbá and Wéétì, they would give their instructions to the other men.

If Bàndàmbá was away, Wéétì would not eat before Bàndàmbá returned, so close was their friendship. When Bàndàmbá arrived, it was he who divided up the food and everything else. The small, round baskets [kátá] that we used for serving food—the ones that we kept up high in the men's verandah [mbánjó]—if Bàndàmbá didn't arrive, we could not take them down. Wéétì had ten wives. Each of his wives prepared food to put in the kátás, but it was Bàndàmbá who distributed the food to everyone. Wéétì and Bàndàmbá always ate together. If they couldn't eat all of their food, they put their baskets back up high in the rafters of the verandah.⁹

This narrative of ethnic intermingling at Ndjàngé highlights several important social patterns. First, it is important to underscore that although Baka and Bakwélé developed close interethnic relations at Ndjàngé, each community retained its ethnic distinctiveness and separate political consciousness. Despite basic differences in their fundamental, ethnic affiliations, Baka and Bakwélé communities were integrated in meaningful ways and in multiple dimensions. The communities shared ecological spaces and had overlapping economic orientations, including hunting, fishing, and gathering. Baka and Bakwélé engaged in intimate partnerships that brought both individuals—such as Bàndàmbá and Wééti—and communities together at Ndjàngé. Importantly, this account locates the temporal as well as spatial point of departure for tracing Baka histories of belonging to Ndjàngé—which is today the heart of Lobéké National Park—and to the collaborative association that Baka shared with Bakwélé at Ndjàngé. As a result, no single community emerges from this historical account as the "original" community of the Lobéké forest region.

Given the high degree of political and economic integration among Baka and Bakwélé at Ndjàngé, and the glowing idealism with which today's Baka remember the abundance and peacefulness of life there, it is not clear what social, political, or ecological pressures precipitated the eventual movement of the Baka community from the Sangha River region westward toward the Boumba River, where the Bangando community had settled. Baka histories indicate that upon the death of Bìákán, a Bakwélé elder who was the father of one of the village heads at Ndjàngé, the Bakwélé abandoned Ndjàngé and returned to Moloundou, the settlement along the Ngoko River where the Bakwélé community is predominant. Baka elders recount that "after the death of Bìákán, the Baka were in charge [of the region of Ndjàngé]."

Despite the wealth of resources at Ndjàngé, Baka also seemed to value political and social alliances with other communities. Thus when they encountered Bangando hunters near Ndjàngé, Baka elders were amenable to the invitation to settle with Bangando families near the Boumba River. It is clear in oral histories recounted by both Bangando and Baka elders that ancestors of the two communities encountered each other during hunting trips near Ndjàngé, and that they developed mutual and robust relationships based on cooperation in hunting and other aspects of daily life. As recalled by Baka elders, the partnership and friendship between Baka and Bangando precipitated quite rapidly from their initial encounter:

> We spent a long time living with the Bakwélé—all of my youth. We walked in the forest, and one time we met Bangando in the forest near *Mɔ̀kòngò*.[10] The day that we met the Bangando, the chimpanzees were high in the trees. We had forbidden them from coming down to the ground. As soon as the chimpanzees started to cry out, the Bangando appeared for the first time. As soon as we met Bangando, they took us as their friends, and we [Baka] all left to join them en masse [*kàlíkíkàlíkí*].

As soon as we arrived among the Bangando, we made our homes here at Bàbélè [a small river near the village of Dioula]. Mbèlá [a Bangando man] contacted us on behalf of the Bangando, so that we could make an alliance [bándí]. He came to greet us with a goat. He cut its throat and we ate together. So we went into the forest, and we killed a wild pig and a buffalo. We brought the meat back to the village to give to the Bangando, because what they did was a good thing.[11]

The initial arrival of Baka families as proximal neighbors to the Bangando seems to have been driven by interethnic sentiments of cooperation and collaboration; memories of this establishment of ties revolve around stories about the reciprocal sharing of highly valued meat. Interestingly, each community describes the initial offering of meat coming from the *other* group: according to Baka accounts, Bangando men first offered meat to Baka elders, leading to reciprocal hunting and offering of meat by the Baka men; in the Bangando elders' accounts of the initial meeting, it was Baka hunters who first presented meat, followed by the Bangando offering of a return gift of meat. In both versions, the exchange of meat led to sustained patterns of collaboration and ultimately to cohabitation. Ambata, a resident of Dioula village, explains the coresidence of a Baka family with his own Bangando family, tracing the alliance back to his great-great-grandfather:

When my great-great-grandfather was young, he hunted on the far side of Ndjàngé, near the Sangha River. He met a Baka man—the great-grandfather of Nakolongjoko—who was also in the forest hunting. This Baka man had just killed an elephant and offered to share it with my great-great- grandfather and his family. So the families came together to share meat. Then my great-great-grandfather also killed an elephant to share with the Baka family. Following their hunting, my great-great-grandfather asked the Baka man to come and join him in the village, so that they could live together and continue their friendship. So the Baka man and his family came to Dioula, and my great-great-grandfather slaughtered a goat in celebration of their arrival. The families and all their generations have lived together.[12]

The narrative of sharing meat, providing the basis for interethnic relations between Baka and Bangando, reflects the trope of commensality that is widely used throughout equatorial Africa to represent the public demonstration of intimate bonds (Holtzman 2006). In this narrative, the public exchange and consumption of highly prized meat reflects the significance that the communities placed on their partnership. That the meat exchanged came from large animals—particularly elephants—suggests that many individuals were brought together through the ceremonial sharing of meat. The narrative of meat sharing is told throughout the Lobéké region by Baka and Bangando, as they recount the forging of their interethnic relations. As will be evident in subsequent chapters, interethnic commensality figures prominently as both a metaphor and vehicle for solidarity in contexts of shared social spaces, conflict resolution, and the forging of interethnic alliances.

Today Ambata's family continues to live in close proximity to Nakolong-joko and his family, the descendants of the Baka man who befriended his great-great-grandfather. The relations between these two families are typical of interfamilial relations throughout the region: families of both ethnicities recognize the special connection between them, a friendship that has been sustained across several generations. As Bangando and Baka began to share joys and sorrows, their alliances linked the communities at several levels of the family: male heads of households formed close friendships and shared

FIG. 2.3 Bangando hunter preparing a packet of meat to give to his Baka partner, *bándí*, Lopondji, 1997

in each other's responsibilities for the physical and social well-being of both families; wives supported each other during times of heavy labor, scant food, and life transitions such as births, deaths, and marriages; children developed fast friendships with their playmates of the other ethnic community, friendships that often developed into more mature alliances as the children grew up and began families of their own. Bangando and Baka boys and youths developed particularly close relations, as many endured initiation and circumcision together, uniting generations of young men in secret societies, interethnic structures of men's responsibility and reciprocity. While maintaining their distinctiveness, Bangando and Baka transcended their linguistic and social differences, ultimately settling down together in the same villages, sharing spaces and forging alliances in the forest, villages, neighborhoods, and within households.

Oral accounts clearly indicate that the initial interdigitation of Bangando and Baka communities was the result of mutual sentiments of cooperation and friendship even as the communities maintained a degree of spatial integrity by living in distinct communities near the Boumba River. Ndjumbé, a Bangando elder of Dioula, recounts childhood meetings with the Baka who had entered into a collaborative relationship with his paternal grandfather, and who lived a short distance from his household:

> In the evenings, we could hear Baka drumming and singing and dancing in the forest. Because we children were curious, we took sticks from the kitchen fire after we ate our meal, and walked through the forest. We had no lamps then, so we would carry the burning embers, waving them through the air to make light as we walked through the forest. The Baka would sing and dance until late in the night. We watched them dance and sing and then we went back home. Other times Baka would come to our house to talk with my father, to discuss hunting and the forest. Sometimes they would bring meat, and sometimes they would take meat from our kitchen back with them.[13]

At least initially, Bangando and Baka families who had established links and alliances of friendship still tended to live at some distance from each other in distinct hamlets comprised of small groups of extended families; increasing interaction among families and across generations led to closer and closer spatial integration.

The ultimate settlement of Bangando and Baka in the same villages alongside the colonial road seems to have been driven by the external political motives of colonial and postcolonial administrators. This permanent resettlement of Baka and the manipulation of Bangando individuals by colonial officials as tools in the sedentarization of the Baka community may have solidified the stratified political and economic relationship between the groups that continues today. As illustrated in the recollections of Sébò, a Bangando elder of the eagle clan, the resettlement of the Baka community among Bangando families and within communal villages introduces questions concerning the relative political power between Bangando and Baka, and the role of Bangando men as "colonizing" agents of the French or Cameroonian administrations and missionaries. According to Sébò,

> The Baka were always in the forest. Then the officials came. . . . The Sous-Préfet said to us: "You must take them slowly, gently. You Bangando, you are not very numerous. You must take the Baka carefully. Don't harm them. Take them so that finally you will be numerous."[14]

Oral stories about the interrelations between Baka and Bangando consistently place the resettlement of Baka along the roadside and their integration into Bangando communities during the late-colonial era or early years of independence. It is unclear in this account whether the "Sous-Préfet" refers to a French colonial-era official or to a postindependence Cameroonian official; in either case Bangando leaders seem to have been manipulated as extension agents of the government, serving as go-betweens in the official attempt to settle the Baka. The implicit assumption of the government officials was that the resettlement of Baka in roadside villages would augment the already politically established and accessible Bangando community, while simultaneously bringing the Baka community under state control.

Other accounts of the settlement of Baka in the predominantly Bangando villages contrast with the recollection that the Bangando were complicit in the project of sedentarization. In these accounts, instead of Bangando facilitation of Baka resettlement, postindependence government officials acted alone as agents of force as they compelled the Baka to move from their villages in the forest to settle in roadside villages. As another Bangando elder, Maga, recalls,

> After independence, the Cameroonian government officials in Moloundou came along to all of the Baka villages in the forest and forced them to move to the roadside, to live in the larger villages. The Sous-Préfet just went into the forest with *gendarmes* and guns and arrested any Baka who refused to comply, and sent them

to prison in Batouri. So the Baka moved out of the forest and settled in villages along the road.[15]

The project of resettlement continued well into the last quarter of the twentieth century, as European missionaries contacted Baka communities that remained in the forest in spite of government efforts to settle them in roadside villages. Perhaps these Baka families had resisted the attempted domination by political authorities altogether; perhaps they had returned to the forest after the wave of sedentarization policies and policing had passed. Baka communities—in both roadside and forest villages—were the target of Catholic missionaries who established their permanent mission station in Wélélé, a sub-hamlet of Salapoumbé, in 1973. Their activities began with taking a census of the Baka, the community that they sought to heal spiritually and physically and to stabilize geographically and socially. Missionary programs, including evangelization, health care, and later, education, were initially directed exclusively at the Baka community; but the missionaries relied on Bangando residents of roadside villages for logistical support and labor. Prior to the arrival of the Catholic mission, a small number of Bangando elders had been baptized by American Protestant missionaries, who had established a mission station and school near Yokadouma during the 1950s. These already converted Bangando men, many of whom were respected elders by the early 1970s, offered an invaluable community of educated Christians to assist the Catholic missionaries' efforts to reach the Baka. In addition, because Bangando and Baka individuals had developed and maintained intricate friendships and partnerships over numerous generations, Bangando collaboration with the Catholic missionaries offered a means to access the more remote Baka families with whom they still had contact. Sébò continues his narrative of Baka settlement:

> There was also a white man who came to count the Baka. He made a new path leading to the Baka [villages] and gave us instructions: "Take them gently; don't force them. Little by little." This was the arrival of evangelization. The Baka of this village, it was the whites who made them leave the forest. There was Aulambang [a Bangando elder of the bò wé clan], who was the catechist. This was the departure of the Baka, coming to the village.[16]

These accounts of the settlement of the Baka in or near Bangando communities suggest that forces external to the Baka, including government authorities (either French or Cameroonian or both) as well as missionaries, and perhaps involving the Bangando as secondary tools but not primary driving forces, propelled the Baka community to leave their forest settlements to live alongside the main axis of colonial transportation, establishing the mixed ethnic communities that still exist today in southeastern Cameroon. Under pressure from external government authorities and mission officials, local groupings of people were encouraged—sometimes under threat of force—to consolidate in larger villages that officials had identified as stable geographical and political entities. That the Bangando were important aides, both to missionaries and to government officials, is clear: the relatively stable and legible social systems of the Bangando made them accessible tools to political authorities and missionaries. Bangando involvement in the settlement of the Baka by the roadside may have constituted a compelling shift in relations between the two communities, with the Bangando occupying newly emerging positions of social and political dominance and wielding an officially sanctioned influence over their now structurally subservient neighbors.

It is unclear to what degree Bangando and Baka relations were embedded in hierarchies of power prior to the resettlement of Baka in the larger roadside villages. Although the bulk of literature on "hunter-gatherers" is based on the assumption that the relatively more sedentary "villagers" were the dominant partners in exchange, labor, and social relations, no evidence offered by Bangando or Baka support this assumption for interethnic relations in southeastern Cameroon prior to the integration of both communities into an externally sanctioned political structure. However, it is also speculative to suggest that the two groups maintained strictly egalitarian relations prior to Baka resettlement in roadside villages. Nevertheless, it is evident that as political relations between the communities became formalized and codified by external authorities, Bangando individuals came to occupy dominant positions in emerging local structures of power.

Yet, because of the lines of friendship and affiliation that Baka and Bangando had developed through their decades-old partnerships of hunting and meat-sharing, when they arrived in Bangando villages as permanent residents, Baka families often forged close residential and neighborly ties with their village-based Bangando allies. Whereas in the past, Bangando and Baka families had to walk some distance between their settlements, now allied families could deepen their relations of cooperation. Although the impetus for Baka movement from their smaller and dispersed forest villages to the larger and more centralized Bangando villages along the roughly hewn road was most likely external pressure, the internal, social magnets that drew certain Baka families to settle among certain Bangando families were probably friendship and cooperation. The power structure that came to place the Bangando in positions of political dominance over the Baka was tempered by cross-cutting relations that fostered intimacy and cooperation among Bangando and Baka families, now not only allies but also neighbors.

Bakwélé: Turbulence and Tension in Interethnic Relations

Whereas interethnic relations between Bangando and Baka have been generally amicable since the communities met and established partnerships, in the region along the Ngoko River relations between Bakwélé and Baka as well as between Bakwélé and Bangando have been, and continue to be, strained. The interethnic relationship between Bakwélé and Baka was initially predicated on Bakwélé presumptions of Baka inferiority, resulting in social distance and tension. Still today, relations between Bakwélé and Baka are generally tense. In contrast, although relations between Bakwélé and Bangando were initially extremely violent, in recent decades Bakwélé-Bangando relations have ameliorated.

Histories of contact and interethnic relations between Bakwélé and Baka at Ndjàngé, along the Sangha River, seem to differ markedly from interethnic relations between Bakwélé and Baka along the Ngoko River. Whereas oral histories in the multiethnic setting at Ndjàngé indicate that the communities were tightly integrated spatially, economically, politically, and socially, histories of contact and current relations between Bakwélé and Baka along the Ngoko River are characterized by tension and mistrust. Elders' narratives have not offered explanations for this divergence, suggesting a compelling topic for further investigation. Preliminarily, it is important to recognize that both Bakwélé and Baka communities are large in total number and are spread out over large geographical areas. Given the size and scope of these communities, perhaps it is not unreasonable to expect that their relations and identities would vary, depending on specific historical and social contexts.[17]

The Bakwélé constitute a diverse community that spreads along waterways through the northern forest zones of contemporary Congo-Brazzaville, northwestern Gabon, and southeastern Cameroon. The far-flung community is divided into at least five distinct linguistic subgroups, reflecting communities that are distinguished from each other by geographical location and histories of migration, variations in political organization, ritual performances, and social cohesion (Siroto 1969; Guthrie 1970). In the face of political conflicts both within and coming from outside the community, Bakwélé have evolved strategies of social fragmentation and fiercely individualistic competition (Siroto 1969). Bakwélé family structure is characterized by both patrilineal and avuncular political relations, allowing individuals to make strategic use of relations through their fathers' line of descent and through maternal uncles. Accessing power and wealth through these competing lines of kinship enable Bakwélé to settle internal conflicts through strategies of fission as well as (and perhaps more frequently than) strategies of reconciliation. Subgroups of the Bakwélé have had diverse relationships with nearby communities; these interactions have been based on relations as divergent as warfare and slave raiding on the one hand, and intermarriage and mutual cooperation on the other. (For detailed ethnographic and historical documentation of the Bakwélé community, see Siroto 1969; Joiris 1998; Rupp 2001.)

The Bakwélé of the Lobéké region have experienced tremendous turmoil and conflict over the past two centuries; external pressures of slave raiding and violence initially drove Bakwélé from the central Congo River basin toward the confluence of the Sangha and Ngoko rivers, where they settled in dispersed communities along the Ngoko River. Some Bakwélé individuals and families fostered meaningful—although not always positive—ties with neighboring Baka and Bangando. Initial contacts between Bakwélé and Baka along the Ngoko River seem to have been peaceful, but were not characterized by equality or amity:

> When the Bakwélé started to build their villages, the forest was empty. There were no other people. We knew that the Baka lived there too, but we never saw or felt them. The Baka came to this part of the forest from the north, from near the Kunabembé. When we first saw the Baka, they had no clothes. But we Bakwélé already had clothes and salt. We gave these things to the Baka, so that they would go into the forest to hunt for us. We gave the Baka things that they didn't have in return for their work, mostly hunting.[18]

This narrative of contact between the Baka and Bakwélé communities highlights initial Bakwélé perceptions that Baka were invisible, generally insignificant people lacking in basic elements of social decency, and simultaneously indicates that Bakwélé were already integrated into long-distance trading networks in the broader Congo River basin. The account, narrated by a Bakwélé elder, also indicates that Bakwélé co-opted their Baka neighbors into relations of economic dependency by offering Baka material items, such as cloth and salt, in exchange for their labor.

Today relations between Bakwélé and Baka along the Ngoko River continue to be predicated on the exchange of Baka labor for goods, involving Bakwélé contributions of local whisky (ngòlòngòló) and salt, as well as occasional clothing and monetary compensation for Baka labor. This skewed exchange relationship generates friction between the communities; Baka resent Bakwélé demands on their time and energy even as they rely on Bakwélé access to material goods that they transport in their canoes from markets in Moloundou to villages along the Ngoko River. Today Bakwélé demand hard, physical labor from Baka in exchange for material goods. Felling trees and clearing gardens are the main activities that Baka undertake for their Bakwélé "patrons" (bosses), as Baka refer to the Bakwélé men for whom they work. But unfair payment of work and overall derision toward the Baka community has fomented a great deal of anger among Baka who live near Bakwélé communities along the Ngoko River.

On a still, hot afternoon in Ndongo, a Baka man named Ndoboyé visited his neighbor to vent his frustration concerning his Bakwélé "patron":

> He asked me to fell a large tree in his garden. So yesterday I went to begin cutting down the big tree. There was not enough time to finish. But the tree fell down anyhow last night, during the big wind. So I went to his home and asked his wife to pay me. He had gone to Moloundou, but before he left he told his wife that she should pay me five liters of ngòlòngòló when I finished cutting down the tree. The wife gave me one glass of ngòlòngòló, and said that she couldn't give me any more because her baby is coming soon, and she'll sell the ngòlòngòló so that she can buy soap and kerosene [items that an expectant mother will prepare for the birth of her child].[19]

Ndoboyé was irate that he did not receive the payment due from his Bakwélé "patron's" wife—especially because when the enormous tree finally fell in the Bakwélé man's garden, it brought down another large tree with it. His Bakwélé "patron" had instructed Ndoboyé to fell this second tree too, in preparation for planting his garden. From Ndoboyé's perspective, he had felled two trees and had been compensated for neither one. The rage swelling as he recounted his travails, Ndoboyé finally announced in a loud voice and with an angry throw of his arm, that the Baka should drive the Bakwélé away, should chase them back to their own place. When asked why he and other Baka continue to work for Bakwélé despite their anger, Ndoboyé answered in a subdued voice, ambivalently flipping both hands palm-side up and shrugging his shoulders: "We work for Bakwélé because we want money."[20]

As Baka ruefully recognize their reliance on Bakwélé neighbors for wages and material goods, Bakwélé acknowledge their dependence on Baka labor; yet both groups seem to prefer social and spatial separation. The chief of Ndongo, an elderly Bakwélé man, imagined life in Ndongo without Baka: "Life would be very difficult, very bad. Without Baka to work for us, Bakwélé would be very hungry and very poor."[21] Yet this interdependence does not foster abiding sentiments of social rapport. Although he maintains ties with his Baka partners and observes their ceremonies from a distance, the chief maintains that Bakwélé and Baka are fundamentally different (lufɔnɔ). From her seat on the edge of the verandah, his daughter added with a cringe, "Their eyes, their spirits, are different. Their eyes do not have the white light shining in them, like the eyes of people. They have eyes like animals. They are not like us."[22]

Because of the constant pressure to work for Bakwélé, and because of ongoing currents of conflict between Bakwélé and Baka as well as among Bakwélé individuals and households, many Baka left Ndongo to settle in their own village called Bàkà in the mid-1980s. The two villages—Ndongo, inhabited by Bakwélé, and Bàkà, inhabited by Baka—are two kilometers apart; close enough to enable Bakwélé and Baka to continue their relations of economic codependence, but far enough apart to insulate Baka from the social friction they feel from their Bakwélé neighbors.

Relations between Bakwélé and Baka in Ndongo are ambivalent. Interactions between the groups are based primarily on economic exchange of labor (provided by Baka) for material goods (provided by Bakwélé), an exchange relationship that elders indicate has served as the basis for interethnic relations between the groups since their initial meeting. This pattern of unequal relations between "pygmies" and "villagers" has been documented by many scholars of "pygmy" communities, and is often held up as the definitive template for interethnic relations. While this dynamic of domination and subordination seems to prevail in relations between Bakwélé and Baka in villages along the Ngoko River, it has no place in the narrative of interethnic relations between Bakwélé and Baka at Ndjàngé. This divergence suggests that localized histories of contact and patterns of interaction may result in dramatically different relations, even among members of the same ethnic communities.

Whereas relations between Bakwélé and Baka along the Ngoko River have remained tense for many generations, relations between the Bakwélé and Bangando have improved and strengthened over the past century and a half. Initial encounters between Bangando and Bakwélé were violent: Bangando terrorized Bakwélé, murdering men, enslaving women and children, and destroying villages. As I prepared for my first trip to Ndongo and other villages along the Ngoko River, Bangando elders of the *bò wé* clan pulled me aside and quietly recounted their initial contact with Bakwélé at Ndongo. During an elephant hunt deep in the forest along the Ngoko River, Bangando hunters of the *bò wé* clan encountered Bakwélé. Surprising the Bakwélé in their village and using hunting spears, throwing knives, and crossbows, the Bangando hunters attacked the Bakwélé village, overwhelming its protective walls and storming Bakwélé houses and *ebaaz* (men's verandahs). The Bangando hunters killed Bakwélé men, burned their houses and gardens, and seized women and children, bringing them back to incorporate them into their own families. This account of Bangando hostility toward Bakwélé was recounted only once; it is not a memory that *bò wé* elders shared with pride. Nonetheless, as I prepared to travel up the Ngoko River to spend several weeks among the Bakwélé in Ndongo, Bangando elders advised me not to mention my close social relations with my neighbors from the *bò wé* clan, and especially not my friendship with Wanguwangu, because his ancestor and namesake had been the driving force in the murderous raid against the Bakwélé.

Relations between Bangando and Bakwélé are no longer violent, but neither are they resoundingly positive. Contemporary relations between Bakwélé and Bangando were reestablished in the region where Bakwélé are predominant when Bangando men moved to Ndongo to take advantage of employment opportunities offered by a French logging company during the mid-1970s. Because of their jobs, strong commercial markets, and excellent climate and soil for cocoa, a handful of Bangando men also began cultivating cocoa plantations and brought their families from Bangando villages to settle in Ndongo permanently. The timber companies have closed, but these Bangando families remain, strongly emphasizing that their interests in staying are commercial, not social. Bangando who live in Ndongo are deeply ambivalent about their relations with Bakwélé, explaining that Bakwélé "laugh with their teeth": they may laugh with you, but they aren't with you in spirit.[23]

Along the Ngoko River, both Bangando and Baka sense profound differences between their communities and the Bakwélé; for their part, Bakwélé reciprocate sentiments of fundamental social distance. A Bakwélé man

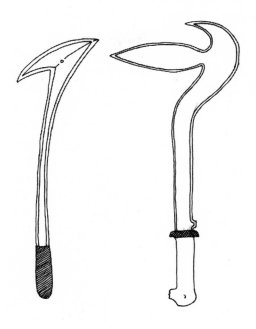

FIG. 2.4 *Kwà* (Bangando throwing knives)

who is training to be a nurse had returned home to Ndongo for a holiday, and articulated his view of the differences between Bakwélé and Bangando: "Bakwélé could never live among Bangando. Do you see Bakwélé men who live in Bangando villages? No way. Perhaps Bakwélé girls who marry Bangando must live there. Bakwélé could never leave the river to go live in the forest."[24] The nurse culminated his discussion of the quintessential difference between the communities through the metaphor of dance: "The dance of the Bangando—*módyâdyâ*—the Bakwélé do not share. Bakwélé could never dance *módyâdyâ*. Bakwélé have our own ways of doing, seeing, living." An elderly woman sitting nearby echoed this sense of underlying, basic difference between Bakwélé and Bangando, asking me with an edge of impatience: "Do people of Yaoundé and Brazzaville have the same problems?"[25]

Despite—or perhaps because of—the social distance between Bakwélé and both Bangando and Baka, Bangando and Baka individuals who live in and around Ndongo express sentiments of cohesion and cooperation, surpassing the already congenial relations that these communities share along the main Moloundou road. Numerous individuals from a variety of backgrounds and in various contexts discussed the close relations between Bangando and Baka, using metaphors of shared identity, shared language, and shared place to evoke their sense of connection. Arriving in the village called Báká that lies two kilometers from Bakwélé-dominated Ndongo, Baka residents eagerly introduced me to two Bangando women to help bridge our language gap; I spoke Bangando, but my Baka hosts in the Ndongo region did not. A small, ebullient woman emerged from a nearby kitchen house and greeted me with a typical Bangando hug: she (and I) exclaimed "*Hèèèèè!*" embracing each other's shoulders, leaning first to one side and then the other. Speaking in Bangando and surrounded by a gathering circle of Baka villagers, she introduced herself, "My name is Lekewe, and I am a Bangando girl. My village is Mbateka." As we spoke, another woman approached and also introduced herself as a *bèmbèkò Bángàndò*, a Bangando girl: Nana from Ngombe, a neighborhood ten kilometers north of Moloundou.[26] These two women had married Baka husbands and moved to Bàkà, their husbands' village. I was relieved to find Bangando speakers who could help me understand the context of Baka living near Ndongo. But I remained confused about why two women who in all respects appeared to be Baka women—Baka spouses, family, and friends, the lilting accent of people who speak Baka as a natal language, and body decorations typical of Baka women—claimed so enthusiastically and adamantly to be Bangando.

During my stay in the Ndongo region, other people who appeared to be fully integrated into the Baka social context of Bàkà village continued to introduce themselves as Bangando. These encounters led to numerous complicated discussions and diagrams of kinship relations extending back over many generations of intimate relations between Baka and Bangando, as I struggled to make sense of these apparently Baka people who identified themselves as Bangando. In several cases, the individuals did have Bangando as biological relatives, but not in immediate, patrilineal relations that would shape their formal ethnic affiliations. Finally a man named Lapo, whose village is in Salapoumbé in the northern end of the Bangando region, explained the deep affiliation that these Baka feel with their Bangando neighbors, partners, and friends:

> We are one thing/concept [*mò*] with Bangando. Baka and Bangando were born on one soil. We come from the same stomach. We are Bangando because we come from Bangando.[27]

This resounding statement of affinity—even unity—with Bangando was echoed by Bangando elders living in Ndongo: "For Bangando and Baka, our villages and even our houses are mixed. We eat together. You rarely see Bakwélé and Baka sitting together to eat. We [Bangando] speak Baka, so we *are* also Baka."[28] Even Ndoboyé, who expressed such animosity toward his Bakwélé "patron" for whom he felled trees, emphasized that if Bangando— here used as a place referent—weren't so far away, he would rather have a Bangando partner. Ndoboyé explained, "Bangando are *good*. They help us well, nicely. They speak Baka *well*. They speak Baka with us *well*"[29] (empha-ses in original remarks). In the region surrounding Ndongo the overriding sentiment between Bangando and Baka individuals is social unity, expressed through the speaking of shared languages, living in shared spaces, and expressing shared identities. This social and emotional proximity between Bangando and Baka seems to be amplified by their distance from home vil-lages along the Moloundou road, and contrasted with the social distance that they perceive between their communities and the surrounding Bakwélé residents of the Ndongo region.

Mbomam: Slaves or Neighbors?

Ethnic solidarity among the Mbomam is based on collective memories of their stamina in surviving migration, dislocation, and the scattering of their community, along with widespread contemporary concerns about their diminishing numbers. Mbomam comprise the smallest ethnic community in southeastern Cameroon, numbering approximately four hundred indi-viduals.[30] The two villages that are considered to be "Mbomam" villages, Ngola and Mikel, lie to the north of the Lokomo River, just north of Sala-poumbé. In these villages, households are primarily headed by Mbomam men but include significant numbers Bangando and Baka wives, as well as one Bangando and numerous Baka households. Because of the small size of the Mbomam community, their history of interaction with Bangando, and their ties of friendship and support with the Baka, many individuals are of mixed parentage; those whose fathers are Mbomam consciously, proudly celebrate their ethnic affiliation with the Mbomam community. Today Mbomam strive to maintain linguistic continuity across the generations; language has emerged as an essential component of their sense of ethnic identity, as well as social and political viability.

Contemporary ethnic pride among Mbomam has its roots in the his-torical struggles of this small, fragmented community. In oral histories, the Mbomam originated in the town of Dumé, which is located in today's political division of Abong Mbang. Toward the end of the nineteenth century, Mbomam were engulfed by attacks perpetrated by neighboring communities and fled their villages toward the Kadeï River. Following the Kadeï River southward to the Sangha River, the Mbomam continued into the Congo River basin, eventually arriving at Ouesso. Because of pressures they encountered from other peoples who had already settled around Ouesso, and to avoid colonial officials and labor recruiters stationed there, the Mbomam continued along the Ngoko River to the west until they reached Moloundou. Arriving exhausted, Mbomam elders approached Nadia, a Bangando elder who served as a liaison between local communities and the German colonial administration. Mbomam elders requested to stay in the region. Nadia agreed that the Mbomam could remain but, on his advice, the German colonial officers split the Mbomam community and scattered individuals and families throughout Bangando villages to prevent large-scale conflict from emerging between the communities. According to elders of both groups, although Bangando did not mistreat their new Mbomam neighbors, they treated Mbomam as subservient and inferior members of the multiethnic community. Some Mbomam elders recall their social status among Bangando as *mòtámbá*: slaves.[31]

According to Mbomam, an elder named Melaamb remained in Moloundou and worked as a personal servant for a German official named Hockmann.[32] One day Hockmann asked Melaamb why he was always so pensive. Melaamb replied, "The Bangando call us their slaves. This is what bothers us Mbomam." Hockmann replied, "Take all Mbomam out of the Bangando villages and go to the other side of the Lokomo River, north of Salapoumbé. There is empty forest there, where you will build a village for the Mbomam people. You will be chief." So Melaamb and many Mbomam left Bangando villages and crossed the Lokomo River to the north, where they built the village of Ngola. Some Mbomam preferred to remain in the Bangando villages where they had settled, especially women who had married into Bangando families. German officials also encouraged the Mbomam to settle a second village north of Ngola, so that the region between Ngola and Yokadouma, the next German colonial post north of Moloundou, would gradually be occupied and become safer for travel. Melaamb appointed his friend, Modyanda, to be the chief of the second Mbomam village, Mikel.[33] Today the Mbomam community is spatially centered in Ngola and Mikel, the two small villages that their ancestors established to achieve autonomy from their engulfing Bangando neighbors. Although the community succeeded in establishing itself apart from the Bangando, today Mbomam continue to struggle for social viability and political representation.

Contemporary Mbomam elders illustrated their subordination to the Bangando community by recounting their failed attempt to gain national recognition and to assert regional political power during the postindependence turmoil of the 1960s. When Cameroonian officials reorganized the territorial layout of their administration and redefined regional structures of political power once the nation had gained its independence, Mbomam elders attempted to persuade government representatives that the headquarters for the subdistrict should be located in Mikel. This location represented the geographical midpoint in the district, would have established the significance of Mikel as a town, and would have enhanced the political and social prominence of the Mbomam community. But, as Mbomam elders recollect, Bangando chiefs protested to the newly independent government, emphasizing that Mbomam held an inferior status, and were neither worthy of the honor nor capable of the responsibility of housing the government's district offices. In their counterproposal, Bangando chiefs suggested that the district headquarters be located just south of the Lokomo River, where Bangando predominate. The Cameroonian officials accepted this suggestion, and the district headquarters were established at Salapoumbé, the historical heart of the Bangando community, just one village south of the Mbomam villages.[34] Mbomam recounted this story to illustrate and underscore their resentment of the political domination of the Bangando, even as Mbomam and Bangando continue to intermarry and share in ceremonial, subsistence, and daily activities.

Without intimate knowledge of social and marital relations in a given village in southeastern Cameroon, it is nearly impossible to distinguish which individuals are Mbomam, so culturally intertwined and linguistically integrated are they with their surrounding Baka, Bakwélé, and Bangando neighbors. Mbomam social invisibility and cultural insecurity are expressed by Maasele, an Mbomam man who is married to a Bangando woman:

> Mbomam traditions are disappearing. There are few and ever-fewer Mbomam who are "pure" [which he expressed using the French term *pur*], and who continue to speak Mbomam with their families. My children speak Bangando with their mother, but they speak Mbomam with me. Just yesterday I had to punish my son for speaking Bangando with his little sister. They should be talking to each other in Mbomam.

But even I speak Bangando more fluently than Mbomam, even though I *am* Mbomam. I know many more names of trees and animals in Bangando than I do in Mbomam. And my little brother knows even fewer names for things in Mbomam than I do. My son knows even fewer Mbomam terms than my brother, and my future grandson might not know Mbomam at all. The Mbomam are dying out, little by little. We Mbomam marry women from other groups—Bangando, Baka, Kunabembe, Mvomvom—because there aren't enough Mbomam women for us to marry. If Mbomam fathers of mixed children continue to let their children speak languages other than Mbomam, the Mbomam will surely die out, as we become completely integrated with people like the Bangando.[35]

That Maasele and other Mbomam interpret the practical loss of their language as the essential loss of their community underscores the very real emotional connection between language and ethnic affiliation among the communities of southeastern Cameroon. This very small community struggles to maintain their linguistic and other social traditions in the face of absorption into the surrounding social landscape through intermarriage and multilingualism.

Despite their small numbers, only individuals from the Mbomam community unequivocally expressed ethnic superiority over their Bangando neighbors, relations with whom they simultaneously acknowledged as inevitable and even necessary. In Ngola and Mikel, discussion of *noblesse*—the essential nobility that Mbomam claim distinguishes their community—resounded in men's verandahs and women's kitchen houses alike. Even as many Mbomam view interethnic marriage as inevitable, and acknowledge that their children grow up speaking Bangando (and other regional languages) as fluently and frequently, or even more so, than the Mbomam language, Mbomam individuals continue to maintain a clear sense of pride and distinctiveness as a community. As explained by Mbomam elders, *noblesse* means not accepting domination by Bangando or any other group. This nobility means "having everything you need to live," including social, linguistic, economic, and political autonomy.[36]

This sense of ethnic chauvinism among the Mbomam is not always appreciated by their neighbors of other languages and ethnic sentiments. Mbomam pride seems to be an inverse reflection of the political and social subordination that Mbomam have had to endure over the generations. As neighbors from other communities moved into their villages during the mid-1990s seeking employment with Société Tropicale d'Exploitation Forestière (SOTREF), a Belgian logging company that actively exploits timber concessions in the region, Mbomam ethnic pride crescendoed. Some Mbomam openly look down on neighbors from other backgrounds who benefit from employment and commercial opportunities provided by the timber company. During a heated discussion among Mbomam men and their Bangando spouses and in-laws, Mbomam again proclaimed their *noblesse*—and thus their superiority to Bangando in particular—by emphasizing their principled resistance to the encroachments of the timber company on the forest. Mbomam men have not sought employment from SOTREF, but continue to maintain their families through the economic pursuits of hunting, agriculture, gathering, and fishing. In an attempt to deflate their Mbomam neighbors' and in-laws' ethnic pride, Bangando men argued that Mbomam men do not work for timber companies such as SOTREF *not* because of their noble resistance to economic imperialism of foreign companies, but because there simply are not enough Mbomam men in the villages for some men to leave their families to seek employment with timber companies.[37] Ultimately the small Mbomam community clings firmly to the cultural anchor of ethnic *noblesse*, as they continue their historical struggle for self-determination and autonomy amid the swelling tide of linguistic, cultural, political, and economic integration in the regional sea of Bangando-dominated villages and foreign-dominated companies.

At the same time that Mbomam experience close but contentious ties with Bangando, Mbomam and Baka consistently share intimate and supportive relations. In Ngola and Mikel, many households comprise interethnic couples of Mbomam and Baka. Moreover, in several families ethnicity and gender are not correlated: husbands and wives may be either Mbomam or Baka. In contrast, interethnic marriages in villages throughout the rest of the Lobéké region tend to bring together Baka wives with Bangando or Bakwélé husbands. This ethnic balance in marital relations is significant, because it suggests that Mbomam and Baka view each other as social equals. Mbomam do not express anxiety about potentially being absorbed into the Baka community, perhaps because both communities are politically and economically less influential than the more predominant Bangando community.

Among all of the communities of the Lobéké forest region, Mbomam families display a higher degree of integration with people of different ethnic affiliations. Mbomam uphold relations of solidarity and support with Baka spouses and neighbors, even as they tend to experience cultural, social, and political tension with Bangando in-laws, neighbors, partners, and friends. Interethnic relations in the villages of Ngola and Mikel highlight variation in social and political attitudes toward both Bangando and Baka.

Structures of Power

Stories of origin, migration, and contact with neighbors provide foundations for ethnic affiliations among the communities of southeastern Cameroon and have provided channels for establishing and negotiating interethnic relationships. Each community—Bangando, Baka, Bakwélé, and Mbomam—has an evident consciousness of ethnic distinction, based largely on stories of their community's particular origin and on collective maintenance of a particular language. But Bangando, Baka, Bakwélé, and Mbomam communities also share a robust core of experiences—precolonial pressures of violence and flight, dislocation and migration, and the building of new relationships in the Lobéké forest region—that provide a firm foundation for shared sentiments of belonging and the perpetuation of interethnic relationships. This chapter has demonstrated that contact and integration among Bangando, Baka, Bakwélé, and Mbomam in different areas of the Lobéké region have varied tremendously, leading to divergent dynamics of social interaction among the communities today.

As is evident from the oral historical accounts offered by Bangando, Baka, Bakwélé, and Mbomam elders, the existence and perpetuation of interethnic relationships does not necessarily produce interethnic harmony or equality. Interethnic dynamics at the time of contact, settlement, and the negotiation of initial social relations among the communities of southeastern Cameroon ranged from violently aggressive (Bangando contact with Bakwélé), to unequal and exploitative (Bakwélé contact with Baka along the Ngoko River), to unequal but tolerant (Bangando contact with Mbomam), to integrated and equitable (Baka contact with Bakwélé along the Sangha River), to amicable and supportive (Bangando contact with Baka; Baka contact with Mbomam).

The formal concretization of relations of power in southeastern Cameroon has also been deeply influenced by outsiders' perceptions of the various communities. The hierarchy of social and political power in southeastern Cameroon was established during the colonial era and persists today. German and then French colonial officials found Bangando communities to be most accessible, initially because of the location of Bangando villages along the Boumba River, the axis of transportation that brought German officials into southeastern Cameroon from Yokadouma to the north. The German colonial administration forcibly resettled Bangando villages along the colonial road that runs parallel to the Boumba River, about fifteen kilometers into the east, after compelling Bangando to build it. Under continued pressure of physical punishment for noncompliance, Bangando were forced to repair and maintain the road, and to undertake other forms of forced labor such as rubber harvesting and porterage, under both the German and French colonial regimes. (See chapter two in Rupp 2001 for detailed discussion of the communities of southeastern Cameroon during the colonial era.) Beginning during the German colonial period, Bangando clan heads were designated as village "chiefs" throughout most of the Lobéké forest region, while Bakwélé "chiefs" were appointed at Adjala and Ndongo along the Ngoko River, and Mbomam "chiefs" were accorded official posts in Mikel and Ngola, north of the Lokomo River. Although Baka communities were socially integrated with Bangando by the turn of the twentieth century, their smaller and more mobile villages—in addition to colonial expectations that "pygmies" are, by nature, elusive—enabled them to evade many direct, colonial pressures. Efforts to resettle Baka in villages along the road were undertaken by French colonial authorities during the 1950s, by the Cameroonian government during the 1970s, and by European missionaries during the 1970s and '80s, with varying degrees of success (see Rupp 2001).

Among the acephalous communities of southeastern Cameroon, alignment with colonial and then postcolonial officials brought unprecedented personal influence to the officially designated "chiefs." These "chiefs" are beholden to the national political system that presides over chiefs' installations and vests them with power. Furthermore, these village chiefs are not always—or usually—the most influential or charismatic leaders of a given village (Geschiere 2004). Alternative avenues for leadership emerge alongside of opportunities for employment and influence, particularly within sectors of forest exploitation and conservation.

Today Bangando remain socially and politically dominant in the majority of villages in southeastern Cameroon; Bakwélé constitute the preponderant community socially and politically in several villages along the Ngoko River; Mbomam struggle to maintain their position of social and political prominence in Ngola and Mikel. Notably absent from formal political and social positions of power throughout the larger region are Baka. Although Baka comprise the majority of the population in numerical terms, they are least likely to hold positions of political prominence beyond serving as the head of the Baka community, a position that is structurally inferior to the officially designated village-wide chief, who is without exception Bangando, Bakwélé, or Mbomam. The relative positions of political power in southeastern Cameroon can be schematically represented as shown in the following figure:

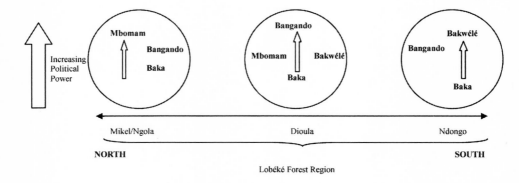

FIG. 2.5 Regional variations in relations of political power

Yet because of the profound social integration that has melded the communities of southeastern Cameroon, relations among individuals and groups are not simply mediated according to structural relations of officially recognized political power, but are negotiated according to feelings of social belonging or alienation as well as considerations of political strategy. A model of monolithic, structural power that places Bangando in a categorically dominant position above their Baka, Bakwélé, and Mbomam neighbors would be misleadingly simplistic. Interpersonal and interethnic relations are formed and reformed taking into account a combination of emotional attachments to language and social origins, shifting social sentiments of friendship or rivalry, cooperation and competition, and political relations of complementary or contradictory political interests. The following chapters demonstrate that the integration of Bangando, Baka, Bakwélé, and Mbomam families in villages throughout southeastern Cameroon has resulted in a dynamic social mix, shaped primarily by intimate friendships and partnerships between individuals and families of various ethnic distinctions, rather than by rigid categories of ethnic belonging, formal structures of political authority, or external paradigms of "pygmy" and "villager."

CHAPTER THREE

Spaces

BEYOND NATURE AND CULTURE

H istories of the confluences and intermingling of Bangando, Baka, Bakwélé, and Mbomam in southeastern Cameroon reveal the extent of spatial and social integration among the communities. In contrast, classic models of forest peoples that insist on dividing communities into categories such as "pygmies" and "villagers" or "hunter-gatherers" and "farmers" emphasize spatial distinctions between "forest" and "village" and corresponding conceptual—even moral—distinctions between people believed to nurture the forest versus those who cut the forest down.

> There are perhaps, 200,000 people living in the Ituri forest who are commonly referred to in the scientific literature as Pygmies. . . . The villages of the farmers who live adjacent to the Pygmies are usually only a bit larger but they are visu-

ally very different. The villagers cut down the forest whereas the Pygmies leave it standing. . . . the village and the forest are diametric opposites. The problem for any anthropologist, therefore, is how to think about the relationship between the farmer and hunter-gatherer. . . . Are farmer communities and the Pygmy communities that live alongside them separate societies, or ethnic groups in a single multiethnic community? Do the farmers dominate the Pygmies or do the Pygmies dominate the farmers? (Grinker 2000: 79-80)

While the dichotomy between nature and culture has been central in European intellectual traditions since the Middle Ages (Thomas 1983; Ritvo 1997), and its power as a simplifying, explanatory framework in various societies has been elaborated (Lévi-Strauss 1969), the uncritical acceptance of this rubric in identifying and analyzing people risks obscuring rather than illuminating social realities (MacCormack and Strathern 1980). Yet within the field of "hunter-gatherer" studies in anthropology, "pygmies" and "hunter-gatherers" continue to occupy a unique niche as people *in* nature. In studies of equatorial African forests, the "pygmy" emerges again and again as the emblem of "natural man," whose life continues to be intimately, even primordially, associated with land and resources. Observers in southeastern Cameroon project the nature/culture dichotomy onto perceptions of people and their spaces, perpetuating oppositional, conceptual models of forest and village as discrete, bounded places, and "people of the forest" and "people of the village" as discrete, bounded communities.

However, the uses of spaces in southeastern Cameroon bring communities together in social and spatial relationships that affirm intercommunal ties rather than segregating communities in distinct spaces. The organization of space in the Lobéké forest region today reflects relationships that traverse ethnic boundaries and socioeconomic categories. Rather than conforming to spatial and social stereotypes of "forest" and "village," the layouts of households, residential patterns within villages, and access to natural resources reflect relations of belonging and multifaceted social identities based on attributes such as gender, kinship, and friendship.

Nature : Culture : : Hut : House

Two architectural house styles predominate in villages throughout southeastern Cameroon: dome-shaped, leaf-shingled "huts" and square, wattle-and-daub "houses." The conceptual differences between hut and house are

FIG. 3.1 "Pygmies in Front of their Hut," 1910 (in Bahuchet 1992: 343)

significant, for they represent basic differences in the position of the structure's inhabitants in either nature or culture and the associated (im)possibility of development and progress. In German, French, and English, the primary languages of formal documentation and discourse on Cameroon, a Bangando home is consistently referred to as a *Haus, maison,* or *house,* whereas a Baka home is called a *Hütte, hutte,* or *hut,* regardless of the actual structure of the building. The moral assumption embedded in these terms is that people who have the capacity to develop socially and culturally live in "houses"; inhabitants of houses are "villagers," and in this context, Bangando, Bakwélé, or Mbomam. In contrast, people whose lives are embedded in nature, and who have little interest in or capacity for development, live in "huts"; inhabitants of huts are "pygmies" and, in the context of southeastern Cameroon, Baka. Similarly, outside observers usually describe a collection of Bangando homes as a "village," whereas a collection of Baka homes is considered a "camp." Even a number of Baka houses made of wattle-and-daub and located in a line along the main road—indistinguishable from nearby Bangando houses—is typically described as a "camp" by missionaries, development agents, and government officials once they are aware that the people who live in these dwellings are Baka. In these stereotypes of domestic space, the actual physical architecture of the buildings and the layout of the communities are less important than the stereotyped identities of the inhabitants of particular houses or neighborhoods. The binary oppositions between nature and culture produce spatial as well as social stereotypes, fitting "pygmies" into "huts" and "villagers" into "houses."

A Cameroonian who had come to the southeastern corner of his country for the first time articulated entrenched assumptions and value judgments concerning houses, huts, and forest peoples:

> I always knew that people live in the forest—I read about them in books in school. But coming here and seeing the pygmies was like seeing the pictures come alive. They really do live in leaf huts! . . . They're like shacks that are about to fall down, but they live in these huts for years and years. In the northwest province, we live in proper, solid houses with tin roofs. . . . The people here seem to like dirt. They like being dirty, and won't even wash if someone gives them soap. Dirt must be a part of their culture. . . . The Baka are stuck in a stage of evolution between gorillas and humans.[1]

Although this man from northwestern Cameroon expresses a clear value judgment between the way of life in his community where people live in "proper, solid houses with tin roofs" and the generally ramshackle domestic context in southeastern Cameroon, he also infers from the style of architecture that Baka are not only unclean but have no civilized way of life. His expectation and perception that Baka live in perpetually dirty domestic conditions lead him to conclude that Baka are frozen in evolutionary time in a primitive, apelike state. An insurmountable conceptual gap seems to separate huts from houses, and inhabitants of huts from inhabitants of houses. Houses are living environments that reflect order, stability, and progress. Huts, in contrast, are living environments that suggest chaos, flux, and poverty. People who live in houses are presumed to be more sedentary, culturally developed, and therefore civilized, while those who live in huts are implicitly presumed to be primitive, nomadic, and embedded in nature.

Confluences: Spaces and Communities in Southeastern Cameroon

Until the mid-nineteenth century, Bangando and Baka lived in neighboring but separate villages. While Bangando built bark houses along the main footpath running along the Boumba River, forming centralized villages that were spatially discrete residential bundles in the forest, Baka families built their dome-shaped, leaf-shingled houses nearby in clusters along paths and streams. As a result of the forging of alliances and partnerships between Bangando and Baka families through the exchange of meat, Baka families began to move their houses closer to Bangando households, ultimately leading to the cohabitation of Bangando and Baka families in united villages. Where Bangando and Baka families did not choose to live as neighbors, colonial policies of resettlement of Baka under the French colonial administration, and continued by postcolonial Cameroonian administrations and missionaries, ultimately forced Baka to live together with Bangando, Bakwélé, and Mbomam in shared villages along the main road. While maintaining their ethnic distinctiveness, Bangando and Baka built social relations that transcend their linguistic and cultural differences, and today continue to foster neighborly relations in shared spaces in villages and in the surrounding forest.

When Germans explorers first arrived in southeastern Cameroon during the 1890s, Bangando families were settled into round clusters of homesteads located along a footpath that followed the eastern bank of the Boumba River. These groupings of homes formed patrilineal villages and provided relatively stable locations of residence. The Bangando did not live in the villages continuously, as they often made family trips into the forest for periods of several weeks to several months for fishing during the dry season when the rivers and streams were low (usually December through February), for collecting wild mangoes during the small, dry season (usually June through July), and for hunting expeditions throughout the year. Bangando houses were constructed of wide lengths of bark called *pàkàdyô*, which Bangando stripped from the thick trunk of the *Triplochiton scleroxylon* tree, a robust hardwood tree. These large pieces of bark were held in place by pairs of poles, whose sharpened ends were buried deep into the ground. Another large piece of bark served as a door, closing off the main entrance at night.

Kebikibele, one of the oldest surviving Bangando elders, recalls her childhood village on the edge of the Boumba River:

> When I was a young girl, we did not live along the road where we live today. We lived along the Boumba River. There was no road along the Boumba, just a long footpath that ran through each village and connected the villages to each other. The houses were all built near each other, and from my family's house I could greet our neighbors to the right and to the left and on the other side of the path, just standing in the doorway of our house. The houses were all built close together, so you could walk from one edge of the village to the other in the rain

FIG. 3.2 Contemporary Bangando house made of *pàkàdyô* bark (Ngilili 1999)

without getting wet, walking underneath the eaves of the thatch roofs. The houses were not made of mud and sticks [*gàlà bílìkì*] as they are today. The houses that we build today are copies of the brick [*bílìkì*] houses that the Germans built.[2] Our houses then were made of bark, wide strips of bark, called *pàkàdyô*. The strips of bark were scraped until they were clean and pounded until they were soft and flat. The Bangando houses were very beautiful, not like they are today. People lived much closer together, and people shared the meat that they hunted, not like today when everyone sells their meat. The Baka did not live in our village, but lived in their own villages nearby.[3]

While the Bangando lived in houses made of bark a century ago, the neighboring Baka lived in small, dome-shaped houses called *mòngúlu*. Baka built (and continue to build) these houses by bending flexible saplings into a dome-shaped framework, attaching the large, waxy, round leaves of the *marantacaea* species in an overlapping pattern of shingles. These rounded houses have become a symbol of the primitivity of "pygmies" in Euroameri-can imagery of equatorial African forests. Today, however, the majority of Baka in southeastern Cameroon live in square wattle-and-daub houses—

FIG. 3.3 A Baka man relaxing in front of his house (Dioula, 1998)

gàlà bílìkì—that are indistinguishable from those of their Bangando, Mbo-mam, and Bakwélé neighbors.

Bangando and Baka families have also designed ingenious hybrid houses, combining the strengths of both architectural styles to meet their needs for functional shelters in various contexts. For example, when moving from their permanent wattle-and-daub houses along the main road to the forest for periods of several weeks to gather wild mangoes and to harvest maize, Bangando families may construct rectangular houses whose frames of vertical posts are similar to their more permanent houses. But rather than filling the walls in with mud, Bangando architects have adapted the Baka technique for shingling their round *mòngúlu* to fit these square house frames. They string vine cords tightly between the vertical posts of the walls, then suspend the large, round leaves from the cords to create a scaly leaf "skin" for the house. The resulting house is sturdy but temporary; when the Bangando family returns seasonally to live in the forest, they can quite easily replace damaged leaf shingles, patch the walls and roof, and quickly move back into their forest home.

Adjacent to this square, leaf-shingled house, the Bangando family also built a wide-mouthed *mòngúlu*, where they relax during the heat of the day,

FIG. 3.4 Bangando house in the forest, using leaf shingles for the wall covering, located in forest behind Koumela, 1997

FIG. 3.5 Bangando adaptation of a *mòngúlu*, located in forest behind Koumela, 1997

adapting the convenient house form that they learned from their Baka neighbors. Baka and Bangando do not conform to the stereotypes of "nature" and "culture" that underlie social designations of "pygmies" and "villagers" and spatial structures such as "huts" and "houses."

Furthermore, just as people defy architectural stereotypes and live in a variety of house structures, social and spatial relations transcend both ethnic and stereotypic distinctions. The spaces and social networks of villages throughout southeastern Cameroon are consistently multiethnic; the constellation of families making up particular neighborhoods within a given village almost always include families of various ethnic affiliations; and even at the household level, interethnic relations are nearly as common as monoethnic families. Rather than indexing ethnic differences or stereotyped models, the spatial layout of the village reflects the social geography of cohesion and conflict, as families and friends come together in cooperation, may encounter conflict or competition, and either reestablish relations as peaceful neighbors or relocate to another region of the long village.

Social Spaces: Overlapping Spheres

Bangando households include three kinds of structures on the central household plot: the big house, the kitchen house, and the men's verandah. Each structure houses a different set of social relations. A Bangando family usually centers around an established, conjugal couple with children of their own, and also often includes their parents, siblings, cousins, nieces, nephews, and sometimes other visitors or acquaintances. Households are not limited to nuclear families, but the nuclear members—mother, father, and children—form the core of the household. The main house, called *ngbà gálà* or, literally, "big house," is the main building where the family sleeps, but is not the focus of family activities. Generally the head of the household, the oldest male of the nuclear family, builds the big house and includes one room for each adult child or conjugal couple in the extended family, if they have not yet established households of their own. It is important that each couple has a room of its own, a space that becomes more and more crowded as the couple has children.

An important rite of passage for a young Bangando man is building his own big house, often with the assistance of his father and older brothers. The construction of his own *ngbà gálà*, which is usually located on the same plot of land as his father's and brothers' houses, marks his passage from being

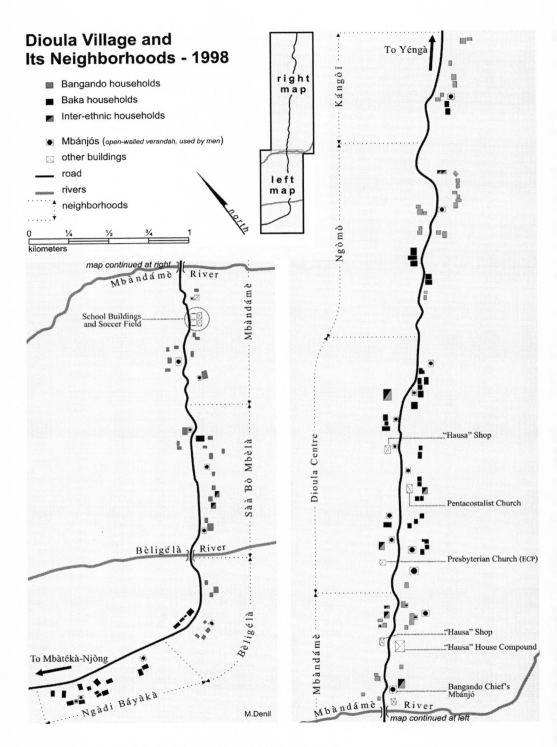

Dioula Village and Its Neighborhoods - 1998

- Bangando households
- Baka households
- Inter-ethnic households

- ⊙ Mbánjós (open-walled verandah, used by men)
- ⊠ other buildings
- road
- rivers
- neighborhoods

0   ¼   ½   ¾   1
kilometers

right map

left map

north

To Yéngà

Kángòï

Ngòmò

map continued at right

Mbàndámè River

School Buildings and Soccer Field

Mbàndámè

Sàà 'Bò Mbèlà

Dioula Centre

"Hausa" Shop

Pentacostalist Church

Bèligélà River

Bèligélà

Presbyterian Church (ECP)

To Mbàtékà-Njòng

Mbàndámè

"Hausa" Shop
"Hausa" House Compound

Ngàdi Báyàkà

Bangando Chief's Mbánjó

M.Denil

Mbàndámè River

map continued at left

MAP 3.1 Dioula Village and its neighborhoods, 1998

his father's dependent to being a self-sufficient, independent man. Thus the household plot of an elder Bangando man may include the smaller houses of his sons and the kitchen houses of their wives, as they move out of the patriarch's big house and establish families and households of their own.

The second architectural structure in a family's compound is the *kísìnì*, or kitchen house. Bangando kitchens are built in a space distinct from the big house to prevent infestation of the *ngbà gálà* by inevitable pests and also to protect the main house from potential kitchen fires. *Kísìnì*, the contemporary word for kitchen, has been adapted from the French term *cuisine*. The original Bangando term for the kitchen house is *twálá*, which is derived from the word *twá* or "nest," perhaps alluding to the nostalgic association of the kitchen as a safe, comforting space where a mother nurtures her children and raises her family. Bangando kitchen houses are the focal point for the majority of the family's activities and socializing. The kitchen house is a space where family and friends, women and men, Bangando and Baka, young and old come together to socialize. The space of the kitchen is organized by and for the needs of women: it is in the kitchen that women prepare meals, bathe children, and store tools, baskets, and machetes for their daily activities in the gardens or forest; it is to the kitchen that women return to rest during the heat of the afternoon, before beginning cooking and other evening activities. While men have their own domestic space for socializing, the *mbánjó*, the woman's kitchen house offers space for economic discussions and transactions, social disputes and resolutions, and other social interactions that cut across gender, generational, and ethnic lines. Perhaps because Bangando women are members of the socially dominant ethnic community but are simultaneously members of the subordinate gender, their social space straddles numerous social boundaries, allowing women of all ethnic communities to feel comfortable, while also drawing in men to the comfort, fellowship, and food of the kitchen house.

The *mbánjó* is the third social area that characterizes Bangando houses; it is also a feature of Baka households. The *mbánjó* is an open-walled verandah that is usually placed apart from both the big house and the kitchen, and is often located near the road or a main path, inviting passers-by to stop and visit. This space is dominated by men; each household typically has one *mbánjó* where male kin and their visitors congregate to share news, discussions, and meals. If the household consists of an aged patriarch whose children have married and remained nearby, the patriarchal network of father and sons will often share one verandah, located in an area central to all of their marital households. If several families live close together, they

FIG. 3.6 Baka neighbors gathered in their *mbánjó* (women joined men for photograph), 1999

may share one *mbánjó* rather than each man building a separate verandah. While the *mbánjó* explicitly excludes women, in general this space fosters communication and community rather than promoting the autonomy and isolation of individual families. Typically, wives send their husbands' food from their kitchens to the central *mbánjó,* where the men will eat together each evening, sharing a kind of pot-luck supper, sampling dishes from each of their wives' kitchens. Often inquisitive younger boys share their fathers' and uncles' meals, absorbing stories and histories, and learning about contemporary issues as they grow into young men.

Access to domestic space is regulated by ascending order of social power: the higher the status an individual holds, the more access he or she has to domestic space within the household. Men have higher social status than women, and elders have higher status than younger family members. Thus sleeping rooms belonging to younger female siblings are accessible to all older siblings of both genders (as well as elder cousins and members of older generations). But younger siblings are prohibited from entering the rooms of their older brothers and sisters, and sisters are not welcome in the sleeping rooms of their brothers regardless of their age. According to this gendered social hierarchy, the *kísìnì*, the domain of women, is accessible to men and women alike, whereas the male-dominated *mbánjó* is open only to men, and sometimes to nongendered individuals such as postmenopausal elderly women and very young children, whose distance from reproductive abilities and responsibilities renders their gender insignificant.

Although the hierarchies of access to domestic space may seem to put women, especially young women and new wives, at structural and social disadvantage within the family, many women skillfully manipulate the social codes of access to send signals about their contentedness or discomfort with relations within the family. For example, women's respect of the men's space can win appreciation from their husbands, providing a source of social and emotional capital. Kebikibele, an elderly Bangando woman, recalled that by warmly welcoming her husband's guests at his *mbánjó*, both her husband and his friend offered her respect and warm appreciation:

> When a visitor would come to my husband's *mbánjó* I would quickly begin to cook plantains and whatever meat I had in the kitchen house. When the food was ready, I would serve it to my husband and his guest, along with fresh drinking water. Sometimes the guest would say, "Ákìbà! Thank you! I was hungry." Later my husband would be glad that I had served his visitor.[4]

While the woman's willingness to serve her husband and his friends in the strictly male space may appear to be simple hierarchical subjugation, a woman's respect of men's space during times of domestic tranquility and cooperation builds social capital to ensure that, in times of conflict or disagreement with her husband or with men's collective decisions, her resistance to domestic codes of conduct produce effective public statements of her displeasure. Kebikibele explained that, if a woman wishes to emphasize her dissent with decisions made by the men of her household, or if she wishes to shame her husband because of a marital dispute, a resounding indication of a woman's dissatisfaction with her domestic situation is her refusal to present her husband and his visitors with food at the *mbánjó*. In addition to respecting men's space, the important and symbolic sharing of food indicates hospitality and solidarity between a man and his guests as well as between husband and wife.[5]

Bangando and Baka households alike are characterized by *mbánjó*. While Bangando men tend to socialize together in their *mbánjó* and Baka men gravitate toward their own verandahs, men of both groups visit each other's *mbánjó* on a daily basis. If a man's friend or neighbor visits his *mbánjó* the friend's presence is an entirely welcome and normal occurrence, regardless of ethnic affiliation.

Baka women and men also visit Bangando women in their kitchen houses. Kitchens often serve as an alternative *mbánjó*, where people come together for informal chats and a drink of cool water if they are passing by, and where neighbors and friends gather throughout the day and into the evening for conversation and socializing. As much as the kitchen is the personal space of Bangando women who cook, tend children, and often sleep there, the kitchen also provides a neutral space where people feel comfortable congregating, regardless of gender, ethnic identity, social identity, or age. Particularly if the elder male of a family is deceased and his wife emerges as the head of household, the kitchen becomes a default *mbánjó*, where meals and conversation are shared, disputes are mediated, and decisions are made. The Bangando kitchen house is usually the context in which Bangando and Baka engage in economic transactions, whether one individual offers a gift of food or tobacco, another borrows a tool or returns a pot, or payment is made for Baka labor. In this way, Bangando women, centered in their kitchen houses, provide an important link among various social groups.

At the village level, the Bangando chief also builds a communal *mbánjó*, where the entire village gathers for important meetings and ceremonies, regardless of ethnicity or gender. The structure of social and political power in the village is reflected in the pattern of seating in the chief's *mbánjó*: political leaders and elders of the village sit at the end of the verandah that faces the road or path. The village leaders who sit on chairs and stools facing outward are a collection of elder men who are predominantly Bangando, but often include a handful of Baka elders. Younger men sit on benches along the edges of the *mbánjó* and often carry on side conversations, exchange and sell tobacco and cigarettes, and share sugar cane while the village meeting is going on. Men at these village meetings (*kɔáni*) include both Bangando and Baka, although the Bangando generally outnumber their Baka counterparts and outspeak them as well. Along the perimeter of the *mbánjó* other young men, women, and children lean on the railing of the verandah and mill about. Although they may attend, women generally do not participate actively in village meetings. But women do take part in the larger ceremonies and celebrations that are also held at the *mbánjó*. These different levels of participation in public gatherings—as reflected in the spatial organization of events at the chief's *mbánjó*—reveal patterns of social interaction rather than formal regulations that determine interethnic political relations. Variations in behavior are common, depending on individuals' interests, personal relationships, and charisma, qualities that do not correlate with ethnic affiliation.

Bangando and Baka draw a clear line of division between communities in which they feel comfortable and communities from which they feel alienated, based on the presence or absence of *mbánjó*. For Bangando and Baka alike, the presence of the *mbánjó* indicates a welcoming family where visitors will be warmly received with offerings of refreshment and companionship. In contrast, Bakwélé households and villages generally lack *mbánjó*, taken by Bangando and Baka as an indication of the inhospitable social environment of Bakwélé villages.

Two Bangando men, Seo and Motupa, have lived for many years in the village of Ndongo, a village that is predominantly inhabited by Bakwélé but also includes a significant Baka population and a very small number of Bangando. In explaining the fundamental difference between Bangando and Baka communities on one hand and the Bakwélé community on the other, Seo and Motupa turned to the *mbánjó* as a metaphor of community that they find lacking in their Bakwélé neighbors. The fundamental difference between the communities, they concurred, is that whereas the Bangando and Baka build *mbánjó* to welcome their visitors, the *mbánjó*-less Bakwélé community in Ndongo is cold, closed, and unwelcoming. They noted that it is a rare occasion when they observe the men of neighboring Bakwélé families sitting together to share a meal, a sociable practice that is common—indeed ubiquitous and quotidian—for Bangando and Baka. Seo and Motupa quickly noted that, although Bakwélé men rarely eat meals together, they often gather to drink together, and drink in abundance. They concluded that "*séé yɔá bò hányáwè*," or "their hearts are hard" (*hányáwè*).[6] Not only in Ndongo but also in villages dominated by the Bangando-Baka nexus located along the Moloundou road, Bangando perceive the Bakwélé as unfriendly people and point to the absence of communal areas for gathering and welcoming visitors—the lack of *mbánjó*—as spatial confirmation of their social analysis.

Whereas Bangando and Baka communities tend to be well-integrated, with interethnic neighborhoods and even interethnic households mixed throughout a given village, in Ndongo all Baka families have moved out of the main village and created their own village two kilometers to the east, citing perpetual difficulties and conflicts with their Bakwélé neighbors as the reason for their collective move. Baka who previously lived in Ndongo and in Leke, the next Bakwélé village, six kilometers to the south, have all abandoned their Bakwélé neighbors to establish the separate village of Bàkà.[7] A handful of Bakwélé families has also moved out of the larger Bakwélé villages and settled in Bàkà, citing the "bad social climate" of Bakwélé-dominated villages. As explained by Gobijan, a Bakwélé man who moved his family to Bàkà, in the Bakwélé-dominated village of Ndongo people look out for their own interests and keep to themselves, creating an unpleasant social climate. Falling back on colonial metaphors to describe the subjugation of the Baka, Gobijan explained the Bakwélé treatment of Baka as a "colonial system" in which the "freedom of the Baka is unknown." Similarly, because the Bakwélé chief of the village of Leke routinely attempted to force Baka residents to work for him and his family, Baka families simply abandoned Leke and came to Bàkà. The chief continues to claim the labor of these former residents, attempting alternately to oblige and to cajole the Baka to return to Leke to work for him.[8] In contrast to social relations in both Ndongo and Leke, in the village of Bàkà, Baka and the few Bakwélé residents "cooperate with each other, rely on each other, are connected with each other."[9] There is no simple, spatial template for representing social relations in southeastern Cameroon. Across the region, differences in the spatial layout of daily life reflect the varied dynamics of interethnic relationships.

Spaces Beyond the Household

The organization of space beyond the household and *mbánjó* also reflects social relationships among individuals, families, and villages. Patterns of access to land and resources in the forest reflect the kind and degree of social relationships among villagers of various ethnic affiliations and social identities. While the Euroamerican dichotomy between nature and culture suggests that the social space of the village and the natural space of the forest ought to be clearly delineated, and that access to resources would then be organized with certain areas open to utilization by the "people of the forest" and other regions available to the "people of the village," access to space and to natural resources is ordered in terms of kinship, friendship, and residency, relationships that often cut across lines of ethnicity and do not involve distinctions between the forest and the village. For example, close friends may share overlapping gardens, working together on the difficult communal tasks of felling trees and clearing underbrush, but maintaining distinct areas of the garden where each family grows basic subsistence crops.

At a the level of intervillage land tenure, villages may engage in rancorous arguments concerning the boundary between two villages, not only along the main road, where demarcation of boundaries is relatively easy, but also where the imputed divisions between villages run back through the forest, allocating some resources to one village and denying access to the other. These disagreements came to the fore during the late 1990s, as conservation organizations encouraged villages to demarcate their territories in preparation for the allocation of community forest areas. At the heart of these disputes was the identification of the spatial boundaries between multiethnic villages, not the allocation of land and resources to particular groups such as "pygmies" as people of the forest, or "villagers," as dichotomies between nature and culture might suggest.

Paths

Paths—channels of movement between spaces—also reflect the topography of social relations. Access to pathways, and to resources along these pathways, is determined by social relations of coresidence, familial relations, and friendship. First, the path directly behind a house, which often leads to a source of drinking water or to fruit trees, is reserved for the family at whose house the path originates. Second, there are paths that run behind a given neighborhood and into the forest, paths that only the resident families of that neighborhood use. Third, there are paths that are used freely by residents of the village as a whole, and that lead back to communal resources. Finally, at a point sufficiently far from the primary resources of any given village—roughly fifteen kilometers from the main road—regional paths link together, offering access to the deeper forest to all inhabitants of the region.

The paths that connect households to gardens, to streams for fishing and shrimping, to cocoa plantations and snare lines, and to hunting areas deeper in the forest, are regulated by residency in particular neighborhoods. Residency is informally determined by social relations between kin and friends. Although there are no hard-and-fast rules of exclusion, the persistent use of a neighborhood path by a nonresident will raise questions as the residents of the neighborhood seek to know where this person is going, and why.

Access to paths is important not only because of the resources located at both ends—the domestic resources located in the village and the resources necessary for subsistence found in gardens, in the forest clearings (for hunting), and in rivers and streams (for fishing). Access to paths is also important because the creation and maintenance of a path offer access to other spaces and resources along its length. Often a family collects its most important daily resources along paths, as they travel to and from gardens or hunting areas. The process of cutting and using a path creates narrow strips of disturbed and often vibrantly productive forest along either side of the path, where the fundamental resources for daily domestic production can be collected. For example, the thick, round leaves of *marantacaea* plants often grow in the forest gaps alongside of paths; women collect bundles of these leaves—which they call *sàà té*—to use for shingling houses and shelters and also as a multifunctional kitchen aid. *Sàà té* leaves serve as all-important containers and wrappers for Bangando and Baka cooking: they are used to wrap up pounded plantains and to store leftovers; they function as packets to steam fish and pounded squash seeds; they serve as potholders, and can be formed into ladles and funnels; they are used to wrap gifts of meat, salt, peanuts, wild mangoes, or mushrooms for friends and neighbors. Paths also offer access to fallen trees for collecting firewood. It is from pathways that Bangando and Baka hunters find smaller animal paths along which to set their lines of snares, and by pathways that women access streams and rivers for fishing. Pathways offer opportunities to gather wild mangos, mushrooms, edible *kúmbí* leaves, caterpillars, termites, snails, and other important elements of the Bangando diet. While the trajectory of a given path generally remains relatively constant over time, the diversity of resources that Bangando and Baka collect along paths varies tremendously from season to season.

In explaining the spatial organization of the village of Dioula, Bangando elders created a map that indicates how social relationships shape access to forest resources. Because paths provide the channels for individuals and families to access materials and spaces for domestic production, elders indicated the name of the head of the family that utilizes each path and thus informally controls access to some of the resources to which the path leads. In addition to smaller pathways that are associated with individual families, there are also pathways that lead to collective resources and are thus accessible to residents of particular neighborhoods and, more generally still, to residents of the entire village. For example, the residents of the Dioula-Beligela neighborhood have certain paths that lead back toward their gardens, as do the people in the *bò mbélá* neighborhood, where the people of the eagle clan live, just north of Dioula-Beligela. Where they share the same pathway, the residents of Dioula-Beligela know that they have access to resources on the south side of the path, whereas the residents of the *bò mbɛ́lá* neighborhood have access to land and resources on the north side of the path.[10] Although these rules regarding shared paths are not formally codified, the generations-long understanding about who has primary access to which areas of the forest ensures that social relations of space remain relatively smooth. At the same time, no one can exclusively control the use of any path or restrict others from gathering and collecting resources along a particular path. Familiarity with space and familiarity with the people who most commonly use that space are the general criteria in determining who has access to spaces, paths, and resources.

Another type of collective path is delineated when individual families' paths merge. For example, the paths that run through the neighborhoods of Dioula-Centre and Dioula-Ngomo link up to a common footpath approximately four kilometers from the village; this shared path in turn leads to a collective area of gardens called Emerson.[11] Emerson is a large area of cocoa plantations that was cleared and planted by Giinde, a prominent Bangando elder, in collaboration with other Bangando and Baka men. Because of the historical collaboration in clearing, planting, and tending the cocoa plantations, the paths leading from individual households soon merge to form a collective path, along which resources are collectively accessible to the families whose cocoa gardens are located at Emerson. Giinde's Baka partner, Mongonga, helped to create the original cocoa plantations and cultivated his own cocoa at Emerson. Together Giinde and Mongonga set snare lines, collected wild mangos and other forest resources, and fished during the dry season. Thus the resources of Emerson—including land for cultivation as well as resources for gathering, fishing, and hunting—have been, and continue to be, communally accessible to the interethnic families of Dioula-Centre and Dioula-Ngomo, from the point where their individual family paths join together to form the collective *autoroute* (or "highway"), as one man described the main path. This relatively large and well-traveled pathway leading to Emerson ultimately joins other paths leading to the river called *Ndjòmbi*, the most distant river and hunting area that residents of Dioula will travel to in a single day.

The pathway from *Ndjòmbi* continues even further eastward toward the Sangha River, to deeper regions of the forest where hunting and fishing grounds are particularly productive. Thus at a broader, regional level the paths of various villages eventually link up with the pathway that heads east beyond *Ndjòmbi*, triangulating to form a common, regional pathway that is shared by Bangando, Baka, Bakwélé, and Mbomam residents of many villages. This path serves as the main route to Ndjàngé, as local communities

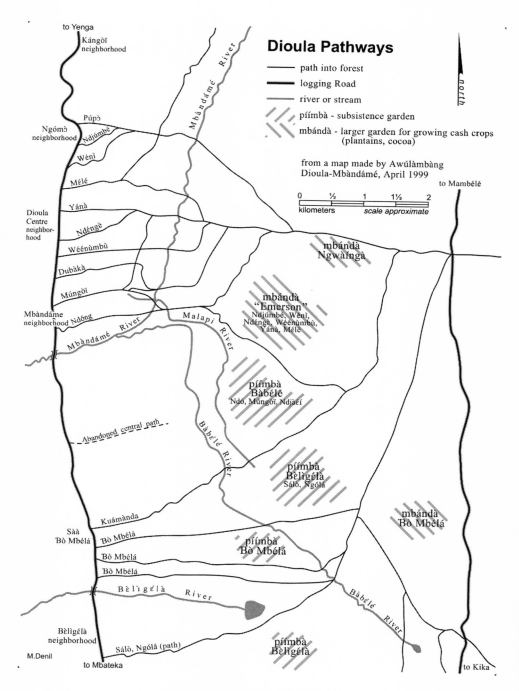

Dioula Pathways

—— path into forest
━━━ logging Road
〰〰 river or stream
píímbà – subsistence garden
mbándà – larger garden for growing cash crops
(plantains, cocoa)

from a map made by Awúlàmbàng
Dioula-Mbàndámé, April 1999

to Yenga
Kángòï
neighborhood

Púpò
Ngómò
neighborhood Ndjúmbè
Wèní
Mélé
Yánà
Ndéngè
Wéénùmbù
Dubàkà
Múngòï
Ndóng

Dioula
Centre
neighbor-
hood

Mbàndámé
neighborhood

Mbàndámé River

Malapi River

Mbàndámé River

mbándà
Ngwàïngà

mbándà
"Emerson"
Ndjúmbè, Wèní,
Ndéngè, Wéénùmbù,
Yánà, Mélé

píímbà
Bàbélé
Ndó, Múngòï, Ndjàéï

Babélé River

Abandoned central path

píímbà
Bèlìgélà
Sálò, Ngólá

mbándà
Bò Mbélá

Kuámànda
Sàà
Bò Mbélá   Bò Mbélá
Bò Mbélá
Bò Mbélá

píímbà
Bò Mbélá

Bèlìgélà River

Babélé River

Bèlìgélà
neighborhood

M.Denil
Sálò, Ngólá (path)
to Mbateka

píímbà
Bèlìgélà

to Kika

to Mambélé

north

0   ½   1   1½   2
kilometers   scale approximate

MAP 3.2 Paths to the east of Dioula Village
(map made by Awulambang, Dioula, April 1999)

refer to Lake Lobéké, where the most abundant hunting and fishing areas lie. Although Ndjàngé lies directly behind Dioula, and Dioula villagers claim that their forebears were the ones who originally cleared the central pathway, this route to rich resources is shared by people throughout southeastern Cameroon.

Ndjàngé is the focal point in Bangando and Baka imaginings of the forest: this fertile, inland delta of the Lobéké River is where the ancestors lived during days of abundance in times past, and where one can find palm nuts, fish, honey, meat, and wild yams, all in the same area. The main pathways of all of the villages along the main road, from Mambélé to Moloundou, converge at a main communal path leading to Ndjàngé, at the heart of the Lobéké forest. Once the paths merge together, access to forest resources on both sides of the path and at its terminus becomes communal.[12]

Specialized Resources

In addition to these regional pathways leading to general resources that are available to many, wild mangoes (*Irvingia excelsa*) and freshwater shrimp are specialized resources that are seasonally available in very specific locations of the forest, to which access is restricted. Wild mangoes, known as *pèkí* to Bangando and *fékí* to Baka, ripen in alternate years during the short dry season and are eagerly awaited not only by people but also by gorillas, monkeys, chimpanzees, and elephants. This interspecies competition for wild mangoes brings Bangando and Baka families into the forest, often together, where they may spend several weeks to two months in temporary camps near the mango trees. The noise of their camps, where parents encourage their children to sing loudly and to play rambunctiously, and the smoke from their cooking fires help to keep the wild competitors for the mangoes at bay. Human access to *pèkí* trees is determined by social ties; relatives and close friends are often invited to join a nuclear family as they harvest *pèkí* and fish and hunt in the forest. For example, Giinde, who initiated the cocoa plantations at Emerson, found a large and productive stand of *pèkí* trees not far from his plantation, and claimed the biennial harvest of the wild mangoes as his family's prerogative. By consistently moving his family to a forest camp near the wild mango trees when the fruits ripened, Giinde staked his claim to the wild mangoes from that particular stand of trees near his plantation. As a result, Giinde's descendants and their families, as well as neighbors and close friends, continue to go into the forest near Emerson

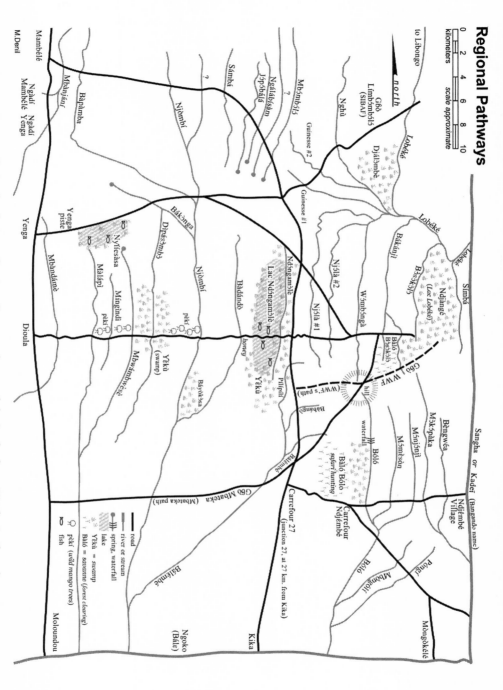

MAP 3.3 Regional paths in southeastern Cameroon (map made by Awulambang, Dioula, April 1999)

to harvest wild mangoes when they ripen. If others wish to access the same *pèkí* trees, they must ask Giinde's eldest son, Ndjumbé, now the head of the family, to grant permission.[13]

The fishing of freshwater shrimp, known to Bangando as *gɓàsà*, poses another dilemma of accessibility and social cartography. Shrimp in any significant quantity are limited spatially as well as temporally. The long, dry season that usually runs from December through February is known as *pèmbé swèè*, or "the season of sun"; during this season the water levels in rivers and streams diminish enough that Bangando and Baka can fish and shrimp effectively in forest streams. Freshwater creatures provide an important source of protein during *pèmbé swèè*, as hunting is especially difficult when there is no mud to facilitate tracking. But despite the seasonal importance of fishing and shrimping, there is only one stream in the entire region of southeastern Cameroon where shrimp are particularly abundant: Mbànjánì, a stream that runs just to the east of Mambélé village.

But even in Mbànjánì, shrimp catches vary dramatically from day to day. During the peak of the dry season, when water levels are at their lowest (known as *òò sá lì*, literally "to spill water out" of the rivers and streams),

FIG. 3.7 Bangando woman resting during a morning of shrimping in the Mbànjánì stream, January 1996

shrimp catches may vary fourfold over several consecutive days.[14] To maximize their returns for the hard work of shrimping and to avoid the bad luck of shrimping only on days when shrimp are scarce, local woman of Mambélé spend a good portion of the dry season in the Mbànjánì stream and its tributaries, shrimping, fishing, and relaxing in the cool shade of the forest. Together Bangando and Baka women wade through the thigh-deep, murky water, sloshing through mud and over fallen trees, stooped over at their waists to scoop their round nets (ndámù) through the water, and tossing the shrimp into the small baskets (tòkídí mbékà) fastened around their waists.

The hard work in Mbànjánì pays off. Shrimp are a very sought-after delicacy; not only do the women of Mambélé and their families enjoy eating tasty shrimp, fish, and crabs during the long, dry season, they also profit handsomely from the sale of shrimp to the local bar at the junction of the two regional roads at Mambélé. The long, dry season also coincides with the start of the annual safari-hunting season, bringing numerous outsiders to Mambélé as employees of a French-owned safari company, which is based just downstream along the Mbànjánì River. The expatriate safari employees often eat their main meals at the bar in Mambélé, whose savvy owner buys as much shrimp as Bangando and Baka women can provide to prepare dinner for her swelling clientele. Despite the delicious and lucrative shrimp of Mbànjánì, people from other villages respect the privileged access of Mambélé residents to the stream and its resources. If a woman who does not live in Mambélé wishes to shrimp, she joins a group of local women when they go to the river. In return for her access to the river for the day, she offers them a proportion of her catch, often giving away half her catch. But by

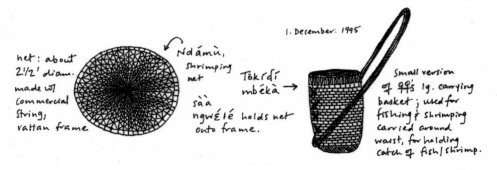

FIG. 3.8 Bangando shrimping equipment

building strong social ties with the women of Mambélé, women from other villages continue to be accepted in the shrimping parties.

Gardens

Like paths and streams, access to land for gardens is intimately linked with social relations of kinship and residence. Bangando and Baka gardens include three types—the *pímbá*, the *mbándà*, and the *sɔ́bɔ́*—each serving a particular agricultural function and each governed by different rules of land tenure. The most basic garden is the *pímbá*, where Bangando and Baka grow their essential daily starches, primarily plantains but also manioc and occasionally maize, as well as an assortment of crops such as eggplants, chili peppers, and peanuts. Baka and some Bangando also supplement their primary, cultivated starches with yams, both wild and domesticated. The *pímbá* is usually located quite near the house, generally within three kilometers, enabling family members, primarily women and children, to tend the crops on a daily basis. Ranging between 50 and 100 meters in length and width, land for this basic garden is used for several years, with a cycle of crops planted (plantains and squashes, then manioc and peanuts) before it is left fallow for ten to fifteen years. Land tenure for *pímbá* is directly linked to the family: each grown child who continues to reside with the family has access to the land surrounding the family's house, up to a midpoint with the neighbors on either side and leading back into the forest for an unspecified distance or until the boundaries coincide with someone else's garden. Because of the low population density, no other system for allocating land has been needed or envisioned.

The location and land tenure of a *mbándà* is quite different. This garden is a longer-term, larger garden that is usually located much further into the forest, generally between five and fifteen kilometers from the village. The *mbándà* is planted on the very best soil; thus in its first season the cultivator often must clear mature forest for this large and usually very productive garden. Bangando and Baka cultivators who invest their time and effort in a *mbándà* usually grow valuable cash crops such as cocoa and plantains, which they haul back to the roadside village to sell to passing trucks, whose drivers serve as middlemen in informal, long-distance trade, bringing the produce to regional markets. Some cultivators also grow maize and manioc at their distant *mbándà*, as these starches can be fermented and then distilled into *ngòlòngòló*, the local whisky, and can turn a modest profit. Otherwise, crops for family consumption that are produced at the *mbándà* are usually small and portable, such as chili peppers, eggplants, and squashes (of which only the seeds are consumed). Sometimes the cultivator and his immediate family live permanently at the *mbándà* and are thus isolated from daily life in the village. In addition to planting cash crops, these forest-based families also raise subsistence crops, a few domestic animals, and gather, hunt, and fish in the forest around their *mbándà* garden. (See chapter six for further discussions of forest-based Bangando.)

Land tenure for *mbándàs* is slightly more flexible than the rules governing *pímbás* for the simple reason that *mbándàs* are often located on vacant—or at least underutilized—land that is deep in the forest. Nevertheless, the same primary importance of kinship ties applies to *mbándàs*: the social ties of kinship bind cultivators to particular plots of land, as individuals inherit space for cultivation from their fathers, and spouses share gardens. In the case of *mbándà,* if a close friend or neighbor outside of the extended family asks permission to cultivate his or her *mbándà* on the land adjacent to the family's *mbándà*, the head of the family will usually acquiesce. In such a situation, the secondary rule of land tenure—the person who makes changes to the land and develops its resources has long-term control over the plot—comes into effect. Once a cultivator has made changes to the land by felling trees, clearing undergrowth, and planting, that piece of the forest remains in his and his family's domain until he decides to give it to someone else or until he and his family abandon the plot.

Access to land for cultivating a streamside garden (*sóbó*) is determined by social relations as well as by competition against potential rivals for such fertile, moist land. A *sóbó* is a particularly valuable garden because it is located alongside a stream or small river and therefore can support crops such as maize and peanuts, even during the dry season when most Bangando have completed their main harvest and are in the process of clearing and burning their *pímbá* for the next planting. The *sóbó* allows cultivation to continue during the dry season because of its location near a stream; the high water table ensures that the soil of the *sóbó* remains moist, enabling the crops to take up water easily. Having a *sóbó* garden in addition to a *pímbá* (and perhaps also in addition to a *mbándà*) means that a family will have something to harvest even during the lean months as they clear land and plant new crops in the main subsistence garden, the *pímbá*. A woman has access to land for a *sóbó* initially through kinship and marriage relations, as her father or husband, or another male to whom her family has close kin or social ties,

FIG. 3.9 Kemongo enjoying the steady growth of maize on her *sɔ́bɔ́*, Dioula Village, 1997

may have inherited access to land along the banks of streams. But because land for *sɔ́bɔ́s* is restricted to relatively small patches along streams, land tenure regulations are strict; kinship alone is not enough to grant a cultivator access to a *sɔ́bɔ́* season after season. Once a *sɔ́bɔ́* is cleared, the principle of control over land that one has "developed" through agricultural work holds, and the woman can return to the same *sɔ́bɔ́* the following year to plant crops that will ripen during the long, dry season. However, she must return to the *sɔ́bɔ́* year after year, or potentially lose access to this valuable land to more competitive, productive cultivators. The *sɔ́bɔ́* is known as the woman's garden, because it is cultivated through the initiative, responsibility, and perseverance of women. The woman who takes primary responsibility for the *sɔ́bɔ́* also has economic and social control over the allocation and utilization of the harvests from this garden. But planting and tending a *sɔ́bɔ́* also increases a woman's workload quite dramatically, as she may simultaneously be preparing her *pímbá* for planting during the dry season and also be tending her family's *mbándà*. In the context of all three types of gardens, Bangando and

Baka access to land for cultivation and to the forest for hunting, gathering, and fishing is guided by ties of both kinship and friendship.

Beyond the Forest-Village Nexus

While paths and gardens are created and maintained through ties of kinship and social alliance, the road was constructed by and continues to be maintained and utilized by people whose relationships with the forest are often commercially and politically exploitative. Today, residents of southeastern Cameroon perceive the main logging road as much as a symbol of their marginalization as a vital facility providing long-distance transportation and links to national flows of markets and power. As foreign-owned timber companies operating in southeastern Cameroon abandon their concessions in the forest, the road falls into increasing disrepair, exacerbating local communities' sense of isolation from towns and cities in Cameroon. But even when the roads are passable, transportation on the logging road is prohibitively expensive for most local people; even hitchhiking on logging trucks or taking the rattletrap public "bus" is a rare event for most people and is reserved for emergencies. Bangando and their neighbors are deeply ambivalent about the road. The road provides the only viable, albeit tenuous, link to distant places and powers, enabling the tendrils of markets to reach their villages and offer basic commodities such as kerosene, soap, salt, and clothing. But because most people cannot afford to travel by road, the movement of others into and through the forest, and the movement of resources *out* of the forest, underlines people's sense of social and political marginalization and economic underdevelopment. The penetration of the forest by commercial hunters whose origins and destinations lie far beyond southeastern Cameroon has opened up the very forest resources that local residents have managed for generations through ties of kinship and alliance to unbridled exploitation by unrelated outsiders. Ironically, the road reinforces local communities' emotional solidarity with the forest and with social relations that take place within the forest, while creating skepticism about their integration into a larger system that clearly maintains the road for the benefit and convenience of external interests. The alienation that Bangando and Baka feel from broader social, economic, and political networks with the rest of Cameroon escalates as the road deteriorates. Although people in southeastern Cameroon move effortlessly between the village and forest on a daily basis, movement from the Lobéké region of southeastern Cameroon to centers of economic and political power—even just to Yokadouma, the nearest town, 220 kilometers north of Dioula—seems next to impossible. The conceptual distinction between distant cities and the forest-village nexus appears to be much more salient to contemporary Bangando and Baka than any distinction between village and forest, settings in which they are situated and between which they move on a daily basis.

Social relations of space in southeastern Cameroon are not based on the presumed divide between the village and forest, nature and culture, that ultimately leads to categories of identity such as "pygmy" and "villager" that are pegged to particular ethnic communities. Instead, Bangando understandings of space and social position are organized according to a division between the forested region of southeastern Cameroon, where villages are embedded within the forest system, and the larger cities and towns of the "rest" of Cameroon.

The social geography of southeastern Cameroon reflects multiple lines of social cohesion and difference. At the household level, spaces are organized with reference to gender, generation, and social affinity. Thus it is not unusual for households to include family members from various ethnic backgrounds, nor is it uncommon for families of various ethnic backgrounds to intermingle in shared neighborhoods. At the same time, domestic space within households is clearly divided between men's and women's social spaces, with women's space welcoming both genders and people of all ethnic backgrounds, and men's space welcoming close friends and associates of various ethnicities but excluding women. At the village level, the organization of domestic space also reflects lines of social integration among the communities. For example, concentric circles of inclusion and involvement in the chief's *mbánjó* serve as a spatial model for the social relations of power, with elder Bangando and Baka men at the core and young Bangando and Baka women on the edge of the social gathering. Layers of social solidarity as well as social difference are clearly evident in the spatial organization at regional, village, and household levels. These layers neither correlate with stereotypes of forest peoples as either "pygmies" or "villagers" in spatial and social opposition, nor reference simple, static ethnic affiliations, but instead reflect the intermingling of forest communities and the shaping of social belonging and identities across numerous generations and in the many, varied spaces of southeastern Cameroon.

CHAPTER FOUR

Ambiguities

INTERETHNIC MARRIAGE AND DESCENT

If one of my children loves a Baka, who am I to stand between
the love of a man and a woman? — *Ngonda, a Bangando elder*

My daughter will marry a Bangando. She cannot marry a Baka. I could
not agree that my daughter would marry a Baka. I could not. I absolutely
could not. — *Pando, a Bangando man who is married to a Baka wife*

The ethnic distinctions among the Bangando, Baka, Bakwélé, and
Mbomam are clearly delineated, with the fundamental social solidarity of speakers of each language linked through a communally
held, sentimental belief in the origins of their community. However, these
seemingly unambiguous lines of ethnic difference are socially permeable.

Intimate relations transcend ethnic lines, often resulting in children whose ethnic affiliations are ambiguous because of their duality.

Many intimate relationships in the Lobéké forest region are interethnic. These crosscutting ties of social and familial intimacy complicate straight and narrow prescriptions for ethnicity, bearing evidence that social affections are at least as influential as formal prescriptions of kinship in shaping sentiments of belonging and social identities. Because Bangando, Baka, Bakwélé, and Mbomam families have lived as close neighbors for many generations, children grow up together, understanding and often speaking each others' languages, and knowing and sharing each others' ways. Such social intimacy leads, not infrequently, to ethnic intermarriage. In addition to the robust core of shared historical experiences that have brought the communities of southeastern Cameroon together, shared everyday relationships and experiences provide common ground for generating senses of belonging among individuals at all ages and stages of life. The social currents that bring people together in friendship, in partnerships to achieve shared economic or political interests, and in daily contact in the forest and in the villages have enabled people to form social ties that transcend lines of ethnic affiliation.

Even as interethnic marriage may serve as a useful barometer of integration among the communities of southeastern Cameroon, it also highlights the countervailing tensions that characterize interethnic relations. For example, children of interethnic parentage embody the discordance between patrilineal inheritance of ethnic affiliation and maternal influence in children's acquisition of language, bringing the fundamental markers of ethnic continuity—descent and language—into tension. Individuals of mixed descent articulate their uncomfortable attempts to reconcile personal preferences for particular individuals and public perceptions of their ethnic affiliation(s). People of interethnic descent express incompatibilities between ethnic affiliation as it is formally declared and ethnic relations as they are socially enacted and emotionally experienced. Discussions about interethnic marriage illuminate the emotional dynamics of amity and animosity in interethnic relations, as individuals simultaneously embrace relations held in the private sphere that may disregard ethnicity, but still recognize and even participate in the perpetuation of ethnic prejudices that may characterize public discourses. The prevalence of interethnic couples and families does not indicate that prejudices based on perceptions of ethnic differences are either nonexistent or irrelevant. On the contrary, examining cases of ethnic denigration within interethnic households brings lines of tension into sharp relief.

Conversations about interethnic marriage with people throughout southeastern Cameroon bring several conceptual issues to the fore: the relationship between ethnicity and gender in the constitution of power; interethnic marriage as cause for ostracism or means for alliance; changing attitudes toward interethnic marriage; and interethnic prejudices. Discussions of these issues comprise the first half of this chapter. The second half of the chapter offers three extended cases of interethnic marriage and descent, underscoring the complex emotional, social, and political dynamics inherent in intimate interethnic relations. The ethnography of ambiguities resulting from interethnic marriage highlights that identification is a process of working out relationships for oneself and between oneself and others, and of negotiating this personal process in the context of structured rules, roles, and expectations of what it means to belong in a family and in a community.

Ethnicity, Gender, and Power

Interaction and mutual support among ethnic communities is the rule, not the exception, of social relations in southeastern Cameroon. Because human relations are formed at both individual and collective levels, and because Bangando, Baka, Bakwélé, and Mbomam communities have lived alongside each other for at least a century and a half, intimate personal relations between individuals of disparate ethnic backgrounds are common. It is also important to bear in mind, however, that residents of southeastern Cameroon interact within contemporary structural relations of power, elevating some communities (notably Bangando) over others (notably Baka) in terms of formal political influence. At the same time, gender is also aligned with social power; men have relatively more social, political, and economic power than women, regardless of ethnic affiliation.

For some individuals, ethnic affiliation and sentiments are seemingly straightforward, as they are perceived to be fixed at birth by the membership of both parents in a single ethnic community. For example, individuals whose mother and father are both Bangando describe themselves and are known by others as *swéngélé* Bàngàndò, where *swéngélé* translates as "pure." Ethnic "purity" is usually traced to an individual's parents' ethnic affiliations, and occasionally back to the individual's grandparents' ethnic affiliations, but almost never beyond these two proximal generations. Given the region's historical patterns of movement and migration, and fission and fusion among communities, it is likely that many individuals who are considered to be *swéngélé* are actually of mixed ethnic background when one traces descent further than two generations.[1] For individuals whose immediate parentage is interethnic, ethnic affiliation is especially ambiguous and malleable, depending on how they, and others, contextually emphasize the various components of their belonging and identity.

Because of the structure of political power in the Lobéké forest region, individuals of mixed ethnic parentage negotiate various layers of power as they assert and experience their identities in different contexts. In general, *swéngélé* Bangando occupy the highest social position in the implicit hierarchy of social relations, whereas *swéngélé* Baka are relegated to the lowest social position. Where an individual's father is Bangando and mother is Baka, he or she is generally considered to be slightly inferior to someone of Bangando-Bangando parentage. Where an individual's father is Baka and mother is Bangando, he or she is considered to have a social standing that is slightly superior to someone of Baka-Baka parentage. In ascribing ethnic affiliation to an individual of mixed parentage, the relative social power attributed by gender seems to play a more decisive role than the social power attributed by ethnicity; thus if an individual's father is Bangando, she will be considered to be nearly Bangando, whereas if an individual's father is Baka, he will be more likely to be categorized by others as Baka.

Although illustrative of relative positions of social and political power based on different combinations of ethnic parentage, the following model of social power is limited in its scope; it includes only two dimensions, in which Bangando are politically and socially more influential than Baka, and in which men are politically and socially more powerful than women. In multiethnic southeastern Cameroon, the social and political influence of Bakwélé and Mbomam individuals who live in villages that are demographi-

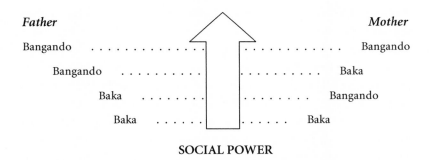

FIG. 4.1 Relative degrees of social power based on ethnic parentage

cally dominated by Bangando and Baka tend to fall between the extremes of relative power. Bakwélé and Mbomam who are integrated into these villages tend to be either women who have married Bangando men, or isolated families that have followed social relations or economic opportunities among Bangando and Baka or have fled from social or political difficulties in villages dominated by their own ethnic community. The influence of Bakwélé and Mbomam individuals tends to be restricted, especially where interethnic marriage places a woman and her mixed-heritage children in a structural position of inferiority to the husband and father, who is frequently Bangando, and then, by extension, to the community at large. If the marriage is mixed between a Bakwélé or Mbomam husband and a Baka wife, the family will have limited social power by virtue of the relatively low political status of Baka and their descendants. Thus individuals of mixed parentage—Bangando-Bakwélé and Bangando-Mbomam or Baka-Bakwélé and Baka-Mbomam—may experience higher levels of social power than *swéngélé* Baka individuals, but generally will not attain the same levels of village social influence as *swéngélé* Bangando individuals. Although this formal structure of power provides a benchmark for locating the communities of the Lobéké region on a relative scale that is determined both by ethnic affiliation and by degree of "purity," it reflects only one factor among many in the formation and maintenance of interethnic relations between individuals and families. As the ethnographic cases in this chapter demonstrate, personal preferences and emotional connections are at least as powerful as hierarchies of social influence in motivating people to engage in and sustain intimate relationships.

Interethnic Intimacy: Alliance or Ostracism?

Until the current generation of mature, established adults, interethnic marriage was considered abhorrent, and sexual relations between Bangando and Baka resulted in social ostracism. In contrast, marriages between Bangando and Bakwélé and between Bangando and Mbomam were encouraged, even among the communities' leaders. Several factors may contribute to this divergence. First, given the structure of power in the Lobéké region that elevates Bangando to a dominant position overall, with Bakwélé and Mbomam retaining influence in the northern and southern areas respectively, interethnic marriage emerged as a powerful means of establishing and consolidating political alliances. As a result, interethnic marriage

between Bangando and Bakwélé or Mbomam partners was neither historically nor is currently unusual. Where the husband is Bangando—therefore
a member of the regionally dominant community—and the wife is Bakwélé
or Mbomam, the ethnic difference between the spouses is nearly invisible
in everyday contexts. Second, given their histories of tension and even
violence as the communities first met, finding channels for building ethnic cohesion between Bangando and Bakwélé and between Bangando and
Mbomam may have been encouraged as ways to resolve frictions between
the communities. Finally, ethnic prejudices held by Bangando typically
portray Baka as lacking not only in political influence but also in morality
and development, as we shall see; these stigmas serve as both a cause and a
reflection of social prohibitions against sexual relations between Bangando
and Baka. The issue of ethnic prejudice against Baka is complex, particularly in relation to Bangando with whom Baka share relations that are,
for the most part, amicable. The context of interethnic marriage provides
an illuminating angle for understanding some of the social tensions that
ground ethnic prejudice, in particular tensions between public categories
and private relations.

Marriages that united Bangando husbands and Bakwélé or Mbomam
wives were accepted soon after these communities came into contact and settled in common, overlapping areas of the forest. Interethnic unions between
Bangando, Bakwélé, and Mbomam tended to couple Bangando husbands
with wives of the other groups, underscoring the position of the Bangando
community at the top of the regional hierarchy of social and political power.
Bangando men married Mbomam women from the outset of their communal relations as a means of integrating the immigrant Mbomam community
into Bangando spheres of familial, social, and political influence. The unions
of Bangando men and Mbomam women assimilated the broader Mbomam
community more intimately into the social and political structures of the
region into which they had migrated, simultaneously offering secure refuge
to the Mbomam as well as increasing the demographic, social, and political
influence of the Bangando community.

Bangando men also took Bakwélé wives, resulting in the integration of
these communities, especially in Moloundou and Ngilili, villages where the
Bangando and Bakwélé spheres of influence overlap. Bangando-Bakwélé
marriages between prominent leaders promoted clear political objectives:
forging closer ties between political elites of the two communities. For
example, the daughter of the Bakwélé chief of Ndongo, a large Bakwélé village along the Ngoko River, was married to the extremely influential Ban-

FIG. 4.2 Bangando currency: *ìnjéwùsó* (left) and *ndùpá* (right) (mechanical pencil in middle measures six inches)

FIG. 4.3 Bangando woman weaving a mat (*fé*)

gando elder named Nadia. Nadia emerged as an unusual, apical political leader among the Bangando, and served as a formal liaison between the German colonial administration and the multiethnic society of the Moloundou region. Matalina recalls their marriage:

> I am the last wife of Nadia, the ɓò dáwà [monkey clan] Bangando chief who came to Moloundou from Salapoumbé because the Germans asked for him. I was the last of his thirteen wives. We are three wives still living. Two are Bakwélé.
>
> My father was the chief of Ndongo. He and Nadia arranged our mónyàdì [wedding].[2] My father took me to Moloundou to see if Nadia would like me. He approved, so we went back to Ndongo to prepare. Later Nadia came to Ndongo on a steamboat to bring my family ndùpá and ìinjéwùsó [iron currency] and fé [woven mats] for the bride price. Then Nadia went back to Moloundou, and I had to go with him. When we arrived, his other wives bathed me and covered me with mɔ́ngwélé [palm oil reddened with mahogany dust, anointment for Bangando brides]. But the colonial officials who were in Moloundou told Nadia that Bangando mónyàdì traditions were bad, and so they sent him away on a tour of villages, all the way to Mikel. They told him to hold a feast with his family in Salapoumbé. So I only had to do one day of mónyàdì.
>
> Because Nadia was the chief, he didn't have to walk to Salapoumbé. He was carried in a kípùi [a sedan chair on two long poles, carried by four men]. I had to walk, even though I was the bride.
>
> I was very sad to leave my family in Ndongo to marry Nadia, because Moloundou is very far away from Ndongo. But now I have lived among the Bangando for so long, that I am already Bangando. I am Bakwélé, and I am also Bangando.[3]

Marriages between Bangando and Bakwélé couples, as well as between Bangando and Mbomam couples, fostered social and political alliances among communities and also enabled individuals to build sentimental attachments and ethnic affiliations with more than one group. At various levels — region, community, family, and individual — interethnic unions promoted increased solidarity.

In contrast to the fostering of political and personal solidarities between Bangando and both Bakwélé and Mbomam, a Bangando elder recalls the social ostracism that resulted if Bangando engaged in sexual relations with Baka:

> In my generation, it was absolutely impossible for Bangando and Baka to marry each other. If family or friends found out that you had had sex with a Baka

woman, you would be completely shut out from your family and friends, and you would take the social level of a Baka. You would not be allowed to eat from the same pot as your family and friends. [Here Ngonda visibly cringed and squeezed his eyes shut, perhaps in disgust.][4]

Commensalism offers a potent metaphor for social intimacy throughout equatorial Africa; ostracism from the intimacy of sharing food served as a clear indication that sexual congress with a Baka individual represented a relationship beyond the accepted boundaries for Bangando individuals. Interethnic sexual philandering was suspected only of men; Bangando women were assumed to remain faithful to their Bangando husbands, and certainly not to be intimately involved with Baka men. (According to numerous Bangando women, these assumptions were faulty on both counts.)

The sexual indiscretions of Bangando men were evident at the blacksmith's forge. Bangando men who had engaged in intimate relations with Baka posed dangers to both the blacksmith (mɔ́kɔ́ndjì dwálà—literally, "the chief of the forge") and to the forge itself, as Bangando believed that this indiscretion would cause ruptures in the carefully constructed clay hearth in which the iron ore was smelted. If interethnically promiscuous men acknowledged their affairs and repented, their ritual cleansing also took place at the forge. As described by Mungoï, one of few remaining Bangando who is a practicing blacksmith, the transgressor inserted his "dirty" hands into the red-hot forge, where the blacksmith symbolically washed them with molten iron ore. Only after this cleansing could the Bangando man resume normal social relations, including eating from a communal pot and sharing intimate domestic activities and space with other Bangando.[5] While in many areas of social life Bangando and Baka cultivated alliances between individuals and families, the line of sexual separation—underscoring political polarity and ethnic difference— between Bangando and Baka was sharply drawn.

Changing Attitudes toward Interethnic Marriage

Today interethnic marriage, even between the extremes of the hierarchy of social and political power—between Bangando and Baka—is increasingly common. Ngonda, a Bangando elder who is well known for his knowledge of Bangando traditions, explains:

Today things are different, and Bangando and Baka sometimes marry. If one of my children loves a Baka, who am I to stand between the love of a man and a woman?[6]

That such a forthright acceptance of intermarriage between Bangando and Baka is expressed by Ngonda, an elder who is known to be a stickler for upholding the values and practices of an older generation, is striking and signals the degree to which interethnic intimacy is accepted today. His comment, however, lacks clarity in what particular "things" are different today that would permit interethnic marriage. A Bangando elder from Lopondji, Maga, is more direct:

In older times Baka and Bangando would never marry each other. But now it's quite common. Three Bangando men in my wife's family are now married to Baka women. In general Bangando don't like to marry Baka because they are dirty. But as Baka become more and more *développés*, Bangando are becoming more and more open about living together, and accept more and more intermarriage. The Baka are now sending their children to school and are learning French, and are becoming *moderne* and are staying clean. So Bangando have an easier time accepting Baka on more equal terms.[7]

As illustrated by Maga, Bangando often point to transformations in the social outlooks and economic status of their Baka neighbors as the change that lowered the barrier to interethnic intimacy. When Baka became more "like us" from the Bangando point of view — "developed" and "modern" — sexual intimacy becomes more acceptable. It is important to emphasize Maga's articulation of increasing social interrelations, at all levels of social intercourse, on "*more* equal terms"; while increasing levels of intermarriage may indicate some leveling of power disparities among the groups, absolute ethnic equality is not a phenomenon that members of Bangando and Baka communities in particular, or Bakwélé and Mbomam communities, claim exists in the social context of the Lobéké forest.

While several generations ago sexual relations between Bangando and Baka were considered utterly reprehensible, today sexual relations and marriage between Bangando men and Baka women are tolerated, indicating a trend toward closer ethnic, social, and political parity. However, evidence of continuing social inequality bubbles to the surface of social discussions about potential — or actual — marriages between Bangando women and Baka men. As bluntly articulated by Maga,

Today the Bangando and Baka live together, but they are not equal. The Bangando are superior. A Bangando man may marry a Baka woman, although if he does, he is not well respected by other Bangando. But a Baka man may not marry a Bangando woman.[8]

Yet even this fundamental prohibition on sexual relations and marital ties between Bangando women and Baka men is changing. As we will see below, open sexual relations between Bangando women and Baka men *do* occur, and it is likely that clandestine sexual relations between Bangando women and Baka men may be more common than most Bangando—especially men— admit.[9]

During an extended interview about interethnic relationships, the parents of a seven-year-old girl expressed concern about the social difficulties that their Bangando daughter might face if she were to marry a Baka spouse. But in the course of the discussion, they admitted the possibility that their little girl might grow up to marry a Baka man. As his wife smiled nervously and looked away, Pito, the father, sought to sidestep the question of their daughter's hypothetical intermarriage by replying, "Bangando girls don't marry Baka boys yet." When pushed further to specify what he meant by "yet," Pito added cursorily, "If things keep changing, maybe someday Bangando girls will marry Baka boys." If what things keep changing? Finally Pito explained his thoughts in detail:

> Now Baka children go to school, and Baka wear *tètè mókàndà* [real clothes][10] and keep clean, whereas before the Baka lived in the forest, away from Bangando villages. In general Bangando girls don't marry Baka boys because the Bangando are stronger than the Baka. . . . But now some Baka have more clothes and keep themselves even cleaner than some Bangando, and some Baka have more money too. The Baka are developing. Baka development is good, because someday they will all change their *gbàsì dáwè* [literally "bad way of life"].[11]

The evolving acceptance of intermarriage between Bangando and Baka indicates that changes in individual relationships accompany developments in social and economic conditions; together, these transformations foster gradual change in ethnic attitudes. At the same time, however, stereotypes run deep; despite positive, even intimate interactions among individuals of the different communities, some stubborn, basic images—each of the other community—persist.

Taken together, these short ethnographic examples outline the changing parameters of interethnic marriage in southeastern Cameroon. In contexts where positions of power are relatively equal, interethnic marriage is accepted and even encouraged, especially when it serves the purpose of building political alliances between communities. As relative positions of political power and social and economic development tend toward equality, interethnic marriage seems to be increasingly common and accepted. At the same time, and in spite of the increasing occurrence of interethnic marriages in all dimensions of ethnicity and gender, interethnic intimacy and marriage highlight tension between public discourse about categories of people, which may be negative, and private relations between individuals, which are often positive. The following extended cases illustrate the emotional, social, and political complexities involved in interethnic relationships of marriage and descent. These examples of contemporary interethnic relationships reveal that, far from being clear-cut, processes of ethnic identification are replete with ambiguities and negotiations as people establish senses of self and other, and forge interrelationships between them in both public and private contexts.

Pando and Laati: Bangando Husband and Father, Baka Wife and Mother

Pando is a relaxed, smiling Bangando man who lives with his elderly, wizened mother, Iinduka, and his vivacious Baka wife, Laati, with their three children in a small house just on the northern bank of the Lopondji River. Pando is devoted to his mother, and has remained by Iinduka's side throughout his life. Although Iinduka has outlived (or divorced) numerous husbands and outlasted several of her children, Pando and Laati have stayed with her for many years.

Pando is as devoted to his wife and children as he is to his mother. He spent most of his young adulthood living with his mother, hunting in the forest and helping her with her garden. But during a visit to some friends in Mbateka, a village twenty kilometers to the south, Pando crossed paths with Laati, a cheerful Baka woman. As their romance unfolded, Pando remained in Mbateka much longer than he had originally planned. Ultimately Pando and Laati married, and they remained with her parents in Mbateka for many months, following the uxorilocal marriage pattern common among Baka newly-weds. Pando was happy living with Laati and her parents:

When we stayed with her family, we were good. I stayed there for a long time. Afterwards, I rejoined my old mother with my wife, and here we are. . . . Oh! Her family likes me too much! The love between my family-in-law and me is too much. My mother-in-law was here just the other day to visit us. She stayed with us here for three days. When my wife comes back from Mbateka, her family always gives her chickens to bring back. There are no problems or worries between Laati and me. What bothers us from time to time is the lack of meat to eat. And the lack of money, too. In our marriage together, we are very good.[12]

Pando's warm sentiments for Laati and her family were reinforced by his eyes, which glowed with warmth as he spoke of their relationship.

Pando and Laati have three children: two boys and one girl. Pando's face changed from contentment to surprise when I ask him if the children are Bangando or Baka. His quick and defensive response—"Bangando!"— emphasized his concurrence with the widespread notion that children naturally belong to the patriline, the father's clan and ethnic group. The idea that his children could be anything other than Bangando seemed to strike Pando as unimaginable and almost insulting. Emphasizing his children's Bangando-ness, Pando turned to the social metaphor of language: "Laati speaks Bangando with the children. They don't speak Baka. They speak Bangando." Pando takes the fact that his children speak Bangando as their primary language to be clear evidence that the ethnic solidarity of the Bangando community includes his children, who as they grow up will come to identify their ethnic affiliation as Bangando. Pando further underscores the Bangando-ness of his children when he clearly, almost severely, states that his daughter will marry a Bangando. Despite the fact that his own wife—his daughter's mother—is Baka, Pando insists that his daughter's future husband absolutely cannot be Baka:

My daughter will marry a Bangando. She cannot marry a Baka. I could not agree that my daughter would marry a Baka. I could not. I absolutely could not. A Bangando, if he marries my daughter, he will give what I want. But a Baka has nothing. A Baka would not give me a goat [for her bride price] as a Bangando would. I would never like my daughter to marry a Baka.[13]

But Pando's remarks are riddled with ambiguity; in the same conversation he emphasizes:

The Baka are people who are very good. When we (his nuclear family, including Laati and the children) go with them into the forest, they take care of us so well. When I was in Mbateka with my in-laws, we went into the forest and they treated me so well. Baka are good people.[14]

These seemingly contradictory sentiments—Baka as potentially stingy in-laws for his daughter and Baka as warm, generous in-laws for himself—highlight the ways that gender and perceptions of socioeconomic development are folded into contemporary discourses on ethnicity. From Pando's point of view, Laati's family offers acceptable in-law relations. Not only are Laati's parents and relatives supportive and caring people, but furthermore, as the family of the bride, they are not obliged to offer either money or manufactured commodities to initiate and nurture the marriage. Whereas the groom, together with his family and social network, is expected to provide cash and commodities—livestock such as chickens and goats, and *ngòlòngòló* whisky—as the bride price, the bride's family and her social network offer woven mats made from readily available rattan fibers (*gàɔu*) in the typical *mónyàdì* exchange. Throughout southeastern Cameroon, Bangando as well as Baka women are excellent weavers of *fé*, woven mats that often include intricate borders and patterns. Bangando fathers fear that their daughters' potential spouses will not have access to the cash and commodities that are expected of their future in-laws, whether these in-laws are Bangando or Baka. These perceptions of Baka as less economically prosperous persist despite increasing levels of socioeconomic development among their Baka friends, partners, and neighbors. Although Pando's comments come across as crass, his clear affection for Laati's family highlights his positive perceptions of Baka as supportive, loving people whose shared intimacies have enriched his life.

Discussions concerning the three children with Laati alone offer a contrasting image of the children's place in the ethnic collage of southeastern Cameroon and in the ethnic double-bill of their parentage.[15] Laati laughs as she holds her toddler daughter in her lap, watching her sons toss ants into the funnel-shaped lairs of ant lions in the sandy dirt nearby. With palpable fondness for her children, Laati reveals that she speaks Baka with her children most of the time, except in collective situations when she and the children are with Pando and his mother or with Bangando neighbors, when they all speak Bangando. She explains that she is most comfortable speak-

FIG. 4.4 Laati with her children, Lopondji, 1999

ing Baka; thoughts come to her first in her own language. From her point of view, there is no conflict between language and ethnic affiliation. Her children speak primarily Baka, because they *are* primarily Baka. She says that she would not be disappointed if her children, including her daughter, grow up to marry Baka spouses. When she visits her family in Mbateka, she often leaves Pando behind as he now must look after his aging mother. With a disarming smile she explains that she plans to visit her family more frequently as the children grow older, so that they can learn Baka customs and stories, hinting that she encourages their sentimental attachment to the Baka community and ways of life.

The contrasting accounts offered by Pando and Laati regarding their interethnic family highlight two areas of tension: evaluations of contributions to marital and extended-family relations, and the correlation between ethnic affiliation and language. Pando's vehement statement that he would not allow his daughter to marry a Baka man betrays ethnic chauvinism. Pando cites the (potential) inability of a Baka man to pay a proper bride price for his daughter, directly contradicting his own experience with generous Baka in-laws and his glowing praise for his own Baka wife. His commentary pivots on the tension between private relationships with individual people and public perceptions of categories of people: Pando's materialist reasoning seems to be guided not by personal experience with his own interethnic marital relations, but by public categories that mark Baka as economically unreliable partners. Perhaps Pando's deeply negative reaction to the prospect of his daughter's potential interethnic marriage also highlights a more fundamental prejudice than stark materialism; that Baka are incapable of properly consolidating the social relations of long-term support and reciprocity that constitute marital ties. In fact, Laati's discussion reveals that she returns to her family frequently—often without Pando—so that the children can nurture their ties with their Baka relatives and, through their care and guidance, learn Baka ways. In expressing his anxieties, Pando reveals the core of Bangando ethnic prejudice toward Baka. Despite manifold examples of intimacy in personal relationships, discussions about intimate relations between Bangando and Baka in hypothetical contexts often conjure images and expectations based on publicly held categories that define all Baka in terms that emphasize social distance. Pando's comments highlight the difference between qualities of individual relationships between Bangando and Baka, which are often characterized by intimacy, affection, and mutual support, and qualities of public categories of Baka, in which Bangando echo prejudicial images of Baka as lacking development, economic means, social reliability, and morality. Despite the ongoing reality of interethnic prejudice, there is gathering evidence that intimate sexual and family relationships that cut across ethnic boundaries provide contexts in which qualities of private relations between individuals provide momentum for the shifting contours of public perceptions of categories of people.

In interethnic marriage and descent, language emerges as another powerful metaphor for belonging and presents another domain for ethnic competition. According to structures of kinship and dynamics of power, ethnic affiliations are understood to flow from and belong to the patriline. Ethnic affiliation is also believed to be manifest in and reinforced by the speaking of a common language. However, interethnic marriages in the Lobéké region are also interlinguistic marriages, and linguistic intimacy and proficiency often follow maternal ties because young children are influenced most profoundly by the social, emotional, and physical nurturing provided by their mothers (Nagata 1981). In the case of Pando and Laati's three children, there is discordance between ethnic and linguistic affiliation—the children's ethnicity derives from their father, making them Bangando, while their intimate language stems from their mother, shaping a deep sense of

Baka affiliation as well. In the case of Pando and Laati's children, the process of identification is still unfolding, and would be fascinating to observe as they develop their own senses of self and relations with others. The relations of affection and support between Pando and Laati, in addition to their ties with extended Bangando and Baka relatives and neighbors, have generated social ties that both transcend and perforate the lines of ethnic affiliation. As a result of their intimacy, their children embody dual ethnic affiliations and dueling ethnic sentiments.[16]

Wetuno: Child of a Baka Father and a Bangando Mother

Wetuno sits with his uncles, cousins, and friends, avoiding the slanting afternoon sun under a low shade tree near his mother's house. His mother, Mokake, grumbles as she prepares manioc, plantains, and *súsúkú*, a hot broth of chilies, eggplants, and pungent bark, which she brings from the

FIG. 4.5 Wetuno and his interethnic family, Mbangoï, 1999

kitchen house to allay the nagging requests for dinner coming from the noisy men under the shade tree. The conversation and annoying demands for supper float back to Mokake's kitchen house in both Bangando and Baka words; the knot of men under the tree includes her Bangando brothers, her son, and her son's Baka uncles, cousins, and friends. In contrast to this animated circle of friends and family, Mokake seems withdrawn and isolated. She and a young teenage niece who has come seeking refuge from conflict in the Republic of Congo[17] are the only women of the household to cook, wash, and domestically support the men of their extended interethnic family.

Mokake has experienced volatile relations with men of many ethnic backgrounds. As a young woman she married, had children with, and divorced a Gbaya man, and later had children by Bangando, Bakwélé, and Baka men. Mokake's relationship with her brothers is strained, as they lean heavily on her for domestic support, even as she complains that the "energy" between them no longer flows and that her brothers speak badly of her everywhere they go.

But despite the unstable personal relationships that she bemoans throughout the afternoon, Mokake speaks fondly of her Baka friends and neighbors, companions whom she has come to appreciate over the course of her life. The Baka neighbors who live in a neighboring cluster of houses were companions of her father:

> My father had many Baka friends. . . . Today there are Baka next to us. It is the Baka who make us numerous here. It is the Baka who make us good here. When they come to visit us, we talk and we laugh. They are our friends. They were the friends of my father, which is why they stay here with us. It is friendship.[18]

The closeness of friendship with her steadfast Baka friends, which contrasts with her bitter relationships with other men from various communities, is deep-rooted and long-lasting, and eventually became intimate. Mokake conceived a child with a Baka man she had known for many years. She delivered their son, Wetuno, at her father's house along the Malapi River, not far from her current house. But when her son was a young boy, Mokake gave him to her older brother to raise. Wetuno recalls his childhood:

> When I was already a little bit big, it was my uncle who raised me, and showed me all of the work that a man should do. I learned to set snares, to weave nets, to clear a garden. So now I know how to do a little bit of everything.[19]

Mokake recalls accepting, eventually, that certain men's skills should be taught to a son by a father-figure. Wanting her son to learn Bangando ways of working, doing, and living, she entrusted her son's practical and cultural education to her older brother. Even today Mokake is critical of what she portrays as a typical Baka approach to work:

> The work that a Bangando man does, a Baka does not necessarily also do. There are things that Baka do that Bangando do not do. For example, a Bangando will not do a *jɔ́p* [paid job[20]] for his brother. But a Baka will leave his own work to go and do a *jɔ́p*. A Baka will leave his garden and go into the forest. But afterwards, he comes back and steals food from a Bangando garden. The Bangando won't do the same thing. This is the difference.[21]

Mokake points to these differences in work ethic as a fundamental distinction between Bangando and Baka; she portrays Bangando as morally superior to Baka, as they would never derail their own work and debase their dignity by performing paid labor for others. Mokake placed her son in the care of her brother to ensure that Wetuno would learn the values and skills needed to live a Bangando way of life.

Today Mokake insists that her son is Bangando. Mokake acknowledges and clearly appreciates the tightly intertwined emotional ties that connect her with her Baka friends and neighbors, and with Wetuno's father and paternal relatives. Still, Mokake vigorously maintains that Wetuno is primarily Bangando, overriding the usual rule that children belong to their father's patriline. In keeping with wider social acceptance of hierarchical organization of ethnic status, Mokake implicitly feels that Baka are socially inferior to Bangando, and she is unwilling to see her son "demoted" to a lower status by affiliating himself primarily with the Baka community.

But under the flat-topped, low-slung shade tree, Wetuno's paternal uncles unanimously—and vigorously—state that the young man is Baka. In defense of their position, they emphasize the overarching rule that a child always belongs to the father's lineage and ethnic community. Furthermore, they point out that Wetuno actually spends more time with Baka relatives, friends, and neighbors than with other Bangando. The Baka relatives view Mokake's attempt to attribute Bangando-ness to Wetuno as just one more Bangando ploy to maintain their overall position of social dominance over Baka, and thus dismiss her claim.

Not surprisingly, Wetuno himself is very uncomfortable about articulating a clear position regarding his ethnic affiliation. He speaks Bangando with the lilting cadence of Baka speech, and in his manner and habits seems more at ease with his Baka relatives and friends than with Bangando. These indicators suggest that, despite his mother's and uncle's best efforts to teach him Bangando ways, Wetuno was most profoundly shaped by the lessons he learned and relationships he formed with his Baka relatives and friends. Through the filing of his teeth, Wetuno has embodied the cultural markings of Baka-ness. He explains,

> For my teeth, they [Baka] tapped them as soon as they were solid [as soon as adult teeth had grown in]. They scraped at [my teeth] with a knife to make them pointed—you see? It didn't take much time. It didn't hurt, but there was a lot of blood. It was my friends who convinced me to do things like that.[22]

When describing his friends, Wetuno speaks enthusiastically about both Bangando and Baka, but finally expresses his desire to be most intimately integrated in relationships with Baka:

> I have Baka friends and Bangando friends. I also want to spend time with Baka as well as Bangando. With the two kinds, I am at peace. . . . I like the two, Bangando and Baka. But I don't want to marry a Bangando girl. This is why I have chosen a Baka wife—my kind [kúlú].[23]

Although Wetuno seems hesitant to articulate a clear affiliation with one group or another, his manner of speaking, his physical presentation, and his preference for a Baka wife all seem to offer clear indications that his sentiments of ethnic affiliation lie primarily with the Baka community. His use of the term *kúlú* to designate his "kind" of people is significant. *Kúlú* is used in various contexts to refer to a particular kind of thing (*kúlú mɔ̀*), including a kind of person or ethnic group (a Bangando is a different *kúlú wì*, or kind of person, than a Baka) and a way of doing something (*kúlú dé mɔ̀*). The link between a kind of person and a way of doing things is thus linguistically indicated. When used specifically to describe different kinds of people, *kúlú* is often translated from Bangando into French as "race."

Perhaps Wetuno's loyalty to his Baka family and friends is also a reaction against the unmistakable social avoidance that he and his Bangando mother have encountered from the larger Bangando community. Mokake and her son have become marginalized members of the Bangando community, living on the edge of Mbangoï with no Bangando neighbors. Her Bangando relatives in other villages laugh uncomfortably when I asked questions about her family and domestic context. Mokake's social exclusion appears related to the perception that she has moved "down" the social hierarchy of power through her open and intimate relations with many men, and in particular with a Baka man. On the other hand, Wetuno's Baka father seems to have maintained his social standing; his intimate relations with a Bangando woman have had no bearing on his domestic relationships with other Baka. In Wetuno's case, discordance emerges among the formal rules of kinship, in which ethnic affiliation passes through the patriline; structures of social and political power in which Wetuno's Baka father occupies a weaker position than his mother; and Wetuno's personal sentiments and friendships. The fact that Wetuno chooses to highlight his affiliation as a Baka indicates that intimate social relations may be preferable to the political power offered by claiming ethnic allegiance with a community that may not fully accept the interethnicity that he embodies.

Nadia: Child of a Bangando Mother and Bamiléké Father

Nadia is the granddaughter of the great Bangando chief Nadia, her name-sake, and his Bakwélé wife, Matalina. Nadia's mother identifies herself as Bangando because her father was Bangando. Nadia's father is Bamiléké, having come to Moloundou from the grasslands of western Cameroon for several years of temporary employment during the late 1970s, when baby Nadia was born. Despite the complex ethnic mixing in her background, Nadia is socially regarded as an ideal Bangando woman by her elders and her contemporaries, and expresses her own sense of belonging in the Bangando community. Nadia speaks Bangando as her natal language, but is fluent in both Bakwélé (by virtue of her grandmother) and Baka (by virtue of her easy sociability with people throughout the community and her diligent work in the forest and gardens). In addition, Nadia speaks fluent French and can read and write at a basic level; it is unusual to find women in southeastern Cameroon who are so well educated, both formally and informally.[24] Nadia has also taken her lessons in Bangando women's work and responsibilities seriously, and is recognized by older women for her abilities to cook and care for children, and to undertake forest activities as well as cultivation. She is a serious woman and a hard worker, but has a robust sense of humor. Once she starts joking, her laughter gathers momentum as she regales her family with stories, puns, and jokes.

When discussing the details of her daily activities and their impact on her sense of identity, Nadia concludes by emphasizing that she is Bangando. Her knowledge, skills, and habits have prepared her for life in the forest, and it is among Bangando that she feels most comfortable. Her emotional sense of connection to Bangando cultural practices also seems to place her squarely within the ethnic bounds of Bangando-ness. Nadia undertook the first stage of her marriage, *mónyàdì*, in February 1999. As she endured the uncomfortable period of several weeks when she was smeared from head to toe with *mɔ́ngwélé*, mahogany-tinted palm oil, wore nothing but a cloth around her naked body, and was weighed down by heavy iron bracelets, anklets, and a necklace, Nadia explained the personal significance that the Bangando ritual of *mónyàdì* holds for her:

> *Mónyàdì* is an essential part of being a Bangando woman. If I had married some-one who wasn't Bangando and I didn't go through *mónyàdì*, I would feel like there was something missing from me. I would not feel complete. *Mónyàdì* is like women's initiation, because the Bangando do not initiate women. Going through *mónyàdì* makes me feel like I'm part of generations of Bangando women, part of Bangando history. *Mónyàdì* is like a Bangando "signature."[25]

In keeping with generations of women before her, Nadia undertook a very traditional Bangando *mónyàdì* and entered into a new phase of her life as an adult married woman, the wife of a well-respected Bangando man.

But Nadia's discussions of her tumultuous birth and childhood, when her mother and father fought over how Nadia should be raised and to which community she belonged, reveal that she is not, according to the widespread convention of patrilineality, Bangando. Instead, she indicates that her for-mal ethnic affiliation is Bamiléké, the ethnic community to which her father belongs and whose regional base lies in western Cameroon, 1,500 kilometers from the Lobéké forest. Nadia's father moved to Moloundou in his profes-sional capacity as a road builder for the Ministry of Public Works. After sev-eral years of work, during which time he met Nadia's mother and they had a baby, construction of the road was complete, and his employment in the Moloundou region came to an end. The parents' relationship also came to an end, and they vehemently disagreed about where the baby Nadia should be raised: with her mother in the forest of southeastern Cameroon, among Bangando, or with her father in the grasslands of western Cameroon, among Bamiléké. This conflict found no simple resolution, as Nadia's father was

FIG. 4.6 Nadia receiving *mónyàdì* advice from her Bakwélé grandmother, Pezam, February 1999

determined to take his child—the blood of his patriline—with him to be raised as the Bamiléké that she, by strict definition of patrilineal descent, is.

But Nadia's mother and maternal relatives refused to let her Bamiléké father take Nadia to his village, for fear that as she grew up she would be discriminated against as a "pygmy." Recalling the bitter arguments over young Nadia's social upbringing, Matalina, Nadia's maternal grandmother, explained that many Cameroonians who live far from the forest assume that all people from southeastern Cameroon are "pygmies," treating them as social inferiors. Matalina recalls her anxiety that Nadia's Bamiléké cousins would force her to eat feces, asserting their power over their lowly, forest-dwelling cousin. As a compromise, Nadia was finally given to her maternal aunt, who ran a restaurant in Bertoua, the capital town of the East Province, far to the north of Moloundou. This aunt had recently lost her own young child, and agreed to raise Nadia as her own so that neither Nadia's father nor mother would have direct influence on or participation in the young child's life.

Because her maternal aunt is Bangando, Nadia grew up speaking Bangando as her first and most fluent language. And because she began her schooling in the larger town of Bertoua, she had the opportunity to solidify her skills in French. When Nadia returned to the Moloundou region for visits, she shriekingly refused to believe that her aunt was anything other than her true mother. But gradually her visits to her grandmother, biological mother, and other relatives in Moloundou grew more frequent and longer, and Nadia returned to Moloundou to finish primary school and attend secondary school. From the time she was about ten, Nadia grew up among Bangando family and friends, learning Bangando ways of playing, working, and living. Today Nadia embraces and supports her mother's family with dedicated loyalty and unbridled affection.

In contrast, Nadia has virtually no connection with her father or her paternal Bamiléké relatives. Nadia does not speak Bamiléké, and does not know Bamiléké customs. She explains:

> I do not know my father, or any of my brothers and sisters, cousins and other relatives who are all Bamiléké. But sometimes I go to the office of Public Works [in Moloundou] and I talk to my father by radio. He tells me the news of his village. I tell him the news of Moloundou.[26]

Despite the geographical, linguistic, and cultural distance between Nadia's circumstances and those of her Bamiléké father, and despite the manifestly intimate connection that she feels with her Bangando mother and cultural heritage, Nadia feels that, as her lowest denominator of ethnicity, she is Bamiléké. In her mind, the question of ethnicity is quite straightforward:

> In my heart [séà, literally, "liver"] I am Bamiléké. Because when a man and a woman have children, the children are the same as the father, not the mother.[27]

For Nadia, then, her ethnic affiliation seems to be determined by the strict rule of patrilineal descent: her father is Bamiléké; therefore she is also Bamiléké. Nadia was not raised within the Bamiléké community because of fears that she would be identified as a "pygmy" by her Bamiléké relatives, reflecting the tension between public categories and private relationships integral to the dynamics of other interethnic relationships. Thus Nadia was raised, despite her formal ethnic affiliation, as a Bangando woman. Her emotional attachments to the collectively held and perpetuated Bangando traditions and language, as well as her sentimental proximity to her Bangando family in Moloundou, seem to be unaffected by the formal, structural fact of her Bamiléké-ness. Indeed, her own marriage followed the customary steps and, in her own words, made her complete in her Bangando womanhood. In Nadia's case, a conceptual line seems to separate her objective acceptance of Bamiléké as her ethnic affiliation and her emotional embracing of Bangando people and traditions as her own.

These examples of interethnic marriage offer a glimpse of tensions between ethnicity and gender as they constitute structures of power, belonging, and individual identities; between patrilineal ethnicity and matrilineal language and cultural acquisition; and between private affections between people and public categories for people (Jenkins 1994). Significantly, no rigid formulas concerning ethnic affiliation and social alignment emerge from these examples. Ethnicity—the collective belief in the ontological, unifying experiences of social origins and communication in a shared, natal language—does exert a powerful influence on how people think about themselves, perceive others, and forge relationships with each other. But, as we see through these examples of intermarriage, which both result from and are a source of ethnic ambiguity, it is apparent that structured and seemingly immutable rules of patrilineal descent, language, and social positioning alone do not constitute ethnic affiliations. While individuals do not choose how to identify themselves independently of cultural assumptions of descent, it is clear that individuals emphasize particular components of their biological, linguistic, social, and economic backgrounds depending on both immediate contexts and proximal relations with both parents' ethnic communities. Cases of interethnic marriage demonstrate that individuals strategically select when and how to articulate ethnic sentiments, and have some choice in the ethnic affiliation(s) that they choose to highlight. When individuals express their opposition to interethnic marriage, ethnic affiliation may be expressed as a rigid outcome of structural formulae of descent. However, in cases in which individuals engage in interethnic marriages and negotiate between their own ethnic sentiments, ethnicity melts into a much more fluid, adaptable criterion for social identification. While the formal structures of power and ethnic affiliation provide a framework for orienting relationships in southeastern Cameroon, interethnic marriages and affiliations highlight the ambiguous process of working out what it means to belong in individual relationships, in a family, and as part of a larger community. Transcending ethnic boundaries altogether, tangles of social networks build compelling and complicating connections among individuals and offer many ways of belonging.

CHAPTER FIVE

Tangles

PARALLEL CLANS, ALLIANCES, RITUALS,
AND COLLECTIVE WORK

E thnic affiliations are thick with historical, linguistic, and ideological value. While not immutable over time, monolithic across communities, or of constant emotional value among individuals, ethnic affiliations are collectively valued, recognized, and upheld. As a result, it is relatively difficult for people to manipulate their ethnic affiliations outright to suit particular interests in particular contexts. In contrast, interethnic social relations are established and nurtured, and interethnic social identities emerge where individuals live in a shared environment, face shared crises and opportunities, and experience shared historical events and social change. Where existential conditions are common, collaborative relationships result in interethnic networks and communal social identities that individuals call on with frequency and ease. While maintaining partner-

FIG. 5.1 Building friendship, Dioula Village, 1996

ships of any kind requires constancy and effort, in southeastern Cameroon individuals are involved in numerous interethnic social relations at once, offering a diversity of ways to interact and to promote mutually beneficial relationships and identities. Moreover, interethnic social relationships have both calculative and affective dimensions, as people balance practical and emotional reasons for coming together in partnerships and networks, or for abandoning these relationships. By exploring the tangles of belonging that bring people of different ethnic affiliations together, it becomes apparent that processes of identification provide multiple channels for people to position themselves in the plural, multiethnic communities of southeastern Cameroon, enabling individuals selectively to emphasize social relationships that transcend their particular ethnic affiliations.

Bangando, Baka, Bakwélé, and Mbomam individuals come together in numerous collaborative social contexts, including parallel clans, interethnic alliances, shared ritual ceremonies and societies, and collective work efforts. These channels of interethnic collaboration highlight the many, varied ways that people in the Lobéké forest region come together, building on and sustaining the core of shared experiences that enable individuals to form meaningful, lasting relationships and fluid, flexible ways of identifying oneself and others. As lianas and vines integrate the forest into a dynamic, interactive ecosystem, so do partnerships, alliances, and collaborative ties integrate the people of southeastern Cameroon in horizontally tangled relationships that cut across vertical trunks of ethnic affiliation.

Clans and Parallel Clans

Throughout the Lobéké forest, families of the four main ethnic communities are internally organized according to patrilineal clans, representing extended families whose narratives of social origins indicate that individuals belonging to the clan have descended from a common, although often mystical, set of ancestors. In addition to sentiments of ethnic affiliation that are based on the sharing of a primary language and story of origin, membership in clans adds another layer of emotional solidarity among individuals of shared patrilineage. As clan members recount stories of the clan's history, uphold taboo restrictions, and overlap in domestic space, individuals belonging to particular clans recognize and reaffirm their deep interconnectedness.[1]

By clan I refer to a kinship group in which members of each group believe themselves to be agnates related by unilineal descent, even though they often cannot trace their relations with other members of the kinship group with genealogical precision (Radcliffe-Brown and Forde 1950; Burnham 1980). Membership in the clan is passed to each individual from his or her father, who in turn "received" his membership from his father, and so on. Membership in a particular clan is represented by three social features that are passed from a father to his children: a clan name, an emblem or totem (which reflects the clan name), and the social rule of exogamous marriage[2] (see Burnham 1980: 83 to compare with Gbaya clans).

Bangando, Baka, Bakwélé, and Mbomam clans offer ligaments of structural parallelism, facilitating interethnic collaboration. The clan systems of all four groups are based on patrilineal, exogamous, noncorporate structures. This organizational alignment across the communities means that their basic kinship structures often correspond and can operate in tandem. Thus if individuals from different ethnic backgrounds marry, the fundamental systems of kinship organization of their respective families are often analogous, allowing the couple and their eventual children to fit within the structural logic of both families. This structural congruence facilitates interethnic marriage, because couples find that despite differences in language and history of origin, the principles and structures of kinship in both families are fundamentally coherent. In addition, certain clan affiliations are held by more than one ethnic group among the Bangando, Baka, Bakwélé, and Mbomam. These overlapping clan affiliations lead to alliances between members of different ethnic groups who belong to the same clan. Each Bangando, Baka, Bakwélé, and Mbomam clan is represented by a totemic symbol, usually a plant or animal found in the surrounding forest, whose consumption is tabooed. Clans rarely recognize apical ancestors.[3] Instead clan origins are based on stories of the rescue of the initial nuclear family by a particular forest animal. A woman of the monkey clan, *bò dáwà*, explains her family's association with chimpanzees and monkeys:

> During the war when the Ndzimou attacked Bangando villages, my family became connected with the family of monkeys. We [Bangando and monkeys] were neighbors living in the forest. When the Ndzimou tried to attack our village, the chimpanzees [*wáké*] saw the Ndzimou approaching, because they were high up in trees. The chimpanzees warned our family that the Ndzimou were coming. The chimpanzees ran ahead of our family through the canopy, showing us the best path for escape and the safest places to hide. Our family was so grateful to the chimpanzees and said that we would never hunt and eat chimpanzees — or other monkeys — again.[4]

Similar stories of rescue are recounted by members of many different clans. In other clans' stories of rescue and alliance, elephants stomped away traces of families that fled into the forest, gathering around them to protect them from advancing enemies. Other clans were saved by birds, which flew into the faces of advancing enemies and blinded them by their flapping as families fled. Still today the rescuing animals serve as the clan totem for the patrilineal descendants from the original families that were rescued; the clan members faithfully observe the taboo restriction on eating the meat of their totem.

In addition, most clans recognize particular insignias that can be used to mark the movement of a clan member, and uphold rituals that pertain to the birth of a new clan member. For example, *bò fɔlɔ* clan members, the people of the elephant, mark their passage at the junction of forest trails by taking a vine and tying it loosely into a circular knot. The ring made by the vine represents an elephant's footprint; the toenails of the elephant's footprint are represented by the crossing of the vine in the loose knot, thus indicating the direction that the elephant-clan person traveled. An example of birth rituals

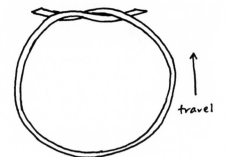

FIG. 5.2 Insignia of the *bò fɔ́lɔ́* clan, "the people of the elephant"

Bò fɔ́lɔ́ clan insignia, indicating direction of travel in forest. "Elephant footprint" is moving forward.

comes from the *bò wé* clan, the people of fire (whose totem is the monitor lizard). *Bò wé* mothers deliver their children in complete darkness. If a child is born at night, no lamp, candle, fire, or even match may be lit. At the first light of dawn, the child is passed over a ceremonial fire (*wé*) at the doorway to the house to purify and protect the child.

Over and above each clan's story of rescue by and alliance with a particular forest animal, the broader history of Bangando migration into the forest of southeastern Cameroon and their ethnic genesis from Ngombé ancestors connect all Bangando lineages. Thus Bangando kinship reinforces agnatic kinship across all clans, even as clans themselves may share important symbolic, ritual, and social ties that are specific to their own lineages, ties that they may share with clan members of other ethnic affiliations.

Bangando clan structures are effectively noncorporate: no internal structure of roles defines positions or formal responsibilities of individuals within a clan. Despite this lack of internal structure within clans, the eldest male of each clan traditionally served as the *mɔ̀kóndjí* or chief of the clan, taking charge of family decisions. If multiple clans lived within a single village, as is usually the case today, traditional political relations would bring the heads of each clan together during times of crisis to make collective decisions regarding the larger multiclan community. But as a result of the political restructuring of communities in southeastern Cameroon and the establishment of village-wide, officially sanctioned chiefs, clans have ceased to function as political structures. Today clans offer extended families a cohesive, sentimental net, as well as a means of internal reckoning of patrilineal relations.

Each Bangando clan tends to have a geographic epicenter where elder male relatives and their families have established their households. The spatial focus of each clan is historically based and is often the location where clan forefathers established a neighborhood of a village. The locations of many Bangando villages have changed over the course of the past century as a result of German and French colonial resettlement policies (Rupp 2001). When entire villages moved, resident clans usually shifted as well. Often these relocations provided opportunities for clans to adjust the layout of their neighborhood with respect to other clans, and for individual families within a clan neighborhood to alter the configuration of their houses, defusing simmering tensions or consolidating new alliances and friendships.

Not all contemporary clans have one single, spatial center. Because economic and social opportunities are distributed throughout the Lobéké forest region, and because mobility was (and continues to be) an entirely acceptable and normal dynamic among the four ethnic groups, young adults were at liberty to establish their own households in other villages. Not infrequently brothers or parallel cousins decided together that their ambitions were best fulfilled in a village some distance from the rest of their clan, which was often dominated by their fathers and grandfathers. In such cases, young men and their families moved to a different village to establish a new neighborhood, or they founded an entirely new village in a new location in the forest. This strategy of internal social mobility and flux enabled the wider, interethnic community to maintain general balance, by neutralizing small-scale conflicts and facilitating new and mutually beneficial relations with individuals from various clans, villages, and ethnic communities. Today when clan members are dispersed in more than one location, members of the clan recognize the various areas where they can find solidarity and hospitality among extended family members, and often visit the other villages of their clanspeople for a holiday or in search of other opportunities. This spatial distribution of clans is significant; family members traveling to a different village, or even to a different region of the forest, can be sure that if they find someone from their clan they will be welcomed and cared for as kin.

If epicenters of clans are predicated on the patrilineal relations of male clan members, the dispersion of the clan is mobilized by women of the clan. Because of the social assumption that an individual's identity derives from the patriline, the children of a couple formally become members of their father's clan, not their mother's.[5] As adults, women marry into the clans of their husbands. Thus wives are affiliated with two clans simultaneously: their patrilineal clan of birth as well as the clan to which their husbands and children belong.[6] In addition, Bangando, Bakwélé, and Mbomam communities follow virilocal marriage patterns; women tend to live and raise their children in the villages and according to the clan allegiance of their husbands. Through the dual clan affiliation of wives and their virilocal distribution throughout villages in southeastern Cameroon (and beyond), the regional spread of clans is convoluted, complex, and wide. Although not every village includes representatives of every clan, many villages are characterized by a surprising diversity of clans, whose representatives are often women who have married into the core patrilineal clans of the village founders. Especially where multiple women from the same family—sisters or female cousins, for example—marry men of a given family, often the households of these women provide important "sub-hubs" of their own patrilineal clan in their marital villages.[7] These multiple marriages between two clans, sometimes involving sibling exchange, also result in the tendency for certain pairs of clans to have particularly strong and affable relations. Through the rigid requirements of exogamous marriage, the extended iterations of virilocal marriage, and the acceptance of social mobility, relationships among the many clans of the four ethnic communities are manifold.

Individual clans reinforce their solidarity through the mythic histories and totemic ideologies that clan members embrace. Each clan name is constructed by placing the prefix *bò* in front of the name of the animal that serves as the clan's totem.[8] Thus the clan name of the forest pig, *ngwéà*, is *bò ngwéà*; the clan members are also called *bò ngwéà*, meaning "people of the forest pig."[9] The evolution of the prefix *bò* as a flexible, nominal marker of identity referring to "people of" in contemporary contexts beyond the clan system also enables speakers of Bangando to construct countless and continually shifting ascriptions of social identity.

Clan affiliation, and thus patrilineal kinship, is one of the fundamental ways that Bangando and the other communities of southeastern Cameroon reckon who is who and conceptualize networks of intimate kin relations. While most Bangando throughout southeastern Cameroon know each other—or at least know of each other—because of their extensive social networks, if strangers meet for the first time, one of first pieces of information that each person inquires about is clan affiliation. Clan membership provides general orienting information about the social and familial back-

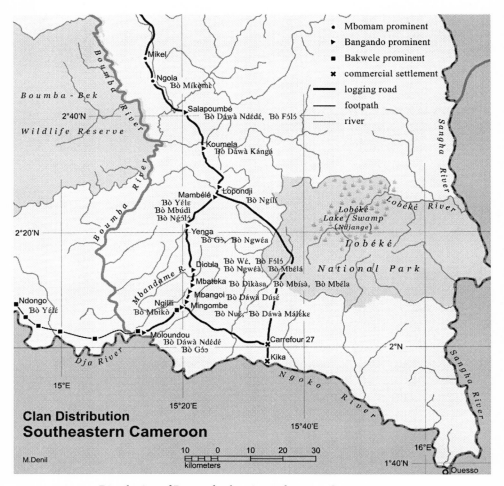

MAP 5.1 Distribution of Bangando clans in southeastern Cameroon

ground of the individual, who her relatives are, and where she may have grown up.

In addition to offering practical support and emotional connections among clanspeople, certain clans have fostered particularly close relations as allies of other clans. These interclan links are often spiritually charged, mythically remembered, and socially reinforced through a high degree of intermarriage of their women. For example, the clan of the monitor lizard, the *bò wé* family, which includes the ancestral line of Wanguwangu, has deep and enduring links with the clan of the elephant, *bò fɔ́lɔ́*. The quasi-apical ancestor of the *bò wé* clan was Wanguwangu, a legendary Bangando warrior

TABLE 5.1 Distribution of Bangando clans in southeastern Cameroon

BANGANDO CLAN	FOCAL VILLAGE	ENGLISH TRANSLATION
bò míkòmè	Ngola	People of the wild cat
bò dáwà[10]		People of the monkey
bò dáwà kángá	Salapoumbé, Moloundou	. . . colobus monkey
bò dáwà málèkè	Koumela	. . . de Brazza's monkey
bò dáwà ndédé	Mbangoï	. . . Guenon monkey
bò dáwà dúsé	Mingombé	. . . ? monkey
bò ngílí	Lopondji	People of the tortoise
bò yélé	Mambélé	People of the buffalo
bò mbúdì	Mambélé	People of the sitatunga[11]
bò ngálá	Mambélé	People of the snail
bò gò	Yenga-Doucement	People of the panther
bò ngwéà	Yenga, Dioula	People of the forest pig
bò mbélá	Dioula, Mbateka	People of the eagle
bò wé	Dioula	People of the monitor lizard
bò fálá	Dioula, Salapoumbé	People of the elephant
bò dìkàsà	Mbateka Njong	People of the hardy shrub
bò mbísà	Mbateka	People of the *mbísa* fruit[12]
bò mbìkò	Ngilili	People of the caiman
bò nué	Mingombé	People of the bird
bò gáá	Moloundou	People of the snake

and elephant hunter. According to the oral mythistories of the clan, Wanguwangu fought enemies with the strength of an elephant. Wanguwangu could also transform himself into an elephant during battle to escape his enemies, and during the hunt to sneak up on elephants that he intended to kill. Kebikibele, Wanguwangu's granddaughter and one of the oldest living Bangando in the region, recalls the merging of attributes from the *bò wé* and *bò fálá* clans, evident in his death and funeral:

> When Wanguwangu died, our family placed two large wooden poles on either side of his grave, sticking out of the ground. The wooden poles had special signs

on them. These poles represented the tusks of an elephant, because Wanguwangu had been a great elephant hunter and warrior. Just as we placed his body in the grave, Wanguwangu transformed himself into an elephant and disappeared into the forest. But an unburied spirit is an unsettled and dangerous thing, so the *bò wé* organized an elephant hunt to find and kill him, so that we could bury him properly. When we finally managed to kill the elephant [Wanguwangu], his tusks had the same markings on them that we had made on the wooden "tusks" that we had placed over his grave. My family took the elephant meat and ate it—we ate Wanguwangu. So the power of *kífí* [transforming from human into animal form] was passed on to younger generations.[13]

It is significant that even though Wanguwangu had the power to transform himself into an elephant, he was not *bò fɔlɔ* (person of the elephant) but *bò wé* (person of fire, represented by the monitor lizard). Usually clans protect their secrets—origin stories and the power of transformation into the form of their totem—from discovery by other clans. But Kebikibele explains that in Wanguwangu's case, he made a pact with elephants because their powers of strength and cunning would be invaluable in battle and in hunting, giving him a strategic advantage beyond any powers that transformation into the form of a monitor lizard, the totem of his patrilineal clan, could offer. Because of the alliance that Wanguwangu had forged with elephants, during the wars and conflicts of the nineteenth century, the *bò wé* clan would flee into the forest along with the *bò fɔlɔ* clan, and elephants would protect them all, people of the elephant and people of the monitor lizard alike. As Kebikibele explains,

> The people would all flee ahead of the elephants, and the elephants would trample over the people's footprints, stomping out any traces of their passage. If the children were crying or the people were making too much noise, the elephants would make noises to cover the people's voices. When the *bò wé* and *bò fɔlɔ* would stop for the night, the elephants would gather around them to protect them.
>
> The same thing would happen today if a war were to break out or if the war comes from Congo. The Bangando and Baka would all flee along the same path into the forest, and the *mòkɛlákɛlá* [elephants, including people transformed into elephants] would follow and stomp out the footprints of the people. The *mòkɛlákɛlá* would protect both Bangando and Baka, because we are all one family.[14]

As a result of the alliance made between Wanguwangu and the elephants, two social articulations were initiated. First, the *bò wé* clan and the *bò fɔlɔ* clan initiated their long-standing relations of interclan cooperation, coresidence in the same village, and intermarriage. Today the emotional bonds between *bò wé* and *bò fɔlɔ* individuals continue to be intimate, as these two clans have intermarried and collaborated closely for numerous generations.

Secondly, Wanguwangu's alliance with elephants and his use of the powers of transformation—*mólómbí*—brought Bangando and Baka together in intimate relations with elephants: both groups share the power of elephant transformation and come under the joint protection of elephants. *Mólómbí* was first a Baka form of sorcery, allowing Baka hunters to move about the forest invisibly, transformed into the bodies of elephants. According to Bangando and Baka elders alike, as their ancestors forged alliances and became partners, Bangando warriors realized that *mólómbí* would offer powerful protection against their enemies in the interethnic conflicts of the nineteenth century. So Bangando warriors added their own magical powers to the Baka expertise in *mólómbí*, enhancing its potency.

> *Mólómbí* is a special power to make yourself invisible, especially for times of war or for hunting, so that others can't see you. *Mólómbí* is a mixture of Bangando and Baka powers; the strongest of both mixed together. You must be initiated to know and practice *mólómbí*. It is *mòbùlè* [very secret].[15]

Today *mólómbí* is used by Baka and Bangando both for hunting and for protection in case of conflict.

Just as both Bangando and Baka families that have affiliations with elephants will be protected by them, numerous Bangando and Baka (as well as Bakwélé and Mbomam) clans share other animal totems, creating an interethnic network of parallel clans and mutual support. It is likely that the social structures of the four communities developed independently of one another, the coincidences of shared clan totems being reinforced by their mutual social and natural contexts once the communities settled in the Lobéké forest region. Names of Bangando and Gbaya clans in some cases are identical, suggesting that at least this structural element of Bangando organization arrived with them intact when they migrated to the forest from the Gbaya-dominated grasslands. Baka clan names refer much more frequently to plants than do Bangando clan names, indicating that Baka and Bangando clans have distinct origins. As Bangando and Baka families developed close affinal ties, deepening their social relations through the sharing of meat and other food, mutual aid, and neighborly cohabitation, the clan systems belonging to these two separate groups also began to intersect. Bangando and Baka recognize a certain mutual reliance on clanspeople of the overlapping, interethnic clan, particularly in situations of stress or need. Some of these shared clans are sketched in table 5.2.[16]

Throughout the Lobéké region, Bangando and Baka alike point to the overlapping of their clan systems as an indication of their intricately connected communities. As a mixed group of villagers in Dioula explain, where two clans intersect, the overlap indicates a special friendship between the Baka and Bangando members of these clans. So if a Bangando *bò dáwà*, a person of the monkey clan, is in a village far away from home, and if there is a Baka *yě kémà* family, also the monkey clan, the *yě kémà* family will take in the *bò dáwà* and care for him. Likewise, if a Baka *yě kémà* comes to a Bangando village where there are *bò dáwà*, the Bangando "people of the monkey" will take care of the Baka "person of the monkey," as they are members of the same family.[17]

Bangando and Baka clans that overlap in the same village know who their fellow clanspeople are, including members of other ethnic affiliations, and know that they can turn to these interethnic clanspeople if they are in need of assistance. Anda, a Baka man who is generally sour about his relations with Bangando neighbors, nonetheless explains the overlap of clans with some appreciation:

> Some Baka and Bangando clans are the same. They have different names, but they ritually avoid [*síní*] the same forest animals. I am *yě gùgà*, so I don't eat monitor lizard. The [Bangando] *bò wé* also don't eat monitor lizard. So the *bò wé* avoid monitor lizards; the *yě gùgà* also avoid monitor lizards. [Then in Bangando he said] *Mí bò bò wé* —I am a person of the monitor lizard. If I have an illness in my family, I can go to Wanguwangu, the elder of the *bò wé* clan, to ask him for help. Wanguwangu will help me by giving me some money or by helping me find medicine. And if Wanguwangu or another *bò wé* comes to me for help, I will try to help him, too. But because I don't have any money, I could only offer Wanguwangu a chicken, which he could then sell, and use the money to sort out his problem.[18]

Although Anda recognizes the links of friendship and support that people who *síní* (avoid) the monitor lizard can fall back on, he also emphasizes that Baka were *yě gùgà* before they met Bangando; there are no compelling historical circumstances that make the *yě gùgà* reliant on or responsible for their parallel Bangando clan, the *bò wé*. The coincidental overlap of their clans' affiliations—the monitor lizard—provides a context in which they can turn to each other for assistance. But other social circumstances, includ-

TABLE 5.2 Interethnic overlap of clans in southeastern Cameroon

BANGANDO	BAKA	MBOMAM	BAKWÉLÉ	TOTEM/TABOO
bò dáwà	yé kɛ́mà		yá dadjak	monkey
bò gɔ́ɔ́	yé mòkùmù		yá zozape	snake
bò wé	yé gùgà			monitor lizard
bò fɔ́lɔ́	yé líkèmbà			elephant
bò yélɛ́	yé ndúmù			buffalo/drum
bò ngwɛ̀à	yé mɔ́ndɔ́			wild pig
	yé mòmbító			kind of tree
	yé ngándá			black civet
	yé sìlò			electric fish
	yé njèmbɛ̀			kind of fish
	yé ngílá			switch, stick for beating
	yé ngɓɛ́			?
	yé kpóngɓò			rattan
	yé ndóngá			?
	yé lɛ́kèmba	yá zɔma		rat
		yá bàngò		green pigeon
		yá mísùlà		?
		yá biótà		weaver bird
		yá ùgól		?
		yá bàng		hornbill
		yá ndyápàngɛi		?
		yá chtíbá		?
		yá msɔla		ground squirrel
		yá sikɛ		?
		yá bɔsɛla		?
bò gò			yá kei	leopard
bò mbélá			yá biel	eagle
			yá kwíɛ̀	blue duiker
			yá bámò	súúm
			yá bomun	?
			yá dada	?
			yá kuaduak	?

ing residence, hunting partnerships, and intermarriage also play a role in their friendships and alliances with Bangando.

Maga, an elder from Lopondji, offers a slightly different explanation for the overlapping of Bangando and Baka clans. He suggests that Baka maintain two clan affiliations: a Baka individual belongs to one clan by virtue of his patriline, and he belongs to a second clan by sharing the clan membership of his Bangando partner. In this case Baka partners do not rigorously uphold the food prohibitions of the Bangando clan. Maga's Baka partner, Andusa, and his extended family are linked to Maga's extended family through a *bándí* partnership. Because of his alliance with Maga, Andusa and his family belong not only to their own patrilineal Baka clan, but also to Maga's patrilineal clan, the clan of the tortoise (*bò ngílí*). Maga and his family, however, are not members of Andusa's clan; indeed, Maga does not know what Andusa's Baka clan affiliation is.[19] This unidirectional "sharing" of clan affiliations seems to reflect the imbalance in social relations of power between Bangando and Baka, in which Bangando hold more social, economic, and political power than their Baka partners.

In practice, Bangando and Baka seem to rely on concentric circles of relations for assistance, turning to wider circles of parallel clan affiliations for support when no other options are available. The most intense and focused support comes from the smallest circle of intimate relations for both groups: their nuclear families, affines, and close friends. If additional support is needed, for example if an individual is traveling beyond the geographic range of her close social ties, or if closely tied friends and relatives are not able to offer help, Bangando and Baka turn to other families and individuals with whom they have social links either through common clan affiliations or, as we shall see below, through other intimate alliances. The existence of clan-based, interethnic relations indicates that the metaphors of kinship and responsibility have coevolved between the two communities, enabling them to support each other in circumstances of need. Parallel clans enable individuals to look for logistical, social, political, and economic assistance through relations that traverse ethnic lines, opening additional avenues of cooperation and support.

Alliances

Because patrilines are often linked through structural alliances that emphasize and reinforce interethnic cooperation, individuals are often connected through lasting friendships and partnerships that transcend ethnic boundaries. At the level of structural kin relations, there are no overlapping terms for kinship relations in the Bangando and Baka languages. One term for a very intimate friend is included in the palette of kinship terms in both languages, however: *bò jáá mù* (in Bangando) and *bò jáá álè* (in Baka), where *bò jáá* in both cases refers to a "person of the same stomach" (and *mù* and *álè* are first person possessive pronouns in Bangando and Baka, respectively). The appellation *bò jáá mù* evokes the intimate connections that siblings share and is attributed to a very close friend or *bándí*. The shared concept for an especially close friend, partner, and ally indicates that sentiments of emotional and social solidarity have developed between individuals of different ethnic groups, affections that can and often do surmount ethnic differences.

In analyzing social relations, however, the literature on relations between "hunter-gatherers"/"farmers" and "pygmies"/"villagers" emphasizes economic relationships between the groups. According to these analyses, labor is provided by "hunter-gatherers" while goods—particularly agricultural produce and commercial goods such as clothes, iron tools, and salt—are provided by "farmers." As classically portrayed by a leading expert on hunting and gathering communities in central Africa,

> Each Pygmy family has exclusive economic relations with a family of farmers. The Aka [Pygmies] provide the villagers with game, forest products, and seasonal agricultural labor (for forest clearing and harvesting). In return, they obtain metal tools and agricultural products. But the two communities are quite independent, with different systems of kinship, and social and religious organizations. The relationship between the two populations is comparable to the "patron-client" relationship in ancient Rome. (Bahuchet 1999: 193)

The summary of socioeconomic relations between "pygmies" and the nondescript "villagers" is typical of much of the literature on forest dwellers. Scholars often portray such exchanges of labor for goods and forest products for agricultural products as the basis of social interaction between groups of "hunter-gatherers" and "farmers."

But alliances between Bangando "villagers" and Baka "pygmies" involve much more than exchanges of labor for goods and forest products for agricultural products. Bangando and Baka families support each other in diverse ways, not only economically but also by providing emotional and political support, formalized through the creation and maintenance of relationships between interethnic partners. While these relationships are often initiated between two men, they frequently develop into alliances between families that pass from one generation to the next, often extending to special friendships between the wives and children of the families as well.

During the tumultuous era of precolonial conflict and the onset of colonialism, when forced labor such as road building and rubber collecting as well as capitation taxes stretched families to the limits of their productive and protective abilities, Bangando and Baka families extended support to each other (for detailed discussion, see Rupp 2001). The pressures wrought on the communities of southeastern Cameroon through the German and French colonial eras, as well as during independence and the postcolonial decades of the twentieth century, brought Bangando and Baka together in mutual support. Little by little, first through internal dynamics of shared affinity and reciprocal support in times of difficulty, and later as a result of the "push" factor of Baka resettlement along the road, Bangando and Baka became more and more intricately involved in each other's lives, struggles, and successes. Intimate relations evolved between men, women, and children of all four communities as daily interactions generated sentiments of affection, providing the contextual foundations for friendships (*bándí*), the sharing of first names (*kɔ́lá*), and alliances (*mbɔ̀ní*). Today, crosscutting relations of amity and alliance transcend ethnic boundaries, weaving together individuals from various ethnic communities.

Bándí — *Friendship*

Whereas intimacy increases the potential for tension as well as affection, the emergence of the *bándí* relationship between Bangando and Baka men, a relationship of formalized friendship that continues to link interethnic partners among men and women today, is testimony to the fostering of interethnic friendship. As explained by Ambata,

> Bangando and Baka are tightly connected. Most Bangando and Baka families have associated families of the other group. Baka families who are allied with Bangando families tend to live in the same neighborhood as their Bangando friends, or even in the same house compound.
>
> The two families are connected as groups. But they are also connected as individual people: the heads of each family are special friends; the wives are friends; and often the children are friends, too. So this *bándí* friendship will pass down to the next generation.

Sometimes the Baka family will give names from the Bangando family to their own children.

The head of the Bangando family is responsible for the actions of the Baka family with respect to other Bangando. The head of the Baka family is responsible for things that the members of the Bangando family do with other Baka. And if someone in the Baka family has a conflict in the village, the Bangando man will help him in discussions or at the *gálá wè*, the tribunal. If a Baka *bándí* has trouble with the government or missionaries, often his Bangando *bándí* will help him. . . . If the Bangando *bándí* has a conflict with other Baka, the Baka partner will help to sort out his problem.

If a woman from the Bangando family gets married to a man from another village, sometimes a member of the *bándí* family will go with her when she moves to her husband's village. Then the *bándí* relationship can be extended to include the new husband's family.

The Bangando family helps to look after the needs of the Baka family, especially in terms of money—buying clothes or pots, paying school fees, and paying for medicine. The Baka family also helps the Bangando family. If someone falls sick, both partners will help find medicines to cure the illness.[20]

A few days after this conversation, Ambata's goat was struck by a passing logging truck, breaking its leg. Nakolongjoko, Ambata's father's *bándí*—who remains a very intimate friend and partner of Ambata's family despite his father's death—found the goat by the side of the road. He set aside his work to splint the goat's leg and to nurse it back to health by means of medicines he collected in the forest, enacting the pattern of care and assistance that *bándí* partners share.

This account of *bándí* relationships reflects elements of the basic exchange relationship often described in "hunter-gatherer" studies. But it also indicates that *bándí* partnerships involve ties at a level of intimacy that surpasses simple exchange. As a result of these *bándí* friendships, Bangando and Baka engage in daily, often prolonged interaction. Bangando and Baka male *bándís* interact informally during hours of leisure and often during activities such as clearing land for a garden or during hunting. *Bándís* support each other formally during village meetings, especially if the men seek to resolve a conflict, either within their own families or between a member of their families and an outsider (or an external element such as the government). Bangando and Baka women interact more frequently and for longer durations of time, because women's work is both more time-consuming and often involves collective tasks during which women can socialize.

Indeed, Bangando women tend to have more frequent domestic and intimate relations with Baka women *and* men than Bangando men have with Baka of either gender. Bangando women may seek but do not rely on domestic and agricultural labor provided by Baka women and men. Baka often help Bangando women by clearing land for planting, carrying water, and collecting edible leaves for preparing the evening meal or useful vines and rattan for weaving baskets or mats. It is not at all unusual for Baka to linger and chat with Bangando women in and around their kitchen houses before and after working, and often to visit Bangando kitchen houses just to socialize. But because of the imbalance of social and political power, Bangando women only occasionally assist Baka families with *their* domestic work; the majority of social and productive activities that involve both Bangando and Baka happen in the context of the Bangando domestic sphere. It is important to take into account the asymmetry in social power between Bangando and Baka, leading Bangando to assume directive roles in public arenas as well as in multiethnic domestic contexts. However, to fully grasp relations between the communities, it is also essential to recognize the voluntary, mutually supportive, and extended nature of *bándí* relations.

To illustrate the quality of *bándí* relations between Bangando and Baka, consider the interaction between neighbors during a period of stress. In the course of one week in early May 1998, a small Bangando family experienced three crises: three babies were born; one of these newborn infants died; and the grandmother's tuberculosis dramatically worsened. Because the family was preoccupied with pressing health concerns, no one was able to harvest plantains, check snare lines, or gather leaves from the forest to prepare the family's meals. Instead, the family's *bándí*, a Baka family that lives just a stone's throw away in a neighboring cluster of houses, provided their Bangando *bándí* with plantains as well as leaf sauce and other prepared dishes. In situations where misfortune or stress befalls this Baka family, their Bangando *bándí* support them in similar ways. The readily forthcoming, mutual support between *bándí* partners is evident in the friendship and assistance that flows in both directions. A few weeks later, when the acute symptoms of her tuberculosis had subsided, the grandmother of this same Bangando family brought her *bándí*, whom she addresses as *mbaié*—"friend"—a basket full of avocados from a tree near her garden, mushrooms that she had collected in the forest, and a block of soap. By sharing their space and resources, work and materials, Bangando and Baka women cultivate deep ties of mutual help and goodwill across ethnic lines.

Wanguwangu offers another perspective on the enduring intimacy of his *bándí* friendship with Ndomonyo, a Baka man who lives with his family just on the other side of the logging road from Wanguwangu's home. He indicates that where *bándí* relationships retain emotional significance over the course of numerous generations between a Bangando and a Baka family, the bonds of mutual collaboration and support generate bonds of fictive kinship, resulting in interethnic sentiments of siblinghood.

> Oh, yes! I have Baka *bándí*. Don't you see me with those neighbors who stay just on the other side of the road? Because our father left them with us, so they are also our friends [*bándí*]. Ndonomyo is my *bándí*; but he is no longer my friend, he is already my brother. My father was the *bándí* of his father, and because his father is dead and my father is dead too—because we were both left as orphans—I consider him to be my brother. And also because I am with him.[21]

In some cases, the melding of intimate relationships between *bándí* partners may reinforce the overlap between parallel clans. Where *bándí* friendships link numerous members of two families, it is probable that parallel clanship was a contributing factor in initiating the friendship; the shared observance of clan rituals also reinforces the close relations between the two extended families. Cooperative engagement during rituals and mutual support during times of family crisis offer clear indications of particularly close interethnic *bándí* friendships and parallel clans. For example, the *bándí* alliance between Mosongo, a Bangando elder and renowned hunter, and Lembi, a Baka elder and renowned spiritual leader, is reinforced by their membership in parallel clans, *bò wé* (Bangando) and *yé gùgà* (Baka), both of which take the monitor lizard as their totem.

Where *bándí* alliances are particularly intimate, such as the partnership between Mosongo and Lembi, which is reinforced by their parallel clanship, *bándí* partners may assume roles of siblings. Lembi and Mosongo live in adjoining house compounds with their wives and families, share meals together, hunt together, and are actively involved in the successes and difficulties that each encounters. So when Lembi's younger brother died during a hunting trip that took him more than twenty kilometers from the village, Mosongo and Lembi together arranged an expedition to retrieve the body and bring it back for the funeral and burial in the village. Several days later, the body was buried and the loss was mourned by Lembi's extended family and network of friends at Mosongo's household. The funeral ceremony, including dancing and singing as well as the bulk of the participants, were

Baka. But, as Lembi's *bándí*, Mosongo and his family organized, hosted, and financed the funeral. Mosongo also undertook the significant task of digging the grave for Lembi's deceased brother. Because of their close *bándí* friendship, Mosongo and his family supported Lembi and his family the way siblings would in such a tragic situation, through logistical, ritual, and emotional help.

Kɔlá — Homonyms

Daily, informal contexts of interethnic friendship serve as a base-level indicator of the high degree of integration among the communities in southeastern Cameroon. Rainy days often find women of neighboring households and mixed ethnic affiliations gathered together in someone's kitchen house near a slowly smoldering fire, smoke and conversation mingling as they rise from the damp thatch roof. The kitchen house of Salo, an elderly Bangando woman who maintains friendships with both her Bangando and Baka neighbors, offers warmth and conversation on rainy days. In the midst of a morning deluge, Bangando travelers passing through Dioula on their way to another destination stopped at Salo's kitchen to take refuge from the rain. Salo invited the visitors to sit on stools near the fire, demoting a Baka woman and her toddler — Salo's close friends — to the floor, where they sat on a mat that is used for drying cocoa on sunnier days. This Baka friend, Alombi, cuddled her little girl in her lap, listening to the conversation which had shifted to topics initiated by the arriving Bangando visitors. The embrace of friendship included neighbors and visitors from various ethnic communities, even as the hierarchy of social power was evident in the seating arrangements.

The next morning the thatch of the kitchen house was steaming as the early sun dried the damp roof after the long rain that fell the day before. The socializing with her Bangando visitors and Baka neighbors was over, the grandchildren had been fed and were washing clothes at the river, and Salo prepared her tools and basket to leave for her garden. Alombi and her toddler came by again to visit Salo. As the women quietly shared the news of the morning, Salo noticed the damp cough of Alombi's young daughter. Reaching back into the black, resin-encrusted storage rack above the fire, she pulled out a bundle of leaves (*sàà ɔ́ngò*) and bark (*kangáá*), the local treatment for a cough (*sábé*). Salo carefully divided her store of cough medicine into two bundles and retied them in large, round leaves, passing one packet to Alombi. Alombi bundled her little girl — whose name is also Salo — into a sling and headed back out into the bright morning sun, going home to treat her child's cough. Salo, the elder Bangando woman, who is well-known for her knowledge of medicinal plants, took up her large carrying basket and went off to her garden to harvest plantains. Arriving at their home just down the road, Alombi gave her daughter, Salo, the medicine prepared for her by her Bangando homonym, the elder Salo.

When Alombi, the young Baka mother, visits Salo, the elderly Bangando woman, they often sit quietly for hours on end, escaping the glare of the after-noon sunshine sitting behind the kitchen house, where they weave baskets, sort squash seeds, or just rest. Alombi brings her daughter to visit Salo each time. When her daughter was born, Alombi named her "Salo" to honor the Bangando elder, and to place the young girl and older woman in special, inti-mate relations as kɔlá—homonyms. When Alombi and Salo visit, the elder Bangando Salo often gives them something to bring back home with them: an enamel pot filled with dried, pounded manioc for their supper; several carefully dried tobacco leaves; some edible leaves, snails, or meat from the forest. Alombi is the daughter of Nakolongjoko, a sprightly, wrinkled Baka man who is the bándí partner of Salo's deceased husband. Alombi named her child after her father's bándí's wife, cementing the relations of friendship and support between the Bangando and Baka families for another generation, despite the death of the initial Bangando bándí partner.[22]

The giving of a first name to an infant initiates intimacy between the child and the person for whom she was named; these explicitly created relationships between homonyms serve as powerful, emotional ligaments between two individuals, who are often of different ethnic affiliations. The establishment of relations between homonyms also serves the practical pur-pose of ensuring, ideally, that the child has a formal, extrafamilial sponsor as she grows—someone who will contribute to her school fees, buy her new clothes for the annual celebration of Children's Day (Fête de Jeunesse), and support her should calamity befall her family.

Relationships between kɔlás are usually imbued with special emotions of affection and respect. Because the role of an elder kɔlá is to support and guide the younger kɔlá from a position outside the nuclear family, kɔlás often enjoy a relationship permeated by positive emotions of giving and receiving, gratitude and guidance rather than one dominated by ambiva-lent emotions of discipline and respect, as between parents and children. Kɔlá relations are recognized and experienced as something special. Thus when the elder homonym does ultimately die, the younger namesake fulfills the role of chief mourner at the funeral. While the most intimate biological members of the deceased's family often participate in the funeral and burial in a state of quiet shock punctuated by intermittent wailing, the *kɔ́lá* of the deceased is the most vocal and consistent of the mourners, often embodying and expressing the collective grief through her continual wailing throughout the several days of funeral activities. Because of the outpouring of grief from family and friends in the name of the dead homonym, a name that by definition the *kɔ́lá* shares, and because the *kɔ́lá's* spirit is searching for refuge now that its body is dead, the living homonym is at great risk of spirit possession by her deceased homonym. During the funeral, the *kɔ́lá* wears protective garlands of braided banana leaves diagonally across her chest and shoulders. When she mourns over the body, she vigorously shakes a ceremonial rattle—which today may simply be an old tin can filled with stones—to keep the spirit of her dead homonym from lodging itself in her body. Thus, while homonyms are still alive, they typically enjoy an intimate relationship of sharing and support; at death, the proximity of their interrelationship is enacted by the younger *kɔ́lá*, who now must protect herself from the wandering spirit of her deceased *kɔ́lá*.[23]

That *kɔ́lás* and *bándí* partners play active roles in rites of passage in the lives of their partners and their families underscores the social importance of these interethnic relations. For example, when a man marries, his *bándís* and *kɔ́lás* will contribute to the *díkwèlí*, the bride price that he will offer to his fiancée's family. If his *bándís* and *kɔ́lás* have means to contribute cash, they will do so. If not, they may contribute meat or local whisky (*ngòlòngòló*) to the wedding feast, or something else that can be sold in order to contribute to the bride price. From the bride's side, her family's *bándí* and *kɔ́lá* partners will contribute woven mats (*fé*) and chickens to her dowry, which will be presented to the family of the groom as a return gift. When the groom's and bride's family have exchanged these marriage gifts, the gifts that have been received by each side will be redistributed to the individuals who contributed to the initial wedding offering. Thus *bándís* and *kɔ́lás* who contributed a woven mat to their partner's daughter's dowry will each receive a return gift of money, whisky, or meat when the marriage rituals (and associated transactions) are complete. Not only with marriages, but also in ritual occasions that mark the beginnings or ends of socially significant relationships such as initiations and funerals, alliances between *bándís* are reinforced by their joint participation in the presentation of gifts and the redistribution of return gifts.[24] *Bándí* and *kɔ́lá* relationships offer individuals formal ways to acknowledge and perpetuate interethnic partnerships that, often begun in generations past, continue to have intense meaning today.

While *bándí* friendships continue to link Bangando and Baka today, even more potent political and social alliances that were founded through a pact of blood—*mbɔní*—are no longer undertaken. The atrophy of social relations between *mbɔní* allies does not necessarily indicate disintegration of overall social ties or interconnectedness. On the contrary, where *mbɔní* served to unite previously warring communities through public commensalism—the eating of collectively shed blood signaling acceptance of mutual peace—the need for such ceremonies has been largely overcome as interethnic coexistence and cooperation have replaced interethnic war in southern Cameroon over the past century.

Conflict, violence, slavery, and flight typified social dynamics among the shifting communities of central Africa throughout the nineteenth century. When two warring communities ultimately resolved their differences, often an *mbɔní* alliance was undertaken to seal the former enemies as allies, as they pledged their mutual loyalty and support in the face of future aggressors. During the ceremony to initiate the *mbɔní* alliance, the elders, warriors, and youths of both groups came together to prepare for a joint circumcision ritual of young men. Meanwhile, women came together to prepare a large feast of pounded maize and meat. The boys were circumcised in the center of the village, with male elders of both sides witnessing the cutting. Blood from the boys' circumcision wounds was caught in a gourd and used to prepare maize meal; this blood-soaked maize served as the centerpiece of the communal feast.[25] As they shared the conciliatory meal, the former antagonists ate the blood of their sons, representing the inextricable mixing of the essences of both groups, the literal and symbolic consummation of the alliance. Through the *mbɔní* alliance, former enemies were now literally "of the same blood." Or, as an elder explained, through *mbɔní* the enemies become "one people" [*gà wì síkínò*].[26] After entering into an *mbɔní* alliance, the two communities were prohibited from engaging in warfare against each other, and instead were obliged to support and defend each other. These allegiances between *mbɔní* partners approximate the obligations among kin; *mbɔní* alliances created kinlike loyalties among communities of different ethnic affiliations.

The incidence of *mbɔní* alliances varied across the communities. Bangando, Bakwélé, and Mbomam seem to have been more directly implicated in the wars and violent conflicts of the nineteenth century, both as victims initially and later as perpetrators. Thus it is not surprising that oral histories recount *mbɔ́ní* pacts among these groups (Bangando with each of the Bakwélé and Mbomam) as well as between each of these groups and other communities beyond the Lobéké forest region (Bangando with Ndzimou, for example). Baka entered into *mbɔ́ní* alliances with Bakwélé and with Mbomam; although oral accounts mention latent tension between some Baka and Bakwélé communities, nothing approximating aggressive conflict characterizes their contact and integration. Perhaps at a later time, when Bakwélé and Mbomam were established in villages in southeastern Cameroon and when friendships and partnerships with the Baka stabilized, Baka engaged in peacetime *mbɔ́ní* pacts to cement their social relations of cooperation with these groups of neighbors, a slight variation of the *mbɔ́ní* pact that was usually made to formalize peace between enemies.[27] It is notable that Baka who live in villages that are dominated by interactions between Baka and Bangando claim never to have engaged in these alliances with Bangando, perhaps indicating the success of *bándí* alliances from the inception of their relations.[28]

Shared Ceremonies—*Békà*, *Jɛngì*, and *Díò*

In addition to relationships that unite individuals, families, and even entire communities through alliances and partnerships that transcend ethnic boundaries, several central ceremonies also serve as interethnic social adhesives that hold men of different communities together in special relations of spiritual fraternity.

Békà is one of the most important ceremonies that men throughout southeastern Cameroon—Bangando, Baka, Bakwélé, and Mbomam alike—undertake. According to Bangando elders, the *békà* ceremony is the initiation of adult men into a men's secret society that is charged with the general protection of society and the maintenance of stability in everyday life in the Lobéké forest region. Men who have been initiated into the *békà* society are also obliged to arrange and undertake the funeral celebrations of fellow members, and to support the families of deceased members (Joiris 1998). Men who are initiated in the same cohort are bound by strong emotional solidarity. For the remainder of their lives, they will share meat with each other following a successful hunt and will offer contributions to a cohort member's bride price payment, constructing relations of kinship and upholding the responsibilities of caring for and supporting each other as brothers. Entrance into this extraordinary society of men requires extraordinary endurance: adult men who are usually in their twenties and thirties are recircumcised, involving the reopening and extension of earlier circumcision scars.[29] While not all men choose to enter into the *ɓékà* society, the ceremonial society refuses entry to no man, regardless of ethnic affiliation.

Entrance into *ɓékà* society was formerly limited to men who had accumulated enough wealth to afford the sizeable contribution of prestige goods required for the initiation to be held. Although the prestige items consisted mostly of items that were consumed during the ceremony, such as meat — both domestic (goats and chickens) and from the forest (elephant, wild pig, duiker) — as well as *ngòlòngòló* whisky, the ability to amass the resources to make such offerings served as an indication that the initiate possessed the means to make future contributions to meet the needs, ordinary as well as urgent, of the community at large. In this way, men of the *ɓékà* society served as community trustees: wealthy, respected, courageous, and presumably wise individuals who could help to see the village through contingencies and conflicts that might arise. Because *ɓékà* initiation required this

FIG. 5.3 Baka candidates for *ɓékà* initiation, with their Bangando sponsor, Yenga, 1995

ability to accumulate and then dispense with significant amounts of wealth, and because Baka typically did not amass property in goods, the first Baka members of *békà* were sponsored by their Bangando *bándí*, who also served as advisors and protectors to their Baka partners who underwent initiation. Thus the process of initiation into *békà* society reinforced the ties between Bangando and Baka *bándí* at the same time that membership in the *békà* society advanced interethnic relations among a larger community of Bangando and Baka (and also Bakwélé and Mbomam) men. Although scholars typically assert that "villagers'" sponsorship of their "pygmy" partners as they enter into ritual initiations and secret societies amounts to coercion and continued unilateral domination by the "villagers" (for example, Turnbull 1965), the relationship between Bangando and Baka men in the *békà* society of southeastern Cameroon appears to be based on willing, even enthusiastic, participation of both Bangando and Baka partners. That Bangando initially sponsored Baka initiates is a reflection of historical conditions of economic, social, and political disparities. Today Baka are initiated into the *békà* society without complete reliance on the economic support of their Bangando *bándí*, indicating their increasing economic parity with other ethnic communities in the region.

Békà is celebrated throughout southeastern Cameroon, although with significant variations in ceremonial structure, proceedings, and ensuing relationships; Bangando elders along the Moloundou road as well as Bakwélé elders in Ndongo emphasized that their respective *békà* ceremonies are distinct. In Ndongo, Baka and Bakwélé men jointly undergo this circumcision ceremony, and together they guide the *békà* society and by extension the society as a whole. In the Republic of Congo, where Baka and Bakwélé also live as neighbors but in different political and cultural contexts from those of southeastern Cameroon, *békà* is also an interethnic affair, although the circumcision takes place in the village rather than in a forest clearing. According to Congolese Baka, joint participation in *békà* reinforces the contemporary mixing of Baka and Bakwélé in villages alongside logging roads.[30] Among Mbomam, Bangando, and Baka living along the main Moloundou road in Cameroon, each community maintains a sense of ownership over the *békà* tradition; Bangando elders are convinced that *békà* was initially their ceremony, into which Bakwélé, Mbomam, and Baka participants were integrated later; Bakwélé argue that *békà* was initially a Bakota ceremony, which passed through the Sangha-Sangha to the Bakwélé, and from Bakwélé was disseminated throughout the Lobéké forest region. And while Baka participants in *békà* do not claim to have been the original initiates, today they take great pride in their unflinching participation in the ceremony, claiming to best represent the potency of men initiated into the *bɛ́kà* society.

Two other important ceremonies bring men together in rites of passage, although each includes active participants from predominantly one ethnic community or another. As explained by Maga,

> Bangando and Baka also take part in each other's ceremonies. Bangando men may join Baka men in celebrating *jɛngì*, and Baka men may join the *dìò* ritual of Bangando men. But usually one group of people won't participate as fully in the other's ceremony. The other group usually watches more than they take part.[31]

Jɛngì constitutes the most important ceremonial occasion for Baka men, who are initiated into the society of *Jɛngì*, a prominent Baka forest spirit. Likewise, *dìò* is the central ritual of Bangando men's spiritual initiation, participation, and death; the powerful and potentially violent spirit *Dìò* is invited to return to the village where an important elder has passed away, to ensure the proper burial and spiritual repose of the deceased.[32] But, despite the ethnic particularities of each ceremony, a significant number of men from the "other" communities actively participate through initiation and continued involvement in the ceremonies.

Jɛngì is the central ritual institution of Baka throughout southern Cameroon. During the ceremony, whose intricate stages take place over numerous months, male initiates live together in an isolated camp in the forest, where they learn about the roles and responsibilities of adults in society, techniques of hunting, and spiritual life in the forest. The process of being initiated into *Jɛngì* is the process of becoming an adult man. At the end of the ritual instruction, the initiates are ritually killed, to be reborn during the culminating ceremony as adult men ready to participate fully in social life (Bahuchet 1992). Once initiated, *Jɛngì* protects his "children," granting Baka men the powers that they need to survive the dangers of the forest (Joiris 1998).

Initiation in *Jɛngì* is not limited to Baka men. Today men of various ethnic backgrounds participate, including Bangando, Mbomam, and Bakwélé, as do young and adolescent boys of various ages. As suggested by Joiris, it is possible that the age of Baka participants is declining, as Baka struggle to maintain control over the changes in their lives, changes that seem to be accelerating with each generation. Perhaps by initiating Baka males at a young age, parents attempt to inculcate their children with values that they hold dear while they feel they still have influence over the younger generation. At a *Jɛngì* ceremony in 1998, a Baka boy of two was initiated.

FIG. 5.4 Interethnic participation in *jεngì* ceremony held in Yenga, December 1998

Although the radical reduction in age of Baka *jεngì* initiates seems to be a recent phenomenon, it is likely that *jεngì* initiates of multiple ethnic backgrounds have entered into the ceremonial society for many generations. Although renowned Baka elephant hunters are the ritual guardians of *Jεngì*, the forest spirit, in the context of Ndongo Bakwélé men initially desired to participate in and learn through *jεngì* initiation because they hoped to benefit from Baka knowledge of the forest as well as from their mystical powers (Joiris 1998). It is likely that motivations for participating in interethnic ceremonies vary from community to community because the dynamics of interethnic relationships vary markedly between different regions of southeastern Cameroon. The interethnic sampling of this research indicates that today Bakwélé participate least intimately in Baka ceremonies, including *jεngì*; Bangando men participate very regularly in *jεngì*; Mbomam men participate most often in *jεngì*, and with the least imbalance of social and ritual status.

While for the most part shared participation in ceremonies enhances solidarities among the communities, occasionally interactions in ritual settings highlight conflicts of interest. In one such case, "outside" participants—observers from neighboring ethnic communities for whom the ritual is not part of their time-honored cultural repertoire—upstaged and upset the smooth proceedings of the ritual. At a *jεngì* ceremony in 1998 in Yenga, a large village with roughly equal proportions of Bangando and Baka residents, several young Bangando men disrupted the initiation rites and threatened to tear down the initiates' *mòngúlu* (dome-shaped, leaf-shingled house), where they were receiving their final ritual instruction from *jengì* elders just prior to their ceremonial death and rebirth, the climax of two weeks of intense activities. The young men charged into the *jengì* ceremonial area with self-important swaggers and an air of self-righteous modernity, wearing stiff new jeans and stylish T-shirts, together with adornments such as a necklace, a watch, or a leather cap. The Bangando youths had no particular conflict with the *jengì* participants, but expressed their condescending judgment of the *jengì* ritual by insulting participants as "primitives" who, they said, were "enslaved" by meaningless rituals. After a few minutes of ruckus, a group of Baka and Bangando elders drove the youths away, shepherding them out of the ceremonial space.[33]

Conversation among participants in and observers of the *jengì* ceremony took a negative turn, as observers criticized the Bangando youths on two counts. For one, some Baka grumbled and muttered that Bangando interfere in Baka ceremonies and spoil the proceedings, whereas Baka treat the Bangando *dìò* ritual with appropriate fear and respect. However, no one suggested that Bangando should not participate in *jengì*, nor Baka in *dìò*; interethnic participation in these ceremonies has been well established. In this particular ceremony, an adult Bangando man was initiated, and took his *jengì* instruction and induction with great gravity. The fact that a majority of Bangando men have been initiated into *jengì* serves as an important indication that, conflicts aside, the structural and emotional participation of both communities in shared ritual knowledge and experience has long been accepted and continues to be cultivated.

The other line of criticism was directed toward youths—of both communities—who follow the lures of money, markets, and commodities to jobs and "urban" life and fall away from "traditional" practices such as *jengì* and the relationships and way of life that *jengì* celebrates and promotes. Analyses of other cases of conflict during performances of power suggest that, although these youths may overtly embrace values of urban society and modernity, evident in their ostentatious display of clothing and commodities, they simultaneously fear and respect ritual power all the more acutely because of their emotional distance from these time-honored values. Thus, perhaps, the Bangando youths' derision of *jengì* initiates stems from their need to dismiss and undermine these expressions of continuing ritual power, power to which they feel they have no access and over which they have no control (Worby 1998).

If *Jengì* is the signature spirit into whose ritual community adult Baka men expect to be initiated, *Dìò* is the quintessential Bangando spirit into whose cult men also enter. *Dìò* ceremonies are conducted very infrequently: only on the occasion of the death of very respected Bangando elders. A short time after the death of a notable elder, Bangando men who have been initiated into the *dìò* community call this potent and potentially violent spirit to come out of the forest and to oversee the settling of the deceased elder's spirit. *Dìò* is the most feared spirit of all communities in southeastern Cameroon, and improper handling of the spirit can quickly result in the death of participants. Because of the violent death suffered by the first woman who encountered the spirit *Dìò*, women are not allowed to see the ritual (for discussion, see Rupp 2001). Instead, women, uninitiated men, and children close themselves into a collective kitchen house near the *mbánjó* verandah where the initiated men and *Dìò* conduct the ceremony; women and uninitiated men listen to and participate in the ceremony by singing and talking with *Dìò* from this safe enclosure.

Even though both *Jengì* and *Dìò* are feared by all residents of the Lobéké region, participation of adult men in both secret societies is widespread. The undertakings of both *jengì* and *dìò* ceremonies are momentous events for the entire interethnic village. Given their deep expertise with the particular ritual preparations and requirements, Baka and Bangando men take responsibility for the ceremonial preparations for *jengì* and *dìò*, respectively; men of all ethnic backgrounds who have been initiated into the societies are expected to contribute according to their ceremonial roles. Although in the past it is likely that Baka did not participate in *dìò* initiation and ceremonies, today their participation is widely accepted. The imbalance in interethnic participation in *jengì* and *dìò* ceremonies, in which it is more common for Bangando men to be initiated into *jengì* than for Baka men to be initiated into *dìò*, reflects continued but narrowing differences in social status between the two communities.

Participation in these central rituals is an indication that a man embraces the traditions of life in the forest and the village, emphasizing these values over and above the potential benefits brought by the increasingly common orientation toward commercial involvement in regional and national markets. While young Bangando and Baka alike embrace the luxuries and changes offered by contemporary music, clothing, and wage labor at timber or safari companies—at least while they are young and relatively free of family responsibilities of their own—a good proportion of these youth will still participate in initiation ceremonies such as *jengì* and *dìò*, but usually in only one or the other. At the same time, men who have chosen to remain in their villages within the forest, following a way of life that is in keeping with the rhythms and patterns of their forebears and upbringing, increasingly participate in *both* communities' initiations and subsequent rituals. This increasing joint participation in central rituals of both communities underscores the increasing integration of interests and values across the ethnic communities of southeastern Cameroon.

Collective Work— *Pɔ́mɔ́* and *Éésɔ̀ngé*

To face occasional circumstances of misfortune, the interethnic communities of the Lobéké region come together through collective work and cooperative networks of support. Collective work has long been a feature of both Bangando and Baka social life, as exemplified in their cooperative hunting of elephants and portaging of baskets of meat back to the village (see chapter six and Rupp 2001). Collective clearing of weeds, however, is less rewarding work. *Pɔ́mɔ́*, the clearing of weeds and undergrowth by means of machetes, has been a feature of collective labor since the colonial era, when communities throughout southeastern Cameroon built the German and French roads by hand and under duress and then were required to maintain the road by clearing away weeds and underbrush and by diverting streams and flows of water and mud. Today *pɔ́mɔ́* activities are carried out by villagers not because of threats of physical abuse by colonial officials, but instead as an attempt to impress Cameroonian government officials or other bearers of development aid, and thus to wring scarce resources from the deep pockets of external powers. In Dioula, for example, villagers come together to clear the central areas near the chief's verandah, where important village-wide political meetings and ceremonies are held, and in front of the small dispensary, where Catholic missionaries arrive occasionally to vaccinate young children.

Political meetings to which government officials are invited arouse village pride and anticipation as residents come together to present the best face of their community. These political meetings also raise village hopes, as well as collective cynicism, that the ever-stingy and deeply corrupt government officials based in Moloundou will finally assist in village development projects such as the rebuilding of the elementary school. Knowing that their chances of receiving any kind of nationally sponsored development aid are slim, and realizing that they have never received the tax on lumber cut from the forest that is legally due to them, villagers nevertheless do what they can to curry the favor of government officials. By presenting a clear, weed-free public space and chief's verandah for the gathering of government officials and village elders, villagers demonstrate that they have done their part to maintain their community to the best of their collective ability.

Early one December morning at the end of the rainy season, villagers from the far ends of the long village of Dioula answered the call of Ndong, the village chief, gathering in the early morning sun to clear the weeds from the chief's central verandah in preparation for an official meeting between village elders, the *Sous-Préfet* of the district, and the mayor of Moloundou. Because of heavy rains, weeds were thick; Bangando and Baka, men and women, worked together from early morning until the sun was high and hot, and finally the meeting area was prepared. *Bándí* partners of Bangando and Baka men had met in their neighborhoods and come together to the center of Dioula to work; when the public meeting area was clear, they set off again together toward their neighborhoods—hot, sweaty, and dirty. Not all villagers came to work. But those who did experienced a cheerful setting for working and socializing and seemed to take genuine pride in investing their efforts for the good of the village. Those who did not come for the collective work session were subjected to criticisms and derision from their irritated neighbors, who had invested time and energy for the good of the community.

When the entourage of officials arrived the following morning, village participation in the meeting was high. Elders, both Bangando and Baka, articulated their disappointment with the government for neglecting to contribute the proportion of timber taxes legally due to the village. The *Sous-Préfet* acknowledged the existence of the village development committee (an official prerequisite for receiving the 1,000 CFA—approximately US$2.00— per cubic meter of wood felled by international timber companies operating in the area) and made note of the overall organization and neat presentation of the village. Although he promised that funds would be forthcoming to rebuild the dilapidated school, not surprisingly, no resources or building materials ever materialized. Yet the positive emotions generated by working together to present their village in the best possible light, the collective courage that numerous villagers demonstrated in standing up to government officials to demand what the villagers knew was their right, and the shared sense of having been swindled by a corrupt political regime all served to reinforce village-wide, interethnic solidarity and helped to generate momentum for future collaborative working groups.[34] The collective

sense that all of the villagers of Dioula, regardless of ethnicity or social identity, were victims of a political system that rewards corrupt officials at the
expense of impoverished villagers is a powerful force that rallies the various
families and neighborhoods to improve the standard of living in their poor
and marginalized interethnic community.

Éésɔ̀ngé

Even as Bangando, Baka, Bakwélé, and Mbomam residents of Dioula come
together to present a unified, organized front to political officials in an
attempt to secure their legal rights to economic resources, women of Dioula come together in cooperation and solidarity to offer internal support to
individual women who may face particularly difficult circumstances. This
interethnic, collaborative association of women is known as Éésɔ̀ngé and
offers women a means of practical assistance and emotional support during
trying times, or during times when a woman suddenly needs to amass great
quantities of resources.

For example, early one morning, before the dew had dried on plants
along the forest paths, women had collected bundles of firewood, hauled
buckets of fresh drinking water from streams, and harvested plantains from
their gardens. The women of Éésɔ̀ngé changed from their work clothes, now
wet from working in the dew-soaked forest so early in the morning, into
their best: a fresh T-shirt, a clean *sándà* cloth wrapped as a skirt, a less tattered head scarf. They washed their feet and rubbed thick palm oil onto
their arms, legs, and faces, preparing to go out to celebrate, even so early
in the day. From the top of the hill, singing trickled down into the center
of Dioula, as the women walked together along the damp red road. Passing households as they walked through the village, more women emerged
from their kitchen houses to join the procession, bearing their gifts of wood,
water, and plantains on their heads or in large carrying baskets slung down
their backs. The parade of women gathered enthusiasm and volume as they
walked and sang together.

Finally, the coterie of women arrived at Mengala's house, where her husband was already busy preparing the ceremonial verandah, covered with
palm fronds. Mengala still wore the black, tattered clothes of mourning that
she had worn for five years since the death of her husband's father. But on
this day, she would finally end her period of mourning; her husband would
present her with a set of fine, new clothes to celebrate her reemergence into

FIG. 5.5 Bangando, Baka, Bakwélé, and Mbomam women participating in Éésɔ̀ngé
Dioula, May 1999

society. Because of the extended duration of her mourning, and because her
husband had returned from his job at a timber company for the ceremony,
scores of guests attended, perhaps as many as two hundred. The ceremony
involved an exchange of mats and chickens for money, foodstuffs, and
whisky (ngòlòngòló) between Mengala's paternal family and her family-in-
law, followed by a banquet of plantains, manioc, and many different kinds
of meat from the forest.[35] With full bellies and glad hearts, the participants
continued dancing and drinking until sunrise.

Mengala's end-of-mourning ceremony would have been infinitely more
difficult to accomplish without the contributions and assistance of the wom-
en's association, Éésɔ̀ngé. Rituals such as marriages, funerals, and end-of-
mourning ceremonies, particularly difficult births and the birth of twins,
and unexpected visitors—these occasions may require more work and productive output than the women of a single household can muster. When the
women of Dioula recognize the sudden or impending difficulties faced by
a fellow woman, the "presidente" of the association organizes the date and
time for the collective donation of supplies. The women are emphatic in

stating that they help other *women*, not men. Even if a woman's husband is sick, women who participate in *Éésɔ̀ngé* will help the woman by easing her domestic work, but will not directly assist her husband. While *Éésɔ̀ngé* expressly excludes men, it actively includes women of all ethnic groups. Bangando and Baka women, as well as the chief's wife (who is Mbomam) and an elderly Bakwélé wife of a Bangando man, participate actively and openly, and know that because of the help that they extend to other women—of any ethnic community within Dioula—when they encounter difficulties, the women will reciprocate and support them.[36] By helping each other, women say that they are developing their community. *Éésɔ̀ngé* is a group of women "of the same heart." The group includes women from all ethnic groups, recognizing that "heart-ness" is not ethnically bounded.

Tangles

It is in the interests of both sides of an interethnic partnership to remain on good terms, providing an informal social insurance policy. Especially in southeastern Cameroon, where the weak and corrupt national bureaucracy tends to undermine rather than support possibilities for economic prosperity and social advancement, there is no alternative to hard work and mutually beneficial collaboration to contend with uncertainties and contingencies. By building reliable and trustworthy partnerships, one friend knows that the other can help her access meat from the forest or plantains from a garden, if she cannot manage to gather enough food for her family's evening meal. Another friend may rely on his partner to help him amass chickens and whisky from their combined network of extended families and friends to pay his bride price. Partners understand that they can turn to each other in case of emergency, illness, or death. Through their participation in collaborative partnerships and networks, peoples' pools of resources for meeting daily needs and contending with unforeseen circumstances are vastly increased.

But the collaborative relationships generated through parallel clans, *bándí* friendships, and alliances are neither uniform nor ubiquitous throughout southeastern Cameroon. The warmth bestowed by a Baka man on his Bangando *bándí's* newborn son as he attached a tiny monkey-tail bracelet onto the tiny wrist to ensure the baby's health and speedy growth, may be contrasted with occasionally bitter experiences between *bándí* friends, resulting in the termination of the partnership. Perhaps as a result of his father's bitter experience with his Bangando *bándí*, the Baka man named Anda who earlier described parallel clan relationships remains acerbic about partnerships between Baka and Bangando. Anda argues that Baka work much harder for the benefit of their Bangando partners than the stinginess of Bangando reciprocation should warrant; Bangando are tightfisted in providing their share of compensation through material goods, money, or work. From Anda's perspective, Baka simply invest more energy and more thought in their relations with Bangando than Bangando partners do for their Baka counterparts. Bangando know that Baka are hard workers, so they call Baka to come do their hard work for them. When Baka work in Bangando gardens, their work will produce a good harvest for the Bangando family, whereas the little bit of food or compensation that the Bangando gives to his Baka partner is hardly enough for the Baka partner to feed his children for that one day. This discourse of inequality between Baka and Bangando is recurrent, and offers a counterweight to overt statements and actions that reflect interethnic amity. When pressed about why Baka would continue to work for Bangando—even voluntarily—if they harbor such negative emotions for their Bangando partners, Anda and his friend Molomb shrugged their shoulders in unison as Molomb replied,

> Some Baka want to work for Bangando, and some don't. Some Baka like Bangando, and some don't. Some Bangando like Baka, and some don't. Baka work for Bangando because people have to do what they have to do for their families. But it's better if Baka work for themselves.[37]

Anda and Molomb then explained that some Baka *do* like Bangando and have Bangando friends, tempering their firmly (almost fiercely) negative comments about Bangando at the outset of the discussion. Anda began to describe his own friendships with Bangando *mbaìé*, people he likes and whose friendship he values. For example, Anda often walks from his neighborhood at Dioula-Mbandame to Dioula-Beligela, four kilometers to the south, to visit Ngola. Anda emphasizes that he goes to *see* Ngola—*a sèbì a sèbì*—only to visit him, not to work for or with him; Ngola is one of his friends, not his *bándí* partner. Anda explained that his wife left home early that morning to visit Ngola's wife, Pauline. Anda walked to Dioula-Beligela to join his wife at Ngola's house at midday, to find that Pauline had prepared a large meal of plantains and leaf sauce with chunks of pangolin meat. Anda also recalled that his wife had carried a basket of plantains and a packet of peanuts when they returned home to Dioula-Mbandame, a gift from Pauline, so Anda and his family ate well again in the evening. Anda explained that he and his wife do not visit Ngola and Pauline because they are obliged to under some kind of collaborative agreement or partnership. Anda enjoys visiting Ngola simply because he enjoys Ngola's company. Just a few days later, Anda and Ngola were sitting together under a guava tree near Ngola's house in the late afternoon, when another Bangando man hurried along the road nearby, and called out that he would meet Anda later in the evening. When Ngola asked what they were planning to do together, Anda's face broke into a sly grin as he replied, "Ɔ̀ɔ bò má yé mbaìé ná?" (Aren't we friends?)[38] Anda articulated the tangle of interethnic relations between Bangando and Baka, explaining "Ɔ̀ɔ bò kínò mɔ̀, bémɔ́ngɔ́ ɔ̀ɔ bò má kìnò mɔ́ nà" — (We are the same thing, *but* we are not the same thing).

This fundamental ambiguity concerning the sentimental unity of Bangando and Baka seems to lie at the core of their interethnic social relations. While Anda is vociferous in his critique of Bangando participation in *bándí* partnerships, alleging that Bangando cannot be counted on as trustworthy, equitable partners who look out for the interests of both parties, he embraces Ngola as a friend, someone whom he can count on not only for companionship, but also for meaningful collaboration. Negative social attributes, when encountered in consistent or parallel contexts, may be conflated with fundamental characteristics of the entire community, generating readily recognized and accepted stereotypes of the ethnic "other." Although these stereotypes are familiar and generally acknowledged throughout the communities of southeastern Cameroon (Bangando as manipulative cheapskates; Baka as unreliable thieves), as individuals of various communities delve into the particularities of their own interethnic relationships, the nuances of other social dynamics and sentiments emerge, and even individuals who begin by criticizing people of a different ethnic community often conclude by affirming their fundamental unity, recognizing but no longer condemning their ethnic differences. Social intimacy does not override ethnic difference; instead the complexities of allegiances, friendships, and long-standing relationships often cut across boundaries of ethnicity, bringing subsets of the various ethnic groups together through shared ceremonies and celebrations, collaborative subsistence activities and cooperative work efforts. The dynamics of belonging that emerge from collaborative efforts and amicable partnerships often result in social identities that offer alternative attributions of self and other beyond those of ethnicity.

CHAPTER SIX

Identities

PEOPLE IN CHANGING CONTEXTS

Yes, Baka go into the forest to look for meat. And Bangando go into the forest to look for meat, too. The village does not have an owner. Baka build their houses in the village. And we [Bangando] do too. And we all live together in the village. Before, Bangando were *bò lé*, that is to say, the people of the village, because they had their houses in the village. And Baka were called *bò kɔ́à*, the people of the forest, because they lived only in the forest. Today we are all *bò lé*, people of the village. Someone is *bò lé* if he dies there [in the forest] and they bring his body back to the village to bury it. Today we don't even bury Baka in the forest as we did before.

— *Mosakamo, Bangando elder, Wélélé, 7 March 1999*

The fundamental boundaries that distinguish one community from another—Bangando, Baka, Bakwélé, and Mbomam—reflect a collective belief in shared origins and in speaking a common language, and provide the foundations for ethnic affiliations. At the same time, individuals from the various communities cultivate complex relationships through intermarriage, alliances, enduring friendships, the sharing of names, and collaborative work; the emotions that are integral to these relationships often cut across ethnic distinctions, uniting individuals through sentiments of social belonging. At this narrower level of analysis that brings particular neighborhoods, families, and friendships into focus, it becomes apparent that social bridges facilitate and foster interethnic relationships, networks, and identities. In addition, people from all four ethnic communities identify themselves and others and build interethnic social relationships that are based on contemporary attributes such as specialized skills, professional occupations, nationality, and emotional qualities. These shared contexts and abilities shape the social identities of people throughout the Lobéké forest region, forming tendrils and creepers that tie this forest of belonging together in dynamic, interactive consociation.

Ethnic affiliations and social identities offer distinct and often simultaneous ways of expressing identity. Both components of identity are variable, but in fundamentally different ways, at different rates, and for different purposes. In contrast to ethnic affiliations, which tend to be relatively stable formulations of historically situated and linguistically based identity, social identities often change substantially over the course of an individual's life, and even in the course of one day in an individual's life, as she moves into and out of various social contexts. An individual may also chose to identify herself by means of different variables, depending on the social contexts in which she interacts and relates with others. Although attributes of social identity are variable, they are not always voluntary; an individual can be identified in particular ways by others, whose objective identifications may affect that person's standing or influence in that context. Thus a Bangando woman may hold multiple social identities as a *bò dáwà*, a person of the monkey clan, a *bò kísìnì*, a person of the kitchen, and a *bò dwá*, a person of sorcery, but while she is in her kitchen healing a patient, she may choose to identify herself, and may be identified by others, primarily as a *bò dwá*. Individuals can manipulate, emphasize, or discard expressions of social identities with relative ease, depending on social circumstances. The social identities of people living in the Lobéké region are malleable and, for the most part, mutable. Individuals move in and out of various expressions of social identity using the conceptual structure based on *bò*—"personting of"—to indicate their social identities in a given context.

Even as the substances of social identities have changed over the past century, and even as particular expressions of social identity shift in different contexts, the linguistic structure that describes who is who has remained consistent. The morpheme *bò* translates as "person of" a particular social category. In the context of kinship and clanship, *bò* refers to a person of a particular patrilineal clan. Thus Bangando recognize the *bò fɔlɔ*, the people of the elephant clan, the *bò dáwà*, the people of the monkey clan, and so on. The bound morpheme *bò* has emerged as a consistent marker for shifting expressions of identity; it is a flexible, nominal prefix that denotes social identity in many contexts beyond kinship. Because the recognizable conceptual structure for denoting social identity consistently introduces the substance of an individual's identity by means of the

FIG. 6.1 Mosua, Bangando healer or *bò dwá*

marker *bò*, individuals are free to sift and sort the stuff of social identity according to the ever-diversifying social, economic, and political contexts that they confront.

Bò Kɔ̀à, Bò Lé—People of the Forest, People of the Village

According to earlier notions of social identification, when the communities of southeastern Cameroon lived in separate settlements, ethnicity was correlated with the spaces that different communities inhabited. Baka individuals were socially identified as *bò kɔ̀à*, people of the forest (*bò*, "people of"; *kɔ̀à*, "the forest"); Bangando were considered to be people of the village, *bò lé*, (*lé*, "village.") While these social identities have remained constant in name, the substance and meaning of the appellations have varied fundamentally over time. *Bò kɔ̀à* and *bò lé* are especially significant and particularly fluid social identities; their meanings have congealed, dissolved, and reformed in varied contexts of social change and political crisis. *Bò kɔ̀à* and *bò lé* are variable social identities that people of the different ethnic communities have used to project their sense of self and their social relationships in particular historical contexts. Today the spatial, social, political, and economic overlap of Bangando and Baka communities has rendered images of identity that posit one ethnic community as "of the forest" and another as "of the village" largely irrelevant.

Bangando and Baka elders alike recall that their families once lived apart: Bangando lived in larger, centralized villages along the main footpath running through the forest, whereas Baka lived in smaller villages a short distance behind Bangando villages, tucked further into the forest. This spatial difference between their village locations provided a salient social variable for distinguishing Bangando from Baka.

> Bangando and Baka have not always lived together along the road. For many generations the Bangando lived in large villages, connected by a footpath and later connected by the colonial road. Bangando villages were located along the Boumba River. . . . Baka lived in their own villages, scattered throughout the forest, sometimes very far into the forest. . . . You could also say that the Bangando did more farming and the Baka did more hunting. But today relations are much more mixed together. Bangando and Baka now both live in villages along the road. And our villages are mixed together.[1]

Another Bangando elder, from a different region of the forest, also describes the spatial differences between Bangando and Baka, even as he emphasizes the close relationships between the communities:

> When I was little, my father lived with the Baka. He went everywhere in the forest with them, but they didn't stay in the village as they do today. Bangando were in the village as we are here, and Baka were in the forest. . . . Bangando left the village to go and visit their Baka *bándí* [friends]. They [Bangando] brought them [Baka] tobacco, salt, and plantains. When the Baka went into the forest, they would come to the Bangando to look for tobacco, salt, and bananas [to take with them], and when they returned from the forest, they brought baskets of meat for their Bangando *bándí*.[2]

Despite the spatial distance between Bangando and Baka villages, the communities developed deep and lasting friendships. Perhaps because of their spatial distribution in different parts of the forest, and because of their divergent historical origins and ecological contexts, early relationships between Bangando and Baka seem to have been built on economic complementarity. Thus Bangando may have been relatively more skilled at growing plantains during the colonial era, at engaging in trade for commodities such as salt; Bangando supported their Baka *bándí* (partners) by sharing these items. In return, Baka offered their Bangando *bándí* meat from their hunt, enabling Bangando to benefit from the relative advantage that Baka may have had at hunting in this region of the forest.

It is this kind of exchange relationship that scholars of "hunter-gatherer" societies emphasize in depicting social relations between communities identified as "hunter-gatherers" and "farmers."[3] But assuming that particular economic pursuits correlate with particular communities based on their ecological positioning in—and of—the forest or village, and that social relations between the groups are premised on and limited to exchanges of economic products, other significant features of relations between forest communities are omitted, especially as these relationships evolved over time. As we have seen, both Bangando and Baka are—and have been for generations—skilled hunters, and gifts of meat and other forest products circulate between families regardless of their ethnic affiliations or their identification as "of the forest" or "of the village."

It is also important to emphasize that Baka have engaged in various economic pursuits in various ecological spheres for much of the twentieth century. Colonial reports dating back to the 1930s indicate that Baka have been cultivating domestic crops for numerous generations.[4] Furthermore, rather than being isolated in the forest, some Baka engaged directly with colonial markets, trading ivory and other forest products for commodities.

> When the Germans were in Moloundou, Moloundou was very full, very busy. There were no other markets, so people came from all over the forest to weigh rubber and cocoa, to trade, and to buy things. There were so many shops in Moloundou! But the biggest shop belonged to Tragos, who had a big belly, like a pot. His shop was *full*. Tragos sold so many different kinds of cloth, and even guitars. The only thing he didn't sell was guns. Kapalani was a Baka hunter who killed very large elephants and sold the ivory to Tragos. The tusks were as thick as the log on this fire! If Kapalani brought Tragos one large elephant's head with tusks, he would trade it for five tin trunks full of cloth, clothes, axes, machetes, salt, and soap—everything you needed! Kapalani had to bring people with him to Moloundou to carry everything back home.[5]

According to a wide array of oral historical and archival sources, Bangando have had extensive experience hunting in forests, and Baka are more practiced agriculturalists and market traders than might be expected if the categories "people of the village" and "people of the forest" were believed to correlate neatly—and exclusively—with ethnic affiliations.

As described by Wanguwangu, a Bangando elder and head of the *bɛ́kà* circumcision ceremony, the union between Bangando and Baka, *bò kɔ́à* and *bò lé*, began numerous generations ago when the two communities ceremonially participated in joint rites of initiation. As Wanguwangu explains,

> There are no longer people whom we call *bò kɔ́à*, the people of the forest. All of us, we all live in the village. If someone leaves the village to go hunt in the forest, we do not call him a person of the forest because he is in the forest. The people of the forest are the animals: the gorilla, the chimpanzee, the monkey, and the elephant. The Baka are not the people of the forest either. They no longer stay in the forest. They go into the forest to look for meat or they work in their gardens, and then they come back to the village. Here are their houses, here in the village. Before, they were the people of the forest. They lived in the forest and made a path that led to the village. We began to live together a long time ago, when our parents still lived at the old road. When we lived along the Boumba River, Bangando and Baka circumcised their boys together. The Bangando and Baka parents organized themselves, and planned the boys' circumcision. Then they cut the boys together. When Bangando and Baka are circumcised together, they already make a union.[6]

The meanings of *bò kɔ̀à* and *bò lé* shifted because of the increased overlap of social, economic, and historical experiences between the communities, as well as their progressively more integrated social, political, and ritual structures. The social categories "of the forest" and "of the village" no longer provided meaningful correlations with particular ethnic communities, Baka and Bangando.

Bò Kɔ̀à and *Bò Lé* during Colonial Years

The social, economic, political, and spatial contexts of southeastern Cameroon, while certainly not static prior to the arrival of colonial explorers and administrators, experienced rapid and profound changes beginning in the 1890s. Colonial activities of forced labor in road-building and harvesting of natural rubber created new dynamics of social difference among local communities. People who lived in villages that were legible to Europeans—for example, in the large, centralized villages along the Boumba River—were counted in colonial censuses and identified as colonial subjects. As a result of this accounting, the Bangando and other village-based communities were levied a semiannual capitation tax and were forced to build the road connecting Moloundou with the next sizeable town, Yokadouma, nearly three hundred kilometers away. In contrast, the Baka community was more difficult to pin down, both as data for colonial censuses and for the practical purpose of extracting labor and taxes. In colonial documents, Baka were usually identified simply as "pygmies" and were assumed to be uncountable, unverifiable, and uncontrollable because of their transient locations within the forest.

Once the colonial road was complete, German administrators forced Bangando to relocate from their centralized villages along the eastern edge of the Boumba River to the shoulders of the new road. This resettlement scheme enabled the colonial officials to count their subjects more accurately, as well as to enlist their services and expertise in extracting valuable forest resources for the colonial coffers. The existence of the colonial road and the resettlement of Bangando along it underscored the conceptual difference between people who lived in the new roadside villages and people who continued to live in the forest, beyond the grasp of colonial authority.

The division of the communities into distinct colonial categories that emphasized spatial differences between village and forest ironically served to tighten the bonds of friendship and support between Bangando and

Baka. Baka remained elusive, keeping to their smaller and more moveable villages at some distance in the forest behind Bangando villages that were now located along the road. Thus Baka were largely insulated from the initial confusion, coercion, and capitation of the early colonial era. Meanwhile their Bangando (as well as Mbomam and Bakwélé) neighbors were pressed into labor, first building the road that connected Moloundou to the rest of the colonial territory, and then harvesting highly valued natural rubber from the forest and hauling it to Moloundou, where it was weighed and shipped off to colonial destinations and bank accounts. It was not physically feasible for Bangando and other "villagers" to sustain this labor in addition to their daily subsistence activities. As men were pressed into labor by the threat of physical punishment (beatings with the flat sides of machetes were common) and imprisonment in Moloundou, Bangando women assumed the bulk of productive as well as reproductive activities. While their husbands, fathers, uncles, and brothers endured the forced labor schemes, Bangando women undertook all the stages of cultivation—felling, clearing, planting, tending, harvesting—in addition to gathering and hunting forest resources to sustain their families. In this context of brutal labor, Baka *bándí* came to the assistance of their partners, helping Bangando men to collect balls of rubber from trees deep in the forest and helping women with their subsistence activities of cultivating, hunting, and gathering. According to numerous elders, the tribulations that Bangando endured during the colonial era were greatly alleviated by the assistance that Baka offered them; the physical and psychological strains of forced labor were offset by the strengthening of social and emotional ties between Bangando and Baka.

From the local communities' perspectives, the benefits of living near the road were minimal: living in roadside villages only increased the chance that one would have to interact with, and endure the vitriol and forced labor of, colonial officials. Thus while Bangando and Baka families maintained and even strengthened their friendships and support through this difficult period, and the emotional differences between people "of the village" and "of the forest" diminished, they continued to reside in distinct domestic spaces. This spatially observable distance provided continuing evidence to colonial administrators that people of the Lobéké region, Bangando "villagers" and Baka "pygmies," could be accurately identified by their relationships to geographical spaces of "village" and "forest" as well as by their relationship with the colonial state; European perceptions of "forest" and "village" as salient social markers of identity persisted. However, the original concepts of *bò kɔ̀à* and *bò lé* that local communities used to differentiate one from another gradually changed during the colonial era, as relations of cooperation and collective resistance to the colonial presence strengthened.

The relationships between communities who had identified themselves as *bò kɔ̀à* and *bò lé* changed again during the second half of the twentieth century, reconfiguring both spatial and social relations. During the 1950s the French administration initiated the resettlement of Baka communities alongside the road, a process that was continued by the independent Cameroonian government during the 1970s and by European missionaries during the 1980s. Because of the lack of success of French resettlement schemes, Cameroonian officials and soldiers penetrated the forest to find resisting Baka families and forced them at gunpoint to move their families from the forest to resettle in villages by the road. Ultimately, because of this pressure from colonial and postcolonial administrators, Baka moved from their small, moveable villages tucked into the forest to the villages that had been established along the main road, living as immediate neighbors to Bangando, Bakwélé, and Mbomam. The *bò kɔ̀à* gradually became *lé*-based—based in the village.

Bò Kɔ̀à and *Bò Lé* during the Marxist Uprising

Communist insurgencies swept through new nations of central Africa during the 1960s, resulting in further changes to social identities of *bò kɔ̀à* and *bò lé* in southeastern Cameroon. In the years preceding Cameroonian independence, the outlawed party *Union des Populations du Cameroun* (UPC) struggled toward its stated goal of a totally independent, prosperous, and unified Cameroon. The declared objective of the UPC was to depose the government of Cameroon's first president, Ahmadou Ahidjo, whom it regarded as a puppet of France.[7]

In the mid-1960s, southern Cameroon and northern Congo (including Ouesso) became the primary locus for the UPC, both because the region's geographical distance provided a buffer from the political and military structures based in the political capital of Yaoundé, and because the UPC found sympathy and logistical support among the Marxist political faction of Congo-Brazzaville. With their operational base first in Brazzaville and then in Ouesso, Osende Afana and other Cameroonian leaders of the UPC used the forests of southeastern Cameroon as their gateway into Cameroon and as staging grounds for their activities. The local communities of the Lobéké forest region were caught in the cross-currents of this political turbulence. With varying degrees of success, the UPC turned to local communities for logistical support, guidance in the forest, camouflage from the Cameroonian forces, and basic necessities such as plantains and meat as well as simple luxuries such as tobacco. Because the local communities of southeastern Cameroon had had unpleasant experiences with political interventions during both the colonial and early independence eras, they were not disposed to assist the Cameroonian state.[8] While elders recall that their families were also terrified of the UPC, they offered tacit support of the UPC under cover of the forest.

Because of the heightened military presence in the Lobéké forest region, local people were surveilled by the Cameroonian military, were forced to remain in their villages, and were required to submit to searches by government soldiers who patrolled the main road. A Bangando elder, Ndjumbé, recalls the fear with which he rode his bicycle thirty kilometers from his home in Dioula back to school in Moloundou following school holidays, encountering government troops along the way. Government soldiers who patrolled the village of Ngilili were particularly severe, as government officials believed that Osende Afana and his rebels were camped in the forest between the Malapi and Ngoko rivers, behind Ngilili. Ndjumbé recounts that more than once government soldiers brusquely confiscated the meat and plantains that his mother had sent with him for his provisions while at school. Sometimes the soldiers commandeered his bicycle to run their own errands, often delaying his return to school until late at night. Other villagers recall the forceful confiscation of supplies such as plantains and manioc, goats and chickens, which government soldiers simply hauled out of kitchen houses or stole from gardens to feed their troops stationed in Moloundou and the five villages to the north, where UPC activity was most prevalent.[9]

In contrast to the soldiers' patrols in villages and along the main road to Moloundou, Osende Afana and his rebels stayed in camps deep in the forest and traveled by forest paths. And in contrast to the government soldiers' expropriation of supplies from villagers, the rebels compensated Bangando and Baka families for the provisions that they took from gardens, leaving payment under rocks or pinned to the stump of a banana tree that they had harvested and felled. Bangando recall with wonder that often the rebels paid them enormous sums of money for the relatively modest provisions that they took.[10] Although local communities feared both the government soldiers and Afana's group of insurgents, the compensation provided by the UPC predisposed local families in favor of the rebels.

While the domestic lives of local people—Bangando and Baka alike—were village-centered, the Communist rebels were scattered throughout the forest. Bangando and Baka continued to aid the rebels with food and provisions, and served as forest guides and informants about the political activities in villages and in Moloundou.[11] Local communities referred to the rebels as the *bò kɔ̀à*—the people of the forest—because of their forest camps and activities. Ascribing this local signifier of identity to the rebels also enabled local people to discuss the rebels without referring to them by name. During this turbulent era, it was in the interests of all local people to differentiate themselves ideologically and nominally from the rebels to prevent government accusations of collusion with the insurgency. Thus *bò kɔ̀à* became the category of social identity used exclusively with reference to the Communist rebels, while all local people, Bangando, Baka, and Bakwélé, referred to themselves and each other as *bò lé*—people of the village—emphasizing their spatial locations in villages and underscoring their nonparticipation in the violent rebellion.

As Ndjumbé recalls, ultimately Osende Afana and a number of his rebels were caught in the forest behind Ngilili, where they were tortured, murdered, and dismembered. Ndjumbé was at school in Moloundou when their bodies were brought back to town. On 16 March 1966, the day after Afana's assassination, government officials forcibly rounded up residents of Moloundou and displayed the severed heads of Afana and his colleagues on sharpened sticks, to impress on the terrified gathering of Bangando, Bakwélé, and Baka the mortal cost of collusion with the UPC.[12] The brutal violence inflicted on Osende Afana and the UPC—the *bò kɔ̀à*—is still remembered in hushed and horrified tones among Bangando, Baka, and Bakwélé families, the *bò lé* of the Lobéké region. As the tumultuous rebellion of the mid-1960s subsided after Afana's murder, and as neocolonial French timber and cocoa companies moved into the forests of southeastern Cameroon during the early 1970s, markers of social identity such as *bò kɔ̀à* and *bò lé* shifted again, taking on a third variation of social significance.

Bò Kɔ̀à—Forest Expertise in a Context of Forest Exploitation

While *bò lé* continues to refer to the broad, village-based, and interethnic community of southeastern Cameroon, including Bangando, Bakwélé, Mbomam, and Baka, *bò kɔ̀à* has come to represent individuals whose skills involve knowledge of and work in the forest, often in the form of commercial labor. This shift in social identity mirrors fundamental socioeconomic changes throughout the forest: people harness their knowledge of the forest for professional, profit-oriented pursuits, hoping to find a lucrative way to be involved in the accelerating forest industries. In the increasingly commercialized economy of southeastern Cameroon, people of all communities make use of the forest to produce and procure resources both for subsistence and for commercial sale. In addition, both Bangando and Baka sell their knowledge of the forest to companies seeking to harvest forest resources—timber, bushmeat, ivory—for large-scale international (and sometimes illegal) markets.

During the last quarter of the twentieth century, the speed of economic penetration into southeastern Cameroon increased markedly, as international timber companies competed with increasing intensity to secure access to diminishing stands of virgin hardwood trees in the forest. Cocoa and coffee production also gathered momentum as companies took advantage of improved transportation and access to markets, a direct result of timber companies' efforts to rebuild and maintain the dirt road that connects the Lobéké forest region with the rest of Cameroon.[13] The increased commercial exploitation of forests required a pool of laborers, attracting local and outside men to positions as forest surveyors, heavy equipment operators, and fellers as well as secretaries, cooks, and cleaners. Increasing opportunities to earn wages, coupled with the expanding needs of the growing nonlocal population, created new and dynamic commercial markets in southeastern Cameroon.

A shift in social relationships accompanied the introduction of the monetized labor economy, commodification of forest resources, and availability of cheap, manufactured goods. With the introduction of money and durable commodities, increasing competition and decreasing cooperation have crept into social relationships, regardless of gender, age, or ethnicity. Today most Bangando and Baka maintain a subsistence household economy, with one big toe, perhaps, dipped into the larger market, yielding annual incomes of approximately US$100 for a family of eight. But with this monetary income, however slight, changes have emerged in relationships of reciprocity, sharing, and exchange. Today people value personal profit in previously unimaginable of ways, not infrequently compromising intimate social ties that are embedded in cooperative relations. The subsistence ethic that lay at the core of social and economic relations of collaboration is shifting, as Bangando and Baka alike become increasingly desirous of and dependent upon basic commodities supplied by the regional and international markets. Daily life in the village is shared by people of all ethnic affiliations, and forest resources are equally accessible to all. But, at the same time, the profit derived from one's ability to bring in income as a professional *bò kɔ́à* and the ensuing economic inequalities in the village context have led to new lines of competition and friction.

Today forest animals are hunted not only for domestic consumption, but also to bring enough money into the family coffers so that they can purchase the minimal necessities of modern life—salt, soap, and kerosene—as well as underwrite expenses such as school and medical fees. If resources remain after the family's needs have been met, individual desires for commodities—clothing, a bicycle, a radio—may be pursued. As a result, hunting forest animals has increased markedly, as local people strive to satisfy appetites for goods as well as hunger for food. Local hunters today comment on the long distances they must travel before they encounter animals in densities that they recall from the past. In addition to local desires for meat and income from hunting, the continued presence of loggers, truck drivers, and

FIG. 6.2 Baka man reading and listening to his radio, Ndongo, 1999

other logging town entrepreneurs, as well as the presence of government officials and other relatively well-off Cameroonians in Moloundou, provides an insatiable market for bushmeat. The increased commercialization of hunting keeps local hunters busy and has attracted outsiders to the Lobéké forest region, where the forests are still relatively rich in animals, compared to other regions of Cameroon. As access to transportation improves, with logging trucks plying the Moloundou-Yaoundé route in three days during the dry season (with good luck), the urban market for bushmeat has exploded, and restaurants in towns and cities across the nation serve meat from remote forests to their cosmopolitan diners. At the same time, Bangando and Baka kitchens resound with the complaint *sìi díà!*—("famine of meat!")—as they see meat in their own cooking pots with less and less frequency. As the economic benefits of hunting for external markets have increased, so too have competition and conflict over increasingly scarce forest resources.

The basic marker of cooperation and mutual support, the sharing and distribution of meat, has dwindled. Instead of sharing meat with family, friends, and neighbors, a hunter's family will often sell his surplus meat to gain cash to meet the family's needs and wants. The social price that Bangando and Baka alike have paid for their access to basic commodities has been the deterioration of the system of mutual support through gifts and delayed-return exchanges that sustained social ties for many generations. As Buba, a Baka elder, explained:

> What our Bangando grandparents[14] did before, it is no longer the same way today. Earlier, they prepared meat and leaves to give to their Baka neighbors. But now, because they know the problem of money, there are no longer the same customs. During our ancestors' times, it was different. Today, if my brother Weenumbu kills meat in the forest, he cannot give me even a little bit. Brothers do not know how to share among themselves because of money.[15]

Differential access to money and markets has introduced new socioeconomic divisions within families, neighborhoods, and villages, even as these same economic forces have brought Bangando and Baka together in cooperative teams of *bò kɔ̀à*, either as coworkers for timber companies or as partners in more time-honored pursuits such as hunting. Both Bangando and Baka hunt extensively, and often elephant hunters will track their prey, make their kill(s), and return to the village carrying meat in ethnically mixed teams, adopting the shared social identity of *bò kɔ̀à* in this newly charged, competitive context of commercial hunting.

Today, even when large animals such as elephants are killed by Bangando and Baka hunters, older patterns of distribution and sharing of meat are often not followed. In the past, when hunters killed an animal that was too large to transport back to the village, the hunters would send a member of the team back to the village to alert others of the kill and to tell them the location of the carcass. The hunters who remained in the forest would begin to carve the meat into chunks and smoke it, while the others organized the mɔkɔpɔlɔ, a team of porters to come to the site of the carcass and to carry baskets of meat back to the village for distribution. But today, especially if the hunters have been commissioned by a "patron"—often a prominent government official or wealthy merchant—to hunt bushmeat and ivory illegally, the hunters see secrecy as a necessary security precaution. The bò kɔà hunters benefit from the wages provided by their "patron" and from the meat that they can carry back to the village. But they are willing to endure the wrath of bò lé—angry friends, family members, and neighbors—to avoid publicizing the location of (and responsibility for having illegally killed) the elephant for fear of having their poaching publicly announced to the authorities in Moloundou, and also to ensure that the profits from their dangerous hunt remain in their pockets.

In 1998 a bitter dispute erupted when a team of bò kɔà hunters did not announce the location of an elephant they had killed, preventing their extended families and networks of neighbors and friends from harvesting meat from the carcass.[16] Throughout the village, bò lé were shocked and angry at the hunters' refusal to reveal the location of the elephant carcass and at their selfish hoarding, keeping both the profit from their wages and the meat for themselves.

From the point of view of hunters, however, the risk and capital required for large-scale hunting today necessitates the sale of meat for money. Offering a lengthy and thoughtful rejoinder to the plentiful objections of hunters' hoarding, Mikome explained his situation:

> I am a hunter. This year I have not worked at all in my cocoa garden, so that I can focus on hunting in the forest. But every time I come back from hunting, people who stay in the village to look after their gardens and cocoa stands demand to have a share of the meat I have hunted. It's not fair that I should have to divide up all of the meat that I have hunted, because I buy the bullets and rent the gun—50,000 CFA each week—on my own.
>
> The meat that I kill is my livelihood. I must pay the expenses of hunting. If I shoot and miss, I alone support the loss of money, time, and effort. But if my

hunting is successful, I am expected to share everything with the whole village. When people sell their cocoa and earn *their* livelihood, I don't benefit at all, not even one cigarette to smoke.

Even if I pay to rent the gun by myself, I can't convince my family and neighbors to help pay for the bullets so that I can hunt for everyone collectively. That way they would have made an investment in my hunting, too.

If I am lucky and I manage to kill an elephant, I might make 80,000 CFA, which is just enough to pay for the gun and the bullets, if it took a couple of bullets to bring down the elephant.

So the villagers who get jealous if I don't share the meat but sell it instead are unfair in their jealousy.[17]

The dynamics of commercial hunting have introduced new antagonisms between *bò kɔ́à* who use the forest and its resources for individual gain, and *bò lé* who sense their marginalization from the economic benefits of commercially exploiting the surrounding forest.

But, importantly, the tension caused by this lack of sharing meat does not seem to have lines of cleavage that follow ethnic distinctions. The label of social identity that once referred to people who lived primarily in the forest, who engaged in a good deal of hunting, and who identified themselves ethnically as Baka—*bò kɔ́à*—is now applied to and assumed by hunters of various ethnic affiliations.

Speaking together, a pair of hunters—one Bangando and one Baka—describes with enthusiasm the complementarity of their skills and knowledge, enabling them to cooperate and compete effectively in the illegal market for bushmeat and ivory. The combination of skills that these hunters bring together enables them to build a successful and mutually beneficial hunting partnership. While one hunter is extremely adroit at navigation in the forest and tracking animals, the other hunter is intimately familiar with timber company roads in a region of the forest where he once worked as a logger, and has access to networks of gun-owning patrons and munitions suppliers in Moloundou and Ouesso.[18]

When Webora is in the forest, he can find anything! Just now we were in the forest for two weeks. We ate our last two plantain fingers; we had no water; we were tired. But then we killed a *mbénjí* [porcupine] to eat, and Webora wandered off into the forest. He made such a racket! I went to see. He had dug up a big pile of wild yams. So I cooked the *mbénjí* and the yams, and we had plenty to eat. I filled up my water container in a stream I knew, and we had plenty to drink. When we are in the forest, we eat together. When we come back to the village, we also eat together.

When we hunt, Webora is very good at finding tracks and orienting our position in the forest. But he also gets distracted, looking for honey and other animal tracks. So I remind him about the elephant. [Grinning.] I fire the gun because I know what distance to shoot from, and I will reload on the spot to shoot again. I always ask Webora if he wants to shoot first, but Webora always says I should do it because it is my talent.[19]

The men exude fondness for each other and respect for the other's abilities to work in the forest; both men describe themselves as *bò kɔ̀à* by virtue of their skill at and reliance on hunting to support their families.

Bò Kɔ̀à, Bò Lé, and Nongovernmental Organizations

Because of the burgeoning activity in the forest from timber companies, hunters, and Bangando and Baka, nongovernmental organizations (NGOs) have arrived in the forests of southeastern Cameroon to protect the fauna and flora of the Lobéké forest. Conservation and development NGOs have introduced new dynamics to the region, including novel ways for local communities to conceptualize their relationship with and control over the surrounding forest and its resources, as well as new avenues for asserting identities and gaining power. Nongovernmental organizations began preliminary research in southeastern Cameroon during the late 1980s, attracted by the opportunity to conserve the endangered fauna of the region by creating Lobéké National Park, which was formally established in 2001. The heart of this protected area is Ndjàngé, the resource-rich clearing west of the Sangha River utilized by Bangando, Baka, Bakwélé, and Mbomam. People throughout southeastern Cameroon are acutely aware of the strain on the forest that sustains them, as a result of the accelerating exploitation of forest resources by entrepreneurial companies and individuals. The widespread sense of diminished quantity and quality of forest resources, coupled with collective concerns about their regional marginalization from economic markets, brings people of all ethnic affiliations together in principled support of conservation and development efforts.

But at the intervillage level, conservation and development organizations have generated new rivalries between villages. Access to substantial benefits such as jobs, and to economically incidental but symbolically significant perks such as T-shirts, transportation in NGO vehicles, and the occasional beer, has not been spread equally throughout the region. Since the inception of conservation work in the early 1990s, NGOs' efforts have been based in the small hamlet of Lopondji, part of the larger village of Mambélé. Over the years, residents of Mambélé have benefited disproportionately from the activities of the NGOs, through their employment as "pisteurs" or path clearers, trackers, and identifiers for visiting foreign biologists and botanists, and as porters for longer expeditions. In addition, several young men are employed as helpers in the tented conservation camp where they cook, wash clothes, and keep the camp tidy. Local men who work for WWF have developed a sense of team spirit that transcends their ethnic affiliations. The solidarity that villagers of Mambélé share with conservation efforts is reflected in the identity of the village soccer team as the *bò dɔbídɔbì*,[20] the "people of WWF." But residents of other villages claim that they do not benefit from the NGOs' activities because they see no short-term, practical benefits, and because the long-term work of establishing Lobéké National Park has been slow and seemingly invisible. Residents of villages that have benefited from the presence of conservation workers have built positive relationships with the extra-local members of their community and have a strengthened sense of solidarity as a result of their collective sense of support for the conservation efforts. At the same time, villagers who feel they have been left out of the process as well as the benefits of conservation have developed a sense of collective resistance to this new dimension of marginalization. Ironically, tensions between villages and solidarities within villages have both increased as a result of varying degrees of alignment with conservation efforts, generating social dynamics that cut across ethnic affiliations and social identities such as and *bò kɔ̀à* and *bò lé*.

Some people have found employment with NGOs, especially serving as local trackers and guides for conservation biologists conducting basic research in the forest. Involvement in conservation efforts has provided a new channel for people from the Lobéké forest region to express their identities as *bò kɔ̀à*, "people of the forest," affirming their knowledge of and commitment to the forest. Mokogwea, a Bangando resident of Lopondji, identifies himself as *bò kɔ̀à* by virtue of his expertise in the forest and his employment as a guide for the conservation biologists of WWF. Mokogwea explains:

> Because WWF has seen that we know the forest, they come each time to look for us. Especially me. Because in the forest, it is I who shows them where to go.

> I know all of this forest. From Ngato, coming out at Ndongo, and even going to Ngoıla, I know this entire forest. So the work that I do for WWF is the work of the forest. . . . Before, it was the Baka who stayed in the forest. But now, Bangando marry Baka wives and Baka also marry Bangando wives. . . . So the forest is for us all. The two kinds of people, Bangando and Baka, stay together in the forest *and* in the village.[21]

Mokogwea emphasizes that he is "of the forest" by virtue of his knowledge, his professional expertise as a guide and tracker for outsider conservation workers, and his emotional connection to the forest through the places and skills that he has mastered. Mokogwea explains that because of the transformations in relationships between Bangando and Baka over the preceding decades, social boundaries that locate one community in the forest and another in the village are no longer relevant. Whereas for earlier generations of Bangando, social boundaries reflected spatial distinctions between forest and village, today social identities such as *bò kɔ́à* and *bò lé* reflect individuals' positions vis-à-vis wider political-economic processes. Today the social identity *bò kɔ́à* marks a point of conjunction between local social identities and global processes—such as international conservation efforts—that offer new opportunities for individuals and communities to reap benefits by crafting and asserting new identities that dovetail with the interests of international institutions (Li 2000). Ironically, however, while *bò kɔ́à* has emerged as a social identity that enables individuals to position themselves in the global context of biodiversity conservation, this identity as a "person of the forest" does not necessarily track with institutional expectations of who the "people of the forest" ought to be: the Baka "pygmies."

Bò Kɔ́à, Bò Lé: Contemporary Relations in the Forest and Village

Bangando and Baka move back and forth between the village and the forest to pursue their subsistence and small-scale commercial activities, while maintaining ties with family and friends in both places. As a result of persistent village disputes about who shares and who doesn't, who works hard and who is lazy, some families have moved away from villages altogether and now spend the vast majority of their time living and working in the forest. These *bò kɔ́à* are Bangando and Baka who return to the villages of their extended families only for occasional visits.

FIG. 6.3
Bangando
ɓò kɔ́à

For example, a Bangando couple, Zoduma and Besombo, live for most of the year at their *mbándà*, or forest garden. Their garden is located fifteen kilometers to the east of Dioula in the direction of Ndjàngé. Zoduma and Besombo return to Dioula on rare occasions, either to celebrate holidays such as Christmas and the New Year with their family in the village, or to address issues or conflicts in the family. Returning to the village brings the mixed sentiments of life in the village and life in the forest to the fore. As Zoduma explains,

> We do not come out [of the forest] very much to the village. In case of sickness, we leave [the forest]. Since our *mbándà* is there along the large path going to Ndjàngé, people arrive left and right. If we leave the *mbándà* for a long time, that would not be good. . . .
>
> We have many goats. Our house is *gàlà bíliki* [wattle-and-daub]. There are six houses. My family has three houses. The Baka who live there with us also have

three houses. There is also a house for Mokan, another Baka woman. In the forest, we are good. . . .

But relationships in the village: they are hard! Living in the village is really hard, too hard. . . . Since I am already at the *mbándà*, I have no more friends in the village. I do not get along well with the people from the village. Life in the village is hard because we Bangando, we do not want someone who progresses. It is because of a hard heart. In this case of a hard heart, we leave progress behind. People do not like that someone is rich, while they stay poor. People do anything to cut down the person who wants to make progress. But in the forest, people get along well.

In the forest, I know a lot. Everything in this forest until Ndjàngé, I know it. I have been everywhere in the forest. Today, everything has changed. Bangando and Baka are all *bò lé* and *bò kɔ̀à* too. Bangando marry Baka, and Baka marry Bangando.[22]

In this discussion, Zoduma points to increasing tensions among people who reside in the village as they struggle to provide for their families in a social and economic context that privileges personal profit over collective, sustained subsistence. Zoduma moved from the village to his forest *mbándà* to escape from the social pressures that he felt in Dioula, where his hard work and success were viewed with envy by his own family, friends, and neighbors. In southeastern Cameroon success is often begrudged by family and friends—even to the extent of fomenting accusations of the use of sorcery to generate profit—unless the successful worker distributes the fruits of his or her labors to the same family and friends who often have not undertaken serious efforts of their own. Because of this compelling social leveling mechanism, incentives to work are diminished: either the products of hard work disappear into the hands and mouths of lazier kin and neighbors, or one may become a target of jealousy and accusations of occult practices to explain both the success and the hoarding.

So Zoduma, Besombo, and their Baka *bándí* retreated to the forest, where the soils are fertile, animals and forest products are plentiful, and they can work to the best of their abilities without daily recriminations for their hard work and daily demands for hand-outs. At the same time, Zoduma struggles to maintain his presence in the village; in 1999 he built a wooden kitchen for his daughters-in-law to use, a rare investment of materials and effort in southeastern Cameroon, especially by someone who actually lives many kilometers away in the forest. Zoduma finds that his visits to the village are still often marked by confrontation, as his orientation, interests, and economic status diverge further from his village-based family and neighbors. In contrast, Zoduma states that "people in the forest get along." Zoduma expresses the social distance that he feels from other Bangando and Baka who live in the village and, at the end of the conversation, describes himself as *bò kɔ̀à*, a person of the forest. He does not relinquish his fundamental ties to the village, however, and notes that the lives of Bangando and Baka alike incorporate both the forest and the village, just as marriages today integrate the personal lives and the social networks of Bangando and Baka.

Social Identities beyond *Bò Kɔ̀à* and *Bò Lé*

Social identities that are structured using the *bò* compound also refer to people whose occupation, skills, or social position distinguish them from other villagers. While they share ethnic affiliations, kinship relations, and other important social ties, individuals whose particular abilities make unusual contributions to the community can variably identify themselves, and are also identified by others, with reference to their special abilities or occupations. Thus people who work for timber companies are often referred to as *bò shàntìé*, "people of the timber camp" (*chantier* in French) by their village-based friends and relations. Also marking people whose livelihoods take them away from the village-forest nexus, *bò màtúà* are "people of the vehicle," people who work in the transportation sector as drivers or touts, or who travel in vehicles on the road that connects the forest-based communities of southeastern Cameroon with towns and cities beyond the region. Other occupational specialists remain in the village and contribute their skills to the health and well-being of the community. For example, the medicinal knowledge and healing powers of *bò dwá*, "people of sorcery," benefit the wider community. Enthusiasm for and some degree of skill at playing soccer among *bò ballon*, "people of the ball," also builds interethnic community solidarity. Finally, the creation of flexible identities using *bò* compounds is also, ironically, well suited to the expression of prejudices and negative social sentiments.

Bò Shàntìé—People of the Timber Camp

Because of the prevalence of logging companies and the intensity of the timber industry, many families throughout southeastern Cameroon have

FIG. 6.4 Mbito,
a self-identified
bò shàntìé

at least one member who has worked for a period of time as a *bò shàntìé*,
a person of the timber camp. Subsistence activities such as hunting have
become increasingly difficult because of the intensification of commercial
markets for bushmeat, markets that are driven in no small measure by the
appetites of extra-local employees of timber companies for forest meat. As
a result of the increasing difficulties that Bangando and Baka hunters have
encountered in finding means to support their families in the forests near
their villages, local people have increasingly turned to timber companies for
employment. Local people are often initially hired as *boussolliers*, literally
"compassers," referring to their responsibility of locating the particular trees
that will be felled. Baka and Bangando alike are engaged as "compassers,"
because their profound knowledge of and ability to navigate within the forest offer valuable skills to a timber company. If the "compasser" is proficient
and hardworking, he may advance to the position of feller's assistant and
ultimately become a feller in his own right. People who work for timber

companies move from one location to another with frequency. At timber camps, people are always coming and going, as new employees arrive and others leave, as individuals change jobs and responsibilities, and as merchants, bar owners, and restaurateurs set up shop to make a profit from timber company employees. Life at logging towns is dynamic—*la vie bouge*. Mbito describes his life in the timber camp:

> Where I work is far away. Life at the timber company is very different from life in the village. Because after two weeks, you "cut the fifteenth," which means that you can take the money that you want, 10,000 or 15,000 or even 20,000 CFA [from your monthly wages].[23] After three weeks, it's payday. This is why there are no troubles at the timber camp. We are not bothered by *la crise* [crisis of hunger, lack of supplies]. . . . It's in the village where there are too many troubles, because there sometimes you can go for one or two months without having even 5,000 CFA.
>
> The life that we lead in the timber camp is always exciting, because you have friends. Sometimes you go out together, four or five of you. You go out today and one person buys drinks for everyone. You drink and you dance, and then you go home. Tomorrow, it's another person's turn to buy, and you all drink again. You also go to visit women.[24]

The differences in lifestyle between the subsistence-based and family-focused daily life of the village and the wage-based and consumption-focused lifestyle of the timber camp precipitate distinct, emotional differences among people who identify themselves as *bò lé* and *bò shàntìé*. Because people of the timber camp often return to the village with expensive clothes and perhaps a watch, the smell of fancy soaps and perfumes, and may come across as arrogant, people of the village often view *bò shàntìé* with suspicion. For example, when Mbito neglected to pay back loans of money and supplies that he had borrowed from his family and neighbors for his wife Mengala's end-of-mourning celebration, people of the village remarked that his violation of their trust was entirely predictable because Mbito is a *bò shàntìé*. Numerous villagers suggested to each other that they should travel to Mbito's timber company to speak with his boss, hoping to recover their loans by withdrawing the money from Mbito's next payment of wages. Because the life of the timber camp is understood to be rough and tumble, competitive and corrupt, the people of the timber camp are perceived to be manipulative and dishonest, making the most of both their wages and their friends.

Southeastern Cameroon is geographically remote and socioeconomically marginalized from the towns and cities of Cameroon. Traveling to and from the region is extremely time-consuming, cumbersome, and uncomfortable. When traveling by bus—small, rattletrap buses that seem either to hurtle along the rutted road at terrifying speeds or to be stuck in mud—it may take as little as three days or as long as a week to reach Yaoundé, the capital of Cameroon, approximately 900 kilometers from Moloundou. The passage of a vehicle along the Moloundou road is an occurrence that people of the village note with interest, turning from their conversations and activities to see who is passing and often identifying the vehicle from a distance, as they learn to distinguish the engine sounds of regular "traffic." A previously unknown vehicle excites interest, as people speculate who the passengers are and what their business is down in the southeastern corner of Cameroon. In Bangando, as in other Ubangian languages, the word for vehicle or car is *màtúà*; in keeping with the structure of ways to identify people, drivers and passengers are referred to as *bò màtúà*, or "people of the vehicle." This appellation is more than simply a transliteration of a generic concept of "passenger," however. For the *bò lé*, Bangando and Baka alike, the people of the vehicle stand—or rather, move—in marked contrast to themselves, the villagers. 'Bò màtúà have access to the resources needed to travel: money to pay the fare and to buy food along the way, as well as social networks at their destination, often including educational opportunities or employment. When Bangando and Baka return from afar, there is often jubilation and communication all along the road as the *bò màtúà* approaches his final destination, usually his patrilineal village. Along the way, the *bò màtúà* and *bò lé* shout out greetings and news to each other as the vehicle whizzes past kitchens, verandas, and houses in a cloud of dust, or crawls along the road, the *bò màtúà* heaving it through mud holes and deep, slippery gullies.

Communication between southeastern Cameroon and the rest of the country is notoriously unreliable. So *bò màtúà* serve as carrier-pigeons, carrying messages home from friends and relatives who live in distant Cameroonian cities, letting the letters fly and flutter behind the bus as it passes by the home villages of the urban-based Bangando and Baka. If a *bò lé* needs to send news to a nearby village or to a more distant city, the only practical means of "posting" a letter is by waving down one of the passing vehicles and hoping that the driver or other passengers—the *bò màtúà*—will be kind (and responsible) enough to drop the letter off (literally) at its destination as they drive past. The *bò màtúà* serve as indispensable links between the villagers and the *bò vílí* (the people of the city, or *ville*), bridges between the social space of the marginalized forest of southeastern Cameroon and the space of political and economic power, the cities and towns.

Although most Bangando and Baka will at some time in their lives be considered *bò màtúà* by those watching the vehicles pass by, the fact that individuals can move in and out of the category of "person of the vehicle" does not undermine the salience of the category as a marker of social difference. The social difference between the mobility of individuals who have access to transportation, and thus access to other resources afforded by networks and opportunities in towns or cities, and the fixity of individuals who remain in the village relying on the forest and kin for basic necessities, is metaphorically expressed through the appellation of the mobile "other" as *bò màtúà*.

Bò Dwá — *People of Sorcery*

Mosua is an elderly Bangando woman who is renowned throughout the region as an expert healer and sorcerer, *bò dwá*. She often spends extended periods of time, sometimes several months, in the forest as she tends her forest garden [*mbándà*] with her husband and collects medicines from sources deep in the forest. Patients visit her for medical advice and healing in the forest; Mosua will also return to her village-based house in Dioula if someone is gravely ill and needs her attention, and cannot move or be brought to her in the forest. Mosua's patients include Baka as well as Bangando, residents of Dioula as well as people from far away. People of sorcery, *bò dwá*, are respected and feared throughout the Lobéké forest. All *bò dwá* possess practical and spiritual knowledge of the forest and are able to manipulate its powers to affect both helpful and harmful change.

Bò Ballon — *People of the Ball, and Nationalism*

Whereas *bò dwá* are imbued with spiritual powers and knowledge of healing, *bò ballon*, or people of the ball (*ballon* in French), are endowed with an extremely popular talent: playing soccer. People of all ages in southeastern Cameroon thoroughly enjoy village soccer matches, in which teams from different villages square off, or the youth (*bwàlá wì*) take on the elders (*tètè wì*), or the safari company employees (*bò safari*) challenge the villagers of Mambélé, many of whom work for WWF (*bò dɔbídɔbì*). The term *bò ballon* identifies all participants in a soccer match, especially the players, but also the spectators. Soccer matches do not engage one ethnic community in competition with another, but reflect village identities, generational differences, and belonging in other social organizations or clubs. The lines of social identity inscribed by the category *bò ballon* cut across ethnic lines, because all residents of a village are welcome to participate on the soccer team. Soccer in the Lobéké region, as at the national level, offers a compelling way to build emotional solidarity among divergent ethnic communities, enabling players as well as spectators to feel the excitement of cooperating well together and supporting each other.

International soccer matches provide one of the few occasions when the residents of southeastern Cameroon express nationalist sentiments. Although there are only three reliable shortwave radios in Dioula (with a population of approximately 500), the coverage of soccer matches by French international broadcasters provides a context for people to come together to cheer for the Cameroon Lions. Soccer enthusiasts in southeastern Cameroon support the Cameroon national team over any other; their support broadens regionally as the teams contesting the match lose immediate political or spatial relevance. Soccer "listeners" cheer for African teams over European, American, or Asian counterparts. Barring any specific loyalties, soccer fans support underdog teams against teams that dominate.[25] Given their proximity to the border of the Republic of Congo (Brazzaville), residents of the Lobéké region are particularly keen to emphasize the differences between *bò Cameroon* and *bò Congo* when national teams from Cameroon and Congo face off in soccer matches, and also when discussion turns to the violent conflict that ravaged Congo during the late 1990s. In both discussions, *bò Cameroon* and *bò Congo* are expressed as opposites: *bò Cameroon* players are clearly the team to support, and not to show your overt support is to risk moral alienation from the other soccer fans, at least for the afternoon. If a Congolese team commits fouls or incurs penalties, listeners sigh and groan as if these infractions were inevitable: the players are *bò Congo*, after all.

In more serious discussions of politics and the violent conflicts that characterized Congo during the 1990s, residents of southeastern Cameroon express fear of crossing the Ngoko River into Congolese territory, a mere thirty kilometers from Dioula. Residents of southeastern Cameroon describe *bò Congo* as dangerous, aggressive, and often drunk. When residents of Dioula behave in ways that others find offensive, they too are sometimes referred to as *bò Congo*. References to others as "people of Congo" evoke collective sentiments of antipathy, based on perceived attitudes or characteristics that are attributed broadly and bluntly to individuals of Congolese nationality. Because Congo is perceived to be a nation rife with political turbulence and social instability, *bò Congo* is often used synonymously with *bò njémúnjèmù* to refer to people of disorder or chaos (*njémúnjèmù*).

Bò X: *Social Identities and Prejudices*

Nationality is not the only frame of reference for stigmatizing labels: derogatory identities are also constructed based on assumptions of characteristics that may be associated with ethnicity. Where interethnic social relations have been prolonged, as among Bangando, Baka, Bakwélé, and Mbomam, prejudices emerge as a nearly universal and unavoidable part of social interrelations and categorization (Allport 1954).

For example, Bangando elders who have lived most of their adult lives among Bakwélé in Ndongo attempted to explain the common Bangando epithet used to refer to Bakwélé in general: *bò kà*. Struggling to find the right words, Ngongo explained that "*bò kà* is someone who is closed off from others, who is hidden [*caché*] or who hides his thoughts." Sensing, perhaps, that his verbal explanation had not captured the sentiments that he wanted to convey, Ngongo enacted what *bò kà* means to Bangando. He put his hands together, palms flat against each other, scrunched his shoulders together while hunching forward, and with a frown and sideways glance turned his back on Sakomo, another Bangando elder who was sitting on a log next to him.[26] Elaborating this negative stereotype of Bakwélé, the men echoed comments that had been articulated by other Bangando throughout the region: Bakwélé do not help each other, much less individuals from other communities; Bakwélé men do not eat together in *mbánjós* (the men's verandah), each man preferring to eat alone or with kin in the kitchen house; Bakwélé often fight with each other, and when they do, the arguments often involve machetes and whisky.

Bangando have also developed stereotyped social identities to describe their Baka neighbors in disparaging terms. In particular, Bangando refer to Baka as *bò kótà*, the "people from behind the kitchen." It is possible that this generalized category of identity derives from the era when Baka *did* live behind—quite far behind—Bangando kitchen houses, in their own settlements and small villages in the forest. But today the label is interpreted specifically as an insult: "going behind" (*mì èlì ná kòtà*) is a euphemism for going to the latrine, which is almost always located behind the kitchen. The contemporary implication of calling Baka *bò kótà* is that Baka live in the dirty areas behind Bangando households, reserved for disposing domestic rubbish and human waste.

Although the negative stereotypes that Bangando use to identify their immediate neighbors are tempered by the daily knowledge of shared intimate relations that are positive as well as negative, Bangando hold consistently negative views of people belonging to the Mpiemu community, which is based approximately 200 kilometers to the north of the Lobéké region.[27] Bangando identify the majority of commercial hunters who arrive in the Lobéké region to hunt bushmeat as Mpiemu. Bangando harbor animosity toward Mpiemu, sensing that their own livelihoods in the forest are directly threatened by these extralocal, profiteering bushmeat hunters. Bangando refer to Mpiemu as *bò ndjómbò*, "people of dirt" or dirty people. This insult reflects Bangando perceptions that Mpiemu live for weeks in the forest as they hunt, without changing their clothes or bathing. This image of filthiness reflects underlying value judgments expressed by Bangando: along with their commercial hunting activities and dirty clothing, the collective morality of Mpiemu is defiled.

Prejudiced social identities also extend to negative characteristics that do not correlate with ethnic affiliation. For example, Bangando may identify someone as *bò dáá sèà* to refer to a "person of bad heart" (*dáá sèà* literally means "bad liver," as the liver is perceived to be the focal point of emotions). This label is used to refer to individuals who are perceived to be conniving, manipulative, or selfish. Bangando ascribe this unfavorable identity to other Bangando as well as to individuals of different ethnic backgrounds. By embedding notions of social identity in the immediately recognizable conceptual structure introduced by the bound morpheme *bò*, Bangando conceptions of self and other are rooted in consistent, historically based linguistic and social frames of reference and have the capacity for unlimited variations in expressions of identity as people encounter, create, and confront unlimited experiences of identity.

Although the repertoire of *bò* identities is vast and varied, several social identities are conspicuously absent. There are no local equivalents for social identities that reference subsistence, as discourse on "hunters" vs. "farmers" would seem to predict. Similarly, there is no local equivalent for the stereotype "pygmy." When the term "pygmy" is used, it is invariably expressed in French and utilized in discussions of institutional or external interventions.

I overheard the term "pygmy" used only once in an intimate context; in a fit of rage and a state of inebriation, one Baka man insulted his Baka neighbor, in French: "*Tu es pygmée!*" This incident demonstrates that external categories and stereotypes—such as "pygmy" as a primitive or debased person—are absorbed into the local frames of reference and vocabularies. But more striking is the lack of Bangando and Baka equivalents for categories of identity—such as "hunter-gatherer" or "farmer" or "pygmy"—that external observers assume reference local ways of life and modes of identification.

In this era of rapid ecological, economic, and social transformation in southeastern Cameroon, there are many orienting nodes of identity other than "the forest" and "the village," even as what it means to be someone "of the forest" and "of the village" has changed markedly over the past century. Social identities are fluid, providing malleable ways of describing who is who as the social landscape changes, allowing people to adopt new ways of seeing themselves and others, and offering contemporary reflections of people's changing abilities and relationships as they learn new skills and become involved in different activities. Contemporary notions of social identity build on the conceptually stable structure for locating individuals in the web of social interactions and relationships by means of descriptions as "people of" various social capacities, qualities, or characters, while the changing substance of these categories highlights the flexibility of local people's ways of expressing and experiencing who is who, and how the "whos" relate to each other and belong together.

CHAPTER SEVEN

Contradictions

IDENTITIES, OPPORTUNITIES, AND CONFLICTS

> It is a question that I should talk to you about, you white people.
> In history, they say that pygmies are men of small size. White people
> say that they come here because of Baka, even though Baka are the
> same size as we [Bangando] are. So are white people sure that
> the people they come to work with are actually Baka?
> —*Medola, Bangando man, Mambélé, May 1999*

Through processes of coming together and engaging with changing contexts, Bangando, Baka, Bakwélé, and Mbomam have built relationships and alliances, negotiated differences and divisions, and contended with political, economic, ecological, and social changes. As a result of these varied dynamics, identities range from relatively stable ethnic affiliations to extremely fluid social identities, with a broad spectrum of collective and individual identities of varying viscosity in between, identities that reflect alliances, partnerships, and shared experiences among the communities of the Lobéké forest region. The tremendous variation in kind, quality, and context of identities indicates the many nodes of commonality among the communities as they have initiated and endured a core of shared experiences over the course of the past two centuries. This ethnography has demonstrated that although Bangando, Baka, Bakwélé, and Mbomam groups are distinct in some fundamental ways, such as language, many historical experiences, intercommunal alliances, social relationships, and ways of identifying self and other bring the communities together. The boundaries that mark distinctions within and among the communities simultaneously serve as social articulations, marking common qualities, contexts, and interests (Barth 2002).

But social systems in their messy glory are too unwieldy for institutional processing and management. Contradictions emerge when outside observers view the integrated, multiethnic society of southeastern Cameroon through lenses that emphasize simplified categories of distinction and opposition. For example, the process of collecting data for the purpose of designing management plans for biodiversity conservation and socioeconomic development is premised on surveying, cataloging, and mapping the components of natural and social systems. In the fields of conservation biology and policy, biodiverse ecosystems are mapped, transects are systematically demarcated and "walked," data are counted and classified, and maps of resources are produced to represent and quantify animal species. In the field of development, communities are identified and categorized, and are surveyed for basic socioeconomic information that often emphasizes the distinctiveness of particular communities. This process of classifying differences creates boundaries that identify and delineate spaces, species, and societies. Through surveys designed for administrative purposes, natural and social boundaries are documented, legislated, and eventually reinscribed as tools to control and patrol the landscapes and socialscapes from which they have been abstracted.

The practical need to categorize forest communities dovetails with analytical models that have been condensed from other seemingly similar environments and that differentiate between communities according to distinctive characteristics of human ecology, economic orientation, social organization, and ritual practice. This attention to divisions among communities has resulted in three prevailing assumptions in policies for forest communities: that differences do, actually, provide the most salient dynamic in social relations; that distinctions in various contexts—ecological, economic, ethnic, and social—are mutually constitutive; and that the distinctions that demarcate analytical categories remain constant across communities and across time. As a result of these assumptions, the analytical frameworks that guide research and policy formulation both draw on and perpetuate sets of oppositional categories that are treated as interchangeable: people of the forest/people of the village; pygmies/villagers; hunter-gatherers/farmers; indigenous people/immigrants; Baka/Bangando. These conveniently interchangeable categories provide stable units of categorization, evaluation, and institutional administration—units that reduce dynamics of social complexity to simple oppositions between paired elements. In the fields of conservation and development, the dominant, pragmatic paradigms of "pygmies" and "hunter-gatherers" appear to serve as convenient conceptual handles for observers who may have neither the expertise nor the time to delve into the details of social life in the forest. However, the actual communities to which these handles are attached may not correspond to the categorical concepts in the ways that outside observers expect.

For policy makers, the muddle of social relations within equatorial African forests poses an administrative quagmire. Institutions that require the distillation of social realities into conceptual categories tend to have particular policy objectives. During the colonial era and early independence in Cameroon, administrators were concerned about cataloging the population in order to resettle them, thus creating legible communities that could be taxed to produce state income, coerced to perform labor, and controlled to produce political subjects. During the last decade of the twentieth century, institutional objectives in southeastern Cameroon have focused primarily on the management of natural resources and secondarily on conditions of poverty, health, and education of local communities. The social and natural systems of southeastern Cameroon that various agencies have attempted to control were, and continue to be, immensely complex; the categories for analyzing and transforming these systems were, and continue to be, static and shallowly schematic.

Having emphasized the polyvalent identities and complex relationships among Bangando, Baka, Bakwélé and Mbomam in the preceding ethnography, this chapter analyzes the creation of institutionally relevant information about the communities of the Lobéké forest region by conservation and development practitioners. Several features of this process warrant analysis: the determination of which social elements constitute relevant, utilitarian information to be collected and catalogued; the use of common units for categorizing social facts; the process of capturing and classifying information according to these established units of analysis; and the analysis of the aggregated, standardized information. This process of identifying, classifying, and assessing social data from the Lobéké forest has produced an institutional view of social relations that is synoptic. Specific details of particular communities are digested, processed, and set aside, so that data can be presented in schematic form and used for practical, administrative purposes (Scott 1998).

The social simplifications "pygmy" and "villager" have been used as a binary rubric to understand and interact with the complex communities of Bangando, Baka, Bakwélé, and Mbomam in various contexts: in designing and implementing policies for conservation and development projects; in promoting and undertaking safari-hunting ventures; and in conversion, health care, and education programs offered through Christian missions in southeastern Cameroon. In each of these cases, the uncritical use of social stereotypes to describe and politically operationalize certain sectors of the complex, multiethnic society has resulted in unexpected outcomes and ramifications. In some cases, the outcomes have been negative, as the aggregate society finds itself marginalized through depictions of derogatory stereotypes. In other cases, unexpected outcomes have been positive for particular subsets of the multiethnic society, sometimes simultaneously fostering increased competition and unanticipated friction among members of the broader community. Marginalized communities are often quick to test and adapt new strategies that may alleviate pressing predicaments. Local people have found ingenious ways of circumventing and subverting categories of social simplification, often strategically manipulating these essentialized identities to their own benefit (Spivak 1988). The resilience of local communities in incorporating external social simplifications into their local discourse, and altering the references and applications of stereotypes to their advantage, highlights the wide array of political skills and social options available to people in southeastern Cameroon, tools that individuals utilize to maintain a sense of control over their social and political circumstances.

Conservation and Development

Baka Songs
The mysterious songs of the Baka are part of the great Congo Basin forest, vast almost beyond imagination. Dark, with dappled patches of sunlight and deep,

silent pools; shrill with the noise of insects and tree frogs; a riot of unfamiliar smells and scents; rich, musky, sharp, rotting, pungent, and spicy. This is the world of the Baka and also of the elephant, gorilla, grey parrot, civet cat and the shadowy, silent leopard, not forgetting the all-devouring forest ant. The Baka have lived in harmony with the forest for centuries both as its guardians and its children. Now, increasingly, their haunting songs are being drowned by the noise of the chain saw and the bulldozer. Poaching camps follow the bulldozer, and the wild animals disappear. In many villages, Jengi has not come for many years; there are no more joyous feasts, no youths are initiated; the culture of the Baka is dying.[1]

Images of forest peoples portrayed in conservation literature evoke intimate connections between endangered nature and endangered culture: just as natural species are at risk of extinction, unique cultural groups are dying out. The twin images of "pristine nature" and "primitive man" make frequent appearances in conservation rhetoric, despite the fact that forests throughout equatorial Africa have been mediated and managed by humans for millennia (Dounias 1993b; Burnham 2000), and communities throughout these forests have been engaged in global flows of economic, political, and social relationships for centuries (Vansina 1995; Klieman 2003). The link between the conservation of natural resources of the Lobéké forest region and the preservation of Baka "pygmies" is made clear by the World Wide Fund for Nature: "an important goal of this project is the maintenance of the forest environment for the long-term survival of the Baka people."[2]

Because of the policy focus on conservation of forest resources of southeastern Cameroon, the people of the region have been consistently classified by reference to their methods of engaging with the forest ecosystem: their subsistence practices. Beginning with the very first surveys of the Lobéké forest region, conducted in the late 1980s under the auspices of the Wildlife Conservation Society, local communities have been identified as either "hunter-gatherers" or as "farmers":

> [S]ixty percent of the population is represented by the Baka ethnic group, a group of hunter-gatherers who continue to use the forest. The Bangando, an ethnic group that practices horticulture (or agriculture) also uses the forest extensively. (Hall 1993: 32)

The classification of people by their apparent subsistence strategy offers convenient paradigms for managing people's interactions with natural resources in contexts of conservation. However, as indicated in this preliminary survey, "both of these ethnic groups consider the entire forest 'their' forest and continue to reap its benefits" (Hall 1993: 32). Over the course of fifteen years of conservation and development efforts that have built on this preliminary research, this nuance—as with many other details of overlapping, shared lives, practices, and spaces—has been lost in the process of simplifying and managing the forest system. As succinctly summarized in a 2006 overview by the World Wide Fund for Nature (WWF) of their conservation efforts, "the southeast forests of Cameroon are homeland to many indigenous ethnic groups, divided between the hunter-gatherer Baka people and the so-called slash-and-burn agriculturalists."[3]

Social analyses of the Lobéké forest region take categories of subsistence as their starting—and ending—points: "hunter-gatherers" and "farmers" provide the basic units for classifying the relations between social groups and their natural surroundings. Reliance on these reductive categories in the conceptualization and analysis of research, as well as in the design and implementation of policy, entails several flawed assumptions. First, subsistence categories and their corresponding ethnic categories are conceptualized as definitively dichotomous. "Hunter-gatherers" and "farmers"; "pygmies" and "villagers"; Baka and Bangando: never the twain shall meet. Subsistence practices are conceptualized as divergent strategies; the people who practice these techniques are conceptualized as discrete communities. Second, because of this trenchant dichotomy, evidence that "hunter-gatherers" also engage in agriculture and that "farmers" also hunt and gather forest resources tends to be disregarded. Similarly, insistence on the categorical conflation between subsistence and cultural identity erases from view any other cultural characteristics that might be relevant to the shaping of identities and relations among the diverse communities. These categories make no analytical room for creative combinations of subsistence strategies, or for cultural and social bridges that might allow ethnic communities to intermingle. Third, if two (or more) ethnic groups are classified according to the same subsistence strategy, then for analytical and administrative purposes, they are treated as equivalent and interchangeable. Finally, this model of opposition between communities characterized by divergent subsistence practices emphasizes a climate of polarization, mistrust, and the marginalization of "hunter-gatherers" while ignoring—or not even being able to recognize—interethnic relationships that are also mutually supportive and beneficial.

Reifying Social Categories through Development

While initial socioeconomic surveys were conducted by researchers and practitioners associated with conservation organizations, starting in 1996 the German development organization *Gesellschaft für technische Zusammenarbeit* (GTZ) assumed responsibility for aspects of research and administrative planning that concerned the social development of the people of the Lobéké forest region. Researchers working with GTZ conducted surveys to identify people of the region based on subsistence techniques, and to record social parameters that reflect spatial, economic, ritual, and social differences that were believed to derive from, and be reflected in, people's divergent ways of engaging with the forest.

While conservationists and development practitioners alike were certain that the main social target of their efforts was the "indigenous" community of Baka "pygmies" or "hunter-gatherers," the identities of the other communities of the forest communities were left vague. Reflecting generalizations in academic literature on "hunter-gatherer" communities throughout equatorial Africa, the category "Bantu" emerged as a catch-all category to identify and classify all "non-Baka" communities whose subsistence techniques were classified as "farming" or "fishing." "Bantu" communities were positioned over and against "Baka," encapsulating all "non-hunter-gatherer" communities. For example:

> The two main ethnic groups of people of the area are Bantus and Baka pygmies. The Bantus in the region make up more than 70% (20,000 inhabitants) of the population and sub-divided into nine tribal groups comprising principally the Mbimo, Movongmvong, Konabembe, Djem-Dzimou of Ngoila, Bakwele and Bangandos. About 20% of the population are Baka (5000 inhabitants) and the rest 10% (3000) are outsiders mainly Muslim traders.[4]

In literature on equatorial African forest, the disjuncture between very general groups of Bantu and very specific "pygmy" communities is pronounced. Development discourse emphasizes the differences between "Baka" and "Bantu" communities while overemphasizing the apparent similarities across all "Bantu" communities. In this binary scheme, being "not pygmy" emerges as a suitable criterion for classifying many diverse communities under a single conceptual umbrella.

As we have seen, Baka is the self-attributed name of a particular community of Baka language-speakers, a community whose cultural traditions are widely similar despite the great distances in southern and eastern Cameroon covered by the community. Bantu, on the other hand, is a linguistic term that refers to a vast and diverse community of speakers of related, but often mutually unintelligible, languages that derive from ancestral Bantu languages. Communities that spoke ancient Bantu languages spread from the Adamawa plateau across central, southern, and eastern Africa several millennia ago. "Bantu," when used as a reference to a specific cultural community, becomes an ethnogracization—an identifying label pinned to a community regardless of other salient cultural characteristics, and often resulting in the creation of an externally generated community where none existed previously (Clammer 1978). Moreover, some communities categorized as "Bantu" do not, in fact, speak Bantu languages; we have seen, for example, that Bangando linguistic roots are Ubangian.

The team of social scientists that oversaw the development component of the integrated conservation and development project in the Lobéké region inherited the categories for research, analysis, and administration from previous researchers and from academic analyses of other forest communities in equatorial Africa. The team's summary report frames the social context of the Lobéké forest by means of categories that underscore distinctions between Baka and other communities and simultaneously project remarkable homogeneity among the many non-Baka communities.

The local or autochthonous population is constituted of two very distinct groups:

The Baka Bagombé pygmies, who were probably the first occupants of the southern forest and who are still the majority in certain areas of the [Lobéké] site. Because of the process of sedentarization that was undertaken since about two decades by the administration and missionaries, the mode of life of the Baka has changed and today a large part of the Baka live temporarily in the villages of the Bantu. . . . Their social rapport with the Bantu has passed from barter for their products and patronage to truly commercial exchanges, even if the inequalities persist between the groups, the pygmies [being] considered by the Bantu as inferior beings.

The Bantu, who constitute several ethnic groups in the area (in its northern part, the Bidjuki, the Mbimu, the Mvongmvong, the Konabembe, and in the southern part the Boman, the Bangando, the Bakwele, the Sangha-Sangha, and in the part to the south-west of Ngoile the Djemnzimou). These groups, even if they belong to different clans, have characteristics that are generally communal. (Augustat 1997a: 2)

This portrayal of social dynamics in the broad region of southeastern Cameroon takes differences between Baka and all others as its starting point. The rigidity of this entrenched opposition between Baka and Bantu hinders the ability of the analyst (and audience) to see and explore social relations across ethnic lines that have proved to be critical in forming contemporary senses of identity and allegiance, or competition and conflict.

As a result of the totalizing classification "Bantu," social differences among distinct "Bantu" communities become difficult or impossible to distinguish. The presumption at the heart of this dichotomy is that all Bantu communities are more or less interchangeable in their oppositional relations with Baka "pygmies"; thus specific details about individual "Bantu" communities, or about relationships between particular "Bantu" communities and their Baka neighbors, do not receive analytical attention. This oversight is critical in the historical context of southeastern Cameroon. To roll the Bangando together with the "Djemnzimou" is to ignore the tumultuous and violent history of warfare and slave raiding that the Bangando and Baka endured at the hands of the Ndzimou, and that the Bakwélé and Baka endured at the detailed hands of the Djem (for discussion, see Rupp 2001).[5] The collective resistance posed by Bangando and Baka against the Ndzimou in the region of Salapoumbé is also significant because through this initial collaboration, Bangando and Baka built lasting relations of mutual trust and affiliation (Rupp 2001). Assuming that Bangando and Mbomam are equivalent, interchangeable "Bantu" communities is also to overlook the history of slavery, competition, and domination that influences these communities' relations even today. Furthermore, assuming that Bangando and Mbomam — as "Bantu" — are equivalent is to misunderstand the qualitative differences in these interethnic relations between each community and Baka. As we have seen, the inferior position of Mbomam to Bangando may facilitate more open and balanced relations between Mbomam and Baka than between Bangando and Baka, because Mbomam and Baka share a position of underdogs relative to the more socially and politically dominant Bangando community. The idea that nine culturally and linguistically distinct communities classified as "Bantu" can be accurately depicted as members of different "clans" who share communal characteristics is misleading, at best.

By homogenizing the cultural characteristics of "Bantu" communities and establishing their relevance through opposition to Baka, the points of tension, negativity, or division that may be typical of relations between one or some "Bantu" groups are extended to all. The analytical and administrative attention to Baka is justified by their equivalent, categorical divergence from *all* of their neighbors, who appear to be interchangeable by virtue of their shared "Bantu-"ness.

> Bantu and Pygmies (Baka): The cultural concepts of these two principal ethnic groups of the area are very different. This demands above all an approach adapted towards the Baka that permits their integration into the modern process of development and at the same time respects and values their specific culture. (Augustat 1997a: 4)

The analysis of Baka and "Bantu" relations argues that the most relevant component of Baka-Bantu relations is the degree of marginalization of Baka from the "modern process of development." In an extended argument, "Bantu" emerge as responsible for the disenfranchisement of "Baka" through their domination of economic, political, and social relations at the village level. Baka culture is degraded by its submission to "Bantu" villagers; thus the GTZ team advocates that the unique Baka culture deserves special protection through external interventions such as conservation and development.

Expressing impatience with academic studies (such as the present one) that attempt to analyze the identities of forest dwellers using internal contexts and criteria, development practitioners argued that analyzing processes of identity formation and change is irrelevant to contemporary conservation and development work. Defending the use of "Baka" and "Bantu" as categories for defining who is who in southeastern Cameroon, GTZ's lead anthropologist explained that "Baka" and "Bantu" serve as operational categories for analyzing identities and relationships among communities that are distinctly different. For the *Gesellschaft für technische Zusammenarbeit*, these categories are "working definitions" for research and policy design, and therefore need not reflect cultural detail.[6]

As has been critically analyzed by many scholars, a serious flaw in generating understandings of social identity is the tendency of social scientists conducting applied research to rely on the methodology of rapid appraisal of cultural contexts (Richards 1995; Green 2000; Biggs and Smith 2001). Both the empirical and practical tasks required of development practitioners are complicated: they have finite time to undertake field studies, to design appropriate plans of action, and to oversee the implementation of these plans. But for management plans to be effective, the initial step of data collection and analysis must be carried out according to contextual realities. Too often rapid assessments of social contexts rely on preconceived units of analysis, leading researchers to overlook cultural complexities and explain away information that contradicts anticipated results. This flawed, basic research results in policies that may contribute to the maintenance of external perceptions and categories rather than supporting local people, relationships, and institutions as they contend with social change and development. Rapid rural appraisals may provide a basis for recording apparent social facts, but do not effectively analyze competing and often discordant voices. Instead, how these "facts" correspond with preconceived categories and units of analysis determines their relevance for policy formulation.

In June 1997 the village of Dioula was targeted by GTZ's socioeconomic team as the site for a trial of the rapid rural appraisal plan that they had designed to gather information on the communities of southeastern Cameroon. For ten days a sprawling team of consultants, government officials, and representatives from regional development committees descended upon Dioula to work intensively with villagers to capture social and ecological information according to the categories that GTZ administrators had deemed to be relevant. Prior to their arrival in Dioula, the GTZ team had identified interest groups that they would target for information: Bangando and Baka; women and men; elders and youth. Following a strict schedule and outline of topics of information to gather, the team solicited responses from these interest groups concerning the layout of their village, areas of the forest that they utilize, land tenure, history of their village, economic activities and their organization in time and space, cultural activities, structures of social organization, and social priorities. Information about these topics is certainly relevant in providing baseline information about natural resource management in the forest. However, the formal and intense format of information-gathering sessions and the division of participants into predetermined groupings based on GTZ's assumptions of the lines of division within the community led to questionable conclusions.

The process of gathering, analyzing, and presenting the data was premised on divergences between the communities, "Baka" and "Bantu," as illustrated in three examples: discussion of spatial, social, and political relations in the village; the use of the contrast between "traditional" and "modern" to frame the analysis of data regarding "Baka" and "Bantu"; and discussions about interethnic relations. Taken together, this methodological approach resulted in a socioeconomic report about the village of Dioula that reflects stereotypes of "pygmies" and "villagers" and serves the administrative purpose of identifying "people of the forest" as the natural recipients of special consideration in the context of conservation of the Lobéké forest and the socioeconomic development of its "indigenous people."

In keeping with the stable stereotypes of "villagers" as institutionally dominant and "pygmies" as culturally preeminent, the GTZ report locates Bangando in square houses and organized villages, while Baka are portrayed as hunter-gatherers who live in "camps" and engage primarily in subsistence activities in the forest (Augustat 1997b: 12). Although the report discusses the increasing involvement of Baka in agriculture as well as in social and commercial networks, the tenor of the discourse suggests that these changes are recent, are imposed by outside institutions with the collusion of Bangando, and are fundamentally detrimental to Baka traditions.

> The process of sedentarization of the Baka pygmies, undertaken for more than a
> decade by the administration and missionaries, has brought well-known changes
> at the level of residential structures as well as at the level of the organization of
> production by the Baka. . . . The missionaries came and emphasized the process
> of sedentarization, and the different lineages regrouped themselves according to
> the alliances they had made with the families of their "friends." They generally
> built their camp next to the villagers and stayed more attached to their allies. . . .
> The different camps and lineages are placed under the authority of a chief (patri-
> arch) but who unfortunately is neither integrated nor recognized at the level of
> village institutions such as the customary tribunal; the inequalities observed
> between the Bangando and Baka explain this. (Augustat 1997b: 15)

This account of sedentarization and social relations raises several misleading implications. First, this account suggests that until very recently Baka were pure "hunter-gatherers," with the further suggestion that because of the short time horizon since their conversion to sedentary and agricultural ways, Baka remain "people of the forest" in their spiritual and cultural essence. But, as we saw in chapter two, Baka began the process of settling near villages and alongside Bangando, Bakwélé, and Mbomam, and diversified their subsistence practices to include some agricultural activities many generations ago, perhaps as early as the mid-nineteenth century.

Second, this account suggests that living alongside Bangando neighbors was fundamentally undesirable to Baka; pressure from the national administration and from foreign missionaries was required before Baka relented to being relocated near their Bangando partners (note that "friends" is placed in quotation marks in GTZ's report, calling into question the reliability of this term). Yet, as we have seen, processes of resettlement and the admixing of the diverse groups of southeastern Cameroon began long before the arrival of missionaries in the mid-1970s and prior to efforts by the German, French, and Cameroonian governments to fix roadside villages as the official unit of residence and most basic unit of political organization. As we have seen, the German colonial administration successfully compelled Bangando to build and then resettle along the colonial road near the Boumba River, and the French compelled Bangando to construct another road—in the current location— and to settle there. Although Baka retained relative autonomy from extralocal political authorities, many Baka families chose to live in proximity to their Bangando partners. The last Baka households that held fast to their forest villages were finally compelled to settle in roadside villages by the Cameroonian government, in collaboration with missionaries, during the 1970s.

Third, in this account the political role of a patriarchal Baka chief appears to have been artificially instituted, with families *placed* under his authority. At the same time, the report suggests that the authority of Baka chiefs is not formally recognized at the broader village (multiethnic) level. But, in fact, the role of elder Baka men as village leaders is not an externally created position; elder Baka men have played a critical role in multiethnic community decision making since the mid-nineteenth century, when Baka and Bakwélé lived together at Ndjàngé. As this ethnography has illustrated, Baka individuals rise to positions of social, ritual, and political leadership through organic processes. Contemporary Baka elders do participate meaningfully in village-wide decision-making bodies; their voices and perspectives are heard in village meetings and decisions, and importantly, Baka perspectives are considered alongside any others in the customary tribunal. External observers consistently present the "relation of submission" (Augustat 1997b: 18) as a straightforward equation of domination (by "Bantu") and submission (by "pygmies"), a relation of structural inequality that is then condemned. But the insistence on fundamental imbalances of social and political power as the central, determining feature of interethnic relations reflects a lack of understanding of the degree to which the multiethnic communities are integrated at various formal and informal levels: through intermarriage, joint participation in rituals, ceremonies, and rites of passage, collaboration in meeting daily needs and desires, and in sorting through political, economic, and social stresses that confront the entire community.

Finally, the representation of Baka as inert social actors in processes of social change unfairly suggests that Baka are incapable of making, or unwilling to initiate, changes of their own accord, and in their own interests.

The final GTZ summary report of their rapid rural appraisal exercise in Dioula presents the "*structures modernes*" that pertain to Bangando and to Baka in discrete sections, imputing a structural divergence of the two communities that does not exist (1997b: 14-15). "Modern" structures of social and political organization are attributed to Bangando, while "traditional" rituals and values are associated with Baka. In presenting Bangando institutions, the GTZ social scientists note several associations and committees, including the committee that oversees the village dispensary, an association of women known by its formal French title and acronym as ASSOFADI (and known locally as *Éésòngé*, discussed in chapter six), an inactive association of young planters of Dioula, and CODEGED, the village committee for development and conservation. In addition, the authors discuss the various religious congregations and communities in Dioula, including the Evangelical Mission of Cameroon (MEEC), the Presbyterian Church (EPC), a small community of Muslims, and a handful of Catholics who attend mass in a small church in Mbateka, one village to the south. Finally, the authors discuss the unanimous village support of the RDPC (Rassemblement Démocratique du Peuple Camerounais), the governing political party in Cameroon, and its *Comité de Base* in Dioula. Although these political and religious institutions in Dioula are presented as if they exclusively involve Bangando, these "modern structures" involve both Bangando and Baka as well as the handful of Bakwélé and Mbomam who are residents in Dioula. In fact, the Evangelical Mission of Cameroon is specifically targeted to Baka, with the goal of "healing their bodies and spirits" through conversion to evangelical Christianity.[7] Even this Baka-specific mission includes a handful of Bangando participants among the largely Baka congregation, indicating the tendency for the interethnic communities to participate in each others' institutions and experiences, even those targeted at one subset of the village. By presenting these "modern" institutional structures in their report as if they pertain only to Bangando, the GTZ authors misrepresent the degree to which Baka actively participate in and are integrated into these contemporary political, social, and religious institutions that serve the multiethnic community in Dioula.

Whereas "modern" social and political institutions are portrayed as belonging to and dominated by Bangando, the GTZ report represents "traditional rites" as almost exclusively the domain of Baka (Augustat 1997b: 11-13). The authors mention the existence of Bangando ceremonies, but do not elaborate on the context, practice, or significance of these ceremonies. The vast bulk of the discussion about "traditional structures" centers on Baka dances, ceremonies, and rites as though the Baka alone maintain a richly textured spiritual and ritual life based on "traditional" practices. But, as we have seen, Bangando and Baka jointly participate in numerous ceremonies and rituals, some of which are central to both communities. Bangando increasingly participate in the crucial Baka initiation ceremony of jengì, while Baka increasingly take part in the fearsome Bangando ritual marking the rite of passage of a deceased elder, dɨɔ. Interethnic participation in these ritual processes is not mentioned until the insertion of a brief and unelaborated comment toward the end of the report. Importantly, nowhere is the multiethnic circumcision ceremony, bέkà, mentioned as a critical way that Bangando, Baka, Bakwélé, and Mbomam men build a coherent and collaborative social and ritual system.

The discussion of "modern structures" and "traditional structures" in reference to Bangando and Baka, respectively, combined with the lack of acknowledgment of the central political institutions and ritual ceremonies that the communities share, only serves to perpetuate inadequate representations of diametrically opposed communities: Bangando as modern, politically controlling, and institutionally dominant; Baka as traditional, culturally valorized, and ritually diverse. In these representations the world of the "villagers" is presented as institutionalized and organized, while the world of the "pygmies" continues to be dominated by images of primitive culture embedded within the overarching forest.

The GTZ report focuses on interethnic conflicts as the seminal interactions that mold social relationships and identities. Although GTZ social scientists parenthetically note that "in the socio-cultural sphere, several parameters demonstrate effective and sincere relations between Baka and Bantu," these mutually supportive and constructive social relations are not elaborated (1997b: 18). Instead, throughout GTZ's reports on communities in southeastern Cameroon, information on the interfaces between diverse communities highlights conflicts that arise between Baka and "Bantu." Not only are communities defined in opposition to each other, but potential contexts of constructive and supportive overlap—such as joint participation in ritual ceremonies, collective participation in shared secret societies, parallel clan structures, and collaborative work efforts—are overlooked at the same time that dynamics of conflict are emphasized. In its portrayal of interethnic relationships, the GTZ report stresses inequality and exploitation as the defining modes of interaction: Baka complain that they are exploited as laborers in Bangando gardens; Baka claim that their views are not represented in village committees; Baka accuse Bangando men of refusing to pay bride price when they marry Baka wives. According to evidence collected through sustained ethnographic research, Baka do complain occasionally that they feel exploited by their Bangando partners and neighbors as manual laborers in Bangando gardens and cocoa plantations. The context of airing such complaints is significant for analyzing their substance and goals: these complaints are often aired in contexts in which Baka hope to gain immediate material support from their Bangando partners who may overhear or be indirectly informed about the complaint. Viewing the accusation of exploitation in a social vacuum promotes a static and preconceived idea of social injustice, but does not facilitate an understanding of the dynamics of social relations that may, or may not, reflect patterns of unjust social relations. In the context of formal interviews conducted by GTZ, the reiteration of limited Baka participation in and representation on village-wide committees seems aimed at the overt goal of securing structural positions of power for Baka individuals on development committees, which is a worthwhile goal. But this antagonistic approach reveals relatively little about the relationships of power and influence in the village when outside investigations are not explicitly arousing sentiments of opposition and prospects for social improvement. Finally, accusations that "Bantu" men do not pay the bride-price to the families of a Baka women when they marry typifies tension between husbands and their in-laws regardless of ethnic affiliation of either spouse. Recall the protestations by Pando, a Bangando man, that his daughter ought not marry a Baka husband for fear that the groom would not pay her bride-price. Accusations of refusal to pay bride-price, or paying a skimpy bride-price, abound between a Bangando man and his Bangando fiancée's family, between a Baka man and his Baka fiancée's family, and between men and their interethnic in-laws. Furthermore, gracious acceptance of an interethnic marriage by both partners and their families is also frequent, as we saw in chapter four through the example of the marriage of Pando and his Baka wife, Laati. By soliciting Baka grievances against their neighbors, external institutions foster an atmosphere that elaborates and emphasizes conflict, to the detriment of both the communities involved and the goals of conservation and development.

The GTZ report presents perceptions of interethnic relations only from the point of view of Baka participants, suggesting that Bangando had no opportunity to articulate their frustrations or joys with their neighbors, had no chance to respond to the issues raised by Baka, or that their views were simply ignored in the analysis. More important still, no discursive space was provided for either community to discuss the positive ways that their communities support each other in daily pursuits, in friendships and other amicable social relationships, in collaborative efforts both in the forest and in gardens, and in cooperation through associations and village committees. Searching for points of tension to the exclusion of looking for points of cooperation reinforces social disequilibrium and discord and may formalize tensions that are a normal part of communal living, while simultaneously withholding official recognition of avenues for reconciling differences. While overstated accounts of social disharmony may bolster the ideological agendas of development organizations, conflicts may be reconstituted through the explicit search for relationships of oppression. Because of the imbalanced context in which information on tensions is solicited—Baka responding to GTZ's preformulated questions about social disharmony— relations of conflict are invariably articulated as the perpetration of social ills by "Bantu" at the expense of "Baka."

Once interethnic relations in southeastern Cameroon are documented and institutionalized, the stereotype of "Bantu"/"villager"/Bangando as oppressor becomes a difficult prejudice to overcome. The categories that GTZ's social scientists utilized to frame their research and analysis—"Bantu" vs. "Baka"—do more than serve as descriptive modifiers for particular communities. More powerfully still, these simplistic, binary categories provide policy parameters within which administrative objectives and methods are established. As a result of the preconceptions, biases, and omissions embedded in the classificatory models, it is not surprising that studies and development initiatives in southeastern Cameroon tend to privilege the perceived needs of Baka at the expense of a more balanced approach to addressing the concerns of the multiethnic community at large. For the purposes of development and conservation in southeastern Cameroon, "Baka" remain rigidly opposed to "Bantu," and "Bantu" remain an undifferentiated mass of equivalent, interchangeable "non-pygmies" who seem not quite "authentic" enough—and too oppressive—to deserve the analytical or policy attention of development practitioners.

Even as their analyses reinforce and reinscribe divisive social categories, GTZ's social science team sees itself as providing a platform for open communication among the communities of the Lobéké forest region.

We hope to provide conditions for dialogue, negotiation, and a partnership in the management of forest space. Communication is important to help the groups in question to know each other, to understand their differences better, to understand better how the others represent their stake, to stimulate a critical reflection that will reveal the scenario and the rules of the game accepted by all. (Ngiunguiri, Mouncharou, and Augustat 1999: 4)

While communication and increased understanding *are* critical to the success of development and conservation initiatives, it is ironic that external practitioners, who consistently demonstrate an inability to analyze local contexts by means of local concepts, present themselves as the medium through which nuanced understandings of the social dynamics among the communities of southeastern Cameroon, and effective communication among various interest groups, can be realized. The communities of the Lobéké forest region have been working out identities and relationships within and among themselves for most of the past two centuries; it is unlikely that they require partial analyses by external observers to know and understand each other better. It is also unlikely that partial analyses will result in impartial policies that advance the socioeconomic interests of the entire multiethnic community.

Missionization

In their dual quest to bring the light of Christianity to communities that are furthest from God and to bring them enlightenment through education and access to health care, missionization efforts in southeastern Cameroon mobilize familiar stereotypes of "pygmies" as remnants of pristine peoples. Images presented by missionaries invoke parallels between the oppression endured by "pygmies" and the early Christian community. Père D'Hellemmes, a Belgian priest who dedicated his life to missionizing the Baka of northern Congo and is a much-celebrated personality in the Catholic community throughout equatorial Africa, offers an introduction to "pygmies" for his European, Catholic audience:

This Pygmy, is he our brother? What will we do to help him? His poverty is unimaginable. It is comparable to that of a new-born baby who came into the world one night, in a stable in Judea. In Africa, Jesus would have chosen to be born in a Pygmy hut. Even more miserable than a stable, there is this circular hut of two and a half meters in diameter and one meter sixty centimeters high in the middle, made of leaves, and where five or six people live. It is their only roof. . . .

In the African countries on the path to development, they voluntarily say that the Pygmy is the man of the forest, the primitive hunter. No insult is intended by this term, even if one pretends to oneself that it is a savage, a being at the margin of civilization. A primitive? That's it, exactly. (D'Hellemmes 1985: 15)

Missionary discourse not only emphasizes the primitivity of "pygmies" and their fundamental, inherent need for liberation from their poverty, but also stresses the inherent need of "pygmies" for liberation from their diametrically opposed and socially oppressive neighbors, variously referred to as the "Big Blacks," the "Bantus," and the "villagers":

He [the Pygmy] lives separately from the other ethnic groups, the "Big Blacks," the Bantus, an important group of African tribes that possess specific, shared characteristics, above all in their linguistics. Nothing to do with the Pygmy language. . . . The Pygmy also distinguishes himself from the Bantu by his mode of life. Whereas the other Africans are sedentary, cultivators attached to their corner of earth, the Pygmies do not stay in the same place. They do not build villages. They live in camps that they abandon without regret, in one night, when they judge it to be good [to leave]. For them, the house is this immense forest, high and without a horizon, this ocean of leaves where others lose themselves, turning around in circles sometimes for days as they search for their path. There [in the forest] the Pygmy feels at home, even at night. He possesses all of its secrets. (D'Hellemmes 1985: 17-18)

Throughout the forests of central Africa, many missionaries have focused their efforts specifically on "pygmies," striving to show the path to God, the path to development, and the path away from perceived dependence on their "Bantu" neighbors. Some missions exclude the much-denigrated "villagers" from participating in missionary activities, justifying this exclusion on the premise that "villagers" are socially, morally, and spiritually distinct from "pygmies." Describing with joy his arrival at a "pygmy" camp and his distribution of free clothing as he banters with the enthusiastic participants, Père D'Hellemmes' tone shifts dramatically when he realizes that a solitary "villager" woman had mingled in with the "pygmies," also hoping to benefit from his distribution:

I take up my work [of distributing clothing and medication] again. At one time or another, my beard straightens out: a Bantu villager woman, very discretely, has infiltrated into the middle of the Pygmies to profit from the free distribution. "What are you doing there? This is not for you! You have nothing to do here. All of these clothes are for them."

The villager woman slowly pulled herself away with a longing look towards the trunk and the tragic air of a martyr. So there are only things for the Pygmies! (D'Hellemmes 1985: 12)

While it would be unfair to attribute this severe exclusion of people perceived as "villagers" to all missionaries working in the Lobéké region, the mission projects are specifically designed to address the needs of the Baka community. The perspectives offered by Père D'Hellemmes are broadly embraced by much of the Catholic mission community in southeastern Cameroon: in Moloundou the dust jacket of his memoir (*Le Père des Pygmées*, quoted above) is pinned prominently to the central bulletin board of the main mission office.

Missionization in the East Province of Cameroon proceeded in fits and starts, initially sponsored by the American Presbyterian church in the Yokadouma region, some 200 kilometers from the northernmost village in the Boumba-Ngoko region. Despite the distance, a dozen or so Bangando men took advantage of both the religious and secular education offered by the American missionaries in the Bulu language, a language that is widely spoken in south-central Cameroon. The majority of the residents of the far southeastern corner of Cameroon, however, did not experience missionization until the early 1970s, when the Catholic mission society of Charles de Foucauld established a mission station at Salapoumbé. Many of the founders had already spent many years working in central Africa; social simplifications of who was who in central African social systems arrived with them and served as the orienting categories for understanding the new social, cultural, and natural context of southeastern Cameroon.

Sister Agathe, an elderly sister who specializes in linguistics, arrived in Salapoumbé in 1974 with the specific goal of learning the Baka language to facilitate the mission's goal of bringing the word of God to the Baka community. Reflecting on the early days of the mission, she explains that her congregation, the *Petites Soeurs de la Fondation,* came to southeastern Cameroon to work specifically with the Baka community because they represent two-thirds of the population of the region but remained the most *éloingés—*

distant. The implications of this "distance" are twofold: Baka are perceived both as distant from the Christian God and from a developed or civilized way of life.

Yet embedded in these perceptions is an odd paradox. For in their primitivity, Baka are represented in missionary discourse as a conflation of the ignoble and noble savage: they are portrayed as eternally impoverished, unable to contend with the vast changes of modernity, while they are simultaneously celebrated for their pure and uncorrupted spirits. Thus, Catholic missionaries such as Père D'Hellemmes and Sister Agathe strive to bring the light of God and the benefits of development to "pygmies," but simultaneously decry the changes that ensue when Baka embrace the social, economic, and technological transformations that are introduced into their lives, actively shaping these changes and incorporating them into their day-to-day experiences.

Today, after dedicating over thirty years of her life to the mission and community at Salapoumbé, Sister Agathe is very pessimistic about the changes she has seen in the conditions of life and the attitudes of Baka. It is economic development, she argues stridently, that has destroyed families and villages. Today Baka struggle to find some money so that they can buy clothes and alcohol, but they forget to feed their children and to keep them clean. Some women come to Mass every Sunday wearing a different piece of clothing, she exclaims. Agathe bemoans the increasing promiscuity of Baka girls, chastising adolescent girls for undertaking baptism even when they are pregnant, pregnant before they have undertaken proper marriage rites. One young Baka woman is the mistress (*femme*) of the mayor of Salapoumbé. Full of doom and doubt, Agathe decries how this young woman is working "double duty" for the mayor, performing household work by day and sex by night. "How can this woman be satisfied with a few clothes and some soap in return?" she laments.

Throughout her discussion of contemporary Baka, Sister Agathe repeated again and again that economic development has brought about the grave decline of Baka society and culture. She openly criticized the idea that Baka are more "developed" today than when she arrived in 1974. From her perspective, Baka who continue to build *mòngúlu* (dome-shaped, leaf-shingled houses) for their families to live in, who hunt and gather and feed their children, who care for their children when they are sick using traditional methods and medicines, are more "progressed" than Baka who live in Salapoumbé, whom Agathe describes as drunkards. Yet Sister Agathe was not interested in discussing possible causes and potential outcomes of the contradictory changes that she has seen. Refusing to discuss the transformation in social contexts and identities that she described and decried, Agathe burst out: "It's not that I can't say [what I've seen]! I live! I see things as they are! The Baka are the Baka. They are as they are!" Several times when discussing Baka participation in economies of money and consumption, sex and alcohol, she pulled her eyelids down over her eyes with her fingers: she so despises the changes she has witnessed that she prefers no longer to see contemporary Baka society. Agathe seems to have concluded with finality that Baka, once noble in their purity and primitivity, are slipping further and further into depravity and vice, the wrong side of development, characterized by greed for money, alcohol, and sex.[8]

Sister Agathe's opinions typify the negativity articulated by numerous missionaries, but are certainly not representative of all perspectives. Another Catholic sister who travels widely throughout the region pointed out that Baka who live near the mission at Salapoumbé are among the most dependent, lazy, and spiritually impoverished Baka that she has encountered in the entire Lobéké forest region. Because initially the mission offered handouts of supplies such as salt, soap, and kerosene to attract Baka to their center, a steady stream of local people in search of easy access to free goods began to flow into Salapoumbé. While the mission today no longer offers free distribution of basic commodities, it remains a context of unmatched support and opportunity. Baka present themselves at the mission seeking casual labor, usually drawing water or cutting grass at the sisters' domestic compound, or offering items such as bushmeat, eggs, and avocados for sale. Baka are fully aware that the mission also provides a source of support for their children through the preschool education program, and Baka children spend hours on the volunteer teachers' verandah, reading books and playing games, and also taking advantage of food or small presents offered to them.

The biases of the Catholic mission in favor of Baka is evident in three integral projects: assisting Baka integration into regional commercial markets, offering preschool education to Baka children, and providing health care at subsidized rates to Baka patients. Missionaries explain the rationale for each of these Baka-centered programs by citing social inequalities that place Baka consistently under the thumb of "Bantu." Sister Thérèse arrived in southeastern Cameroon in 1995 because the escalating chaos and violence in Congo-Brazzaville, where she had served for thirty-seven years, finally forced the mission station to close. Thérèse wholeheartedly took up the mission of evangelizing and assisting Baka in southeastern Cameroon, fervently committed to her calling to help Baka develop socially, economically, and spiritually to show that they are no different from and not inferior to any of their "Bantu" neighbors.[9] Spending time with Thérèse as she interacts with Baka, it is evident that she is passionately dedicated to helping them—through sedentarization, education, and conversion. Passing by enormous gardens carved out of the forest alongside logging roads, she exclaims with utter delight, "What lovely gardens!" Sister Thérèse's activities focus on promoting what she considers a "healthy work ethic" and the integration of Baka into the local economy by means agricultural production. When discussing the difficult balance between large-scale agriculture and forest conservation, she emphatically argued that the goal *should* be "the conservation of Baka and their forest, not simply conservation of nature." After all, she argued, the Baka *are* the first inhabitants of the forest, and thus they should be protected and preserved.[10]

This cultural preservationist approach is seemingly at odds with her campaign to integrate Baka into the regional commercial agricultural markets, by focusing on the production of plantains and the manufacture of banana flour for use in baking. Sister Thérèse makes frequent trips in the mission pickup truck to a cluster of Baka gardens located east of Dioula, which she reaches by following forty kilometers of abandoned logging roads from the mission station at Moloundou. These deep forest gardens—*mbándà*—were initially planted by Zoduma and Besombo, a Bangando couple, and their Baka partners (see chapter six). Many years ago Zoduma and Besombo decided to live at their *mbándà* to take advantage of the fertile soils, rich hunting grounds, and abundant streams. Two Baka families—their long-term, intergenerational partners (*bándí*)—moved with them into the forest and planted gardens of their own. These gardens and the surrounding forest provide for the subsistence needs of the Bangando and Baka families, and also enable them to grow plantains and cocoa for the regional commercial market. Five Baka families now live at the settlement in the forest in addition to Zoduma and Besombo; collectively they have cleared a swath of the forest for their gardens. When Thérèse arrives, she stops her truck at a small but growing pile of green plantains, tied together into bundles to be sold for 300 CFA (about US$ 0.60) each at the Moloundou market. As Baka women carry their plantains toward the truck, Zoduma and Besombo remain out of sight, at work in their garden; Thérèse has come to assist Baka, not Bangando, in keeping with her mission to help Baka help themselves. As she prepares to leave the gardens, she advises the knot of Baka planters to have seventy-five bundles of plantains ready for her next collection in a few weeks' time instead of the forty bundles that they had prepared for this visit, as she will charge them 5,000 CFA (about US$ 10.00) to cover the cost of petrol.

While Sister Thérèse's efforts, and the broader work of the Catholic mission in Moloundou, are laudable in bringing much-needed and greatly appreciated aid to a very poor community, the situation facing many Baka families is not so much more difficult than that experienced by other families in southeastern Cameroon to justify their exclusive assistance. As Baka planters in the distant forest gardens watch Sister Thérèse drive off, their plantains piled high in the back of her truck, with a handful of their relatives perched atop the load to oversee the sale of the produce in Moloundou, Zoduma and Besombo prepare their heavy baskets to carry their produce by foot back to Dioula, where they will sell their plantains and cocoa in front of their house to whatever truck may stop along the road. Not only do they incur the additional costs in time, energy, and frustration in carrying their heavy baskets back to the village along fifteen kilometers of slippery, twisting forest paths, but the decentralized market of the village offers a much riskier economic context for making their sale. At the same time, their Baka partners did manage to include some of Zomduma and Besombo's plantains in the load that the mission transported to Moloundou, undermining the missionaries' perception of the clear social and economic divide between "pygmies" and "villagers" and of their own efforts to target their aid specifically at Baka planters, to the exclusion of others.

Another program sponsored by the Catholic mission in southeastern Cameroon is the preschool program, the educational component of the mission's "Projet Pygmées." This program, called ORA, is based on the principles "*Observir! Reflechir! Agir!*" (observe, reflect, act), and is intended to prepare Baka children to enter the dilapidated Cameroonian public school system. As with the economic development assistance offered by the mission, the education program is based on the fundamental assumption that Baka children can justifiably be singled out to benefit from special assistance. Yet the structural collapse of the school system throughout southeastern Cameroon has effectively rendered children and young adults throughout the entire region functionally illiterate and innumerate, regardless of their belonging to any particular ethnic group.

Recognizing the educational needs of the broader community of southeastern Cameroon, the ORA school program does accept small numbers of Bangando, Bakwélé, and Mbomam children in the preschools, provided that the majority of students are Baka. Their inclusion in the schools is enormously appreciated by all the families whose children benefit. Standing in the shade of a mango tree for his self-portrait, a Bangando father held two items that represent his most cherished goals: in one hand he held his child's ORA school book, explaining that his future lies in his children, and that his children's future lies in their education. In his other hand he held a machete, describing it as the foundation of his life. He relies on his machete to work in his garden to feed his family, and to work in his cocoa plantation to earn enough money to pay school fees to send his children to the ORA school program.[11]

Despite the acute need for education across all ethnic communities in southeastern Cameroon, the mission preschool education program is clearly targeted at Baka children. When a conflict between the mission's requirement of monogamy and a Baka teacher's marriage to a second wife erupted at an ORA school in Ngola, Baka families withdrew their children from the school in solidarity with the teacher. With no Baka children attending the school, leaving only a handful of Bangando and Mbomam pupils in attendance, the mission closed down the entire ORA program in Ngola, pending resolution of the conflict. The Catholic mission certainly has the perogative to suspend programs that they organize and support through their own resources; yet the narrow vision of social relations and perceptions of social inequality hinder their ability to effect broad, positive changes in the lives of the people of southeastern Cameroon, who are poor and structurally marginalized in broader regional, national, and international perspectives. The ideological and practical emphasis on Baka over and above all other local people, who are lumped together into the monolithic, opposed category of "Bantu," obscures the high degree of overlap in the socioeconomic, political, and cultural contexts that are directly relevant to the shared experiences of poverty and marginalization that typify the multiethnic society of this corner of Cameroon.

Beyond efforts at socioeconomic development and preschool education, the most important service offered by the Catholic mission is the health care center and dispensary, which provide the most comprehensive, reliable, and affordable health care in the entire region between Moloundou and Yokadouma. The health care center was established to meet the needs of the Baka community, although, even in its early days, the missionaries did not refuse care to others who sought treatment. However, consultation and treatment were provided to Baka free of charge, while local people who were categorized as "Bantu"—including Bangando, Bakwélé, and Mbomam—were charged full price for medical services. Because of the tension generated by this policy of unequal treatment, a nurse convinced the mission that Baka should pay something toward their health care, taking a step toward acknowledging that the multiethnic community in southeastern Cameroon collectively faces extremely difficult social and economic conditions, and that Baka cannot be justifiably singled out for such imbalanced benefits without provoking conflict.

Today Bangando and Baka come in roughly equal numbers to the health clinic at the Catholic mission in Salapoumbé for serious illnesses that require hospitalization. And roughly equal numbers of Bangando and Baka are actually hospitalized. Bangando use the clinic for general consultations more frequently than Baka, however. When Baka receive treatments they pay whatever they can pull together—a little bit of money, a couple of eggs, some plantains. Fees for Baka patients are reduced; for example, they pay 5 CFA per quinine tablet, whereas a "Bantu" patient would be charged 10 CFA per tablet, and a timber company employee or government official would be charged 15 CFA per tablet.[12] In addition to the higher price charged for medication, "Bantu" patients are assessed a consultation fee, which is waived for Baka. Furthermore, if Baka arrive with no money to pay for their treatment, the nurses will give the consultation and medical advice for no fee and will give the patient one day's worth of medication, requiring the patient to return the following day to collect the remainder of the dosage and to pay for the medication.[13]

Identifying who is who for the purposes of health care is not always a straightforward or transparent process. Because most Baka and many Bangando do not have identity cards that definitively state their official ethnic designation, nurses' discretion is required when assessing charges for medical treatment. In addition, because interethnic parentage is common, clear distinctions between the communities are not always evident. Although initially, extralocal nurses claimed that they could identify the ethnic identities of their patients with certainty, after discussion they admitted that it is sometimes difficult to know who is who. Nurses indicated that they rely on physical traits such as height and facial appearance, filed teeth, ragged clothing, and the lilting, rhythmic accent of the Baka language to identify their Baka patients. As long as patients cannot be clearly categorized at the other socioeconomic extreme, as a government official or a timber company employee, the nurses treat all other patients as "Bantu." According to Cécile, a volunteer French nurse, if she is unsure about a patient's identity, she asks the patient if he is Bangando. If the patient is Baka, he will not accept the label Bangando as it means he must pay a higher price for medication. And if the patient is Bangando, the nurse argued that he will usually accept this label even though it entails paying a higher price for the medical treatment because it signals his position within the more influential community in the region. Baka individuals in Salapoumbé, however, are convinced that many Bangando manipulate the system, presenting themselves in accordance with outsiders' expectations of Baka to take advantage of reduced fees for medical treatment. Such speculation of manipulation of ethnic affiliations reveals the degree to which perceptions of social identity are multiple and slippery. Local people are acutely aware that outsiders hold particular expectations and images of the various communities, and in many contexts local people are willing to play along with these stereotypes where the practical outcomes are beneficial. In practice, the director of the health center, Sister Geneviève, accepts whatever payment she feels a patient can afford to pay. She is more tolerant of her Baka patients' inability to pay, although if an evidently poor Bangando arrives at the clinic, especially to treat a child, Geneviève will reduce the charges. This approach acknowledges the overall context of poverty and marginalization that faces the multiethnic community of southeastern Cameroon, regardless of externally generated, "official" categories or internally manipulated expressions of social identity.

Safari Hunting

Throughout the tourist literature on hunting in central Africa, perceptions abound of the African equatorial forest as the last sliver of true wilderness supporting exotic fauna and housing the last shreds of primitive man. In colonial as well as contemporary hunting, "pygmies" consistently serve as trackers, the guiding link between the civilized world of the tourist hunters and the savage, wild world of the equatorial forest. The context of trophy hunting in southeastern Cameroon reveals the enduring quality of Euroamerican stereotypes of "pygmies" as expert hunters and trackers— quintessential forest people—while also demonstrating local hunters' strategic manipulation of these stereotypes to ensure personal profit and burnish their own identities as hunters.

Safari companies that operate in southeastern Cameroon advertise their adventures through the linked images of the primitive hunt of exotic forest game and the expert tracking skills of primitive "pygmy" trackers. Tourists who specialize in safari hunting in Africa consistently cite hunting bongo with "pygmy" trackers as a highlight, even a pinnacle, of their hunting experiences. As promoted by Safari Club International, the official body representing thousands of hunters internationally:

> There is no other country in the last decade that has developed its forest hunting so well that nearly every hunter seeking western Bongo will first look at the safaris being offered in the equatorial rain forests in the southeast corner of Cameroon. Hunting Bongo with Pygmy trackers and their dogs has produced almost 100 percent success. This is not an easy hunt by any interpretation, but if a hunter can walk well and can put up with constantly high humidity and heat, and can shoot reasonably well, he or she has an excellent chance to collect this most beautiful antelope. The concept of hunting Bongo with Pygmies and dogs is by no means new in that part of Africa. It is, after all, the way Pygmies hunt. (Safari Club International 1997: 2)

Images of the central African forest portrayed in promotional literature for trophy hunting in the twenty-first century echo images of primeval forest, pristine wildlife, and primitive man evoked in memoirs of colonial-era hunters. Describing his hunting expedition in the Ituri forest during 1912-14, Cuthbert Christy captures the common colonial sentiment that all of the primitive species of the tropical forest have remained static since time immemorial.

> [T]he Ituri Pygmies, whether primitive or indigenous, or introduced and degraded as regards stature, are the last remaining representatives of the inhabitants of forest-covered Africa. . . . This forest is a partially isolated equatorial remnant of the vast primeval forests which at one time covered the continent. It is, moreover, still a portion of "darkest Africa," one of the spots yet almost undisturbed by modern man. . . . the original stock left in the forest, such as the little red buffalo, the okapi and the forest elephant, have remained like the Pygmies unmodified, or at any rate less changed, to the present day. (Christy 1924: 50-51)

Themes of African forests, animals, and hunters resonate across the century and a half of European experiences in "darkest Africa," and find concrete expression in contemporary images of southeastern Cameroon. Images of the mysterious forest filled with exotic animals continue to prevail in popular literature on and advertising for hunting expeditions in the Lobéké forest region.

Bongo Hunting in Cameroon: The Land of the Pygmies
Tucked away in the extreme southeast of Cameroon . . . lies the deep jungle, the mystic land of giant trees, mighty elephants, elusive Bongo and the most proficient

hunter/gatherers of all: the pygmies. Our outfitter was the first commercial safari operator in this secluded spot of the dark continent, with the owner establishing his first camp there 15 years ago. . . . [T]o this day our outfitter has the very best area, the best pygmy hunters and the most experienced PH's [Professional Hunters] for the demanding, challenging and unique safaris, in quest of the most elusive of all African game species, the Bongo, as well as Dwarf Forest buffalo, Giant Forest Hog, Forest Elephant, Sitatunga and a variety of forest Duiker species.[14]

The tropical forest seems to be replete with creatures and trees of fantastic sizes—giant trees and giant forest hogs, dwarf buffalos and small forest elephants, pygmy chimpanzees and pygmy people. These beings are portrayed as living and breathing examples of perpetual primitivity for as long as their species defy extinction, a compelling image of the forest that has stood the test of time.

In addition to bringing home animal trophies from the Lobéké forest, tourist hunters often seek "pygmy" artifacts as emblems of the timelessness of the people of the forest. Taking advantage of tourists' appetites for cultural objects that authenticate their encounter with primitive "pygmies," a handful of local artisans waits each evening as the tourists return from their afternoon hunt, hoping to interest them in their crafts. But rather than arriving with readymade crafts to sell, the artisans—both Bangando and Baka—describe the various kinds of items that they can produce within the remaining time of the hunting expedition, and receive orders and specifications. Thus "pygmy" crossbows and spears, drums and mats, can be fabricated according to the desires of the tourists. These cultural constructions of primitive "pygminess" offer a way for tourists to validate their hunting experience according to Euroamerican perceptions of both the forest and its people, and allow them to take into consideration the dimensions of their suitcases and space left between their trophies on their living room walls.

The constructedness of the cultural artifacts parallels tourists' willingness to believe that all people who live and hunt in the forest are "pygmies." Contemporary tourist hunters assume that all local hunters who track their trophy animals *are* actually "pygmies."[15] However, "pygmy" hunters who are hired to serve as trackers for tourists include Bangando as well as Baka hunters. Safari operators are less concerned that the men they employ as "pygmy" trackers *are* "pygmies" than that they contribute their skills in reading tracks and animal signs to the hunt, ensuring the wealthy clients the chance to shoot their trophies. Thus each year in early February, when the French safari operators arrive in southeastern Cameroon to prepare for the opening of the tourist hunting season, Bangando and Baka hunters report to the safari camp in the hope of being hired as "pygmy" trackers. Based on previous years' employment with the company, and on their performance as general forest workers as they prepare for the arrival of the tourists, the most capable and cooperative employees are retained for the tourist season. While many of the trackers are Baka, a significant minority are Bangando. According to Sombale, a Bangando hunter from Dioula, he fully realizes that the tourist hunters assume that he, along with all the other trackers, is a "pygmy." Sombale is also cognizant of the contradictory values held by Euroamerican hunters as they embrace "pygmies" as pure and pristine forest people and simultaneously deride them as primitive and ignorant. Dismissing the derogatory connotations inherent in images of "primitive pygmies," Sombale cheerfully explained that he is quite content to be regarded as a "pygmy" by strangers who come to hunt for a short time. His work for these strangers provides him with income as well as with meat from the hunt, which he can send back to his family in Dioula. Like many local hunters, Bangando and Baka alike, Sombale is quite willing temporarily to assume the image of "pygmy hunter" as projected by Euroamerican clients; the money and meat provided by these wealthy outsiders go far to assuage the assumptions of primitivity held by many tourist hunters.[16]

The employees of safari-hunting outfits also enjoy an elevation in social status during the hunting season. Not only do they provide their families, friends, and neighbors with windfalls of meat, earn generous salaries, and benefit from perks and presents from the tourists, they also burnish their reputations as great hunters themselves, providing their forest knowledge in the hunt for large, symbolically valued animals. Local employees of safari-hunting companies ride with great gusto in the open backs of the pickup trucks and four-wheel-drive vehicles as they hurtle through villages, ferrying tourist hunters to and from their hunting sites; the machismo of the Great White Hunt permeates Bangando and Baka hunters as they show off to their home-bound friends and neighbors, benefiting both materially from their salaries and burnishing their reputations as skilled—even professional—hunters.

The unanticipated outcomes of uncritical use of images of "pygmies" among foreign trophy hunters reveal the stark contradictions between the static, shallow stereotype and the deeply complex cultural issues of belonging, intimate relations with the forest, and hunting aptitudes. In stark contrast to static images of the forest held by tourist hunters, inhabitants of the forest and villages of southeastern Cameroon have learned to mold and shape facets of their social reality in accordance with the expectations of outsiders. In conforming to and manipulating external stereotypes of the forest, local people are able to profit through the salaries and tips that they earn as artificial representations of an imagined reality: primitive man in primeval forest.

Contradictions and Conflicts

While missionaries and development agents, conservationists and safari hunters readily dismiss their stereotypes of local people in southeastern Cameroon as both insignificant and unintrusive—insignificant to the molding of their ideas and unintrusive in the shaping of their practical agendas for activities and programs in the Lobéké forest region—local people's perceptions of outsiders' images of them are incisive. A new brew of tension is simmering between Bangando and Baka, despite the clear movement over the past century and a half toward increasing social overlap, economic cooperation, joint ritual participation, interethnic friendship, and intermarriage. The imbalanced allocation of resources for development, employment, and aid flowing consistently from Euroamerican institutions and individuals to the Baka segment of the multiethnic society in the Lobéké region is generating a new source of friction. During a long afternoon conversation, Medola, a young Bangando man from Mambélé, articulated clearly and eloquently the various experiences of social change that have emerged because of the complex dialectic of changes from within and from outside of integrated Bangando-Baka society.

> Actually, everyone here is *bò lé*. Because a Baka builds [his house] here in the village too, and also sleeps on a mattress like me. But what is different between us has to do with the development that the white people bring here. When they arrive, they are not coming for Bangando. When they give Baka money, they also show them [Baka] what they should do with it, how to use it well. This is good. . . . But I would like to ask you, because if a white person arrives here, it is only for the Baka. Why do they all come for the Baka?
>
> It is you white people who cause the spiteful feelings between the Baka and Bangando. Because if a white person arrives here, he says that he comes for the Baka, and when he sees Bangando he chases them away. If we tell you right now that you have to leave because you are white, is that good? No, that is not good. But it is you white people who cause these rifts between us.

You know, the Baka say that if a Baka dies, he transforms himself into a white person. And if a Bangando dies, he transforms himself into a gorilla. All of this is because when a white person comes, he directs himself to the Baka. He doesn't like anything but the Baka. When a white person spends a lot of time with a Baka, he [the Baka] says that it [the white person] is someone from his family who died and has come back. And when he [the Baka] dies, he will also come back as a white person. When this white-Baka sees a Bangando, he says "Go away, Bangando. I am a white person." And after that, the white person [reincarnated Baka] comes to ask for salt, but the Bangando cannot give it to him. The white-Baka will say that Bangando are gorillas, even though we share the same blood. . . .

The white people believe that Baka are the people who know things of the forest, more than Bangando. . . . They believe that Baka still do the things from before. Bangando have changed things from before, and there is already evolution for them. This is why white people love the Baka. But you see, the Baka have stopped eating wild yams, and it is already rare to see a Baka digging the earth to look for wild yams. They have already forgotten.

It is important that you, you white people who come to study Africans, tell your brothers to stop coming here only for Baka. This causes conflicts between Baka and Bangando. It is bad. Baka are no longer like the ones from before, who saw Bangando and fled. They already live together with Bangando, to sleep, to drink, to eat together with Baka. Me, when I hunt with Baka I eat with them from the same plate.

You white people, you are stupid because instead of coming to look for Bangando to teach them about everything that's happening in the world, you attach yourselves to Baka men and women. What is it that you will say to us [Bangando]? You don't believe that you are causing conflicts between us? We cannot love them [Baka] because you bring them to hate us.

When white people come, they stay in the homes of Baka. Another arrives in the village, and he doesn't even say hello or talk to the other people [Bangando]. He doesn't even tell the chief of the village that he is there, to do this and to do that. He goes directly to the Baka houses, to stay with the Baka. But when the people will see that, they will think many things. They will say that it's for collecting the bones of Baka.[17]

But you white people, you cause conflict. You know that we are all poor people here. When you come, if it is for a little work, it is necessary that you take at least two Bangando and two Baka [to work with you] because that will help everyone. But when you come, you say that you are here for Baka and only for them. The others [who have no work] are dying of famine, so should Bangando love Baka? No way. Your way of doing things brings problems between us and Baka.[18]

Several points in this account deserve emphasis and clarification. First, contemporary Bangando and Baka recognize that Euroamerican outsiders perceive Baka as more isolated, exotically primitive, and compelling recipients of their intellectual attention, economic resources, and campaigns for social justice. Outside observers and practitioners tend to dismiss Bangando as lacking in interest because they are too acculturated to materialistic modernity and, as "farmers," do not fit paradigms of "indigenous people." Second, outsiders' interventions invert the contemporary relations of authority between Bangando and Baka. As we have seen, both historically and today, Bangando have tended to occupy positions of political and economic power. Outside aid workers, aware of the political and economic marginalization of Baka, offer access to education and health care as a means of remedying these perceived imbalances, even as they contribute to long-standing Euroamerican fascinations and fantasies about how contemporary "pygmies" embody pure and primitive human culture and historical origins.

This discussion of changes in social relations and relative positions between Bangando and Baka captures the sense of disequilibrium and disquiet that has penetrated the contemporary, multiethnic society. Medola's discourse certainly reveals his own loyalty to his Bangando ethnic affiliation and highlights his recognition that his "non-pygmy" social identity is ascribed, at least in part, by outsiders. Medola clearly implies that the discomfort experienced by Bangando is related to an imbalance of power as a result of outsiders' intense and prolonged attention to Baka. Many outsiders who are active in the region, particularly missionaries and development practitioners, would likely dismiss Medola's discomfort with this inversion of an older system of inequality as a fully justifiable correction to the domination of Baka by "Bantu." But a fundamental problem with outsiders' easy acceptance of such massive changes in social relations is the lack of nuanced understanding of the integrated, multiethnic society that must contend with external programs of social and religious development as well as nature conservation and tourism.

Perhaps the disquiet that Medola articulates reflects the disjuncture between institutional privileging of "indigenous" identities and the local histories, relationships, and experiences of belonging within and among forest communities (Pelican 2009). Furthermore, the categories projected by conservation and development practitioners, missionaries, and safari hunters offer people in the Lobéké forest region new avenues for adapting, shaping, and asserting new identities and new relationships in strategic ways, allowing them to take advantage of new opportunities. These extralocal institutions and personnel constitute "culture brokers" (Vail 1989): extracting bits of sociocultural information from the context of the Lobéké forest, practitioners craft newly validated categories of identity that their institutional programs sustain (cf. Comaroff and Comaroff 2009). Without analyzing the particularities of local social relations beyond the confines of rigid stereotypes of "pygmies" and "villagers," outsiders are unable to see or assess the changes that their actions might bring about, and then perhaps reconsider the approaches and design of their activities and programs.

Rethinking

SOCIAL IDENTITIES, ETHNIC AFFILIATIONS,

AND STEREOTYPES

The central argument presented in this book suggests that by analytically slotting African equatorial forest communities into predetermined categories of "pygmy/villager" and "hunter-gatherer/farmer," the field of social relations is flattened into two dimensions based on contrasting subsistence strategies and polar relations of power. As a result of this narrow focus, other relationships and dynamics of belonging that are experienced by forest peoples are rendered analytically invisible and ideologically irrelevant to outside observers. Far from conforming to the simplified, paired classifications of social identity based on presumed economic strategies and assumed political relationships, the diverse communities of southeastern Cameroon pursue various adaptable economic strategies, engage in many different kinds of social and political relationships, and

FIG. 8.1 Bangando elder
Kebikibele, Dioula, 1999

identify themselves and shape relationships with others in dynamic ways.
Thus an understanding of how forest peoples conceive of and express who
they are, both as individuals and as groups, is fundamental to an analysis of
social and cultural-ecological dynamics among forest communities. Conceptions and transformations of self and other provide the bases for ethnic
affiliations and social solidarities, components of contemporary reality that
orient individuals in these tangled forests of belonging.

Classification—the meaningful construction of the world—is a necessary condition of social existence (Durkheim and Mauss 1963 [1903]). This
ethnography demonstrates that two systems of social classification run
alongside of each other, working dynamically to provide frameworks for
conceptualizing belonging and identities among the people of the Lobéké
forest region. One system of categorization is influenced predominantly
by extralocal expectations of forest communities and is utilized primarily by institutions to describe and analyze the communities of the region.
This system of institutional classification is particularly powerful because
it provides the conceptual foundation for policies that legislate local communities' access to natural, economic, social, and political resources. The

other system of classification is influenced predominantly by local histories, relationships, and concerns, and is used primarily by local people as they experience social relationships and express shifting senses of self and other in changing contexts.

Institutional categories of identity tend to be oriented around oppositional pairs that are utilized as equivalent and interchangeable units: "pygmy"/"villager"; "person of the forest"/"person of the village"; "hunter-gatherer"/"farmer"; "indigenous"/"immigrant." Included in this stacking set of oppositional categories is a pair of local referents — "Baka"/"Bantu" — based on the assumption that ethnic affiliations also serve as functionally equivalent, oppositional categories. The intersection of local referents with stereotyped categories highlights the dynamic reflexivity between the systems; while different, these systems of classification ought not to be interpreted as distinct or oppositional. To insist that one system is strictly outside/etic and the other inside/emic would replicate the conceptual flaw of insisting on identifying people by categories of distinction in contexts in which relations of negotiation and influence predominate. But it is also fundamentally misleading to assume that institutional and local categories of identity are equivalent and interchangeable. As this ethnography has demonstrated, "people of the forest" connotes different experiences, relationships, tensions, and opportunities, depending on which system the category references. Recalling one example, "people of the forest" refers to an entirely different set of actors and historical dynamics in the context of twenty-first-century conservation discourse than those of the Marxist rebellions in 1960s Cameroon.

Categorical boundaries in institutional systems of classification indicate social, ecological, and economic differences that extralocal observers deem to be relevant to their studies or policy prescriptions. In this case, the categorical boundaries serve the purpose of highlighting divergences among communities, offering a pragmatic, simplified scheme to facilitate the allocation of resources or to enable regional comparisons with similar contexts. This study illustrates that local conceptions of self and other *also* build on differences between people; however, because of the multiplicity of dimensions for building shared experiences, affiliations, and identities, social boundaries provide opportunities for articulation and collaboration as much as they mark distinctions (Barth 2002). Fundamentally, this ethnography demonstrates that the boundaries predicated on divisions between nature and culture, resulting in categories such as "pygmies" and "villagers" in all of their iterations, do not overlap easily or predictably with local boundaries, categories, or relationships. The following diagram illustrates conceptual relationships between institutional and local systems for classifying social belonging and identities, as together they shape processes of identification in the Lobéké forest region.

The aim of this diagram is to illustrate the disjunctures as well as the parallelisms between institutional and local categories of identity. As a result, it depicts only those local orientations that correspond to prevailing institutional categories such as "pygmy" and "villager," which are rooted in the conceptual opposition between nature and culture. In addition to the intricate interplay among identities and relationships depicted in this diagram, nuanced analyses of social constellations in the Lobéké forest region must *also* consider the multiethnic, multiangular context of the Lobéké forest, which includes Bakwélé and Mbomam communities in addition to those of Bangando and Baka. This ethnography has illustrated that relations between Baka and each of the other communities (Bangando, Bakwélé, Mbomam), and between Bangando and each of the other communities (Baka, Bakwélé, Mbomam)—vary in social, political, ritual, and emotional integration, and cannot be boiled down to a template of "pygmy"/"villager" relations (chapter two). Analysis of social dynamics ought also to consider the ambiguities that characterize interethnic marriage and descent (chapter four). The social context in southeastern Cameroon is also shaped by relations of amity and alliance forged through overlapping clans, *bándí* partnerships, relations between *kɔ́lá*, and *mbɔ̀ní* alliances, as well as ritual collaboration in

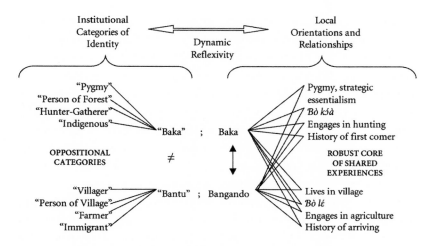

FIG. 8.2 Divergences and reflexivity between systems of identity categorization

bɛ́kà, jɛngì, and *díɔ* ceremonial practices and secret societies (chapter five). Furthermore, understanding local orientations and relations also requires attention to the fluid and overlapping social identities that reflect skills, occupations, nationality, and emotional character (chapter six). By what it omits, this diagram demonstrates that models of identity that are oriented around basic, binary oppositions overlook substantial areas of integration and interaction among the peoples of the Lobéké forest region.

Importantly the diagram also illustrates that institutional categories of identity and local orientations and relationships function in shared contexts such as the politics of contemporary conservation and development efforts (chapter seven). Moreover, institutional categories of identity are *also* relevant in the formation and transformation of local identities. However, local orientations and relationships are far more intricate than the simple, oppositional categories that typify institutional discourse. For example, the diagram illustrates the lack of correlation between ethnic affiliation and spatial orientation, mode of subsistence, and history of arrival—relationships that institutional categories depict as direct and exclusive. Note that neither community, Bangando nor Baka, offers a history of having been resident in the forest when other groups arrived, calling into question the assumption that one community can be identified as the "first comers" or the "indigenous people" (chapter two).

Reliance on the clear-cut distinctions that underlie institutional categories of identity may be pragmatic, allowing policy makers to simplify the social context for which policies must be designed and legislated. However, such distillations also render the complexities of local identities and relationships invisible and irrelevant. This ethnography has demonstrated that it is exactly the complexities and dynamism, ambiguities and nuances of local orientations and senses of belonging that enable the people of southeastern Cameroon to engage in a robust core of shared experiences that sustains their multiethnic community. Indeed, this robust core of shared experiences *includes* the contemporary process of engaging with institutions such as conservation and development NGOs, missionaries, and safari-hunting companies and clients that impose—to various degrees—institutional, extralocal views and categories onto local people. What is analytically interesting and politically crucial is to look at the ways in which these systems of classification interact, rubbing up against and blurring into each other, producing new ways for people to identify themselves, negotiate relationships, take strategic advantage of opportunities and, in the process, produce and mediate new dynamics of friction. But despite the articulation of these two broad systems of classifying who is who, one system predominates in authoritative power. For it is through the application of the binary opposition "pygmies"/"villagers" to practical social and political tasks that these stereotypes gain institutional power and momentum, generating a practical, potent, and homogenizing force with which local people must contend, either by conforming to or resisting the external categories (Foucault 1980; Scott 1998; Keim 1999).

Ethnic Affiliations and Social Identities

Social scientists have made a compelling call to reject the concept of "identity" as a valid category of analysis. Analytical conceptions of identity seem at once too hard to account for the flexibility of people's conceptions of self and other, and too soft to account for the stark realities of identity politics (Brubaker and Cooper 2000). I sympathize with this frustration about discourses of identity, and have taken their call to action seriously in my attempt to analyze expressions of self and other as articulated, performed, and manipulated by Bangando and Baka, Bakwélé and Mbomam of the Lobéké forest region. However, I do not concur with the argument that scholars should reject "identity" as a valid analytical concept because, as the authors concede, categories of identity *do* have important practical and political effects on the lives of people all over the world. Rather than rejecting identity outright, perhaps a more productive approach would be to look at how expressions of self and other are variable, and what we might conclude about the differences that arise from this variability. Perhaps it is the tendency to conflate what appear to be many distinct ways of knowing self and other into one category that undermines the ability of "identity" to serve as a useful analytical tool. In differentiating among kinds of "identities" that operate simultaneously in any society and that vary from society to society, scholars might come to a more nuanced understanding of processes of identity formation and change.

During my research in the Lobéké forest region, it became clear that there are some ways that individuals express notions of self and other that change quite quickly, are relevant only in particular contexts, and that people can assume and shed with ease. At the same time, other ways of expressing boundaries of self and other are relatively stable and constant. Field observations and conversations produced a wide range of shifting notions of self, such as *bò kɔ́à* (person of the forest), *bò lé* (person of the village), ɓò shàntìé (person of the timber company), ɓò dwá (person of sorcery), ɓò cameroon (person of Cameroon), and ɓò kísìnì (person of the kitchen). At the same time that an individual used one—or several—of these shifting notions of identity to describe herself, she invariably selected one—and only one—ethnic affiliation as representing her language community and sense of personal social history: Bangando, Baka, Bakwélé, or Mbomam. Thus a relatively stable layer of affiliation evokes sentiments of permanent belonging to a collectivity of individuals who share emotional attachments to a common history of social origins and a shared language.

I consider the first set of shifting expressions of self and other to be manifestations of *social identities*, while the latter, more stable notion of self and other to be a manifestation of *ethnic affiliation*. Bangando and their neighbors talk about relationships and experiences of social identity and ethnic affiliation, but do not refer to these notions using equivalent terms; I use these terms to clarify to myself (and hopefully to other outside observers) the fundamental differences in ways that people in southeastern Cameroon reckon the various boundaries of self and other, and the different dynamics of belonging that result. It is of critical importance to recognize that expressions of social identities in Cameroon *do* shift and change, but they are not limitless—they are contextually contingent. It is of critical importance to note as well that expressions of ethnic affiliation are *relatively* more stable than expressions of social identities, but that they are not static.

In addition, characteristics that might seem inalterable, such as belonging to a particular patrilineal clan or gender, are not necessarily fixed in the individual's social experience. Thus a woman who is born into her father's clan will marry into her husband's clan; as a married woman, she will hold two clan affiliations at once (for example, ɓò dáwà and ɓò fɔlɔ). Similarly, a woman may identify herself, and be identified by others, as ɓò kísìnì by virtue of the social responsibilities that center on women's domestic space, the kitchen. As she becomes an elder, this woman may also be considered ɓò mbánjó—a distinctly male category—by virtue of her distance from woman's activities of reproduction and production and of her movement into male spheres of overseeing and advising, which take place in the men's verandah, or mbánjó. In the case of both descent and gender, the social relevance of these categories is variable and is not imbued with the same mythistorical potency as ethnic referents. Thus, although it can be argued that descent and gender are determined at birth, in the context of southeastern Cameroon these attributes of identity are social referents that are relatively variable, as opposed to ethnic referents that are relatively more stable.

Individuals' experiences of identifying self and other are not uniform either at a particular moment in time across numerous individuals or for a given individual across time. The following chart may help to clarify the different components of ethnic affiliation and social identity as they have been expressed by people of the Lobéké forest region. I intend for this schematic diagram to offer only an illustration of the differences between ethnic affiliation and social identity among Bangando, Baka, Bakwélé, and Mbomam individuals, and as a way of understanding the variability of components that may contribute to people's experiences and expressions of their identities in a larger sense.

By examining relationships of ethnic affiliation and social identity in southeastern Cameroon, I have tried to study Bangando and their neighbors in the spirit proposed by Hocart (1953): by means of the categories expressed by the people themselves. Bangando, Baka, Bakwélé, and Mbomam recognize distinctions and differences among them—and within each community. Some of these differences are oppositional; others are oblique. By looking at social boundaries not simply as delineations of division between particular groups of people, but as offering variable points of articulation among different groupings of people in diverse contexts, it becomes clear that modes of identification vary in substance, quality, and purpose. This book has explored the cultural logics and social histories that enable the Bangando, Baka, Bakwélé, and Mbomam communities to live together, maintaining ethnic distinctiveness even as their past and present social experiences melt certain differences into cohesive relations of mutual sup-

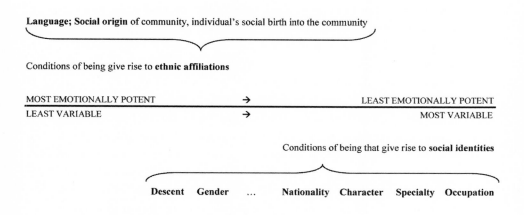

FIG. 8.3 Variable dynamics of ethnic affiliations and social identities

port and reliance, coupled with occasional relations of social friction as the communities negotiate the shifting lines of social allegiances, ethnic affiliations, and institutional stereotypes.

This ethnography has illustrated the varying viscosities of particular modes of identification, demonstrating that modes of identity congeal and dissolve at different rates, in different ways, and for different purposes. I submit that social identities are fluid, allowing individuals to move in and out of many different social positions and relationships over the course of a single day or a single hour. At the same time, ethnic affiliations are more viscous: stickier, even tarry. Individuals experience and express ethnic affiliation through metaphors of shared language and common social origins, emphasizing the stable substance of collective affiliation that provides a lowest common denominator of identification. Finally, stereotypes such as "pygmy" and "villager" represent crystallized categories that result from the distillation of social particularities of any given context. This crystallization makes such rigid categories useful for both policy and comparative studies, but also results in categories whose substance individuals cannot shape. People can strategically opt to align themselves with essentialized categories (Spivak 1988), but when they do, they shift their self-presentations rather than altering the stereotype itself. Understanding the different viscosities of categories of identity—from fluid to sticky to crystalline—may offer a helpful analytical approach for addressing various and divergent processes of identity.

Social identities, ethnic affiliations, and stereotypes are all ways that people experience belonging and actively position themselves and relate with others; they are distinct processes in the creation and negotiation of identities. These different processes of identity are neither equivalent nor interchangeable: each process reflects different criteria for belonging and identification; processes change at different rates and for different reasons; and individuals have different degrees of agency over these processes of identification. The social identities *bò kɔ̀à* (people of the forest) and *bò lé* (people of the village) may appear to be equivalent with the ethnic affiliations Baka and Bangando, but such a simple equivalence overlooks generations of cooperation among the communities in both the forest and the village, as well as distinct modes of belonging and strategies of identification with either the forest or the village among individuals of both communities. It may also appear that stereotypes such as "indigenous people" or "pygmies" correlate clearly with people whose ethnic affiliation is Baka; but the histories of

STEREOTYPES ◀▶	ETHNIC AFFILIATIONS ◀▶	SOCIAL IDENTITIES
RIGID	VISCOUS	FLUID
Criteria have deep, ideological histories that are independent of the Lobéké region.	Criteria reflect enduring local histories, relations, and qualities; may change over time, but slowly.	Criteria reflect cultural qualities that are salient to contemporary, everyday experiences.
Substance of stereotypes reflect values of external observers and institutions.	Affiliations that an individual is raised to embrace: language, origins (of self, clan, and larger community).	Identities reflect partnerships, groups, and skills that people emphasize and shift with ease.
Stereotypes are imposed on local people; people may opt to identify with stereotypes for strategic gain of resources.	Boundaries marking ethnic affiliations tend to be porous because of frequency of interethnic marriage.	People hold many different social identities simultaneously; social identities are useful for understanding relationships in specific, contemporary contexts.

FIG. 8.4 Processes of identification

migration demonstrate that the quality of "indigenousness" is not unique to any single community in the Lobéké region, and in contemporary contexts of engagement with forest industries and conservation, people of various ethnic affiliations identify themselves as "pygmies" and "people of the forest" for various, strategic reasons.

Marginality

The political implications of shattering the stacking paradigms of "hunter-gatherer"—"forager"—"pygmy"—"indigenous people" are both enormous and potentially disempowering to communities for whom conformity with the stereotypes produces beneficial relationships, services, or economic outcomes. The communities represented—however accurately or inaccurately—by these stereotypes remain among the most politically and economically marginalized communities in the world. If maintaining images of "hunter-gatherer" and "pygmy" constitutes an important political tool for pulling on the heartstrings of Euroamerican donor agencies and on the head-strings of scholars and researchers, perhaps these stereotypes serve an important, practical role that can be effectively utilized by some forest communities. But, nevertheless, responsible scholars and practitioners need to recognize that where individuals conform to external expectations and categories, these models may be based on simplified representations that diminish the complexity and diversity of relationships that *also* help communities to remain resilient and resourceful. Where labels such as "pygmy" and "hunter-gatherer" continue to be attached to forest communities by external analysts, these terms ought to reflect self-attributions articulated by the communities and individuals themselves, not reductionist stereotypes imposed by Euroamerican researchers, aid practitioners, or tourists. But at the same time, the attempt by well-meaning researchers to call categories such as "pygmy" and "villager" into question also threatens to remove one possible tool for resistance and self-determination that is available, and increasingly so, to people of the multiethnic society of the Lobéké forest region.

We have seen that southeastern Cameroon has become more ethnically integrated and socially, politically, and economically complex over the course of the past century and a half. In particular, communities have become *less* socially differentiated from each other, resulting in a leveling of political relations of power at a local level simultaneously as southeastern Cameroon as a region has become *more* marginalized with respect to Cameroon as a nation (and Cameroon with respect to the rest of the world). The attempt by conservationists, development practitioners, and missionaries to continue to impose categorical divisions of "hunter-gatherer"/"farmer" and "pygmy"/"villager" threatens to undo much of the ethnic collaboration that these communities have generated over the past century and a half, as these external social identities carry with them particular opportunities and accesses to tangible benefits (such as health care, or access to good hunting grounds). Sharing a common space and collectively enduring historical and contemporary political-economic pressures has brought Bangando, Baka, Bakwélé, and Mbomam intimately together. The Lobéké forest region of southeastern Cameroon is painfully marginalized from the rest of the nation. Yet the people of the Lobéké forest have fostered an unprecedented degree of interethnic solidarity through this marginalization, and through the collective attempt to provide for their increasingly interethnic families and villages in their increasingly complex social and political-economic context (Eder 1987). Where the categories "pygmy," "hunter-gatherer," or "indigenous people" can be harnessed by local people to the benefit of the multiethnic community at large, the stereotypes may serve a useful purpose. But where such categorical social distinctions offer benefits to some communities to the exclusion of others, the prejudicial use of such categories could destabilize ethnic relations in this very marginalized and very poor region of the world. Identifying marginalized forest communities through stereotypes of "hunter-gatherer" and "farmer" or "pygmy" and "villager" may well mask other more relevant and more potent relationships—local, regional, national, and international—of structural inequality, institutionalized power, and social injustice that threaten the natural and social communities of southeastern Cameroon and other tropical forests.

The efforts of conservation and development organizations in southeastern Cameroon—for all their flaws in identifying the people on whose behalf they work—offer an unprecedented opportunity to empower the multiethnic community of the Lobéké forest region. In concrete terms, the socioeconomic improvements in the years since 2001 offer a concerted attempt to alleviate conditions of poverty, disempowerment, and marginalization for the first time in the region's history. Bangando, Bakwélé, and Mbomam communities are evidently displeased with the prejudiced exclusion of their communities from forests they have utilized for generations, forests that are now at the heart of national parks (Lobéké, as well as neighboring Boumba-Bek and Nki national parks). The privileged allowance of Baka into protected areas, together with preferences that Baka typically receive in other institutional contexts, have generated frictions between neighbors. But at the same time, communities throughout the region have received monetary compensation for the commercial felling of timber and tourists' hunting of animals in their newly legislated community forests. These institutionally recognized "communities," moreover, have the authority to determine how this infusion of resources should be used; communities have rebuilt school buildings and desks and hired additional school teachers. Because of the efforts of extralocal institutions and agents, local people are, for the first time, experiencing meaningful improvements in the conditions of their lives.

This moment may provide a tectonic shift in relations of power and dynamics of belonging. A process of social transformation is unfolding in southeastern Cameroon. Legislating "community forests" and managing collective resources demands that "communities" be identified and belonging be negotiated. If the metrics of belonging are institutionalized according to division, there is potential for tremendous conflict. Other contexts in which boundaries have been politically influenced to emphasize difference have resulted in tragedy (Bringa 1995; Strauss 2006). In southeastern Cameroon, many elements and experiences come together to shape a common core of experiences that influence identities and anchor relationships. Individuals and institutions that have the power to effect large-scale change in the Lobéké forest region would strengthen the positive outcomes of their projects of community building through conservation, development, and missionization if they consider seriously the integrated, interconnected identities and relationships of mutual belonging that are embraced by Bangando, Baka, Bakwélé, and Mbomam.

Notes

Notes indicate where ethnographic data are recorded, including field notebooks and field cassettes. These data were collected in the Lobéké forest region of southeastern Cameroon between 1995 and 2000. The African Collection at Sterling Memorial Library, Yale University, has kindly agreed to archive these primary sources permanently, so that scholars may consult them in their research.

INTRODUCTION

Discussion with Maga about relations between Bangando and Baka, recorded in Field Notebook #3, pp. 142–51. Lopondji, 5 October 1998.

1   See, for example, Vallois 1950; Frasez 1952; Althabe 1965; Vallois and Marquer 1976; Demesse 1980; Bahuchet 1992; Sato 1992, 1998; Dounias 1993a; Joiris

1993a, 1993b, 1996, 1997, 1998; Dongmo and Loung 1993; Boursier 1994, 1996; Leonard 1997; Leclerc 1998, 2000; Abéga 1998; Tsuru 1998; Brisson 1999; Leonhardt 1999; Hewlett 2000; Kimura 2003.

2   My preliminary research resources in Epulu included Schebesta 1940, 1952; P. Putnam 1948; A. Putnam and Keller 1954; Turnbull 1961, 1965; J. Hart 1979; T. Hart and J. Hart 1978, 1986; Bailey and Peacock 1988; Bailey and Aunger 1989; Headland and Bailey 1991; Grinker 1990.

3   Several significant studies do highlight the role of farming and "swidden agriculture" in maintaining biodiverse ecosystems. See, in particular, Fairhead and Leach 1996, and Conklin 1961.

4   Anthropologists who work in the forests of central Africa are generally quite certain that they can readily distinguish a "pygmy" individual from a "non-pygmy" (Cavalli-Sforza 1986). Perhaps my powers of observation are limited; however, discussions with Catholic missionaries who have worked with Baka and Bangando (as well as Bakwélé and Mbomam) for many years also admit that they are not always able to distinguish "pygmies" from "non-pygmies" based on appearance. For example, a Baka resident of Dioula measures 5 feet 8 inches tall.

5   In total, my field research among the Bangando, Baka, Bakwélé, and Mbomam communities of southeastern Cameroon covered twenty-six months, from 1995 to 2000. In citing the many individuals who contributed to my research, I have maintained some informants' names if they expressed this preference. For other informants, particularly those who spoke to me about delicate matters or preferred anonymity, I have provided pseudonyms.

CHAPTER ONE: PARADIGMS

1   MINFOF, the Ministère des Forêts et de la Faune, is now responsible for managing forest resources in Cameroon. This domain was formerly the responsibility of MINEF, the Ministère des Eaux et Forêts, which no longer exists.

2   Http://ld.panda.org/jengi_news.html. Accessed 15 July, 2005.

3   Discussion with Bertin Tchikangwa, recorded in Field Notebook #5, pp. 14–15. Yaoundé, 26 January 1999.

4   This inversion of the anticipated pattern of technology exchange, in which "hunter-gatherers" could be expected to teach "farmers" how to hunt, has also been noted in other forest communities, notably among the Mbuti and Aka. (Turnbull 1983; Bahuchet and Guillaume 1982; Bahuchet 1993a). Further examination of histories of technology transfer is warranted.

5   Among many examples, see "Cultural Survival" at http://www.culturalsurival. org. Accessed 10 August 2005.

CHAPTER TWO: BELONGING

1   Rupp: "Ɛ́nɛ́ Bàngàndò, ɛ́nɛ́ bò né ɔ̀ɔ̀?" Wanguwangu: "Yé Bàngàndò bò yé Bàngàndò. Bàngàndò bò nú ɔ̀ɔ̀, kà ɔ̀ɔ̀ bò Bángàndò. Bò má hànyàwé nà!" Conversation recorded in Field Notebook #5, pp. 23–25. Dioula-Beligela, 14 February 1999.

2   Discussion of Bangando history with Kouamanda Kallo and Wanguwangu, recorded in Field Notebook #3 pp. 69–72, 114–16. Dioula, 7 and 18 July 1997.

3   *Ndjámbé* or *Ndjámbé mòkákè* is the Bangando creator deity, and is often portrayed in stories as the ancestor of the entire community. *Ndjámbé* is also often portrayed as a buffoon, a fallible father figure whose mistakes often lead to unexpected but important lessons for his family, and ultimately for all Bangando descendants. *Ndjámbé*, who is considered to be an all-powerful spirit, nonetheless combines qualities of both godliness and humanity. Catholic missionaries in the region have translated the Judeo-Christian concept of "God" into Bangando as *Ndjámbé*.

4   Today a community identified by the ethnonym "Ngombé" lives in the forest of the Republic of Congo, on the western side of the Sangha River. I am not certain if this community constitutes the other "half" of the original Ngombé community prior to the schism; however, Bangando in southeastern Cameroon claim that they can communicate with Ngombé in Congo, suggesting that their languages—and communities—are perhaps historically related. Interestingly, scientists working in these forests identify "Ngombé" as a "pygmy" community (Paul Elkan, personal communication, 1997)

5   Discussion of Bangando history with Kouamanda Kallo and Wanguwangu, recorded in Field Notebook #3, pp. 69–72, 114–16. Dioula, 7 and 18 July 1997.

6   Archaeologists working in equatorial Africa interpret hardened palm oil kernels (one of the few organic items that survive in the acidic and moist soils of the forest) as evidence of relatively permanent human settlements. Palm oil trees are domesticated, and thus must be planted by human communities. Since palm oil kernels mature slowly, the planting of these trees indicates that the people intended to inhabit the site for numerous years.

7   "Lake Lobéké" is a site of intense contestation, as Western conservation organizations have sought to place the region beyond the reach of local communities by making it the heart of a nature reserve.

8   Discussion of Baka history by Buba, Weenumbu, and other Baka elders, recorded on Field Cassette #9. Dioula-Mbandame, 22 April 1999.

9   Ibid.

10   The geographical reference *Mɔ́kòngò* is vague. However, "Kongo" could well refer to Congo, which would indicate that Baka and Bangando hunters met near the Sangha River, which forms the border with Congo, placing the encounter in the vicinity of Ndjàngé.

11　Discussion of Baka history by Buba, Weenumbu, and other Baka elders, recorded on Field Cassette #9. Dioula-Mbandame, 22 April 1999.

12　Discussion of family history by Ambata, recorded in Field Notebook #1, p. 24. Dioula-Beligela, 14 October 1995.

13　Discussion with Ndjumbé about Bangando history, recorded on Field Cassette #34. Dioula-Mbandame, 9 May 2000.

14　Discussion with Sebo about Bangando history, recorded in Field Notebook #3, p. 128. Dioula-Sà Bò Mbélá, 20 July 1997.

15　Discussion with Maga about Bangando history, recorded in Field Notebook #3, pp. 143–44. Lopondji, 5 October 1998.

16　Discussion with Sebo about Bangando history, recorded in Field Notebook #3, p. 128. Dioula-Sà Bò Mbélá, 20 July 1997.

17　It is possible that the Bakwélé community that today inhabits the Moloundou region, including the large village of Ngilili as well as villages along the Ngoko-Dja River, represents the merging of two formerly discrete Bakwélé communities, one on the west bank of the Sangha River and continuing toward its confluence with the Ngoko at Ouesso and then up toward Moloundou (the *Djáchɛ,* "people from downriver"), and the other on the north bank of the Ngoko-Dja River, to the west of Moloundou (the *Djákò,* "people from upriver").

18　Discussion of Bakwélé history with Mwalu, recorded in Field Notebook #5, pp. 127–30. Ndongo, 20 March 1998. Mwalu's grandson translated from Bakwélé into a combination of French and Bangando.

19　Discussion with Ndoboyé, recorded in Field Notebook #5, pp. 143–44. Ndongo, 22 March 1999. The issues of ethnicity and gender become entangled in this example of inequality. Women throughout southeastern Cameroon struggle to maintain control over a small portion of the family's income to purchase necessities such as soap, petrol, salt, and clothing, and to pay school and medical fees. Ndoboyé was emphatic that if the husband had been present to pay him the local whiskey for his work, he would have received his compensation, stating numerous times that women are very "difficult" (*hányáwè*) when it comes to questions of money. In this case the wife was less willing to part with resources that she relied upon as well, to ensure that she would be able to care for her new baby. The Bakwélé wife and the Baka man are in parallel situations of economic inferiority vis-à-vis the Bakwélé husband/"patron."

20　Ibid.

21　Discussion with Kouamanda Marcel, chief of Ndongo, recorded in Field Notebook #5, pp. 123–26. Ndongo, 19 March 1999.

22　Comment by daughter of Bakwélé chief, recorded in Field Notebook #5, p. 126. Ndongo, 19 March 1999.

23　Discussion with Bangando men living in Ndongo, recorded in Field Notebook #5, pp. 142, 146–49. Ndongo, 21 March 1999.

24 Discussion with Jean-Pierre, recorded in Field Notebook #5, p. 132. Ndongo, 18 March 1999.

25 Discussion with Atchio and Paulina, recorded in Field Notebook #5, p. 133–34. Ndongo, 18 March 1999.

26 "Lìì mú à Lékéwɛ. Mì bò bèmbèkò Bángàndò! Lé mú à Mbàtékà." Discussion with Lekewe and Nana, recorded in Field Notebook #5, p. 106. Bàkà, 14 March 1999.

27 "Ɔ̀ɔ bò síkìnò mɔ yɔ̀ yé Bángàndò. Ɔ̀ɔ bòàvàà kpè na búnù síkìnò. Ɔ̀ɔ tòlì ná jàà síkìnò. Ɔ̀ɔ bò Bángàndò péká ɔ̀ɔ tòlì ná Bángàndò." Note that the speakers used the term "Bangando" as a spatial as well as social referent. Discussion with Lapo and Lekewe, recorded in Field Notebook #5, p. 112. Bàkà, 12 March 1999.

28 "Ɔ̀ɔ wélà Báyàkà; ɔ̀ɔ bò kà Báyàkà." Discussion with Ngongo, Sakombo, and Albert, recorded in Field Notebook #5, pp. 142, 146–49. Ndongo, 21 March 1999.

29 "Bàngàndò bò dɔ̀làwè. Yɔ̀à gbàdè ɔ̀ɔ dɔ̀làwè. Yɔ̀à wélà nú Báyàkà dɔ̀làwè. Yɔ̀à wélà nú Báyàkà ná ɔ̀ɔ dɔ̀làwè." Discussion with Ndoboyé, recorded in Field Notebook #5, p. 144–45. Ndongo, 22 March 1999.

30 Virtually no research has been conducted among the Mbomam, outside of one brief comparative study of household diets and food preferences by Kaori Komatsu (1998), which included some Mbomam data. In addition, a master's thesis by Edjondji Mempouth Andre Innocent (1994) examines the history of the Mpo'oh, a community that is linguistically (and perhaps also culturally) related to the Mbomam of southeastern Cameroon.

31 *Mòtámbá* was translated into French as *esclaves* (slaves) by Mbomam who were listening to the history. Although it does not seem that Mbomam were forced unwillingly to work for Bangando, the sense of Mbomam social and political subjugation to their Bangando "hosts" was clear.

32 I have not yet found Hockmann in German archival documents concerning southeastern Cameroon. However, Hockmann's historical role during the German colonial period in Moloundou is corroborated by Bakwélé elders who also mention his colonial policies (cited in Joiris 1998: 251).

33 Mbomam history recounted by Ando Daniel and neighbors, recorded in Field Notebook #5, pp. 92–95. Ngola, 5 March 1999.

34 Ibid.

35 Discussion with Maasele, recorded in Field notebook #5, pp. 95–96. Ngola, 5 March 1999.

36 Discussion with Mbomam and Bangando men in Ngola, recorded in Field Notebook #5, p. 83. 3 March 1999. *Noblesse* seems to be a characteristic that Mbomam men, rather than women, are particularly concerned about maintaining. Perhaps this male sense of nobility is a display of Mbomam chauvinism, especially because Mbomam men have difficulty finding Mbomam wives, and often marry Bangando, Baka, Bakwélé, or Mpiemu wives instead.

37 Discussion with Mbomam and Bangando men, recorded in Field Notebook #5, p. 83. Ngola, 3 March 1999.

CHAPTER THREE: SPACES

1 Discussion with an Anglophone cook working for WWF about his impressions of southeastern Cameroon. Mambélé, 27 April 1999.

2 Bangando call wattle-and-daub houses *gàlà bílìkì* in reference to the sun-dried bricks that German colonists used in constructing their own houses and buildings. *Bílìkì* is the Bangando rendering of "brick" as it was adopted from pidgin English, which was widely spoken throughout the German colonies of Togo and Cameroon. The rectangular compartments of mud that are separated by bamboo framing are reminiscent of the brick architecture that Germans introduced to the region.

3 Discussion with Kebikibele about Bangando history, recorded in Field Notebook #2, pp. 252–53. Dioula-Ngomo, 30 March 1996.

4 Discussion about women's relations with Kebikibele, recorded in Field Notebook #5, p. 27. Dioula-Beligela, 14 February 1999.

5 Discussion with Jeanne, recorded in Field Notebook #1, p. 133. Lopondji, 7 February 1996.

6 Discussion with Seo and Motupa, recorded in Field Notebook #6, p. 1. Ndongo, 21 March 1999.

7 The name of the village of Bàkà has falling tones, whereas the name of the Baka people is properly pronounced with rising tones: Báká.

8 Discussion with Gobijan, recorded in Field Notebook #5, pp. 150–51. Bàkà, 22 March 1999.

9 Ibid.

10 Discussion with Ngola and Njela, recorded in Field Notebook #4, p. 142–45. Dioula-Beligela, 5 February 1999.

11 The name Emerson is curious, as it is evidently neither a Bangando nor a French name. This area of the forest was named after an American Presbyterian missionary who was the teacher of several Bangando elders when they were young men and attended school at Moumjepoum, the site of the Presbyterian mission station (in the region of the Bulu community, near Yokadouma).

12 Discussion with Buba, recorded on Cassette #8. Dioula-Centre, 10 April 1999.

13 Discussion with Ndjumbé concerning land tenure, recorded on Field Cassette #34. Dioula-Ngomo, 9 May 2000.

14 Observations recorded in Field Notebook #1, pp. 83. Mbànjánì, 6 December 1996.

1   After a lengthy discussion of *swéngélé* Bangando, elders indicated that relative degrees of Bangando "purity" could also be expressed using various contrasting terms and metaphors. For example, the "purest" Bangando are referred to as *kárnákárná mbú bɔ̀tòmbɛ*, of which there are probably fewer than five households in the entire region between Mikel and Moloundou, according to the elders. These *kárnákárna mbú bɔ̀tòmbɛ* Bangando are considered to be *bè ngómbè*, or the descendants (children: *bè*), of the Ngombé, the ancestors of the Bangando (as discussed in chapter two). At the same time, these "purest" Bangando are contrasted with *bè jéléjélé* or Bangando of mixed blood. Thus, while the discussion of Bangando sentiments of solidarity based on language and social origin most often involved discussions of *swéngélé* Bangando as representing contemporary ethnic Bangando-ness by virtue of having Bangando parents and grandparents, deeper explorations revealed more thorough explanations of what ethnic "purity" means to Bangando elders, even if these notions are seldom raised today and seem to have a limited impact on contemporary discussions of ethnicity and identity. Discussion with Kebikibele and Ndjumbé, recorded in Field Notebook #6, p. 94–95. Dioula, 5 May 1999.

2   *Mónyàdì* is the wedding process, which unfolds along very similar lines among the Bangando, Bakwélé, Mbomam, and Baka of southeastern Cameroon. Customarily the groom will announce his wish to marry a woman by presenting a needle—a symbol of attaching or sewing the man and woman together into one couple—to her parents. He will arrive very early in the morning to place the needle, which is stuck into a corncob, on the floor in front of the woman's parents as they receive him in the main house. The woman's mother asks her daughter if she accepts the man. If she does, and if her parents also agree to the match, the woman's mother accepts the needle and gives it to her daughter, who keeps it safely with her personal items. In the near future, the bride will accompany the groom to his village, where she will stay with his family for the period of *mónyàdì,* during which she will learn from the groom's mother about the responsibilities, skills, and knowledge that she will need as a wife. When she arrives at her fiancé's house, the women of his family bathe her as she stands on a stone, representing the stability of the family and the honorable position of the new wife (her feet stay clean as she is bathed). During the period of *mónyàdì*, the bride will be covered with palm oil that has been reddened with the dust of mahogany wood (*mɔ́ngwélé*), she will wear only a cloth *sándà* (a cloth wrap), and she will be served the best food that the family can offer, often in large quantities. Typically, she will wear heavy iron bracelets, anklets, and a thick iron necklace, items of family pride and wealth, decorations that, together with the sticky, itchy palm oil rub, prevent

her from undertaking heavy labor. Thus the bride remains at her mother-in-law's side in the kitchen house, weaving baskets and mats, and undertaking activities that she can do without exertion, for her secondary responsibility is to grow plump. Many women dislike the process of *mónyàdì* because the palm oil rub, the iron decorations, and the social position at the center of the groom's household place the new bride in quite an uncomfortable situation. The bride is expected to endure *mónyàdì* with patience and good humor, a sign of how she will endure the ultimate marriage. When the *mónyàdì* period (usually several weeks to several months) is complete, the bride returns to her paternal household to visit her family and to show her parents the baskets, mats, and foods that she has learned to prepare. After a short time, the groom and his family will return to the bride's house with her completed bride price and will claim her as their new wife. The families will celebrate together and will ceremonially exchange woven mats (presented by the bride's family) for chickens, goats, local whisky, and money (presented by the groom's family). The bride then returns with her husband and his family to their village, where she assumes her responsibilities as his wife.

3 Discussion about marriage with Matalina, recorded in Field Notebook #5, pp. 37–39. Pezam-Moloundou, 16 February 1999.

4 Discussion with Ngonda recorded in Field Notebook #5, pp. 50–51. Moloundou-Pezam, 17 February 1999.

5 The role of Bangando blacksmiths as cleansers of social transgressions may be related to notions that blacksmiths occupy the lowest rung of productive society, perform the dirtiest and most unpleasant physical work, and are thus marginalized from mainstream society. The low social status of blacksmiths is common throughout central Africa.

6 Discussion with Ngonda, recorded in Field Notebook #5, p. 51. Pezam-Moloundou, 17 February 1999.

7 Discussion with Maga, recorded in Field Notebook #3, pp. 141–49. Lopondji, 5 October 1998. While Maga offered his comments in Bangando, he used French words to express "developed" and "modern." Field Notebook #3, pp. 141–49. Lopondji, 5 October 1998.

8 Ibid.

9 During conversations with Bangando women about interethnic relationships, women often initially articulated the common reaction of disgust at the idea of sexual relations. As conversations became more relaxed and intimate, however, numerous Bangando women indicated that sexual relations with Baka men were neither disgusting nor unusual, but were actually quite common.

10 "Real" clothes, referring to western clothing bought from merchants who sell secondhand clothing that has been discarded by Euroamericans, bundled into large bales, and brought to Africa (and other regions of the developing world) for resale.

11 Discussion with Pito and Marie, recorded in Field Notebook #5, pp. 52–53. Pezam-Moloundou, 17 February 1999. Bangando occasionally discuss the "bad habits" or the "bad way of life" of Baka, referring to Bangando stereotypes of Baka as irresponsible and lazy people who cannot be bothered to keep their own gardens, so instead they steal from Bangando gardens and otherwise take advantage of Bangando. Interethnic stereotypes and insults will be discussed in chapter six.

12 Discussion with Pando, recorded on Field Cassette #11B. Lopondji, 30 April 1999.

13 Ibid.

14 Ibid.

15 Discussion with Laati, recorded on Field Cassette #12. Lopondji, 2 May 1999.

16 It would be very interesting to return to Pando's and Laati's children in a decade or two, to discuss their experiences with and understandings of ethnicity.

17 Mokake's sister married a Congolese man in Ouesso and lives there with him and his family. She sent her daughter to Mokake in Cameroon to protect her from the violence of the political upheaval in the Republic of Congo during the late 1990s.

18 Discussion with Mokake, recorded on Field Cassette #24B. Mbango1, 27 May 1999.

19 Discussion with Wetuno, recorded on Field Cassette #25A. Mbango1, 27 May 1999.

20 The Bangando term *jɔ́p* indicates short-term labor, borrowed from the Pidgin English term "job."

21 Discussion with Mokake, recorded on Field Cassette #25A. Mbango1, 27 May 1999.

22 Discussion with Wetuno, recorded on Field Cassette #25A. Mbango1, 27 May 1999.

23 Ibid.

24 The vast majority of women in southeastern Cameroon are illiterate, and many speak only broken French, if they speak French at all. Education for girls in this region is critically lacking.

25 Discussion with Nadia about *mónyàdì*, recorded in Field Notebook #5, pp. 31–32. Dioula, 15 February 1999.

26 Discussion with Nadia, recorded in Field Notebook #5, p. 37. Pezam-Moloundou, 16 February 1999.

27 Ibid.

CHAPTER FIVE: TANGLES

1 Burnham offers a detailed description of Gbaya social organization and structural fluidity in chapter four of *Opportunity and Constraint in a Savanna*

Society (1980). It is quite clear that Bangando social organization is closely related to that of the Gbaya, in keeping with the historic, linguistic, and cultural relations between these communities. In addition to the strikingly parallel structure of Bangando and Gbaya clans, there is also a small degree of overlap between the totems. Bangando and Gbaya both recognize the people of the leopard as *bò gò*, and while the people of the elephant are *bò fòlò* in Bangando terminology and *bò fòrò* among the Gbaya. In addition, although the Bangando call the people of the monitor lizard *bò wé*, in reference to their taboo on the use of fire during the birth of a clans-baby, the word for monitor lizard in Bangando is *mbáwálá,* which bears striking similarity to the Gbaya clan name for the people of the monitor lizard, *bò mbáráwárá.* These overlaps in terminology for clans as well as for animals indicate that Bangando and Gbaya share a history of social intimacy and overlapping knowledge of faunal resources (cf. Burnham 1980: 85, 89). Bangando clans have not remained static, however; since their arrival in the forest of the Sangha-Ngoko corner of Cameroon, clan symbols, interclan relationships, and clan rituals have changed, reflecting their forest surroundings.

2   Clans of all four ethnic communities in southeastern Cameroon are exogamous. In rare cases individuals of the same clan may marry, provided the bride ceremonially disassociates herself from the clan prior to the wedding. If the spouses are members of the same clan but belong to different ethnic groups — especially ethnic groups beyond the Lobéké region — their marriage does not usually pose any structural prohibitions.

3   However, members of the *bò dáwà* clan revere their powerful chief Nadia as an especially important ancestor. He consolidated the Bangando community following their tumultuous migration to the Lobéké forest region, organized their successful defense against subsequent attacks by the Ndzimou, and oversaw their relations with German and French colonial officials. A second example of a quasi-apical clan ancestor is Wanguwangu, the renowned elephant hunter and warrior of the *bò wé* clan; Wanguwangu descendants regard him as the prototype of courage and strength that characterizes all *bò wé* clan members.

4   Story of the origins of the *bò dáwà* clan recounted by Jeanne, recorded in Field Notebook #2, p. 222. Lopondji, 16 March 1996.

5   However, we have seen that in some contexts ethnic affiliation through shared language is not inherited from the patriline, but is shaped by an individual's relationships and experiences with the maternal family. It follows that clan membership, as with ethnicity, may be more malleable than the social "rule" of patrilineality would seem to dictate.

6   With her marriage to a man who, by definition, is not a member of her father's clan, a woman relinquishes neither her membership in her patrilineal clan

nor her responsibility to refrain from eating the taboo meat of her clan. In addition to her patrilineal food prohibition, she is obliged to prepare food that conforms to the husband's patrilineal clan affiliation for her husband and for the couple's children (who by rule of descent belong to the clan of their father). As long as a woman is fertile and has the potential to produce children for her husband's clan, she is prohibited from eating the meat of her husband's clan, for fear that the taboo meat should be "eaten" as well by the unborn child, potentially resulting in complications during the pregnancy or birth. Thus a woman belongs to two clans when she marries: she retains her association with the clan of her father while abiding by the food prohibitions of the clan of her husband and her children, whose food she prepares.

7   There are two situations in which a man may marry more than one woman from the same family. First, if a man and his wife have difficulty conceiving a child, the woman's family may provide a younger sister or niece as a reproductive substitute for the initial wife. This second relationship may or may not be formalized through marriage. In addition, if a man desires to marry a second wife, he may request that his first wife select one of her female relatives for his additional marriage. Granting his first wife a choice in his subsequent marriage may help to soothe the potential frictions of polygyny. In addition, by choosing to marry another woman from his first wife's family, the husband increases the chances that his co-wives will have deep emotional attachments to each other, further minimizing potential marital conflict. Finally, marrying two women from the same family builds strong ties of support between the two families.

8   Moniño interprets the prefix *bò*, as it is used by speakers of Gbaya-Kara in clan names, as meaning "people of." I follow this usage. Gbaya-Kara is a subgroup of the larger Gbaya community that resides in the grasslands of east-central Cameroon.

9   Drawing on analyses of clan names offered by scholars of Gbaya language and culture, the bound morpheme *bò* appears to be a vestigial remnant of Bantu name classes, particularly as the formal, structural role of a particular prefix serving as a consistent element in naming is not found elsewhere in Bangando or in other Ubangian languages (cf. Burnham 1980: 85; and Moniño 1988 concerning the syllable *bò* in Gbaya clan names).

10   The people of the monkey, the *bò dáwà*, are divided into patrilineal subclans. The *bò dáwà kángá* subclan is represented by black-and-white colobus monkeys, (*Colobus guereza uellensis*). The *bò dáwà máleke* subclan is represented by De Brazza's monkeys (*Cercopithecus neglectus*). The *bò dáwà ndédé* subclan is represented by white-nosed guenon monkeys (*Cercopithecus nictitans nictitans*). Unfortunately, I am unable to correlate the *bò dáwà dúsé* subclan with a particular species of monkey. It is interesting that, while the overarching *bò dáwà* origin story recognizes chimpanzees as the saviors of the apical *bò dáwà*

ancestors, chimpanzees do not represent a particular subclan of the larger monkey clan. Nonetheless, chimpanzees and gorillas (great apes), as well as all other monkeys, are taboos of the *bò dáwà* clan.

11   Sitatunga is the common name for *Tragelaphus spekii*, an elegant, medium-large russet-gray antelope that frequents marshy clearings in the forest.

12   The *mbísà* is a small, sweet, yellow fruit of *Carpholobia alba* of the *Polygalaceae* family. (Thanks to Dr. Edmond Dounias for making this identification.) I am not sure why this fruit is among the other animal-based Bangando clans, although it has been known to produce a severe allergic reaction—swelling of the trachea—and may therefore be avoided ritually to ensure its complete avoidance.

13   Discussion with Kebikibele recorded in Field Notebook #4, pp. 81–84. Dioula-Beligela, 23 November 1998.

14   Ibid. Bangando and Baka both recognize people of the elephant (*bò fɔ́lɔ́, yɛ̃ líkɛ̀mbà*) and people of the monitor lizard (*bò wé, yɛ̃ gùgà*).

15   Discussion with Kebikibele, Ndjumbe (Bangando), and Kito (Baka) about *mólómbí*, recorded in Field Notebook #7, pp. 66–67. Dioula Beligela, 6 May 2000. According to Susa, a young Baka man from the Republic of Congo, Baka on the Congolese side of the Ngoko River do not know *mòkɛlákɛlá*: "[T]hat's only for Baka of Cameroon." Interestingly, Susa claims that Bakwélé of Congo do know *mòkɛlákɛlá*, but call this human transformed into an elephant form *mimbeng*. As far as I know, Bakwélé in Cameroon do not practice elephant transformation.

16   I regret the paucity of information concerning the clans of the Mbomam and the Bakwélé. Having focused my field research primarily on the Bangando and secondarily on the Baka communities, I was unable to carry out extensive field research concerning Mbomam and Bakwélé social structure. Further hampering my efforts to analyze the parallels and intersections between the social systems more thoroughly, none of the research—published and unpublished—concerning the Bakwélé discusses the clan system or social structure in depth. Joiris mentions several Bakwélé clans in her thesis (1998), although her differentiation between clans and subclans, as well as clans' names, totemic emblems, and taboos, is confusing. It is also curious that included among the Bakwélé clans is the *yɛ̃ kwíè* clan, which, according to a translation offered by Leon Siroto (personal communication, December 1998), takes the blue duiker as its taboo. The blue duiker is among the most commonly eaten animals in southeastern Cameroon; that a clan would ritually avoid this meat is surprising. A comprehensive study of Bakwélé social structure would be very useful. In addition, aside from one brief ethnobotanical article (Komatsu 1998), no materials have been published on the Mbomam community at all.

17   Discussion with Anda and Yana, recorded in Field Notebook #7, pp. 35–36. Dioula-Mbandame, 28 April 2000.

18 Discussion with Anda, recorded in Field Notebook #7, pp. 35–36. Dioula-Mbandame, 28 April 2000.

19 Discussion about Bangando-Baka relations with Maga, recorded in Field Notebook #3, p. 148. Lopondji, 5 October 1998.

20 Discussion with Ambata, recorded in Field Notebook #1, pp. 23–25. Dioula-Beligela, 14 October 1995.

21 Discussion with Wanguwangu, recorded on Field Cassette #33A. Dioula-Beligela, 28 April 2000.

22 Observations recorded in Field Notebook #6, p. 75. Dioula-Beligela, 15 April 1999.

23 Observations and discussions at funeral, recorded in Field Notebook #4, pp. 139–42. Mbateka Njong, 4 February 1999.

24 In his dissertation on the Bakwélé, Siroto also notes the custom of *contredot* or return gift, in which the bride's family offers a return gift of chickens, mats, and brass anklets to the family of the new husband (Siroto 1969: 102).

25 That the central dish of reconciliation was maize meal indicates that the origins of the *mbɔní* ceremony may lie in the grasslands of central Cameroon or the Central African Republic, perhaps among the Gbaya and other Ubangian communities, rather than in the equatorial forest, where plantains provide the staple starch.

26 Discussion with Mungoï, recorded in Field Notebook #7, p. 22. Dioula-Mbandame, 21 April 2000.

27 According to Baka who live in Ndongo, in the past, Baka and Bakwélé friends made *mbɔní* alliances to cement their friendship. But with the constant friction between the communities today, they no longer make these alliances. Discussion with Lapo and Lekewe, recorded in Field Notebook #5, p. 116. Ndongo, 15 March 1999. At the other end of the Lobéké region, Baka and Mbomam established intimate friendships in the past and continue to do so today. As explained by a Mbomam elder in Ngola, Mbomam forefathers participated in the Baka initiation ceremonies of *Jengì*, and so they became brothers ("frères"). Mbomam and Baka also undertook *mbɔní* alliances to solidify their friendship. Mbomam also formed *mbɔní* alliances with Bangando. ("Friend" in Mbomam and Bakwélé is *ésò*. "Alliance" in Mbomam is *bón*.) Discussion with Ando, recorded in Field Notebook #5, p. 93. Ngola, 5 March 1999.

28 Discussion with Yana and Michel, recorded in Field Notebook #7, p. 37. Dioula-Mbandame, 28 April 2000.

29 Boys are circumcised for the first time at the age of ten to fourteen years.

30 Discussion with Sousa, recorded in Field Notebook #4, p. 131. Tala-Tala (Republic of Congo), 19 December 1998.

31 Discussion with Maga about relations between Bangando and Baka, recorded in Field Notebook #3, pp. 142–51. Lopondji, 5 October 1998.

32 *Jengì* and *Dʼíò* are both the names of powerful forest spirits as well as the

names of ceremonies in which the spirits are called to visit the village from the forest, when uninitiated men are ritually inducted into the ceremonial society. Where the terms refer to the proper names of the forest spirits, they are capitalized. Names of the ceremonial practices are denoted by lowercase letters.

33 Observations of *Jengì* ceremony recorded in Field Notebook #4, pp. 126–30. Yenga, 13 December 1998.

34 Observations of village meeting with *Sous-Préfet* recorded in Field Notebook #4, pp. 112–13. Dioula-Mbandame, 5 December 1998.

35 Note that this exchange of chickens and mats for money and whisky parallels the bride-price and return gift of the *mónyàdì* wedding ceremony described in chapter four. In both cases the woman's family presents chickens and mats to her husband's family, while the husband's family presents money, food, and whisky to his wife's family in recognition of her sacrifice during the mourning period.

36 Discussion with the *presidente* of Éésòngé, about women's issues, recorded in Field Notebook #4, pp. 26–27. Dioula, 5 November 1998.

37 Discussion of Baka-Bangando relations with Anda and Molomb, recorded in Field Notebook #7, pp. 34–42. Dioula-Mbandame, 28 April 2000.

38 Anda's comments, recorded in Field Notebook #7, p. 38. Dioula-Mbandame, 28 April 2000.

CHAPTER SIX: IDENTITIES

Historical discussion and self-narrative, Mosakamo. Recorded on field cassette #9A. Wélélé, 7 March 1999.

1 Historical discussion with Maga, recorded in Field Notebook #3, pp. 142–49. Lopondji, 5 October 1998.

2 Historical discussion with Wanguwangu, recorded on Field Cassette #19, sides A and B. Dioula-Beligela, 14 May 1999.

3 See, for a few examples among many, Museur 1969; Peterson 1978; Blackburn 1982; Bahuchet and Guillaume 1982; Bahuchet 1984, 1988; Hoffman 1984; Bailey and Peacock 1998.

4 "La mort des Pygmées" in *Illustration*, no. 4947 (25 December 1937): 503. Centre des Archives d'Outre Mer, box 353, file 169.

5 Discussion with Kebikibele, recorded in Field Notebook #4, pp. 60–62. Dioula-Mbandame, 9 November 1998.

6 Discussion with Wanguwangu, recorded on Field Cassette #19, sides A and B. Dioula-Beligela, 14 May 1999.

7 "Declaration Générale"—Union des Populations du Cameroun (UPC), Section Kamerounaise du Rassemblement Démocratique Africain (RDA). Conférence des Cadres de l'UPC, 25–27 September 1964.

8 Report from the Chef de Poste Frontiére de Sûreté Fédérale de Moloundou

to M. le Directeur de la Sûreté Fédérale, Yaoundé, 5 March 1965, concerning "Activités rebelles." National Archives of Cameroon, file no. 19929.

9   Discussion with Ndjumbé, recorded in Field Notebook #3, p. 58. Dioula-Centre, 11 July 1997.

10 Discussion with Ngangue, recorded in Field Notebook #3, p. 45. Mbateka, 23 June 1997.

11 Discussion with Wanguwangu, recorded on Field Cassette #19, sides A and B. Dioula-Beligela, 14 May 1999.

12 Discussion with Ndjumbé, recorded in Field Notebook #3, p. 58. Dioula-Centre, 11 July 1997.

13 Logs are brought from the Lobéké forest region over 1700 kilometers of fairly atrocious logging roads to Douala, the port from which the logs are shipped to markets, primarily in Europe and Asia.

14 Buba here specifically referred to the Bangando elders with whom his own father had close relations as his "grandparents," alluding to the familial relations that were often shared between Bangando and Baka.

15 Discussion with Buba, recorded on Field Cassettes #7B and #8A. Dioula-Mbandame, 31 March 1999.

16 Incident recorded in Field Notebook #4, pp. 97–105, Dioula, 3 December 1998. See also Woodburn (1982: 440–41) for discussion of hunters' ownership of meat, and Lee (1979: 247–48) on increased hoarding and social conflict in the sharing of meat as markets become monetized.

17 Discussion with Mikome about hunting, recorded in Field Notebook #5, pp. 6–8. Dioula-Mbandame, 9 February 1999.

18 According to elephant hunters today, most commercial hunts are undertaken with automatic weapons such as AK-47s, which are widely available in the Republic of Congo. The hunter bought four rounds of ammunition in Moloundou for 60,000 CFA, approximately US$120.

19 Discussion about elephant hunting with Mikome, Webora, and Motapa, recorded in Field Notebook #5, pp. 16–22. Dioula-Mbandame, 9 February 1999.

20 Dɔ̀bídɔ̀bì is the nickname for WWF, derived from a local pronunciation of the letter "W" —dɔ̀bí.

21 Discussion with and self-narrative by Mokogwea, recorded on Field Cassette #17, sides A and B. Lopondji, 4 May 1999.

22 Discussion with Zoduma, recorded on Field Cassette #28B, #29A. Dioula-Saa Bo Mbela, 13 June 1999.

23 In 1996, 500 CFA was approximately US$1. Thus, 10,000 CFA amounts to US$20; 15,000 CFA to US$30; and 20,000 CFA to US$40.

24 Discussion with Mbito, recorded on Field Cassette #24, sides A and B. Dioula-Centre, 28 May 1999.

25 When Calais (a French division IV team) defeated Bordeaux (a French

division I team) in a massive upset during the spring of 2000, soccer fans in southeastern Cameroon overwhelmingly and enthusiastically supported Calais from the outset of the match. The surprising victory of the underdog was a topic of conversation for days afterward.

26   Discussion with Ngongo, Sakomo, and Monigia, recorded in Field Notebook #5, p. 142. Ndongo, 21 March 1999.

27   Historical discussion with Mosakamo, recorded on Field Cassette #9A. Wélélé, 7 March 1999.

CHAPTER SEVEN: CONTRADICTIONS

1   Http://ld.panda.org/jengi_songs.html. Accessed 15 June 2001; site now discontinued.

2   Http://www.wwfcameroon.org/cpoprojects/seandjengi.htm. Accessed 1 November 2002; site now discontinued.

3   Http://www.wwfcameroon.org/cpoprojects/seandjengi.htm. Accessed 1 November 2002; site now discontinued.

4   Http://www.wwfcameroon.org/cpoprojects/seandjengi.htm, Accessed 1 November 2002; site now discontinued.

5   According to oral historical accounts of these conflicts, the Nzimou and the Djem are distinct communities.

6   Discussion with Karin Augustat about social categories, recorded in Field Notebook #5, pp. 13–15. Yokadouma, 1 February 1999.

7   Discussion with Brother Matthias, the Pentecostal Christian minister in Dioula, recorded in Field Notebook #6, p. 55. Dioula-Centre, 31 March 1999.

8   Discussion with Sister Agathe, recorded in Field Notebook #5, pp. 61–62, 67, 76–80. Salapoumbé, 1 March 1999.

9   Discussion with Sister Thérèse, recorded in Field Notebook #1, pp. 102–3. Moloundou, 24 January 1996.

10   Discussion with Sister Thérèse, recorded in Field Notebook #1, pp. 104–5. Forest *mbándà* behind Dioula, 24 January 1996.

11   Interview with and self-portrait by Seo, recorded in Field Notebook #6, pp. 38–39. Ndongo, 26 March 1999.

12   Discussion with nurse at Centre de Santé, recorded in Field Notebook #7, pp. 48–49. Salapoumbé, 2 May 2000.

13   Discussion with nurse at Centre de Santé, recorded in Field Notebook #4, pp. 68–69. Salapoumbé, 18 November 1998.

14   Http://www.ameri-cana.com/bongo_hunting_in_Cameroon.htm. Accessed 15 July 2001; site now discontinued.

15   American client of Safari Alain Raoul, recorded in Field Notebook #7, pp. 53–55. Mambélé-Mbanjani, 2 May 2000.

16 Discussions with Medola, recorded in Field Notebook #6, p. 91. Mambélé, 27 April 1999.

17 "Stealing the bones of the Baka" refers to the widespread belief that certain body parts contain supernatural essences of life and power. If someone seeks power, it can be gained by stealing body parts, such as bones, and extracting and consuming the powerful essence of that person. In southeastern Cameroon, the fear of stealing and using body parts is common among all local communities.

18 Discussion with Medola, recorded on Field Cassette #29. Mambélé, 20 July 1998.

Glossary of Non-English Terms

The Bangando language has three tones: falling, flat (neutral), and rising. The tones shift based on the grammatical context in which the word is used. This glossary reflects the tones of words used in the grammatical contexts in which the terms are first used or quoted in the book.

GUIDE TO SOUNDS:

ɛ   pronounced as the "e" in "pet"
e   pronounced as the "e" in the French word, "bébé"
ɔ   pronounced as the "o" in "not"
o   pronounced as the "o" in "no"
ɓ   implosive "b"
ɗ   implosive "d"
ʏ   "y" sound that combines the consonants "djy"

a to

à to be

à third-person pronoun: he/she

àààà no

ákìbà thank you

álè first-person possessive pronoun: my (Baka)

bàló forest clearing (*savanne* in French)

bándí alliance of friendship

ʼBàngàndò Bangando

baaz open-walled verandahs, used by men; plural form *ebaaz* (Bakwélé)

bè little; little one; child

ʼBékà men's circumcision rites and secret society

bèmbèkò young woman

bémɔ́ngó but

bè ngándò little crocodiles

békà male circumcision ceremony

bílìkì brick

bò to be

bò person or people of a particular quality

bò ballon people of the ball (soccer players and enthusiasts)

bò Cameroon people of Cameroon

bò Congo people of Congo

bò dáá sèà people of bad heart (literally, "liver")

bò dáwà people of the monkey

bò dáwà dúsé people of the monkey subclan (species unidentified)

bò dáwà kángá people of the monkey subclan: colobus monkey (*Colobus guereza uellensis*)

bò dáwà málèkè people of the monkey subclan: de Brazza's monkey (*Cercopithecus neglectus*)

bò dáwà ndédé people of the monkey subclan: white-nosed Guenon monkey, (*Cercopithecus nictitans nictitans*)

bò dìkàsà people of a hardy shrub (species not identified); Bangando clan name

bò dɔbídɔbì people of WWF

bò dwá people of sorcery

bò fɔ́lɔ́ people of the elephant; Bangando clan name

bò gɔ̀ people of the panther; Bangando clan name

bò gɔ́ɔ́ people of the snake; Bangando clan name

bò jáá people of the (same) stomach; siblings through alliance

bò kà people who are closed or hidden

bò kísìnì people of the kitchen

bò kótà people from behind (the kitchen)

bò kɔ́à people of the forest

bò lé people of the village

bò màtúà people of the vehicle

bò mbánjó people of the verandah

bò mbélá people of the eagle; Bangando clan name

bò mbísà people of the *mbísà* shrub (*Carpholobia alba*); Bangando clan name

bò mbìkò people of the caiman; Bangando clan name

bò mbúdì people of the sitatunga (*Tragelaphus spekii*); Bangando clan name

bò míkòmè people of the wild cat

bò ndjɔ́mbò people of dirt or filth

bò ngílí people of the tortoise; Bangando clan name

bò ngɔ́lɔ́ people of the snail; Bangando clan name

bò ngwéà people of the pig; Bangando clan name

bò njémúnjèmù people of disorder or chaos

bò nué people of birds; Bangando clan name

bò safari people of the safari hunting companies

bò shàntié people of the timber camp (*chantier* in French)

bò tú sàà people of the snare; commercial bushmeat hunters

bò vílí people of the city

bò wé people of fire; Bangando clan name (totem is the monitor lizard)

bò yélé people of the buffalo; Bangando clan name

bón alliance (Mbomam)

boussolliers (French) logging assistants who locate trees to be felled (literally, "compassers")

búnù soil

bwàlá wì youth

dáwè bad

dé to do

dèí kíà What is it? How are you?

díà meat

Dɔ̀bídɔ̀bì nickname for WWF (World Wide Fund for Nature)

díkwèlí bride-price

díò Bangando ritual to commemorate a deceased notable

Ɖíò Bangando spirit

dɔ̀làwè good; well

dwá sorcery

dwálà forge

Ɛ́ɛ̀sɔ̀ngé interethnic women's association (also known by French acronym ASSOFADI)

èlì, èlè to go

éné you (plural)

ésò friend (Bakwélé)

fé woven mat

fékí wild mangoes (*Irvingia excels*; Baka)

fɔ̀lɔ̀ elephant

gà kind; type

gàlà house

gàlà bílìkì wattle-and-daub house; "brick house"

gálá wè tribunal

gàɔ́u rattan

gbàdè to help

Gɓákɔ̀lɔ̀ Boumba River

gbàsà freshwater shrimp

gbàsì dáwè primitive way of life (literally, "bad way of life")

gbò road

hányáwè difficult; complicated; hard-hearted

ììnjéwùsò iron currency

jáá stomach

jéléjélé mixed

jɛngì initiation ceremony for Baka males

Jɛngì Baka forest spirit

jɔ́p paid labor; job

kà so; therefore

kàlíkíkàlíkí all at once; all together

kangáá bark of the *ayous* tree (*Triplochiton scleroxylon*)

kátá small, round baskets

kífí transformation between human and animal form

kínò same

kípùí sedan chair mounted on two long poles and carried by four men

kísìnì kitchen

kòlò rain

kótà behind

kɔ́à forest

kɔ̀ánì meeting

kɔ̀lá people who share the same name; homonyms

kpè to be born

kúlú kind or type of thing; way of doing something; "race" in French

kúmbí leaves of the *Gnetum africanum* plant, used for making a leaf stew

kwà Bangando throwing knife

lé village

lì water

lìì name

lufɔ́nɔ̀ different

má . . . nà compound indicating negative phrase

Máánú territory near the Nile River, legendary place of Bangando origin *mbándà*   long-term garden located five to fifteen kilometers from village

Mbànjáni   river near Mambélé village

mbánjó   open-walled verandah, used by men

mbaìé   friend

mbáwálá   monitor lizard

mbékà   carrying basket

mbénjí   porcupine

mbɔní   ritualized peace alliance

mì   first-person pronoun: I, me

mimbeng   human-to-elephant transformation (Bakwélé)

móbùlè   very secret

módyàdyà   Bangando dance

mòkɛlákɛlá   herd of elephants that includes humans transformed into elephants

mólómbí   ability to transform oneself into an elephant (initially a Baka form of sorcery)

mòngúlu   dome-shaped Baka houses

mónyàdì   wedding process

mòtámbá   slave

mɔ   thing; concept; entity

mɔkóndjì   chief

mɔkóndjì dwálà   blacksmith (literally, "chief of the forge")

mɔkɔpɔlɔ   team of porters who carry meat from the forest to the village

mɔngwélé   palm oil colored red by mahogany dust, used to anoint brides

mù   first-person possessive pronoun: my (Bangando)

na   conjunction: and

ná   preposition: to, from

ndámù   round nets for catching shrimp and small fish

Ndjámbé   God

Ndjàngé   Lobéké swamp; inland delta formed by the Lobéké River

Ndjòmbi   a river fifteen kilometers east of Dioula

ndùpá   iron currency

né   conjunction that accompanies "to be"

ngàdí   hill

ngándò   crocodile

ngbà   big

ngbà gálà   main house, especially for sleeping (literally, "big house")

ngílí   tortoise

ngòlòngòló   local whisky, distilled from manioc and maize

Ngombé   ancestral community of contemporary Bangando

ngwéà   forest pig

ngɔlɔ   honey

njémúnjèmù   disorder; chaos

nú   language; mouth; source

nú kòlò   source of pure water

Nyàwúndì   vine bridge created by Ndjámbé (God)

ɔɔ   we; our

òò   to spill out; to break open

pàkàdyò   a light-colored hardwood tree (*Triplochiton scleroxylon*)

pánò   Bangando cross-bow

patron (French)   boss; superior

pèká   because

pèkí   wild mangoes (*Irvingia excelsa*), known as *fékí* in Baka

pèmbé swèè   hot, dry season

Pényé   lighter-skinned people, whose skin turns pink rather than brown in the sun, and who ride on horseback. Translated into French as *Arabe*.

pímbá   subsistence garden, located within five kilometers of a village

pɔmɔ   clearing underbrush and weeds

sà   neighborhood

sáá   snare

sàà   leaf

sàà té   thick, round leaves of *marantacaea* plants

sàà ɔ́ngò   leaves of the *ayous* tree (*Triplochyton scleroxylon*) used to treat a cough

sábé   cough

sándà length of calico cloth, worn as a skirt or headscarf, used as a sling to carry children, or used for other domestic purposes

sɛ́ɛ́, sɛ́à heart; biophysical location of emotions (literally, "liver")

sèbì to see; to visit

sɛ́kɛ́sɛ́kɛ́ sáá ngɔ̀mbé tall, straight, very strong tree, perhaps referencing the ancestral Bangando community, Ngombé

shàntìé timber camp

sìì famine

síkínò one; same

síní ritually avoid

sous-préfet (French) official in charge of the district of Boumba and Ngoko, equivalent to the district commissioner

sɔ́bɔ́ small garden located on the edge of a stream

súlòwè very (much)

súsúkú broth made from chili peppers, eggplants, and a particular kind of bark

swɛ́ngɛ́lɛ́ pure

tètè real

tètè mókàndà real clothes; i.e., manufactured pants, shirts, and skirts rather than raffia fiber, bark, or leather clothing

tètè wì elders (literally, "real people")

tòkídí small

Tòkídí tòkídí bò dɔ́ɔ́ dà wè "Little by little the pieces come together"

tòlì ná to come from

tú to set a snare

twá nest

twálá kitchen (archaic form)

wákè chimpanzee

wélà to speak

wè problem; conflict

wé fire

wì person

yã̀ bàng people of the hornbill; Mbomam clan

yã̀ bàngò people of the green pigeon; Mbomam clan

yã̀ biel people of the eagle; Bakwélé clan

yã̀ biótà people of the weaver bird; Mbomam clan

yã̀ dadjak people of the monkey; Bakwélé clan

yã̀ kei people of the leopard; Bakwélé clan

yã̀ kwíè people of the blue duiker; Bakwélé clan

yã̀ msɔla people of the squirrel; Mbomam clan

yã̀ zɔma people of the rat; Mbomam clan

yã̀ zozape people of the snake; Bakwélé clan

yé the (plural)

yɛ̃ gùgà people of the monitor lizard; Baka clan name

yɛ̃ kpóngbò people of rattan, Baka clan

yɛ̃ kémà people of the monkey; Baka clan name

yɛ̃ lɛ́kèmbà people of the monitor lizard; Baka clan name

yɛ̃ líkèmbà people of the elephant; Baka clan

yɛ̃ mòkùmù people of the snake; Baka clan

yɛ̃ mòmbító people of the mombito tree; Baka clan

yɛ̃ mɔ́ndɔ́ people of the wild pig; Baka clan

yɛ̃ ndúmù people of the buffalo/drum; Baka clan

yɛ̃ ngándá people of the black civet; Baka clan

yɛ̃ ngílá people of the switch/beating stick; Baka clan

yɛ̃ njèmbè people of the njembe fish; Baka clan

yɛ̃ sìlò people of the electric fish; Baka clan

yɛ̃kù swamp

yɛ̃lì Baka ceremony to initiate an elephant hunt

yɔ̀ with

yɔ̀á their

Bibliography

Abéga, Séverin Cécile. 1998. *Pygmées Baka: Le Droit à la Différence*. Yaoundé, Cameroon: INADES Formation.

Akolea Alfred. 1994. "L'évolution historique d'une ville du Cameroun 1896–1982: Le cas de Moloundou." Master's thesis, Université de Yaoundé I.

Allport, Gordon. 1954. *The Nature of Prejudice*. Cambridge, MA: Addison Wesley Publishing.

Althabe, Gérard. 1965. "Changements sociaux chez les pygmées Baka de l'est Cameroun." *Cahiers d'Études Africaines* 5 (20): 561–92.

Ango, Mengue. 1982. "L'est Camerounais: Une géographie du sous-peuplement et de la marginalité." Ph.D. diss., Université de Bordeaux II.

Arcand, Bernard. 1988. "Il n'y a jamais eu de société des chasseurs-cueilleurs." *Anthropologie et Sociétés* 12 (1): 39–58.

Augustat, Karin. 1997a. "Concept de la cellule socio-économique (CSE). Projet de conservation des forêts naturelles au sud-est Cameroun." Yokadouma, Cameroon:

Programme de Conservation et Gestion de la Biodiversité au Cameroun (PRO-FORNAT).

——. 1997b. "Rapport de l'étude socio-économique participative (selon la méthode MARP) à Dioula, sud-est Cameroun. 20–29 June, 1997." Yaoundé, Cameroon: Gesellschaft für technische Zusammenarbeit.

Bahuchet, Serge. 1984. "Circulation et échanges en Afrique tropicale: Relations entre chasseurs-cueilleurs pygmées et agriculteurs de forêt en Centrafrique." *Revista de Pré-Historia* 11: 86–97.

——. 1988. "Food supply and uncertainty among the Aka Pygmies (Lobaye, Central African Republic)." In *Coping with Uncertainty in Food Supply*, ed. Igor de Garine and Geoffrey A. Harrison, 118–49. Oxford: Clarendon Press.

——. 1992. *Dans la Forêt d'Afrique Centrale: Les Pygmées Aka et Baka*. Paris: Éditions Peeters/SELAF.

——. 1993a. *La Rencontre des Agriculteurs: Les Pygmées parmi les Peuples d'Afrique Centrale*. Paris: Peeters/SELAF

——. 1993b. "History of the inhabitants of the central African rain forest: Perspectives from comparative linguistics." In *Tropical Forests, People, and Food: Biocultural Interactions and Applications for Development*, ed. Claude Marcel Hladik, Annette Hladik, et al., 37–54. Paris: UNESCO.

——. 1993c. "L'invention des pygmées." *Cahiers d'Études Africaines* 129 (33–1): 153–81.

——. 1995. "Changements culturels et changements linguistiques dans la forêt d'Afrique centrale." *Revue d'Ethnolinguistique (Cahiers du LACITO)* 7: 43–69.

——. 1999. "Aka Pygmies." In *The Cambridge Encyclopedia of Hunter-Gatherers*, ed. Richard B. Lee and Richard Daly, 190–93. Cambridge: Cambridge University Press.

Bahuchet, Serge, and Henri Guillaume. 1982. "Aka-Farmer Relations in the Northwest Congo Basin." In *Politics and History in Band Societies*, ed. Eleanor Leacock and Richard Lee, 189–211. Cambridge: Cambridge University Press.

Bailey, Robert, and Nadine Peacock. 1988. "Efe Pygmies of northeast Zaire: Subsistence strategies in the Ituri Forest." In *Coping with Uncertainty in Food Supply*, ed. Igore de Garine and Geoffrey A. Harrison, 88–117. Oxford: Clarendon Press.

Bailey, Robert, and Robert Aunger. 1989. "Humans as primates: the social relationships of Efe pygmy men in comparative perspective." *International Journal of Primatology* 11 (2): 127–46.

Barnard, Alan, and Justin Kenrick. 2001. *Africa's Indigenous Peoples: "First Peoples" or "Marginalized Minorities"?* Edinburgh: Centre of African Studies, University of Edinburgh.

Barth, Fredrik. 1969. *Ethnic Groups and Boundaries: The Social Organization of Culture Difference*. Boston: Little, Brown and Co.

——. 2002. "Boundaries and connections." In *Signifying Identities: Anthropological Perspectives on Boundaries and Contested Values*, ed. Anthony Cohen, 17–36. London, New York: Routledge.

Baumann, Hermann, and Diedrich Westermann. 1948. *Peuples et Civilisations de l'Afrique*. Paris: Payot.

Bayart, Jean-François. 1993. *The State in Africa: The Politics of the Belly*. New York: Longman.

Biggs, Stephen, and Grant Smith. 2001. "Beyond methodologies: Coalition-building for participatory technology development." *World Development* 26 (2): 239–48.

Blackburn, Roderick. 1982. "In the land of milk and honey: Okiek adaptations to their forests and neighbours." In *Politics and History in Band Societies*, ed. Eleanor Leacock and Richard Lee, 283–306. Cambridge: Cambridge University Press.

Boursier, Daniel. 1994. "*Depuis ce jour là...*" *Contes des Pygmées Baka du Sud-Est Cameroun*. Paris: Éditions L'Harmattan.

———. 1996. *Pöli: Mémoire d'une Femme Pygmée: Témoignage Auto-biographique d'une Femme Pygmée-Baka (Sud-Est Cameroun)*. Translated by Daniel Boursier. Paris: Éditions L'Harmattan.

Bringa, Tone. 1995. *Being Muslim the Bosnian Way: Identity and Community in a Central Bosnian Village*. Princeton, NJ: Princeton University Press.

Brisson, Robert. 1999. *Mythologie des Pygmées Baka (Sud-Cameroun): Mythologie et Contes*. Vols. 1 and 2. Paris: Peeters/SELAF.

Brubaker, Rogers and Frederick Cooper. 2000. "Beyond identity." *Theory and Society* 29:1–47.

Burnham, Philip. 1980. *Opportunity and Constraint in a Savanna Society: The Gbaya of Meiganga, Cameroon*. London: Academic Press.

———. 1996. *The Politics of Cultural Difference in Northern Cameroon*. Washington, D.C.: Smithsonian Institution Press.

———. 2000. "Whose forest? Whose myth? Conceptualisations of community forests in Cameroon." In *Land, Law and Environment: Mythical Land, Legal Boundaries*, ed. Allen Abramson and Dimitrios Thodossopoulos, 31–58. London: Pluto Press.

Burnham, Philip, Elisabeth Copet-Rougier, and Philip Noss. 1986. "Gbaya and Mkako: Contribution ethno-linguistiqué l'histoire de l'est Cameroun." *Paideuma* 32: 87–128.

Cavalli-Sforza, Luigi Luca, ed. 1986. *African Pygmies*. Orlando, FL: Academic Press.

Cavalli-Sforza, Luigi Luca, Paolo Menozzi, and Alberto Piazza, eds. 1993. *The History and Geography of Human Genes*. Princeton, NJ: Princeton University Press.

Christy, Cuthbert. 1924. *Big Game and Pygmies: Experiences of a Naturalist in Central African Forests in Quest of the Okapi*. London: MacMillan and Co.

Clammer, John. 1978. "Concepts and objects in economic anthropology." *The New Economic Anthropology*, ed. John Clammer. New York: St. Martin's Press.

Comaroff, John L., and Jean Comaroff. 2009. *Ethnicity, Inc*. Chicago: University of Chicago Press.

Conklin, Harold. 1961. "The study of shifting cultivation." *Current Anthropology* 2 (1): 27–61.

Copet-Rougier, Elisabeth. 1998. "Political-economic history of the upper Sangha." In *Resource Use in the Trinational Sangha River Region of Equatorial Africa: Histories, Knowledge Forms, and Institutions*, ed. Heather Eves, Rebecca Hardin, and Stephanie Rupp, 51–71. New Haven, CT: Yale School of Forestry and Environmental Studies, Bulletin No. 102.

Coquery-Vidrovitch, Catherine. 1972. *Le Congo au Temps des Grands Compagnies Concessionnaires, 1892-1930*. Paris: Mouton.

————. 1998. "The upper-Sangha in the time of the concession companies." In *Resource Use in the Trinational Sangha River Region of Equatorial Africa: Histories, Knowledge Forms, and Institutions*, ed. Heather Eves, Rebecca Hardin, and Stephanie Rupp, 72–84. New Haven, CT: Yale School of Forestry and Environmental Studies, Bulletin No. 102.

D'Hellemmes, Ignace. 1985. *Le Père des Pygmées*. Paris: Flammarion.

Demesse, Lucien. 1980. *Techniques et économie des Pygmées Babinga*. Paris: Institut d'Ethnologie, Musée de l'Homme.

Dongmo, Jean-Louis, and Jean-Felix Loung. 1994. "Identification des groupes-cibles dans la region de l'est." Report prepared for SNV-Cameroon, 1–22. Yaoundé, Cameroon.

Dounias, Edmond. 1993a. "Perception and use of wild yams by the Baka hunter-gatherers in south Cameroon." In *Tropical Forests, People, and Food: Biocultural Interactions and Applications for Development*, ed. C. M. Hladik, A. Hladik, et al., 621–32. Paris: UNESCO.

————. 1993b. "Dymanique et gestion différentielle du systéme de production à dominante agricôle des Mvae du sud Cameroun forestier." Ph.D. diss., Université des Sciences et Techniques du Languedoc.

Durkheim, Emile, and Marcel Mauss. 1963[1903]. *Primitive Classification*. Translated by Rodney Needham. Chicago: University of Chicago Press.

Eder, James. 1987. *On the Road to Tribal Extinction: Depopulation, Deculturation, and Adaptive Well-Being among the Batek of the Philippines*. Berkeley: University of California Press.

Edjondji, Mempouth Andre Innocent. 1994. "Étude historique des Mpo'oh et apparentes du sud-est Camerounais des origines 1916." Master's thesis, École Normale Supérieure, Yaoundé, Cameroon.

Fairhead, James, and Melissa Leach. 1996. *Misreading the African Landscape: Society and Ecology in a Forest-Savanna Mosaic*. Cambridge: Cambridge University Press.

Forni, Eric, and Alain Karsenty. 2000. "Potentiel de bois d'œuvre exploitable et gestion durable dans le domaine forestier permanent du Cameroun." In *Audit Économique et Financier du Secteur Forestier au Cameroun*. CIRAD-Forêt. Report prepared for Ministère de l'Economie et des Finances, Yaoundé, Cameroon.

Foucault, Michel 1980. *Power/Knowledge: Selected Interviews and Other Writings, 1972–1977*. Edited by Colin Gordon. New York: Pantheon Books.

Frasez, P. 1953. "Pygmées de la Boumba-Ngoko (Cameroun)." In *Encyclopedie Mensuelle d'Outre Mer* 3 (31): 83–88. Aix-en-Provence: Centre des Archives d'Outre Mer. Box 353, file 169.

Friedman, John. 1981. *The Monstrous Races in Medieval Art and Thought*. Cambridge, MA: Harvard University Press.

Geertz, Clifford. 1973. *The Interpretation of Cultures*. New York: Basic Books.

Geschiere, Peter. 2004. "Ecology, belonging and xenophobia: The 1994 Forest Law in Cameroon and the issue of 'community.'" In *Rights and the Politics of Recognition in Africa*, ed. Harri Englund and Francis Nyamanjoh, 237–60. London: Zed Books.

————. 2009. *The Perils of Belonging: Autochthony, Citizenship, and Exclusion in Africa and Europe*. Chicago: University of Chicago Press.

Geschiere, Peter, and Francis Nyamnjoh. 2000. "Capitalism and autochthony: The see-saw of mobility and belonging." *Public Culture* 12 (2): 423–52.

Giles-Vernick, Tamara. 1999. "We wander like birds: Migration, indigeneity, and the fabrication of frontiers in the Sangha River basin of equatorial Africa." *Environmental History* 4 (2): 168–97.

———. 2002. *Cutting the Vines of the Past: Environmental Histories of the Central African Rain Forest.* Charlottesville: University of Virginia Press.

Gnangue, Jean-Claude. 1998. "Évolution des techniques de chasse chez les Bangando du sud-est Cameroun: Des origines 1994." Master's thesis, École Normale Superieure, Yaoundé, Cameroon.

Green, Maia. 2000. "Participatory development and the appropriation of agency in southern Tanzania." *Critique of Anthropology* (20) 1: 67–89.

Greenberg, Joseph. 1955. *Studies in African Linguistic Classification.* New Haven: Compass Publishing Company.

———. 1963. *The Languages of Africa.* Bloomington, IN: University of Indiana Press.

Grinker, Richard Roy. 1990. "Images of denigration: structuring inequality between foragers and farmers in the Ituri Forest, Zaıre." *American Ethnologist* 17 (1): 111–30.

———. 1994. *Houses in the Rainforest: Ethnicity and Inequality among Farmers and Foragers in Central Africa.* Berkeley: University of California Press.

———. 2000. *In the Arms of Africa: The Life of Colin M. Turnbull.* New York: St. Martin's Press.

Gupta, Akhil. 1998. *Postcolonial Developments: Agriculture in the Making of Modern India.* Durham, NC: Duke University Press.

Guthrie, Malcolm. 1970. *Comparative Bantu: An Introduction to the Comparative Linguistics and Prehistory of the Bantu Languages.* Farnborough: Gregg Press.

Guyer, Jane. 1995. "Wealth in people as wealth in knowledge: Accumulation and composition in equatorial Africa." *Journal of African History* 36 (1): 91–120.

Hall, Jefferson. 1993. "Lobéké report" in *Proceedings of the Workshop on Community Forest/Protected Area Management.* 12–13 October 1993. Yaoundé, Cameroon: MINEF/WWF.

Harms, Robert. 1979. "Oral tradition and ethnicity." *Journal of Interdisciplinary History* 10 (1): 61–85.

———. 1981. *River of Wealth, River of Sorrow: The Central Zaıre Basin in the Era of the Slave and Ivory Trade, 1500–1891.* New Haven, CT: Yale University Press.

Hart, John. 1979. "Nomadic hunters and village cultivators: A study of subsistence interdependence in the Ituri Forest, Zaire." Master's thesis, Michigan State University.

Hart, John, and Terese Hart. 1984. "The Mbuti of Zaire: Political change and the opening of the Ituri Forest." *Cultural Survival Quarterly* 8 (3): 18–20.

———. 1986. "The ecological basis of hunter-gatherer subsistence in African rain forests: The Mbuti of eastern Zaire." *Human Ecology* 14 (1): 29–55.

Headland, Thomas, and Lawrence Reid. 1989. "Hunter-gatherers and their neighbors from prehistory to the present." *Current Anthropology* 30 (1): 43–66.

Headland, Thomas, and Robert Bailey. 1991. "Have hunter-gatherers ever lived in tropical rain forest independently of agriculture?" *Human Ecology* 19 (2): 115–22.

Hewlett, Barry. 2000. "Central African government's and international NGOs' perceptions of Baka Pygmy development." In *Hunters and Gatherers of the Modern World: Conflict, Resistance, and Self-Determination,* ed. Peter Schweitzer, Megan Biesele, and Robert Hitchcock, 380–90. New York, Oxford: Berghahn Books.

Hocart, Arthur Maurice. 1953. *The Life-Giving Gift and Other Essays.* New York: Grove Press.

Hoffman, Carl. 1984. "Punan foragers in the trading networks of Southeast Asia." In *Past and Present in Hunter-Gatherer Societies,* ed. Carmel Schrire, 123–49. Orlando: Academic Press.

Holtzman, Jon. 2006. "Food and memory." *Annual Review of Anthropology* 35: 361–78.

International Labor Organization. 1989. Convention on Indigenous and Tribal Peoples. Convention No. 169.

International Tropical Timber Organization (ITTO). 1998. "Annual Review and Assessment of the World Tropical Timber Situation 1998." Available online at http://www.itto.or.jp/ (accessed 23 July 2000).

Jahoda, Gustav. 1999. *Images of Savages: Ancient Roots of Modern Prejudice in Western Culture.* London: Routledge.

Jenkins, Richard. 1994. "Rethinking ethnicity: Identity, categorization and power." *Ethnic and Racial Studies* 17 (2): 197–219.

Joiris, Daou Veronique. 1993a. "The mask that is hungry for yams: Ethnoecology of *Dioscorea mangenotiana* among the Baka, Cameroon." In *Tropical Forests, People, and Food: Biocultural Interactions and Applications for Development,* ed. C. M. Hladik, A. Hladik, et al., 633–41. Paris: UNESCO.

———. 1993b. "How to walk side by side with the elephant: Baka pygmy hunting rituals in southern Cameroon." *Civilizations* 32 (1–2): 51–81.

———. 1996. "A comparative approach to hunting rituals among Baka Pygmies (Southeastern Cameroon)." In *Cultural Diversity among Twentieth-Century Foragers: An African Perspective,* ed. Susan Kent, 245–75. Cambridge: Cambridge University Press.

———. 1997. "La nature des uns et la nature des autres: Mythe et réalité du monde rural face aux aires protégées d'Afrique centrale." *Les Peuples des Forêts Tropicales: Systémes Traditionneles et Développement Rural en Afrique Équatoriale, Grande Amazonie et Asie du Sud-Est.* Special volume, *Civilizations* 44 (1–2): 94–103.

———. 1998. "La chasse, la chance, le chant: Aspects du systéme rituel des Baka du Cameroun." Ph.D. diss., Université Libre de Bruxelles.

Karsenty, Alain. 1999. "Vers la fin de l'état forestier? Appropriation des espaces et parage de la rente forestière au Cameroun." *Politique Africaine* 75: 147–61.

Keim, Curtis. 1999. *Mistaking Africa: Curiosities and Inventions of the American Mind.* Washington, D.C.: Smithsonian Institution Press.

Kelly, Robert. 1995. *The Foraging Spectrum: Diversity in Hunter-Gatherer Lifeways.* Washington, D.C.: Smithsonian Institution Press.

Kenrick, Justin. 2001. "Present predicament of hunter-gatherers and former hunter-gatherers of the central African rainforests." In *Africa's Indigenous Peoples: "First Peoples" or "Marginalized Minorities"?* ed. Alan Barnard and Justin Kenrick, 39–60. Edinburgh: Centre of African Studies, University of Edinburgh.

————. 2005. "Equalising processes, processes of discrimination, and the forest peoples of central Africa." In *Property and Equality: Ritualisation, Sharing, Egalitarianism*, ed. Thomas Widlok and Wolda Gossa Tadesse, 104–28. London: Routledge.

Kenrick, Justin, and Jerome Lewis. 2004. "Indigenous people's rights and the politics of the term 'indigenous.'" *Anthropology Today* 20 (2): 4–9.

Kent, Susan. 1996. *Cultural Diversity among Twentieth-Century Foragers: An African Perspective*. Cambridge: Cambridge University Press.

————. 2002. *Ethnicity, Hunter-Gatherers, and the "Other": Association and Assimilation in Africa*. Washington: Smithsonian Institution Press.

Kimura, Daiji. 2003. "Bakas' mode of co-presence." Supplementary issue, *African Studies Monographs* 28: 25–36.

Klieman, Kairn. 2003. *The Pygmies Were Our Compass: Bantu and Batwa in the History of West-Central Africa, Early Times to c. 1900*. Portsmouth: Heinemann.

Komatsu, Kaori. 1998. "The food cultures of the shifting cultivators in central Africa: The diversity in selection of food materials." Supplementary issue, *African Studies Monographs* 25: 149–77.

Konings, Piet. 2001. "Mobility and exclusion: Conflicts between autochthons and allochthons during political liberalization in Cameroon." *African Dynamics* 1: 169–94.

Kuper, Adam. 1988. *The Invention of Primitive Society: Transformations of an Illusion*. New York: Routledge.

————. 2003. "Return of the native." *Current Anthropology* 44 (4): 389–402.

Leclerc, Christian. 1998. "Social space, natural space, and development (Baka pygmies, southeastern Cameroon)." *APFT-News* 5: 5–8.

————. 2000. "Des pygmées entre la forêt et la savane: Étude comparative de deux campements Medzan (vallée du Mbam, Cameroun)." In *Challenging Elusiveness: Central African Hunter-Gatherers in a Multi-Disciplinary Perspective*, ed. Karen Biesbrouk, Stefan Elders, and Gerda Rossel, 169–86. Leiden: Research School for Asian, African, and Amerindian Studies.

Lee, Richard. 1979. *The !Kung San: Men, Women and Work in a Foraging Society*. New York: Cambridge University Press.

————. 1992. "Art, science, or politics? The crisis in hunter-gatherer studies." *American Anthropologist* 94 (1): 31–54.

————. 2005. "Power and property in twenty-first century foragers: A critical examination." In *Property and Equality: Encapsulation, Commercialization, Discrimination*, ed. Thomas Widlok and Wolde Gossa Tadesse, 16–31. New York: Berghan Books.

Lee, Richard, and Richard Daley, eds. 1999. *The Cambridge Encyclopedia of Hunter-Gatherers*. Cambridge: Cambridge University Press.

Leonard, Yves. 1997. "The Baka: A people between two worlds." Master's thesis, Providence Theological Seminary.

Leonhardt, Alec. 1999. "The culture of development in Bakaland: The apparatus of development in relation to Baka hunter-gatherers." Ph.D. diss., Princeton University.

Lévi-Strauss, Claude. 1969. *The Raw and the Cooked*. Translated by John Weightman and Doreen Weightman. New York: Harper and Row Publishers.

Lewis, Jerome. 2001. "Forest people or village people: Whose voice will be heard?" In *Africa's Indigenous Peoples: "First Peoples" or "Marginalized Minorities"?* ed. Alan Barnard and Justin Kenrick, 61–78. Edinburgh: Centre of African Studies, University of Edinburgh.

Li, Tania. 2000. "Articulating indigenous identity in Indonesia: Resource politics and the tribal slot." *Comparative Studies of Society and History* 42 (1): 149–79.

Lovejoy, Arthur O. 1936. *Great Chain of Being: A Study of the History of an Idea.* Cambridge, MA: Harvard University Press.

MacCormack, Carol, and Marilyn Strathern, eds. 1980. *Nature, Culture and Gender.* Cambridge: Cambridge University Press.

Mbembe, Achille. 2001. "Ways of seeing: Beyond the new nativism." *African Studies Review* 44 (2): 1–14.

Monga, Yvette. 2000. "'Au village': Space, culture and politics in Cameroon." *Cahiers d' Etudes Africaines* 160: 723–49.

———. 2001. "The politics of identity negotiation in Cameroon." *International Negotiation* 6 (2): 199–228.

Moñino, Yves. 1988. *Lexique Comparatif des Langues Oubanguiennes.* Paris: Librairie Orientaliste Paul Geuthner.

———. 1995. *Le Proto-Gbaya: Essai de Linguistique Comparative sur Vingt-et-une Langues d'Afrique Centrale.* Paris: éditions Peeters.

Museur, Michel. 1969. "Récentes perspectives sur la culture des Mbuti." *Cahiers d'Études Africaines* 9 (33): 150–59.

Nagata, Judith. 1981. "In defense of ethnic boundaries: The changing myths and charters of Malay identity." In *Ethnic Change,* ed. Charles Keyes. Seattle: University of Washington Press.

Neba, Aaron. 1987. *Géographie Moderne de la République du Cameroun,* 2nd ed. Camden, NJ: Éditions Neba.

Ngombe, Lucien. 1995. "L'évolution des Bangando du sud-est Cameroun: Des origines 1894." Master's thesis, L'École Normale Supérieure, Yaoundé, Cameroon.

Nguinguiri, Jean Claude, Georges Mouncharou, and Karin Augustat. 1999. "Gérer le pluralisme dans l'Est et dans le Sud du Cameroun." Paper presented at the Conférence Internationale sur la Conservation des Écosystémes Forestiers et le Développement du Sud et de l'Est du Cameroun. Yaoundé, Cameroon, 16–17 February 1999.

Njoh, Ambe. 2007. "Politico-economic determinants of forestry policy in Cameroon." *GeoJournal* 70: 109–20.

Oyono, Phil René, Jesse Ribot, and Anne Larson. 2006. "Green and black gold in rural Cameroon: Natural resources for local governance, justice, and sustainability." Working Paper Series. Washington, D.C.: World Resources Institute.

Jon Pederson and Espen Waehle. 1988. "The complexities of residential organization among the Efe (Mbuti) and the Bagombi (Baka): A critical view of the notion of flux." In *Hunters and Gatherers: History, Evolution and Social Change,* ed. Tim Ingold, David Riches, and James Woodburn, 75–90. New York: Berg.

Pelican, Michaela. 2009. "Complexities of indigeneity and autochthony: An African example." *American Ethnologist* 36 (1): 52–65.

Peterson, Jean Treloggen. 1978. "Hunter-gatherer/farmer exchange." *American Anthropologist* 80: 335–51.

Putnam, Anne E., and Allan Keller. 1954. *Madami: My Eight Years of Adventure with the Congo Pygmies*. New York: Prentice Hall.

Putnam, Patrick. 1948. "The pigmies of the Ituri Forest." In *A Reader in General Anthropology*, ed. Carleton Coon, 322–41. New York: Henry Holt.

Radcliffe-Brown, Alfred Reginald, and Daryll Forde. 1950. *African Systems of Kinship and Marriage*. London: Oxford University Press for the International African Institute.

Richards, Paul. 1995. "Participatory rural appraisal: A quick and dirty critique." *PLA Notes* 24: 13–20.

Ritvo, Harriet. 1997. *The Platypus and the Mermaid, and Other Figments of the Classifying Imagination*. Cambridge: Harvard University Press.

Rupp, Stephanie. 2001. "I, you, we, they: Forests of identity in southeastern Cameroon." Ph.D. diss., Yale University.

Safari Club International. 1997. *SCI Record Book of Trophy Animals. Africa Field Edition*. Edition IX, (1): 2. Tuscon, AZ: Safari Club International.

Sato, Hiroaki. 1998. "Folk etiology among the Baka, a group of hunter-gatherers in the African rainforest." Supplementary issue, *African Study Monographs* 25: 33–46.

———. 1992. "Notes on the distribution and settlement pattern of hunter-gatherers in northwestern Congo" *African Studies Monographs* 13 (4): 203–16.

Saugestad, Sidsel. 1998. *The Inconvenient Indigenous: Remote Area Development in Botswana, Donor Assistance, and the First People of the Kalahari*. Uppsala, Sweden: Nordic Africa Institute.

———. 1999. "Contested images: Indigenous peoples in Africa." *Indigenous Affairs* 2: 6–9.

———. 2001. "Contested images: 'First Peoples' or 'marginalised minorities' in southern Africa." In *Africa's Indigenous Peoples: "First Peoples" or "Marginalised Minorities"?* ed. Alan Barnard and Justin Kenrick, 299–322. Edinburgh: Centre of African Studies, University of Edinburgh.

Schebesta, Paul. 1940. *Les Pygmées*. Paris: Gallimard.

———. 1952. *Les Pygmées du Congo Belge*. Bruxelles: Institut Royal Colonial Belge.

Schweinfurth, Georg. 1874. *Im Herzen von Arika. Resien und Entdeckungen im Afrika während der Jarhre 1868–1873. Ein Beitrag zur Entdeckungsgeschichte von Afrika*. 3 vols. Leipzig: F. A. Brockhaus.

Scott, James. 1998. *Seeing Like a State: How Certain Schemes to Improve the Human Condition Have Failed*. New Haven: Yale University Press.

Sharpe, Barrie. 1998. "First the forest: Conservation, 'community' and 'participation' in south-west Cameroon." *Africa* 68: 25–45.

Silberbauer, George. 1994. "A sense of place." In *Key Issues in Hunter-Gatherer Research*, ed. Ernest Burch and Linda Ellanna, 119–46. Oxford: Berg.

Simone, AbdouMaliq. 2001. "On the worldling of African cities." *African Studies Review* 44 (2): 15–43.

Siroto, Leon. 1969. "Masks and social organization among the BaKwele people of western equatorial Africa." Ph.D. diss., Columbia University.

Socpa, Antoine. 2006. "Bailleurs autochtones et locataires allogènes: Enjeu foncier et participation politique au Cameroun." *African Studies Review.* 49 (2): 45–67.

Solway, Jacqueline, and Richard Lee. 1990. "Foragers, genuine or spurious? Situating the Kalahari San in history." *Current Anthropology* 31 (2): 109–46.

Spivak, Gayatri. 1988. *In Other Worlds: Essays on Cultural Politics.* New York: Routledge.

Strauss, Scott. 2006. *The Order of Genocide: Race, Power, and War in Rwanda.* Ithaca: Cornell University Press.

Terashima, Hideaki. 1986. "Economic exchange and the symbiotic relationship between the Mbuti (Efe) pygmies and the neighboring farmers." *Sprache und Geschichte in Afrika* 7 (1): 394–405.

Tessmann, Günter. 1934. *Die Baja: Ein Negerstamm im mittleren Sudan.* Stuttgart: Verlag Strecker und Schröder.

Thigio, Innocent. 2007. "Opportunities for community-based wildlife management: A case study from the Korup Region, Cameroon." Ph.D. diss., University of Göttingen.

Thomas, Keith. 1983. *Man in the Natural World: A History of Modern Sensibility.* New York: Pantheon.

Tsuru, Daisaku. 1998. "Diversity of ritual spirit performances among the Baka pygmies in southeastern Cameroon." Supplementary issue, *African Study Monographs* 25:47–84.

Turnbull, Colin. 1961. *The Forest People.* New York: Touchstone Books.

———. 1965. *Wayward Servants: The Two Worlds of the African Pygmies.* Garden City, NY: The Natural History Press.

———. 1983. *The Mbuti Pygmies: Change and Adaptation.* New York: Holt, Rinehart & Winston.

Tyson, Edward. [1699]1894. *The Anatomy of a Pygmy Compared with That of a Monkey, an Ape and a Man.* London: Thomas Bennett at the Half Moon.

Union des Populations du Cameroun. 1964. "Declaration Générale." Cameroonian Section of the African Democratic Assembly, Conference of Officials of the UPC, 25–27 September 1964.

Vabi, Michael, and Fondo Sikod. 2000. "Challenges of reconciling informal and formal land and resource access tenure: Evidence from WWF-supported conservation sites in Cameroon." Paper presented at the *2nd Pan-African Symposium on the Sustainable Use of Natural Resources in Africa,* July 2000, in Ouagadougou, Burkina Faso.

Vail, Leroy, ed. 1989. *The Creation of Tribalism in Southern Africa.* London: James Currey.

Vallois, Henri Victor. 1950. "Les pygmées du Cameroun." *Sciences* 67: 271–79.

Vallois, H. V., and Paulette. Marquer. 1976. *Les Pygmées Baka du Cameroun: Anthropologie et Ethnographie avec une Annexe Démographique.* Paris: Mémoires du Muséum National d'Histoire Naturelle.

Vansina, Jan. 1986. "Do pygmies have a history?" *Sprache und Geschichte in Afrika* 7 (1): 431–45.

———. 1990. *Paths in the Rainforests: Toward a History of Political Tradition in Equatorial Africa.* London: James Currey.

————. 1995. "New linguistic evidence and 'The Bantu expansion.'" *Journal of African History* 36 (2): 173–95.

Waehle, Espen. 1986. "Efe (Mbuti Pygmy) relations to Lese Dese villagers in the Ituri Forest, Zaïre: Historical changes during the last 150 years." *Sprache und Geschichte in Afrika* 7 (2): 375–411.

Wilmsen, Edwin. 1989. *Land Filled with Flies: A Political Economy of the Kalahari.* Chicago: University of Chicago Press.

Wilmsen, Edwin, and Patrick McAllister, eds. 1996. *The Politics of Difference: Ethnic Premises in a World of Power.* Chicago: University of Chicago Press.

Woodburn, James. 1982. "Egalitarian societies." *Man* (N.S.) 17 (3): 431–51.

————. 1997. "Indigenous discrimination: The ideological basis for discrimination against hunter-gatherer minorities in sub-Saharan Africa." *Racial and Ethnic Studies* 20 (2): 345–61.

————. 2001. "The political status of hunter-gatherers in present-day and future Africa." In *Africa's Indigenous Peoples: "First Peoples" or "Marginalized Minorities"?* ed. Alan Barnard and Justin Kenrick, 1–14. Edinburgh: Center of African Studies, University of Edinburgh.

————. 2005. "Egalitarian societies revisited." In *Property and Equality: Ritualization, Sharing, Egalitarianism*, ed. Thomas Widlok and Wolda Gossa Tadesse, 18–31. New York: Berghahn Books.

Worby, Eric. 1996 "Not to plow my master's field: Discourses of ethnicity and the production of inequality in Botswana." *Journal of Social Studies* 67: 73–108.

————. 1998. "Tyranny, parody, and ethnic polarity: Ritual engagements with the state in northern Zimbabwe." *Journal of Southern African Studies* 24 (3): 561–78.

World Resources Institute. 2005. *Interactive Forestry Atlas of Cameroon: An Overview.* Washington, D.C.: Global Forest Watch. Available online at http://archive.wri.org/publication_detail.cfm?pubid=3864 (accessed 25 June 2008).

Index

Note: page numbers in *italics* refer to figures, maps, or tables; those followed by "n" indicate endnotes.

Groupes d'Interêts Communitaires (GICs), 29–31

GTZ. *See Gesellschaft für technische Zusammenarbeit*

guns, 199, 275n18

heads of household, female, 106

healers (*bò dwá*), *186*, 209

health clinic, missionary, 238–40

hierarchies of power, domination, and subordination: Baka becoming more "acceptable," 131; *bándí* friendships and, 164; Bangando collaboration with state and missionaries over Baka, 75–78; Bangando over Mbomam, 86–87; in conservation literature, 226; economic dependence of Baka on Bakwélé, 80–81; ethnic affiliation and, 90–92, *92*; ethnic parentage and, *125*, 125–26; gender and ethnicity, 265n19; "indigenous people" concept and inequality, 51; inverted by outsider intervention, 244–47; *mòtámbá* ("slaves"), 86, 265n31; in narratives of "hunter-gatherer"–"farmer" relations, 41–43; outsider intervention and, 246; social belonging or alienation and, 92

hoarding by hunters, 198–99

Hocart, Arthur M., 255

Hockmann (German official), 86, 265n32

homonyms (*kólá*), 166–68

hospitality and *mbánjó*, 105, 107

houses and households: house types, 96–101, *98*, *100*; "hut" vs. "house," 94–96; *kísìnì* (kitchen house), 103, 106; *mbánjó* (open-walled verandah), 103–7, *104*, 154; *ngbà gálà* ("big house"), 101–3

"hunter-gatherer" studies, 39–46, 94, 161

"hunter-gatherers": absence of local equivalent term, 212–13; in conservation literature, 218–19; continued use of category, 44–47; as convenient, misleading gloss, 43–44; ethnicity and, 58; "former-foragers" or "postforagers," 46; history of concept, 38–40; interchangeability with "pygmies" and "indigenous people," 36, 39, 47–48; relations with "farmers," ethnographic accounts of, 40–43. *See also* "pygmies"; stereotypes, external

hunting: commercial hunters as *bò ndjómbò* (people of dirt), 212; commercialization of, 197–200; elephant hunting, 197–200, 275n18; meat sharing, 71–73, *73*; as "primitive" icon, 33–34; technology exchange, history of, 34, *35*. *See also* safari hunting

"huts" vs. houses, 94–96, *95*

identity. *See specific topics, such as* ethnic affiliations *or* social identities

illiteracy, 269n24

"indigenous people": as contested in Africa, 48–49; exclusion and, 50–51; history of concept, 46–48; institutional privileging of, vs. belonging, 246; interchangeability with "pygmies" and "hunter-gatherers," 36, 47–48; Kuper's critique, 49; Lobéké National Park access and, 32–34; multiethnic contexts and, 49–50; as relational concept, 50–51; rights in constitution of 1996, 52. *See also* stereotypes, external

initiation. *See* rites of passage

institutional administration. *See* colonial rule; conservation and development NGOs

institutional vs. local systems of identity categorization, divergences and reflexivity between, 248–53, *251*. *See also* stereotypes

interethnic relations: overview, 57–58; Baka and Bangando affiliation, 71–74, 83–85; Baka and Bangando cohabitation, 97; Baka move to settle with Bangando, 71–78; Bakwélé and Baka, 69–71, 78, 79–81; Bakwélé and Bangando, 82–83; categorical divisions as threat to, 258–59; clan alliances, 154–57; clans, parallel, 157–60, *159*; as cluster of issues, 16; commercial hunting and,

market integration campaign, 236–37; oppositional categorization and, 214–17, 232–33; ORA preschool program, 237–38

mixed parentage. *See* marriage and descent, interethnic

"modern" structures opposed to "traditional" rituals, 227–28

módyàdyà (Bangando dance), 83

Mokake (Bangando woman, interethnic parenting), 138–42

mòkɛlákɛlá (elephants and transformed human), 156, 272n15

Mokogwea (Bangando man, employee of WWF, *bò kɔ̀à* "person of the forest"), 201–2

mɔ̀kɔ́ndjí (clan chief), 151–52

Molomb (Baka man), 182

mólómbí (transformation), 157

Moloundou, 22, 189, 190

monetized economy, 194–200, 207, 234–37

Mongonga (Baka man, *bándí* of Giinde), 111

mòngúlu (domed Baka houses), 95, 95–96, 99

monitor lizard clan, 82, 151, 154–57, 158, 165–66, 270n1, 270n3

monkey clan, 150, 158, 270n3, 271n10

mónyàdì (wedding process), 129, 135, 143, 267n2

Mosakamo (Bangando elder), 184

Mosongo (Bangando elder and hunter, *bándí* of Lembi), 165–66

Mosua (Bangando elder, *bò dwá* "person of sorcery"), *186*, 209

mòtámbá ("slaves"), 86, 265n31

Motupa (Bangando man, living in Ndongo village), 107

Moumba-Ngoko district, 21–22

mourning and end-of-mourning, 179–80, 274n35. *See also* funerals

Mpiemu, 212

Mpo'oh community, 265n30

multiangular approach, 13–14, *59*, 59–60, 251–52

multiethnic systems, 42–43, 49–50. *See also* ethnic affiliations; interethnic relations

Mungoï (Bangando man, blacksmith), 130

Muslim invasions of northern and central Africa, 65–66

myths of origin. *See* origin metaphors and myths

Nadia (Bangando chief), 86, 129, 270n3

Nakolongjoko (Baka man, *bándí* of Ambata), 72, 163

Nana (Baka woman, identifies self as Bangando), 84

nationalism, 210–11

nature/culture binary: endangered nature and culture in conservation literature, 217–19; institutional vs. local catagories and, 250–51; people of nature vs. people of culture, 31, 94; spatial relations and, 93–94, 108–9, 121

navigation by *boussolliers* ("compassers"), 206

Ndjámbé (creator deity), 67, 263n3

Ndjàngé (Lake Lobéké), 32–33, 34, 68–72, 78, 113, 200, 203–4, 226, 263n7

Ndjumbé (Bangando elder), 74, 193, 194; wild mangoes and, 115

Ndoboyé (Baka man, angry at Bakwélé "patron"), 80–81, 85

Ndomonyo (Baka man, *bándí* of Wanguwangu), 165

Ndong (Bangando man, chief of Dioula village), 178

Ndongo village, 80–81, 82–83, 107–8

Ndzimou, 150, 222

neighborhoods, 26, 110–11. *See also* houses and households

ngbà gálà ("big house"), 101–3

Ngilili village, 193

Ngola (Bangando man), 182–83

Ngola village, 85–89

ngòlòngòló (local whisky), 80, 117, 135, 171, 180

Ngombé, 65–68, 263n4, 267n1

Ngonda (Bangando elder), 122, 130–31

NGOs. *See* conservation and development NGOs

noblesse (nobility), 88–89, 265n36

nongovernmental organizations. *See* conservation and development NGOs

nú ("language," "source," or "mouth"), 62

oppositional binaries: administrative use of, 214–17; "Bantu"-Baka, 220–24, 230; institutional vs. local catagories and, 250. *See also* nature/culture binary; *specific identifications, such as* "pygmies"

ORA preschool program, 237–38

origin metaphors and myths: Baka, 69–70; Bakwélé, 265n17; Bangando, 64–68; clans, 156; Mbomam, 85–86; social birth, 62–63

pàkàdyò bark houses, 96, 97–98, *98*

palm oil, 263n6

Pando (Bangando man, married to Baka woman), 122, 133–38, 229

paradigms of belonging: autochthony and politics of belonging, 51–54; as cluster of issues, 16; forest environment, 21–24; forest peoples, 24–27, *25*; land and resources, institutional control over, 26–35; relation to processes and communities, *17*; simplified notions of "pygmy," "hunter-gatherer," and "indigenous people," 35–51; Southeastern Cameroon setting, 19–21, *20*. *See also* stereotypes

partnership and collaboration, interethnic: overview, 147–49; ambiguity and flux in, 181–83; *bándí* (friendship alliances), 162–66, 168, 172, 191; *bò jáá* friendships, 161; ceremonies, shared, 170–77; clans and parallel clans, 149–60; economic complementarity and,

188–89; *Éésòngé* women's association, 179–81, *180*; intermarriage and, 123, 139; *kólá* (shared first names), 166–68; *mbòní* (blood pacts), 169–70, 273n27; scholarly overemphasis on economic relations, 161; work, collective, 177–79

paths, 109–13, *112, 114*

patriarchy, 103–5, 226. *See also* clans

patrilineality, 97, 123, 149, 152

Pauline (Bangando woman), 182–83

pèkí (wild mangoes), 113–15

pèmbé swèè (dry season): shrimping and, 115

Pényé, 65

"people of the . . .". *See* entries at *bò*

pímbá (subsistence garden), 117–19

Pito (Bangando man), 132

Plato, 37

political meetings. *See* village meetings

polygyny, 153, 238, 271n7

pòmò (collective weed clearing), 177–79

"post-foragers," 46

power hierarchies. *See* hierarchies of power, domination, and subordination

prejudice against Baka: "bad habits," 269n11; as *bò kótà* (people from behind the kitchen), 211–12; individual relationships vs. public categories, 137; intermarriage and, 127, 129–30, 134–35, 137; shifts in, 131; on work ethic, 140. *See also* stereotypes, external

prejudicial social identities, 211–13

Presbyterian missionaries, 233

preschool program, 237–38

"primitive": Cameroonian perceptions of, 96; "indigenous" as euphemism for, 49; missionaries and, 232, 234, 235; nature and, 218, 228; outside aid and, 246; "pygmies" as, 33–35, 38, 232, 243; safari hunting and, 240–44. *See also* "huntergatherers"; "pygmies"

processes of identification: as cluster of issues, 16; relation to paradigms and communities, *17*